ESMÉ OF PARIS

ESMÉ
of PARIS

BY

ESMÉ DAVIS

Drawings by
CONSTANTIN ALAJÁLOV

D. APPLETON-CENTURY COMPANY
Incorporated
New York   London

FOREWORD

FOR YEARS whenever I have brought up incidents from my past, people have either looked at me dubiously or asked me why I didn't write a book. To the latter I have invariably replied that I had neither the time nor the ability for such an undertaking. The skeptics I haven't even tried to convince, for it is hard to make those outside the theater, and especially the circus, understand how varied are the experiences that fall to the lot of every performer who tours the world. Not until I met Eckert Goodman in New York did the idea of doing an autobiography come out of moth-balls again, and only his enthusiasm and knowledge of circus people and their lives gave me confidence to start in.

According to him, the fabric of my life, as I unravel it, shows a strange weave, with many isolated and unrelated threads, a couple of bad tears, and some moth holes. If that is so, it is because circumstances have forced me to vary my type of work so frequently. Yet I have never entirely left "show business," the *leitmotiv* of my life. It has given me, in recompense for years of hard work, some experiences I wouldn't trade for the world, and a lot of fun.

Through the pages of this book, I have told of friends, who with their interest and advice, have helped me to achieve some success and to avoid many pitfalls. I can only hope that some of them may read these pages and know that I have not forgotten.

I should like to express, at this time, my thanks to my husband, Robert Matz, Jr., for his long-suffering patience during the preparation of this book, which was almost more than any mate should be required to endure; and also to

Eckert Goodman, whose articles in *Town & Country* under the same title, served as an impetus and inspiration. Without the united efforts of these helpful enthusiasts, these memoirs might never have reached the press.

ESMÉ DAVIS MATZ

New York

PART I

IF I WASN'T born precisely in the traditional dressing-room trunk, it was the next best thing, for I spent the first years of my life in theater and circus dressing-rooms in many lands, playing between wardrobe trunks and slumbering in an atmosphere of *poudre de riz* with the distant throb of the orchestra as my lullaby.

My mother had spent the summer before my birth by the seashore. She loved the sea and used to walk alone on the beach praying over and over again that should God grant her a daughter, the child would grow up to have self-reliance, courage, and some sort of talent to assure her independence through life, adding that, if possible, she would prefer another son, for she adored my brother, then about ten years old.

Grandmother often told me that I had been inconsiderate enough to arrive in the world feet first. But perhaps I should begin at the beginning. . . .

I was born on January 18, 1906, in Wheeling, West Virginia, during one of the wildest storms and coldest winters ever known in that region. Mother was visiting my grandmother, who was assembling her company for the southern tour of the Sells-Floto Circus, Wheeling being in those days a sort of taking-off point for acts going south for the winter circus dates.

My father was in Canada, and mother had intended joining him for the "blessed event," but I was born three weeks prematurely, the result of an accident mother experienced while out driving with grandmama, in which she broke her wrist. The shock not only precipitated my birth but caused complications which nearly cost mother her life.

My mother, Sofía Oswaldo, was an exceedingly beautiful woman, with a dead-white skin and copper-colored hair that

3

contrasted strangely with her vividly green eyes. She was very tiny, with exquisite little feet but ugly hands of which she was morbidly ashamed, especially when this defect was reproduced in me.

Grandmama used to say that mother was a seventh child of a seventh child and as a result had second sight. I don't know just how true this is, but mother insisted that she encountered ghosts almost everywhere we went, often announcing she had just seen "Tio Enrique," a favorite uncle, or some other defunct relative who sent his regards to everybody. This happened so frequently we eventually took it as a matter of course.

In addition to her beauty, mother had a magnificent soprano voice and was a finished musician. She played both piano and guitar perfectly and had a vast knowledge of music. I have seen her, during the rehearsal of an opera, criticize the rendering of a passage in the Partitura, interpreting it better than the director. She had made a considerable reputation for herself as a concert and grand opera singer, under the stage name of Maria de Lisle, both in Europe and in the Americas. She had a childish disregard for the practical things in life, living only for music, yet she was devoted to me, and looking back, I have a feeling of intense admiration for her and the things for which she stood.

In appearance she was totally different from my grandmother, who was also very tiny but with a dark, almost oriental beauty frequently seen in the Andalusian gipsies, lovely feet and hands, and jet-black hair so long she could almost stand on it. She smoked black Cuban cigars incessantly, loved to gamble, and, like all gipsies, preferred to "borrow" rather than buy anything she wanted.

Grandmother married very young, in the Spanish custom, and couldn't have been more than sixteen when she was already a famous flamenco dancer known throughout Spain as "La Maravilla" (the Marvel). Her diminutive green satin slippers are still preserved in a glass case in the Posada de la Sangre, an ancient hangout of bullfighters and their *cua-*

4

drillas in the Albaïcin gipsy quarter of Seville, where the autographed dancing slippers of many great dancers of Spain are reverently kept, together with the glowering black heads of famous bulls who have given the public their money's worth in the *corridas.*

Grandmama's maiden name was Lolita Bazil de Delgado, and her husband, my grandfather, was Guillermo Oswaldo. He must have been very handsome, to judge from the little faded photograph grandmama always carried. His family had been owners for three or four generations of a fleet of small freighters that plied in and out of the Port of Cadiz with cargoes of fruit. Grandfather was also an *abogado,* as lawyers are called in Spain, and he died rather young to have had such a large family, for grandmama managed to have fourteen children—and keep her figure.

She was very slender as I first knew her, and as she got older, she seemed to shrink till there was nothing left but her great black eyes. After grandfather's death she found herself obliged to return to the stage, for he had left very little money. As far as her own people were concerned she could look for no assistance whatsoever, having married out of the gipsy race, and thus, in their eyes, automatically forfeited her right to make any call on them.

The Andalusian gipsies are as proud as they are poor, and if my grandfather's narrow-minded relatives turned up their noses at grandmama because she was a gipsy, her family returned the compliment with interest. The gitanos looked with humorous contempt on bourgeois people who worked for their living, for they preferred the primitive *cuevas* on the sunbaked hillsides of Granada and their fiestas of dancing and singing for their own pleasure and the entertainment of tourists. Only when it was absolutely necessary did they turn to making *canastros* (baskets) to sell: for the most part, they were content to dream their lives away in the sun.

In Spain a woman in her early thirties is considered almost decrepit and far too old to dance professionally, so after months of struggling to make a "come-back," grandmama

5

conceived the idea of turning to account her gift of snake-charming, which she had learned from her infancy and for which she had an uncanny talent.

Among some tribes of gipsies, the snake from time immemorial has been a mystic symbol. When a seventh child is born, if it is a girl, they look in her eyes to see if she has been endowed with the gift of Pythias, the gift of prophecy and wisdom which they called the "Power." Grandmama had this power in a big way, so from earliest childhood she was taught to handle snakes and to perform snake-dance routines.

With this talent and her great beauty, grandmama created her famous act, "A Night in India," which rapidly became a star attraction throughout Europe and the United States. She had her own orchestra of Indian musicians playing specially written music on native instruments, with marvelous drum effects, and wore vividly colored Indian costume. All this, together with her ability as a dancer, produced a sensational artistic triumph.

It is not surprising, considering the evil reputation snakes enjoy in Spain, that grandmama, in spite of her spectacular success, succeeded in widening the breach between herself and my grandfather's family.

Her power over snakes was fantastic: she bought them wild and trained them herself and could handle any poisonous reptile without getting bitten, often demonstrating this ability to directors of zoölogical societies and scientists. She said it was because snake-charming was done not by force but through the eyes and with the mind.

Most people, when recalling their childhood, have memories of cherished toys or games. Looking back on mine, I see snakes. Big snakes, little snakes, and all kinds of snakes, crawling through a succession of hotel bedrooms and hallways: they lie benumbed in tin bathtubs and *bidets,* coil and weave on stages and circus rings, and dully hibernate, squirming over my crib, behind trunks, and into beds.

Hercules is said to have had an encounter with snakes when

6

he was a child, so I suppose that gives us something in common, except that, if I remember correctly, he strangled them. Had I tried that, I would have been thrashed within an inch of my life, for the snakes represented my grandmother's livelihood, and when anything happened to them, as it did occasionally, it upset her peace of mind—and sometimes her bookings—for weeks.

When I was old enough to understand, she would tell me long and complicated gipsy folklore about snakes and the "Power." I never attempted to read or study anything about

it, for grandmama said it was useless for me to try and develop the gift, on account of my Irish father: any one connected with a country whose patron saint was revered for having driven out the snakes would just be wasting time. Frankly, I think she was considerably influenced by the fact that she always thought of snakes in terms of their cost—her own represented a considerable investment—so in her eyes Saint Patrick's miracle was just extravagant waste.

She did, however, teach me to handle, wash, and oil them, and help her extract their poison, when I grew older. Her pythons and big snakes were kept in huge tanks which were left backstage if we were appearing in a theater, and in the menageries if we were under canvas. The smaller ones were kept in baskets in our hotel bedrooms.

Snakes have to be washed daily, and this was one of my duties. I would put them in a bathtub of tepid water, stir them around for a while, then take them out and dry them carefully, after which I rubbed them with warm olive oil. Snakes love to be oiled because it helps them to slide. Some big ones (like the boa I later kept for years in my apartment in Paris) lubricate themselves by spitting out something that looks like whipped cream. This has an awful effect on servants, especially if they happen to suspect where it came from.

The business of "milking" poisonous snakes was a more serious proceeding. Grandmama used to put a piece of absorbent cotton in a wine-glass and cover it with antiseptic gauze; then she took the glass in her left hand and the snake in her right, and with a gentle pressure of her fingers forced its mouth open and pushed the fangs into the soft gauze. The infuriated reptile would eject his venom where it would drop harmlessly on to the cotton.

Most snake handlers tie threads around the poisoned fangs and pull them completely out, but my grandmother would never do this because the roots might rot in the mouth, and the snake would die. She was genuinely fond of the snakes, and though it was not necessary for her to have poisonous ones (very few acts do), they were nearly always the most beautiful.

She took the greatest care of her snakes, holding them in deep respect, and I can still recall her when some momentous decision was to be made, consulting with them in the middle of the night, by the light of a small lamp. The greatest benefit I ever derived from them was their usefulness in getting unwanted guests out of the house in a hurry and in negotiating the customs when traveling.

I used to put a small one around my neck under my coat. He was very curious about people, and when the customs officers wanted to go through my mother's mountain of luggage, I would let "Pushkin" push his head out and

8

wiggle his tongue at them. They chalked the luggage out immediately.

My father, Charles Holland, was a wonderful person: he had a wistful sweetness and charm that attracted people. He was six feet two inches tall and very strong, with kind blue eyes and coal-black eyebrows. A true Irish type with a great sense of humor, he adored animals and the country and was a magnificent rider. I have heard people in Ireland say that there was never a horse foaled that he could not ride, or a child born that did not love him. His ability to administer his father's estates was marked in his boyhood, for he had that love of the soil so dominant in the Irish character.

His forebears were an old Catholic family, many of whom served in the British Army and Navy at different times throughout the family history, probably because wherever there was a fight going on, they had to be in it, no matter whose side they were on. Kipling was indeed right: "The Irish move to the sound of the guns, like salmon to the sea." Their crest was a round shield with a hand pointing upward to a star in the center, and the motto read *"Forti Favet Cœlum"* (Fortune Favors the Brave).

My father was educated at Beaumont and Sandhurst Military College. He served as a subaltern in the Irish Guards and had seen service in India. He loved music and was a good amateur violinist, and he met my mother when she was singing at a reception in London. He married her three weeks later, despite the bitter opposition of his family to his marrying a foreign artist. They never would receive mother. After they were married, father left the army and joined a brother in Canada. They had a farm in British Columbia for a while, but eventually my father became a director of several companies and general manager of the Dominion Bank of Canada in Toronto.

I spent the first two years of my life shuttling between New York, California, and Hawaii, where my mother sought

9

to regain her health. She had been seriously ill after I was born, and father never wanted her to return to the operatic stage. Her determination to do so, however, created a break between them that widened with the years, until they eventually became separated.

This situation was a great grief to my father and made him unhappy on my account, for I never had a home life in the sense that most people think of one. That is to say, I can not remember a single warmly familiar spot from which I could set out or to which I could return.

I was two years old when we sailed to Europe to join my grandmother, then at the height of her theatrical triumphs. My brother was sent to school in England while mother resumed her singing, and I was placed in the charge of grandmama and a younger sister of mother's. This aunt, Elisabetta Concepción, was even more beautiful than mother and also a singer, but she never became one of any consequence. Aunt Lisa was the wife of Nolan de Lisle, a teacher of singing in Paris and a descendant of Rouget de Lisle, composer of the ''Marseillaise.'' It was Nolan de Lisle who ''discovered'' mother, sponsored her career as a singer, and gave her her stage name.

Mother and grandmama often told me about my first appearance on any stage. It happened during the year of 1908 in Turin, Italy. Mother was singing there in Puccini's operas in an effort to condition her voice for heavier rôles after her long *relâche*. The child used in the last act of *Madame Butterfly* to impersonate the baby was taken ill during the performance. Grandmama, a hound for punishment, offered my services as a solution to the dilemma.

I was, of course, too small to walk properly and used to do most of my traveling by crawling on the floor. In the last act of the opera, Madame Butterfly sets the child in the middle of the stage and gives him American and Japanese flags to play with, then retires behind a screen upstage to commit *hara-kiri* and sings the aria, ''Piccolo Idolo, Addio.'' This is the

10

"punch" of the whole opera, and the audience is supposed to be filled with deep emotion. Although used to peculiar noises in theaters, the row mother was making behind the screen aroused my curiosity. I probably thought some one was murdering her and she needed help, so, true to the motto of my father's crest, "Fortune Favors the Brave," I turned my back on the footlights and started to crawl toward the screen on my hands and knees, showing to the audience a little pair of white buttocks.

It stopped the show. The orchestra leader, an excitable Italian who took himself seriously, could not keep his musicians together, for they wanted to see what was causing the mirth, and mother behind the screen was forced to signal frantically to the wings for somebody to come and remove me. Fortunately, the woman who sang the rôle of Suzuki, Butterfly's maid, was awaiting her cue, and she finally rushed out and got me off.

After a year of almost constant traveling, we returned to the United States, grandmama to fulfil circus engagements and mother to sing at the Metropolitan. (I believe this was the year she sang with Adelina Patti.) Father, always thoughtful and generous, took a charming little house for us on Riverside Drive, and apart from grandmama's snakes, this house formed one of my earliest recollections, impressing me as being the first place we had stayed in for more than a week at a time. Vaguely I can remember a white staircase leading from the hall and my grandmother trying to stop me from pushing my head through the banisters to look at my mother in an evening dress with glittering things in her hair.

After mother finished her contract at the opera, we spent a short vacation with father in Florida and left again for Europe.

We toured France and the Riviera and were in Spain when I first realized what a beautiful person my mother was. Everybody stared at her in the hotel lobbies, and she was run after and fêted everywhere. Consequently I was left almost entirely in grandmama's care.

In that period of my life grandmother was not kind to me: whenever I did anything she did not approve of, she used to whip me across the hand with a small switch. She continued this custom until I was about six years old, when one day I took the switch away from her and walloped her across the face with it. Strangely enough, she was much kinder to me after this, and although we never spoke of the matter again, I know she was secretly delighted because it showed her I had some of the gipsy spirit in me.

Mother was singing in the Teatro Real of Madrid, and grandmama with natural pride wanted her sisters in Seville to know about it, so she wrote them glowing accounts. In answer to her letter, and without any invitation, a perfect deluge of relatives descended upon us in the exclusive Ritz Hotel. They arrived with luggage composed of untidy bundles, old boxes tied with string, two hoot owls in a wicker cage as a *porte-bonheur* for grandmama and a dilapidated rubber plant for mother. They presented me with an evil-looking doll, an unfortunate choice, because from my earliest infancy I hated dolls, absolutely refusing to play with anything but animals, live ones if possible.

The party consisted, first, of two sisters of grandmama's who had also married out of the tribe. They had been models for the famous Spanish painter, Ignacio Zuloaga, and one of them, Dona Constantina, who was considered the perfect type of gitana, gave herself quaint little airs on the strength of it. She had brought her married daughter, Paquita, a rather sweet woman with three small children—a modest brood compared with that of Dona Inocencia, grandmama's other sister, who arrived with her entire family, of four giggling girls and two boys aged twelve and fourteen, plus her second husband.

This man was a most repulsive-looking person, tall, emaciated, and yellow-skinned, wrapped in a rusty black cape and looking more like a recently disinterred corpse than anything

12

else. Extremely gloomy, he never opened his mouth except to spit, but in spite of his unprepossessing exterior, he was one of the best guitar players in Spain and known as the "Tres de Copas" (Three of Cups), meaning a playing card in the Spanish deck, which is different from ordinary cards.

Our relatives, having installed themselves in the Ritz at our expense, proceeded to invade our suites. They talked, laughed, and screamed at the tops of their voices and dived into mother's perfume and wardrobe until she nearly had a nervous breakdown. Their idea of a good time was to sit in a circle around the room and hold what is called in Spain a *tertulia* and drink manzanilla.

Everybody spoke at once, and the Tres de Copas played his guitar incessantly and sang *trianerias* all through their chattering. The conversation, when it did not sound like a birth, death, and marriage column, was punctuated with regrets that María Esther, another sister of grandmama's, had not come with them. This calamity had apparently been averted because they did not have the price of the train fare.

The children and grandchildren that our guests brought with them were funny little dark creatures, like Jeroboam, who sat in corners and never spoke a word, but their enormous dark eyes took in everything. Mother had the bright idea of sending them down to the Prado gardens in front of the hotel in charge of her maid, to play with me and get acquainted.

As soon as we got to the gardens, they changed from timid little mice to devils incarnate. They yelled and ran about pushing each other, climbed the railings and benches like lunatics for about five minutes, then turned their attention to me. Their comments on my appearance were anything but complimentary.

I was never allowed to wear a hat or shoes and stockings, and this seemed to cause them amusement, as did the yellow linen tunic I was wearing. Apparently they thought that the daughter of so wealthy a mother should be decked out in ermine and red plush at least, and they started pulling me about between them.

13

I had never been permitted to play with other children: in the circuses and theaters, mother gave strict orders that I was not to speak to children of the performers, especially in the circus acts, whose members she treated with an icy contempt. For this reason I was at a disadvantage with my cousins, but eventually I reacted with energy, and the most God-awful fight took place, with the unfortunate maid trying to separate us and coming off with a badly bitten thumb.

The Tres de Copas was finally sent for, and I was dragged into our apartment with one of my front teeth loosened, and covered with scratches. Mother was furious, and relations became very strained. That night our relatives invaded the Teatro Real with a collection of friends they had looked up in the meantime, and they wanted to bring them all to mother's dressing-room after the opera to drink more manzanilla. They stayed for the bullfight on Sunday afternoon and were then prevailed upon to return home by my grandmother, who had to give them half of mother's wardrobe to get rid of them.

I saw my first bullfight in Madrid. Mother always refused to go all week, then never missed the one on Sunday. Usually rather calm and dignified, unless angry about something, her character changed as soon as she was in the Plaza de Toros. The spectacle seemed to intoxicate her. Her eyes would turn almost black, and she would get white to the lips whenever there was any particularly sensational incident: all her Spanish ancestry seemed to come to the surface. In San Sebastian, she once had to be forcibly restrained by grandmama from throwing her diamond earrings into the arena to Bombita, the great fighter. I was so young when I saw my first fight that I don't remember much about it except the music and color and my mother's face.

In Europe we always made our headquarters in Paris, and some of my happiest childhood memories are associated with walks in the Bois or under the chestnut trees on the Champs-Élysées, or looking at the Marly horses on the Place de la Concorde. I used to love to visit the toy kiosks near the Grand Palais, where old women selling dolls made of chestnuts dressed in little bits of cloth gossiped with my grandmother.

I was a lonely child and used to invent my own games, and had a language I had made up. At one time I insisted on asking for things by the names I had invented for them. It drove grandmama nearly frantic, but mother was interested and thought it a sign of genius. It served a useful purpose, for she engaged a nursery governess for me and I started learning to read and write. Another peculiar phase I went through about this time, and which I can not account for, was my refusal to wear any clothes. I struggled out of them as soon as I was dressed, thereby causing considerable embarrassment on several occasions.

This eccentricity I certainly did not inherit from my mother, for when we were in Paris, she had veritable orgies of buying clothes. She dressed well and loved beautiful furs, and sometimes, when in a good temper, allowed me to play with her jewels, of which she had a costly collection, and to which, in true gipsy fashion, she added substantially every time she received a pay check. The favorite occupation of any spare time she had was gloating over her treasures with my grandmother.

Grandmama had her usual success in London's Crystal Palace, after our Spanish trip. She had made her début in England at this place of entertainment when she was a young girl, and she often told me she was so beautiful that people would stop in the street to stare at her. She won a command performance before Queen Victoria, together with one of her sisters, who was a sensational high-wire performer billed as "La Bonita."

In later years, when grandmother had her snake act going, she again played the Crystal Palace and this time also was sent for to perform before the Queen, in the gardens of Windsor Castle. Her Majesty was so thrilled by the performance that she had grandmother wait after the other artists had been presented, and according to grandmama (and to use a good old English expression) they became very "matey." She showed the Queen all her snakes and how she called them with different inflections in her voice and various drum beats from the native musicians. Her Majesty was particularly interested in these men, for she loved all things Indian, and grandmother said two enormous Sikh servants were standing behind her chair.

Some people believe snakes can not hear, but I think they are wrong. The snakes' sense of smell is much more highly developed, but they can hear vibration. Grandmama would clap her hands on a monotonous musical phrase produced by the drums and flutes and accompany this with staccato stamping of her feet, which her snakes knew and responded to. She would call Rajah, her white cobra, in this way.

Casting about for a novelty for her act, she heard of a species of albino cobra that grows enormously big in certain parts of Burma and Java. Because the natives believe them sacred and make offerings to them of bowls of rice and the entrails of sacrificial animals, the cobras collect around the temples, where the worshipers never molest them. They hiss and spit if anybody approaches them, and the priests read fortunes from the designs their spittle makes in the sand.

A dozen leading animal firms in London were commissioned to try and get her one of these snakes. Finally, she obtained Rajah. He was, I believe, the first white cobra anybody had ever attempted to train or keep in captivity. He was nearly six feet long (enormous for a cobra) and as wild as a March hare. The "spectacle" markings on the back of his hood, instead of being white on darkish brown as in ordinary cobras, were black on white, and his scales had a strange pink glow about them which was rather disgusting.

Grandmama's act depended greatly on dramatic musical effects arranged for each snake. With the smaller varieties the music was high and fast; with the great lumbering pythons she used for an encore, it was deep and slow. The python had to

16

be carried in by three or four men and placed over her shoulders. She then draped him around her body below the ribs, because a snake is not so apt to constrict on soft flesh but may be tempted to crush if he gets a grip on a comparatively bony section of the body, like the thorax. He was so heavy that about all grandmama with her frail body could do, was stand with him wound around her, holding his head in one small hand and looking steadfastly into his eyes in a way that never failed to sell the act.

With the exception of the python, all the snakes were brought on in wicker baskets, one at a time. The baskets were then placed on individual rugs in front of the musicians. I can still see grandmama whirling and pirouetting on her tiny feet in a circle of snakes of different types and varieties, till with a clash of her silver anklets she reached the climax of the first part of her act. Then Rajah was brought on, coiled on his rug, his head poised about three feet from the ground.

Rhythmically he would sway backward and forward, following her every movement as she danced before him, whirling her brilliantly colored skirt. Every now and again he would strike at her and hiss, then go on swinging, only to strike and hiss again. It was a thrilling performance.

The year 1911 was one of intense work for mother; in fact, she overworked all her life. She was extremely ambitious but did not have the physical strength to stand the hours of rehearsal and study she put in, combined with the nervous strain she underwent at every performance. She had sung Elsa in *Lohengrin* when only eighteen and had received a command performance in the Imperial Opera in Vienna from the Emperor Francis Joseph. With this brilliant début, it was understandable that her whole life was filled with the one idea of more and more triumphs, to the exclusion of everything else.

We toured Austria and Romania in a concert tournée with the Philharmonic Orchestra of Vienna under the direction of

17

Arthur Nikisch, giving command performances for Queen Marie of Romania in Bucharest, and I was five-and-a-half years old when we arrived in Russia.

I commenced ballet school almost at once, going to a school for children kept by an old Frenchwoman, Madame Verdain. I do not have any of the usual happy childhood recollections about the place but remember there was always a Russian priest in black robes sneaking in and out of doorways, and my grandmother slapped me almost every time she came to call for me, because it was so cold and because I fought with most of the pupils, especially a boy phenomenon who played the piano and wore thick glasses. I don't remember much about it, but I think I must have done a good job on him, because they took me away after that to another school for a year, where I progressed to music and languages.

The Nelidova Ballet School held examinations in dancing which were decisive for professional children, and the weeks before them were filled with constant naggings and slappings from my grandmother, on the "spare the rod and spoil the child" principle, and rare moments with my mother when she deplored my hands. I have always had powerful hands, a handicap in ballet (no pun intended) but good for piano. I played extremely well for a child, and they told mother I could be a concert pianist. I learned the guitar from grandmother, the concertina and banjo for fun. They overworked me at home, and I was always tired and cold.

There were long discussions about my appearance. Mother decided I had good feet and eyes, but grandmama thought me hopeless, on account of my Irish blood. The inferiority complex brought on by these criticisms nearly cost me my exam. In addition, there were arguments over my dress, a white *tutu* with rosebuds.

On the examination day they tweaked and poked at me for an hour before I danced, until I was completely worn out; then mother sat down with the teachers and some decrepit old gentlemen who were, I suppose, "balletomanes" looking for future Pavlovas. Everything I had learned went out of my head. I seldom cried as a child but bottled up my emotions, which made matters worse.

There is a movement in ballet called a *grande jetée*, really very simple, needing only balance on arrival. Unfortunately I overdid it when I stopped on my toe, lost my balance, and landed flat on my *tutu* in a sitting position amid a horrified silence.

All the same they passed me, for I eventually recovered my composure and outdid the other pupils in a "Pizzicato" by Drigo, on my toes, which were always my best feature. The exercises in the Russian method of ballet training, combined with the weight of the body, force the soft bones in children's feet into an arch, but it is often necessary to bend and press the foot after dancing, while it is still warm. I needed very little of this, and as my toes were unusually strong, I could stand on them in my bare feet, even making a few steps— which is more difficult than it sounds.

My mother traveled extensively in Russia, collecting folksongs. She had a rare gift for arranging simple melodies, and these lieder were a great success, winning for her a command performance and a decoration.

After a performance of *Boris Godunov* in Moscow, mother became very ill with a sore throat that developed into quinsy. Grandmama gave up contracts to nurse her, and as the allowance my father could send was not enough for so much expense, we gradually became financially embarrassed. Princess Soltikoff, an old friend of mother's, took me to stay with her. She had three children, two daughters and a son, all older than I. They were at school in Paris but came home for holidays.

The princess had a magnificent house in the outskirts of Moscow and one on the Nevsky Prospekt in Petrograd. The Russia of those days was wonderful but unfortunately I was too young to appreciate or know much of its splendor. Outstanding in my memory are the huge bonfires that were lighted on the street corners on winter nights, where the policemen and guards of the palaces warmed themselves. The private carriages and cars of the great ladies along the smart streets had footmen to open the doors for the ladies to alight. They wore *cashoubas* (overcoats) lined with mink, and the carriage rugs were of sable and stone marten.

In Moscow, I once went with mother and the princess to the perfume shop of Manioulieff, a tiny place with gothic windows and cases filled with rare bottles of jade and crystal. The perfumes that floated out of their warm interiors haunted me for days and started me on the love for good perfumes, of which mother was a great critic.

After her illness, mother went with grandmama for some time, to regain her health in the warmer climate of the Crimea, and on her return it was decided something had to be done with me. I think mother must have been too ill to be consulted about the future, but obviously I could not accept the hospitality of Princess Soltikoff indefinitely, so grandmama took the situation in hand, arranging for me to work in a children's troupe called the "Ograinsky Wonder Children." Ograinsky, owner and director, agreed to train me, and I was to receive a small salary for my work in the act, for a period of three years, the contract then to be renewed.

I never knew where grandmama unearthed Ograinsky. He was an enormous broken-nosed ex-wrestler of Polish extraction, married to a thin, bitter, cockney Englishwoman. She looked after the wardrobe and always had a cold in her head. Between fights with her husband, and in her more cheerful moments, she used to sing most amusing cockney songs. I remember one which went:

Every Saturday afternoon we loves to drown our sorrows,
So we always visits the waxwork show and sits in the Chamber
of 'Orrors;
There's a beautiful statue of mother there wot gives us
pleasure—rather,
For we likes to think of her as she looked, the night she
strangled father.

20

The Ograinskys had five children of their own, four boys and a girl, all born in different countries and all speaking different tongues with their parents—a family tower of Babel. There were three other children in the troupe, also of diverse nationalities, and to hear old man Ograinsky conducting a rehearsal was something to marvel at. Despite his brutality, he was a fine trainer and built a good act with us. I was a very powerful child, supple and with a good back, also considerably more advanced in dancing than other children in the troupe.

My best friends among them were Paul, the eldest boy, and Toto, a little Italian foundling who was frail and frightened and never could do backbends. Ograinsky used to tie Toto's head to his ankles and leave him in a corner for twenty minutes to punish him. I have always regretted a thing we once did to him: children can be cruel.

In the Morelli Circus, when we worked in Romania, there was an aged black panther called "Bogie" who was in the menagerie just for show. I liked her, and she knew me. In spite of the bad reputation these animals have, she was gentle, and it was easy for me to push up a wooden bar and get into her cage. This I did a few times, when nobody was around and I wanted to be alone.

One day the children decided to shut Toto into the cage. I can't imagine what the idea was, but we got hold of him when he was tied up and shoved him in. Bogie woke up and stared with a strange look in her eyes, and the poor child started yelling, which was the worst thing he could have done. The kids all ran, but me: I started for the wooden bar to get him out when a menagerie cleaner came in. His cries brought the ringmaster from a card game just in time. Ograinsky beat Paul almost to death, and over what my grandmother did to me, I prefer to draw a veil....

II

ALL MY LIFE, I have had reason to remember Stanislas Ograinsky and his training methods. He was of the old school and had no use for gentleness or culture. To him either people were acrobats or they weren't, and he had every intention of making them learn to do tricks and incredible feats, whether or not he ruined their health in the attempt.

Like many ex-wrestlers, he had something sadistic about him, and if he saw any of the children, especially his own, sick from exhaustion, he would get a mad gleam in his eye and work them until they dropped on the floor. He taught us tumbling, back somersaults, and full twisters in a "mechanic" or harness till we learned the timing. Then we had to do these tricks alone without any help.

A mechanic is a stout leather belt which fits around the body under the armpits, with a ring in the back to which a rope is attached with a snap. The rope goes up to a pulley in the roof, passes through it and down to the hand of the trainer, who can manipulate his pupils' bodies by lifting them, or save them from falls by pulling on the rope as they do their tricks. This apparatus is used in all kinds of acrobatic work, aërial trapeze, and vaulting on horses.

Ograinsky started me off in this as basic training, and for a while everything was fine. All the other children were more or less advanced in it, but the trouble really began when I had to learn to turn in the air without the mechanic. For some reason I could not learn to "tuck," which is to roll one's self into a ball, touch the knees with the head, and make a complete turn landing on the feet and producing a somersault.

This position affords protection for the head in case of a fall and also helps the body revolve. Ograinsky, impatient to have me work in the act as soon as possible, used to yell at me till I became flustered and had some nasty falls. This went on for two or three days till he finally got a knotted rope and hit me over the knees with it to make me turn higher and faster. Welts and dark bruises were the result, and grandmama made him stop. Then he used to cup his hand and hit me on the back of the neck to send me over and

make me keep my head in, explaining to grandmama that it was the only way I could be saved from a fall on my head and a possible broken neck. It did teach me to do the trick but eventually resulted in chronic headaches which threatened to affect my eyesight.

Despite his Spartan methods, the thorough grounding Ograinsky gave me has been invaluable all through my professional life, and in many ways I have had reason to be grateful to him.

We danced a ballet on the points and did an equestrian act, practically ballet, vaulting on and off the horses' broad backs, the girls wearing old fashioned ballet *tutus* and the boys white silk tights with black velvet jerkins, similar to costumes worn in the *Sylphides* ballet. We did graceful poses while the fat white horses (chalked by us before every show) galloped around the ring. Then we had the tumbling act and the cross flying trapeze act, which was our star number and really outstanding.

A flying trapeze act is done with a group of people over a net, and the first thing I was taught was how to fall in the net without injuring myself, and with grace. This is so important that I can now understand Ograinsky's fury when I could not learn to tuck, for the same movement is used to turn in the air before landing in the net. I was younger than the other children working in this act, and being fairly tall, I could do graceful "cuts" with my feet while swinging, and so I got into Ograinsky's good graces over that.

Later we learned a "Cossack" riding display and a "Wild West" number, in which I excelled, and in addition to our work, we helped groom and care for two horses each. We mended their harnesses and whitened them, for Ograinsky could never keep any of his helpers long. He used to shout and hit them all the time, and the only one who stood it was a deaf-and-dumb Russian who wasn't much help.

I loved my work, of course, and began to get the thrill of danger and the thirst for applause. We worked all our acts in circuses but only a few single trapeze and ring numbers when booked in vaudeville. All children working with parents were allowed to perform in theaters and music-halls, provided they were out of the theater by eleven every night, and provided their parents could furnish proof of their attendance at a school for part of the year.

While in Moscow I continued school, which took time out from my training and exasperated Ograinsky. He had plenty of trouble about his own children and always tried to keep out of England, where the Child Labor Act was far more strictly enforced than on the continent. Where or how his four children had learned to read and write was a mystery, for they never stopped anywhere long enough to attend school, but somehow they had managed to pick up just enough to make out easy words from the newspapers in the various

24

tongues they spoke, according to the various countries they had been born in. Whether their mother screamed at them in English, or their father swore at them in Polish, they obeyed just the same. The rest of the Ograinsky League of Nations was rounded out by three more children besides myself: Toto, the Italian foundling, Fritzi, a fat complacent little girl from Essen, Germany, and Anna, the daughter of a Greek wrestler, one-time partner of Ograinsky.

We played a few weeks in and around Moscow; then Ograinsky signed a contract with a relatively small one-ring circus playing a winter route through Romania, the Balkans, Poland, Finland, and crossing by boat to Scandinavia. The circus was run by three Romanian gipsy brothers with the Italian name of Morelli. They had been acrobats themselves, and their families for generations back had owned small traveling shows.

The entire circus traveled by train and did not carry large animal acts. What animals they did carry were boxed in the worst possible way, but I don't think they could possibly have suffered more than the performers did.

Of course it was valuable experience for me, and in a way I enjoyed it, but this must have been very hard for grand-mama, who was convinced some one had cast the evil eye on us. She traveled with me for the first few weeks, then had to return to mother, who was so ill she could not be alone, so I was left in the care of Mrs. Ograinsky.

When the circus reached the end of the tour and we were in Scandinavia, grandmama got Ograinsky a booking in Copenhagen with her own act, in the famous Schumann Circus there. I had not seen her for six months and was shocked to see how she had aged. I never knew her age, but she was such a fierce bright little person it seemed impossible to believe she was really very old.

I had received very few letters from her but knew she had taken mother to a sanitarium in Vienna, where her health was improving under a famous throat specialist, but grandmama never told me in her letters that she was suffering tortures

25

herself, with rheumatism, and was desperately in need of rest and sunshine. She forced herself to play that month in Copenhagen for me and for her orchestra, and that was when I really started to be of some use to her with the cleaning and care of her snakes.

The Schumann Circus is an institution in Denmark, run by two brothers who were and still are horse trainers of international fame, and it was only through grandmama's prestige that Ograinsky got the booking. It was an agreeable contrast to the circus we had been working with, but I was sorry to leave the many performers with whom I had made friends. They were true flotsam and jetsam of the theatrical profession and most of them elderly people who had once been headliners. Perhaps typical of them all was an old equestrian, "Lady Gretchen," and her horse Barney.

How old she was nobody knew, and Barney's date of birth was lost in the mists of antiquity. Lady Gretchen was a very tall fair woman from Montana, of Irish and German descent. She spoke German fluently, but her English had a violent twang to it, with so many peculiar words and so much slang that even the English artists on the bill had a hard time following the thread of her conversation. In appearance she resembled the late Marie Dressler as "Tugboat Annie" more than any one else I know, and she claimed her professional career started when she was a cowgirl in Buffalo Bill's Wild West Show and she came to Europe with their world tour.

She had photographs (which she always gave for the programs) that had probably been taken some twenty years previously, when she was an attractive girl with a really stunning figure. On one she gave me was written the classic dedication among circus and vaudeville performers when they exchange pictures: "Some Time, Some Day, Remember!"

As a general rule she talked very little about her past, and I have always felt she had been some one important once. The only thing in the world she truly loved was her horse Barney, who, despite his age and fatness, was still a beautiful snow-white animal, perfectly trained. When she did her high

26

school act with him, in her black riding habit and high silk hat, they made quite an impressive picture.

She was a deeply religious woman, which was in sharp contrast to her habit of using appalling language to all and sundry when anything annoyed her. I have heard her curse out a group of roustabouts in four different languages, leaving them flabbergasted, and the three Morellis, who were pretty hard-boiled themselves, invariably ran for cover when she started on them. But she always read her Bible, and every Sunday morning she would go to Barney's stall, no matter where we were, on trains, or playing somewhere, and read him the Twenty-third Psalm.

The old horse used to nuzzle her neck as she read to him, seeming to understand the lines about ''He maketh me to lie down in green pastures: He leadeth me beside the still waters.'' All the circus kids used to steal up and listen, and gradually she started a sort of Sunday School for them, too.

Most of the children, particularly the Ograinskys, had only a hazy knowledge of the Scriptures, their parents not having given a great amount of consideration to their religious training, so that by the time Lady Gretchen had expounded her version of the Bible to them, they had a confused idea that the Good Lord must have been an outstanding animal trainer who made the lions lie down with the lambs.

She was extremely fond of children, and it was only rarely that she did not have time to play with us and tell tales about Buffalo Bill. Sometimes she would sit on an upturned bucket beside Barney and describe America and the rolling foothills of Montana, where she hoped to return some day and have a little ranch with green pastures, like the ones in the Psalm, where Barney could spend his old age. It was her dream, and I know she saved every penny of her modest salary to this end.

She despised the performers in the show who neglected or mistreated their children, and more than once she tackled Ograinsky and his wife about their treatment of Toto. She also got after a Hungarian family from the east side of New

27

York, who half-starved their three little girls and spent their salary on drink.

These people had all sorts of mediocre acts involving complicated material, but the worst was a perch act the three girls did. It consisted of a high wooden pole their father held on his shoulders, while they climbed up and did different routines of balancing tricks on it: there was a sort of perch or skeleton platform on which they stood on their heads and hands, lay on their backs, turned round and round on a revolving bar, and made all sorts of other complicated revolutions requiring perfect balance.

When their father was working after one of his frequent alcoholic bouts, those poor girls went through absolute hell. They were tense with fear, for the pole was a high one and a fall meant a serious injury. The Morellis would never have put up with this but for the fact that three girls on a high pole held by one man is an exceptional act. But despite their light weight, it was a terrible strain on the father. In the finale of this act the youngest girl did a handstand on the top of the perch, with her sisters spinning around on the revolving bars on each side of the pole. One night the inevitable happened.

We were in Budapest, and the father had been celebrating for three days. He got sobered up somehow for the evening performance but was too shaky to work, which everybody knew but did nothing about. The act was a shambles, and most of the other performers were watching from the ring entrance with clenched teeth: among them was Lady Gretchen, who was particularly fond of little Yoli, the girl on the top.

As the weight of the girls increased when they started to revolve, their father began to waver and wobble beneath them. In a split second, the pole—which always looked to be in the last stage of dry rot—snapped near the top. The three girls fell, the heavy steel perch on top of them. Two of the girls were not badly hurt, but Yoli struck the ring curb and broke her back. She had such serious internal injuries that she died in Lady Gretchen's arms two hours later.

28

The next night the act was, of course, cut out for the time being, but the Morellis made an announcement and a man carried in another pole with the same perch rigged on it, and in the place where Yoli used to stand there was an enormous bouquet of flowers tied with black crape, a tribute from her fellow artists. The lights went down while they played her music for a minute, with the spotlight on the bouquet; then the pole was carried out, lights went on again, and the show continued. Artists and hard-bitten circus help alike had a hard time hiding their wet eyes.

Ograinsky put Toto in Yoli's place a few days later. He was the lightest child in the circus and had no parents or guardians to prevent such a horrible thing, for the poor child had seen Yoli fall and was so terrified of the pole that he almost fainted two or three times during the first rehearsals. This was followed by the usual cuffings and cursings from Ograinsky.

Lady Gretchen tried to comfort the poor little fellow, even offering to pay out of her pocket the few dollars Ograinsky was getting for him, to obtain his release, but Ograinsky flatly refused. As I said before, he had a sadistic complex: it made me feel sick when I saw the expression on his face as he watched Toto on the pole.

Another strange personality in that circus was an old clown called Moreno. This was not his name, but the story about him was that he had at one time been a top-ranking opera singer and had even sung at the Metropolitan. He was an inveterate drunkard, and his voice had been gradually destroyed by alcohol. In order that nobody might recognize him, he did a clown act in which he burlesqued arias from the great operas he had once sung, wearing the usual heavy grease-paint make-up which served as a perfect disguise.

He still had the remains of a good tenor voice which, on the rare nights he was sober, rang out with some fine notes, especially when he sang the "Celeste Aïda," although he filled it with slapstick comedy. The other men in the company who dressed with him said he always carried a dilapidated

29

portable phonograph in his trunk and played over and over again records which were worn thin and from which he had carefully removed the labels. When anybody would listen to him he would hint that these records were his and that he had made them at the height of his triumphs.

Nobody believed this, and most of the men disliked his drinking, for there is not much of it going on in the average circus, most performers being hard-working folk who despise drunkenness and vice in any form and especially those who have allowed such things to ruin them professionally. His only friends were the animals and a little midget called Beppo who worked in a troupe billed under the astounding title of "Muller's Midgets in Terpsichorean Tid-bits."

Lady Gretchen detested the old clown and seldom spoke to him, but somehow all the children and animals loved him, for he was kind and gentle. Whenever Lady Gretchen came into the menagerie and saw us with him, she would call us away and start a long tirade in English and German about the evils of alcohol and how it made "bums" out of people. Her attitude toward Moreno is what makes the final phase of this saga of the circus seem unbelievable, but, unfortunately, it is tragically true.

The Morelli Circus laid off for three months after we finished in Copenhagen and started out again in May for the summer tour under canvas. They played all the small towns and villages in one-night stands, and their headquarters were in Bucharest, where the Morellis had stables for their horses and a shabby menagerie. They traveled by road, with only a small troupe of inferior artists who would put up with old-fashioned horse-drawn caravans for living quarters and who were immune to the bedbugs and other enterprising insects that infested them.

Lady Gretchen had signed up as star of the summer tour only after a desperate hunt for other work in Scandinavia. I suppose both she and Moreno were "has-beens" and could find nothing else. The same thing occurred with the Hungarian family, whose tragic accident had been noised abroad so that nobody wanted them, with only two girls to work the perch act and their father's reputation as a "booze artist."

We were in New York later that summer when we heard from some performers who had been in Romania that the Morelli Circus had been destroyed by fire. It seems that the Hungarian couple had got drunk and started a fight in their trailer, which was backed up against the big tent, knocked over an oil lamp, and started a blaze that spread rapidly with the wind.

The men fought desperately to save the animals, and Lady Gretchen managed to get Barney out unhurt. Most of the performers escaped, including Moreno, who was more than usually drunk. When the local fire engines arrived, the flames were raging everywhere, and the little group of performers huddled together watching their props and few personal belongings being destroyed.

Suddenly Moreno was missed. Some one said he must have gone back to the men's dressing-tent for his portable phonograph, which he had been playing when the fire broke out. The men's dressing-tent was ablaze and so filled with smoke that nobody dared attempt to go in—except Lady Gretchen.

She gave Barney to the men to hold and before they could stop her dashed inside the tent. It was about to collapse in burning ruins: even police and firemen were unable to approach it. Lacking adequate equipment, they formed a chain and passed buckets filled with water, but this was of little help, and one of the sides collapsed. Minutes passed; then they saw Lady Gretchen stagger out, dragging Moreno. He was so terribly burned that the doctor could do nothing for him, and he lay stretched out on a blanket on the ground. It was then they saw that he had, tightly clasped in his arms, the phonograph he had given his life to save.

Lady Gretchen had burns on her arms and hands which kept her in the hospital for several weeks afterward, but that night she refused treatment, ignoring the pain of her burns as she knelt beside old Moreno, trying to get him to hear her voice and the prayers she kept repeating.

He managed to whisper something to her; and the astounded onlookers saw her open the phonograph by the flickering light from the burning wagons and try to get a cracked record to play. It was the aria from *Aïda*. As she supported the dying clown's head on her knees, she cried out to the gaping crowd to applaud the finale of the music. Interspersing curses, she shouted an explanation that it was for Moreno, so that he could die happy, hearing through the agony of his burned body the applause of the public for the last time.

They never knew whether he really heard or not, but he died with a faint, triumphant little smile on his lips, and who knows, perhaps he saw himself again on the stage of the Metropolitan, with the glittering audience of the Diamond Horseshoe applauding him, instead of a crowd of gaping yokels and shabby heartbroken performers.

The circus was a complete loss to the Morellis, and the artists were stranded for some time. When Lady Gretchen came out of the hospital she found that her fellow artists had given a benefit performance for her and, as a surprise, they presented her with a sum of money, just enough for her passage to the United States with Barney.

Then she found out that the two little Hungarian girls had been left destitute, both parents having perished in the fire. They had no relatives, nowhere to go, and nobody else wanted them, so she decided to take the girls with her. It was then that she made her supreme sacrifice and sold Barney to pay their fares.

Nobody ever knew what became of her or the girls. Several times grandmama tried to locate them in theatrical agencies in both the United States and Europe, but they had disappeared completely. I am sure she left the stage, and I like to think she is somewhere on the ranch in the foothills of Montana that she so loved to talk about.

While we were working in the Schumann Circus, our act began to attract the notice of agents and the press. I personally had a nice success, which resulted in Ograinsky's redoubling his efforts to improve my tumbling. He resorted to his old habit of hitting me on the nape of the neck to increase my speed, and I developed chronic headaches that made me so ill I was hardly able to get through the performance. One night my eyes started blurring while I was on my trapeze, and I nearly fell, which alarmed grandmama so that she called the doctor. His diagnosis was that the frequent blows were causing the trouble; besides, I was very anemic and would have to rest for the entire summer. The row between Ograinsky and grandmama that followed the doctor's visit was sensational, with grandmama coming off the winner.

It was funny to see that great hairy ape, with his cauliflower ears and hands that resembled legs of mutton, writhing under the lash of grandmama's tongue. She frightened him so much that he finally quieted down and became almost human for the last few days in Copenhagen.

It was compulsory for me to have a rest and for grandmama to take care of herself, too, so we met mother in Rapallo, on the Italian Riviera, where we stayed at the quiet, old-fashioned Hotel Nervi overlooking the bay and blue waters of the Mediterranean. Rapallo is a favorite resort for singers who find the air and sunshine excellent for their throats and nervous systems.

Nellie Melba, the Australian soprano, a friend of mother's, spent a few days with us. Titta Ruffo, Montesanto, and Toti Dal Monte were all staying at the hotel, so it proved amusing for mother. They sang private concerts together for their own amusement after dinner, and to hear Melba, who was so tall and dignified, sing an English cockney song was a joy.

We had rooms opening on a private terrace with orange trees all around it, where grandmama could bask in the sunshine with her three pet snakes. They were the oldest and best beloved of her reptiles, and it did not occur to us that there was anything very odd in her having them, but they produced a startling effect on the guests and the staff of the Hotel Nervi as they crawled around her chair on the terrace.

It was like old times, being together again in a decent hotel with private bathrooms, but grandmama was very depressed about her rheumatism, which was especially painful in her wrists, and also because her hair was so gray. Every two or three days she would announce that she had made up her mind to retire from show business; then she would follow this up with a letter to Mr. Sherek, her agent, demanding to know why he had not sent her more bookings.

After a six-week stay in Rapallo, we went to London. Mother decided to make a trip to Canada and see my father, partly for business reasons and partly to give my brother an Easter vacation. He had just finished the winter term at Beaumont College, the Catholic equivalent of Eton. It is one of the most famous of English schools, a stately old place on the River Thames, full of beauty and tradition. I must say, the ship mother booked passage on was hardly in keeping with the dignity of the school, as far as my brother was concerned, for the S.S. *Lake Erie* was one of the more modest ships out of Liverpool for Quebec.

Our party consisted of grandmama with her three snakes in a clothes-basket "borrowed" from the Carlton Hotel in London, mother with a sable coat she had just bought on the instalment plan—which, I suspect, was the reason she chose a cheap ship—her bag of jewelry, a Spanish maid constantly seasick, myself, and my brother, very sulky on account of the snakes.

The second day at sea grandmama discovered some Spanish emigrants in the steerage and, in spite of mother's indignation, spent most of her time there playing cards with them. Her prolonged absences from her cabin were what enabled my brother and myself to carry out a plot of thoughtless adolescent cruelty concerning her senile and malodorant python, Lulu. She was my grandmother's favorite, and together with Susie, an African desert snake, and a nameless black king snake with a wandering complex, was retired from her professional career in "A Night in India."

I can only give as an excuse for my part in the affair my
34

extreme youth at the time; also, I was bored to tears and had nobody to play with. It is true I had followed grandmama to the steerage and struck up an acquaintance with some of the emigrants' children, but this was put a stop to when mother found out about it and discovered that there were cases of scarlet fever in the steerage infirmary. So I was disinfected, slapped, and that was that.

The odor of Lulu was historic and had already caused a stir in the Hotel Nervi, where the management had put it down to the smell of grandmama's cigars, but only after they had torn up the floor boards to see if something had clogged up the drain. When pythons, especially elderly lady pythons, change their skins, they are particularly fruity.

Lulu had just started to change hers when we got on the ship and was torpid and unpleasant to a high degree, especially in a small cabin. But grandmama refused to be separated from her pets and had developed a system of tipping the personnel wherever we went to keep their mouths shut. My brother, however, fresh from one of England's most exclusive public schools, lived in a constant state of worry lest the stewardess or cabin boy, in spite of tips, spread a report about the snakes among the passengers and cause embarrassing criticism.

One afternoon he came into the cabin and with my assistance dug Lulu out of the clothes-basket and inched her out of the port-hole into the sea. It took a bit of doing, but we managed it. When grandmama returned and discovered that Lulu was nowhere to be found, she had the entire ship searched and accused everybody from the captain down of having something to do with it. Grandmama when mad was not easy to handle, and the row she kicked up was terrific— but she never suspected us. Whether or not she put a ''hex'' on the ship out of rage (some people thought she did) I don't know, but the next night the good ship *Lake Erie* struck a submerged iceberg in the Strait of Belle Isle, off the coast of Newfoundland.

The usual scenes of confusion followed, with part of the

ship's lights out of commission, the emigrants stampeding and yelling to have the boats lowered, and pushing the first-class passengers about. The captain, with a Lancashire accent, bellowed through a megaphone that all women and children were to get into the first-class dining saloon and stay there.

Mother behaved with superb calm. She grabbed her sable coat and bag of jewelry and gave me an apple to eat. I don't know why, unless she thought I would have my mouth full and be unable to cry, which I had no intention of doing to begin with. Then she told grandmama and me to follow her to the bridge, where we were to remain whatever happened.

I don't remember much about what my brother did, except that after a consultation with grandmama, mother sent him to our cabin to fetch a small concertina. When he got back with it she started singing "Abide With Me" to calm the passengers. I accompanied her, but grandmama said it was not so hot because mother could not remember the words, so we went into Gounod's "Ave Maria," which sounded much better, although nobody listened to it as far as I know. There was an awful noise going on anyway. They were sending rockets up to give our location, and we kept being interrupted by mother's maid who wanted to be lowered in a lifeboat, despite the fact that the ship was not sinking, and when she was, insisted on being pulled up again immediately. Mother finally got a hairbrush out of her dressing-bag and rapped her sharply over the head with it. She was much better after that and confined her activities to wailing by herself on the steps of the bridge.

When dawn broke the ship was pronounced "not in danger," so everybody quieted down and went back to bed. At six o'clock the pilot tug came alongside to take off any passengers who wanted to proceed on another boat, but the *Lake Erie* righted herself while I was asleep in my cabin, and we continued on our trip to Quebec to meet my father.

He met us when the ship docked, and I noticed how his face lit up when he saw mother. We went to the Château Frontenac, where he had taken a suite for us: our rooms were filled with bowls of mother's favorite flower, lilies of the valley. He was always doing sweet things for people and remembered what they liked. The following day was the first time I ever saw him become cross with anybody, and that was with my brother.

Ever since we had left London, there had been scenes about the snakes and their feeding equipment which grandmama had handed over to my brother to take charge of. This equipment consisted of a large box with a wire top and a heavy metal tray which was used to keep the mice, frogs, and guinea pigs for the snakes' food. Certain varieties of snakes must kill their food at least twice a month or they will not thrive. Susie, the smallest snake, got by on raw eggs, milk, and desserts of meal worms and ant eggs which can be purchased at any pet shop, but the larger snakes had to have bigger game.

It was a messy business, especially when traveling, and took up hours of canvassing markets and pet shops. Of course the disappearance of Lulu was a big help, since we no longer had to buy baby rabbits for her, but the king snake simply had to have his menus prepared, and my brother refused to have anything to do with it. He was so rude to grandmama that she appealed to my father to take him to task.

Of course father did not enjoy the addition of the snakes and their livestock to our party and could appreciate my brother's point of view, but he really got upset when Bunnie (as my brother was nicknamed) complained bitterly that grandmama would not wear a hat, smoked cigars, and did not look like anybody else's grandmother, and he would not be seen with her. Father put it down to a youthful lack of poise, but at the same time told him there is nothing more detestable than a "snob."

I will never forget my brother's account of another grievance that caused him to sulk. Like all Spanish women, grandmama wore many petticoats, and whenever dressing or undressing, she had the habit of stepping out of them and leaving them in circles on the floor of her bedroom, or any other room she happened to be in. When asked why she didn't pick them up, she invariably replied, *"Los españoles nunca se rebajan"*—"Spaniards never stoop!"

Grandmama was deeply hurt about my brother's being ashamed of her, for she was very fond of him and proud of his good looks, but after this little upset she packed her things, said she was going off by herself with her snakes, and would meet us in New York for the return trip to Europe. Mother took Bunnie's part in the whole affair but oddly enough got it into her head that it was all father's fault that grandmama went wandering off alone, and that he had insulted her. She took my brother and went to visit some distant cousins in Montreal, and I was left with my father.

He took me to Toronto, where he had a house near the University, and I was happier than ever before. It was the first time I really got to know my own father. When he left his office in the afternoon, we used to go for long walks, and he would talk to me almost as if I were a grown person, teaching me English words and reading to me every night before I went to sleep. All this was too good to last, and one day he received a frantic telegram from mother announcing that Bunnie had suffered a serious motorcycle accident while out racing with some of the cousins they were visiting. He had a ruptured kidney and she was taking him to New York for medical treatment. We started packing immediately to join her there.

My father had given me everything I wanted, and our luggage included an Angora cat and a bowl of goldfish, which latter I fitted into a spittoon in the pullman car on the train: I had never seen a spittoon before. The water spilled out of the goldfish bowl over the feet of an old gentleman in the smoking compartment, but father smoothed everything over and never scolded me once. He was wonderfully patient, and I tried to be as little trouble as possible, for I sensed how worried he was that my brother had been moved by train while suffering such a serious injury.

Mother always made impulsive mistakes with the best possible intentions and generally managed to do the wrong things whenever she was left alone. When we arrived in New York, we found that my brother's condition had been aggravated by the traveling and he was very ill. Poor mother blamed herself for moving him against the advice of the Canadian doctors and never left his bedside. It was impossible to locate grandmama until she received the letters we sent in care of her agents in New York.

Father had to continue looking after me. I wore no hat and spoke very poor English, and everybody stared at me. The first time he took me to lunch in a very elegant restaurant, I tried my best to be on good behavior but got into serious difficulty with a lamb chop. I had just tackled it in the approved manner when it flew off my plate, landing on the carpet in the middle of the aisle just at the moment when some very elaborately dressed ladies were being shown to their table by the headwaiter. I was on the verge of tears and expected that this time I really would get slapped, but Daddy just laughed and got me another chop.

Grandmama turned up in New York in answer to the letters we sent to her agents, and as soon as Bunnie was out of danger, mother announced she was taking him to Europe. I will always remember the day we left and the New York docks in the hot sunshine: my brother could not walk, so was carried to the ship on a stretcher, and father seemed unusually sad. I could not understand why he didn't come with us, and saw tears in his eyes when he kissed me good-by.

We disembarked in Cherbourg and went on to Paris where my brother was first placed in a sanitarium in St. Cloud. He craved the sea, so mother decided to take a house somewhere on the coast of France for his convalescence. The place she rented, on the Island of Guernsey, was once Victor Hugo's house where he wrote *Toilers of the Sea*. It was very old, built of gray stone and something like the houses in Normandy, but wings and towers had been added to it at different times till it rambled all over the high cliffs overlooking the sea. The gardens were beautiful despite the winds, and the moors stretching behind the house were covered with bracken and yellow gorse. I used to imagine I could see the coast of Brittany on a clear day and the land where Iseult

Blanches Mains lived, and where King Arthur sailed on the black barge that came for him.

Mother had taken the house from a phony estate agent she had met, a bogus "count" of some sort. She was always getting herself mixed up with funny people she met on trains and in hotels, believing everything they told her. That was why grandmama always hung on to the bag of jewelry and kept the snakes in our bedroom.

Mother took the house because she wanted to watch the sea all day and sing up in the tower-room at four in the morning if she felt inclined: we always had trouble in hotels over the latter habit. The tower-room was a studio, built with windows circling the walls like a lighthouse. Migrating birds used to dash themselves against the glass on stormy nights when the lamps were lighted.

The tower overhung great black rocks where the waves thundered all day, and there were so many storms, even in the summertime, that it got on grandmama's nerves. She used to wander about the countryside looking for dead animals and herbs to make spells with, for she said the place was *embrujada* (bewitched). She was probably right, for mother found that all the water had to be pumped from a well and the lavatories wouldn't work, so she had to go to endless expense, getting a plumber and the nearest engineer to come and fix up the mess.

She had hauled an enormous Steinway concert grand piano from London for the tower-room, and part of the staircase caved in as it was being taken up. Then she found that the drawing-room, which she insisted on calling her "salon," had mildewed walls from the damp, so she went to London again to get material to cover them, rolls and rolls of brocade, and also bought a set of rosewood furniture.

She had everything shipped on a small steamer, the *Ibex*, which went aground on the Casquets, a group of dangerous rocks between Southampton and the Channel Islands. Weeks later the insurance company retrieved the things, which were of course ruined with seawater.

40

No servants would stay because the town of Guernsey was eleven miles away and there was no bus, making it a very unfortunate choice for a permanent residence. Grandmama said she could hear the voices of drowned sailors calling out of the sea at night, strange old Breton names of their wives and sweethearts, and this frightened the servants out of their wits and our employ.

We had no visitors except on one occasion—a call from the vicar and his wife, an impossible fat woman with a red face. When they came, mother, like the Lady of Shalott in Tennyson's poem, refused to descend from the tower-room, so I had to receive them in the "salon" to the best of my ability, which was hampered somewhat by my lack of knowledge of the English language and the startling effect produced by the spectacle of grandmama sitting in the middle of the floor smoking a black cigar and darning a Spanish shawl hung over two chairs.

We had put the big wooden shipping case belonging to the piano in a summer-house in a sheltered corner of the garden, and an old handy-man who pumped water for us and did what he called "tidying up," gave me a rabbit. My brother and I hid it in the piano case with supplies of lettuce and carrots, and shortly afterwards it had young ones and trouble really started. Rabbits swarmed all over the place, eating everything they came in contact with and continuing to reproduce more and more families in the greenhouses and under the veranda. Mother became worried by this and the situation in general, especially the incredible bills she kept receiving from the "count" for repairs on the house.

Finally father came over from Canada to see what was going on, his arrival coinciding with a notice from a lawyer in Southampton that the house had been bought the previous year from the Hugo estate by the government, to be used as a museum, and they could not understand how the agent had managed to rent it to us. In the meantime the "count" disappeared with three months' advance rent and the check for the plumber.

41

III

WHATEVER HARM the summer in Guernsey may have done to my father's bank account, it did at least restore my brother's health in an almost miraculous fashion. He loved the island so much that father arranged to leave him there in a Catholic seminary conducted by the Jesuit fathers, who maintained a lighter discipline than at Beaumont College with its compulsory games and outdoor sports, which were considered too strenuous for Bunnie. Father stayed with us long enough to conduct what the army terms "mopping up operations" on our family affairs and then returned to Canada.

After spending a few weeks in Düsseldorf, mother, grandmama, and I went to Berlin in October, and I rejoined Ograinsky's troupe for the coming three-month tour of the famous Hagenbeck Circus, which was to cover all Germany, Belgium, and Holland, and play a Christmas engagement at the Winter Garden in Berlin.

This great circus was an impressive organization run with almost military discipline. Its acts were the best obtainable, especially the animal acts, and it was a joy to see how well the animals were taken care of—with scrupulous cleanliness and hygiene. Night watchmen slept in cots beside their stalls and cages all night, and old Dr. Karl Hagenbeck, head of the family, was always on the prowl to see that nothing was ever neglected.

I used to spend hours watching him train his own acts, especially the bears, which were his specialty. He had a marvelous act with polar bears, which are very hard to handle and inclined to be wicked as a general rule. People said he had received countless maulings from them but would go right back to training them as soon as he got better. He was a rather small man, as I remember him, with a white beard and kindly blue eyes; he walked with a limp probably caused by a clawing from some refractory bear. His animals were trained with common sense and a firm gentleness, prongs or whips seldom being used except as a threat, and Dr. Hagenbeck insisted that the trainers who worked under him use the same system.

All the children who were considered trustworthy were allowed to walk the lion and tiger cubs in their spare time, so through this, I had a chance to learn about "big cats" and leopards (which interested me even more). While I took the cubs back and forth to the menagerie, I made friends with the different trainers and animal men, and they were nearly always willing to tell me about how they worked their animals.

To find a child with a special aptitude for wild-animal training is not so easy as people think, for it requires nerve and patience as well as physical strength and many other qualities. Some of the trainers had watched me hanging around the cages, unafraid of passing between them or along the dark aisles beside the "run"—which is quite a test in itself—and so gave me the chance I was looking for to learn to handle cats. I was never afraid of them and learned quickly.

My new hobby did not please Ograinsky. One afternoon he came looking for me. There was no matinée, and I was learning to school a lioness for the trainer, Hermann Paats. Ograinsky began storming at me and creating a scene outside the cage when suddenly a quiet voice came from the back of the bleachers. It was Doctor Karl. He told Ograinsky never to shout at animals or children around his circus, that I was a good child and had the makings of a trainer; he also suggested that I be allowed to work with the animals until I could handle some of them and get paid for my work as an extra act, instead of stunting the growth of my body by doing too many strenuous acrobatic feats, as I had been forced to do. I was in an ecstasy of pride and gratitude toward Doctor Karl, for Ograinsky got red and stammered something

43

foolish—but from that day on, he let me have two hours to myself every afternoon when there was no matinée.

After the Winter Garden we played a music-hall tour through Austria and Poland. My mother was touring with her concerts in Germany. One night in Warsaw, grandmama saw the World War in the cards—she was sometimes very clever in predicting things—and she was filled with such grave forebodings that she prevailed upon Ograinsky to get a booking in Paris. Sherek was cabled and got a date for us at the old Cirque Nouveau, and we arrived in Paris just two or three days before the declaration of war.

Paris was in an uproar, and everything was disorganized. Foreign artists (many from enemy countries) were being hustled about, so between one thing and another our opening was postponed. Mother was trying to get back to Paris from Germany and had succeeded in involving herself in a terrible mess on the Swiss-German frontier. Grandmama was worried to death about what might happen for she knew the difficulties mother could manage to create in normal times, and she foresaw troubles on a grand scale if we could not get hold of her quickly. We haunted the consulates, tourist agencies, and railway stations where mobilized troops leaving for the front sang the "Marseillaise," and crowds of people stood cheering and weeping. All Paris was in a delirium of patriotic fervor. Grandmama was greatly perturbed because nobody would take any gold louis or English pounds. They wanted paper notes instead, and these were practically impossible to get.

Finally mother arrived by train in a horse car crowded with refugees. Her only remaining piece of luggage was a round hat-box with a mauve feather boa in it. She had been treated with the greatest discourtesy by the German officials at the frontier, and her fur coat had been stolen. It was only by a dispensation of Providence and my grandmother's foresight that she had not taken her jewelry with her, or they would have seized that, too.

As soon as mother had recovered from her fatiguing experience and bought some more clothes, we decided to go to

44

London, grandmama's agents Sherek and Braff having booked us to play the Coliseum, which was then considered the best music-hall in London. We made a hurried exit from Paris at the last minute—for we had waited in vain for Ograinsky to get the horses out of France. Every available horse was needed by the French Army, and the authorities made all sorts of difficulties. We were finally obliged to leave without them for it meant losing the Coliseum if we waited any longer.

Two months later, Ograinsky did manage to get his horses shipped to England and through the Quarantine. Fortunately, nobody in France wanted grandmama's snakes or the Indians, and so they all embarked successfully. Our trip across on a crowded channel steamer was an exciting one. The ship was jammed with Belgian refugees and many well-known French artists, including Alice Delysia (made a famous revue star through the notoriety of the Fragson case), Randall, the Anglo-French comic, and Jacqueline Forzane, one of the most beautiful of the French actresses. Another lovely lady was accompanied by her lover, a Russian Grand Duke who insisted on carting an enormous antique bed around with him everywhere he went. In the flurry of the departure, the bed, wrapped in burlap, had been deposited on the forward deck and left there, where it came in very handy for the refugees to lie down on whenever they felt seasick. The ship took nine hours to navigate the submarine-infested waters of the English Channel, but we finally arrived in London and went to the Piccadilly Hotel.

That was a caravanserai of all the smartest French *cocottes* and artists, who made the Grill Room their rendezvous every night till it looked like the Café de la Paix in Paris. Gaby Deslys and Harry Pilcer were there; Marilyn Miller, the American dancer with her family (working in the 400 Club); Mado Minty; Valeska Suratt, and all sorts of well-known people. When the first of the British wounded arrived from France, they used to hobble down to the Grill Room on crutches or heavily bandaged but immaculately dressed in dinner jackets.

45

We opened at the Coliseum and were immediately booked for the London Music-Halls circuit and the Moss Stoll Northern tour through England and Scotland if we wanted it. The Ograinsky Wonder Children were beginning to go places, and we got a better spot on the bill after our opening night. We played two shows a day, so I was able to have a governess in the mornings, and three times a week we went for dancing lessons at the Lupino School of Acrobatic Dancing near Shaftesbury Avenue.

The English vaudeville of that epoch was a revelation to me, and I often think that the younger generation of to-day, which has never really known vaudeville, is losing a great deal, for the talent in some of those acts was marvelous. There were then such artists as Marie Lloyd, the comedian, with her sly guttersnipe humor which was so clever it never became offensive; Grock, the great French musical clown, who played the Coliseum year after year, as did Sarah Bernhardt and the first of the Russian ballet troupes; and Harry Tate and George Robey, whose acts were classics in England and whose gags and jokes will never die. We played a huge charity benefit for the Red Cross while we were at the Coliseum, and I saw this marvelous group of artists all together. One of the numbers that most impressed me was called "Joe Boganny and His Lunatic Bakers." It was something like the "mumming birds" that Charlie Chaplin worked in and was composed of acrobats ranging from tiny dwarfs to the biggest giants I have ever seen. They were dressed as bakers and did tumbling at such speed that it was almost unbelievable. Another act was the beloved "coster," Albert Chevalier, who became a star with his singing of "My Old Dutch." He must have been in his seventies, and I will never forget his old withered hands and tired face as he stood in the spotlight and sang,

"We've been together now for forty years
And it don't seem a day too much—
For there's not a lady living in the land
That I'd change for my dear old Dutch . . ."

46

Circus acts had gravitated to London from all parts of war-
torn Europe and had amalgamated to form an immense spectacle called the "International Circus" under a syndicate of
prominent showmen and newspapermen. The recovery of the
horses and the list of head-liners booked for the circus were
sufficient to throw Ograinsky into a veritable frenzy of rehearsing, and he decided that from the end of October on we
would take no more bookings but concentrate on polishing up
the different acts for the big show at the Olympia, the huge
stadium equivalent to New York's Madison Square Garden.
We had just started when a cable came from my father saying that his mother was seriously ill in Ireland and wanted
to see my brother and me. Since he could not come himself we
were to start immediately.

My brother was sent for from the Channel Islands, and we
left from Liverpool. I had never seen my paternal grandmother and was not very keen on the idea: I had enough of
grandmothers with the one I did know. However, it was an
adventure, and the trip alone with my brother was fun—we
sat on the deck of the little steamer crossing to Ireland and
listened to the eerie sound of the foghorns in the night and
wondered what our father's relatives were like.

The house where our grandmother lived was at Gorfe, a
tiny village on the coast of Antrim looking across the sea
to the Firth of Clyde. The ruins of the original Castle Gorfe
date back to Cormac mac Cuillenáin in the tenth century. It is
near Ballymena, where most of the family lived and still
live. The modern wing which formed my grandmother's house
was a great gray-stone building that had been added on in
the eighteenth century and it was sometimes called "Friend-
ville." It fascinated me because the stairs had red cords for
banisters. There were black wood panels on the walls, dark
passages, and an incredibly depressing drawing-room. Gray
sea fog filled every corner of the great house, laden with
the smell of sea wrack, and this mingled with the smoke of
peat sods burning in the fireplaces. It was the end of October
and cold as Charity, and there was an English nurse who

47

rustled about and constantly complained about the lack of hot water.

We were received by the village priest and two dreary old gentlemen who were, I think, lawyers. I could not understand a word they said, but I remember that my brother was very rude to them because they said my mother could not be buried in the family vault when she died. There was also a thin, red-nosed woman called Miss Cameron—lady's companion to my grandmother—who kept staring at me as if she thought I would bite her and continually asked me personal questions. While we were waiting to see my grandmother, who had pneumonia, I got out by myself and found two foxhound puppies and a very nice groom who took me through the grounds. He told me that the night before we arrived, the Banshee had called twice from the old castle and that there had been a loud ringing at the front door at midnight. When they opened it, there was nothing there, but everybody with the exception of the English nurse (he referred to her as a "foreigner") knew that the hearse had come for "the Mistress," my grandmother. He said he looked from his window over the stables and saw the hearse go down the drive with black plumes and four black horses. And he told me how the Banshees came from the back of the bog and said that lots of people who had seen them declared they were big gray birds with eyes like drowned women. He explained to me that the house and the family were finished because there was a curse on them—that there would be no more men to carry on the race. Then he showed me a round stone table in the middle of the courtyard in front of the house, where there had at one time been a big tree.

The legend of the family was that there should always be a place set at this table for the "uninvited guest," for "holy men often came as beggars to try out the hearts of men." The legend ran that the day the place was not set any more, the tree would wither and the last of the men of the house would die, one by one, without heirs to the name.

It appeared that some years previously my father's oldest

48

brother—who had retired from the Navy, drank like a fish, and spent his spare time hunting, gambling and having illegitimate children—came home one summer evening on the eve of the Holy Day and found the servants eating and dancing and a place set on the stone table under the tree, with an old tramp feasting as the "uninvited guest." This seems to have annoyed my uncle, for he flew into a terrible rage, knocked the plates from the table with his whip, beat the tramp, and gave orders in the house that thereafter there was to be no more of such superstition. My grandmother tried to reason with him for the sake of the old tradition, but he would not have it.

That night a great storm came in from the sea: the tree was struck by lightning and so completely shattered that it had to be cut down. A few weeks later, my uncle was thrown from his horse and brought home dying. He was unmarried and had no heirs, so the first part of the curse had already started working. The groom said my uncle's last words were, "There is a woman in the village—" They supposed she was the mother of one of his many illegitimate offspring, but they never discovered who she was. When I told my brother about these things, he asked the lawyers and they said it was true about the tree, the legend, and my father's brother, but they did not believe about the Banshee and the hearse. They also said I was not to be allowed to talk to the servants any more or to go out without Miss Cameron.

I saw my grandmother the next day: she was lying wrapped in a white shawl in a great four-poster bed and looked as if she were made of yellow wax. She cried when she saw me. Her lips moved but I could not hear whether she said anything. Then Miss Cameron and the nurse took me out of the room and down to the drawing-room, where the lawyers and a lot of elderly people sat drinking port.

They gave me a horrible amethyst brooch with my late grandfather's hair in it as a souvenir from my grandmother (I still have it). Then my brother went up to see her and came down green in the face. He proceeded to get violently drunk on port wine, which did not seem to surprise anybody (they appeared to like him better than me). The blinds were kept down all day until my grandmother died at midnight—just as the groom had said she would.

After we returned to London, we joined grandmama who had found a studio apartment in Earl's Court. The day before we moved in, mother suddenly stopped in one of the bedrooms and said, "Oh, this is terrible! Somebody has died here."

Grandmama replied immediately, "You're not going to mix me up with your spirits. You can sleep in this room yourself."

They began to argue about it in excited Spanish, gesticulating wildly and pushing each other about. In the end, I was given the room. I will never know whether or not it was because they had stirred my imagination, but I felt at once there was something wrong with that room. All night long I heard choking breathing, heavy panting, the sound of some one shuffling about, and bottles on the mantelpiece being shifted. At about four in the morning I could stand it no longer, so I got up and, groping my way down a dark corridor to mother's room, woke her.

She didn't like the house much anyway, because she discovered it was damp, so the next morning she told grandmama there definitely were spirits in the place and we wouldn't have to pay any rent. We left after breakfast for the estate agent's office, and after much haggling he finally admitted that the former owner, an elderly gentleman, had died of asthma in my bedroom.

Mother sang several concerts at the Royal Albert and Queen's Halls, then left for a concert tournée with the London Symphony Orchestra, while grandmama and I again started rehearsals for the Olympia. Ograinsky kept us children practising almost beyond the limits of our endurance.

He rented an old riding academy near the Olympia which was without heat and far too low for the height we would have to work in the circus. Naturally we were all ill from the

50

cold, and we suffered from stiff muscles that prevented our sleeping at night, but Ograinsky put any ailment in children down to overeating. He had a book we had to sign every morning before working, to record whether we had functioned normally. If not, it was castor oil immediately, or some other equally fœtid concoction of grandmama's. I got disgusted with it all and had no relaxation except the hour I had managed to obtain in the studio of Weidmar von Teiplitz, a famous Polish painter of miniatures.

During the summer we had spent in Guernsey, I had dabbled a little in watercolors and was intensely interested in learning to paint—particularly miniature portraits. Von Teiplitz was a wonderful teacher. He lived in a very dark churchlike house off Kensington High Street, and grandmama used to go there with me. She struck up a friendship with Madame Teiplitz, who had a weakness for spiritualism. While I took my lesson in the big vault-like studio, the two old ladies used to hold a séance in a corner. I am sure grandmama faked the whole thing, but it got Madame Teiplitz in such a dither that she kept her husband awake all night because she was sure the studio was filled with astral bodies. In spite of all the other work I was obliged to do, I made progress in my painting lessons, which I took between the functions at the Olympia.

The management tried to run the show as much like the American three-ring circuses as possible, a different system entirely from the one we were accustomed to, and until we became familiar with working to a whistle—which marked the finish of our acts—we had to do a lot of extra rehearsing in order to get things running with their usual smoothness, especially the horses, and we took more than one spill during the first few days.

We had a brilliant opening and quite a lot of publicity on our own work: the entire show was a success, playing to capacity houses at every performance. There were two famous flying acts, that were of course adult performers. They did double and triple turns in the air and many other feats which we children were not able to do. One of them—the original troupe of the Zimgannos whom we knew from the Cenicelli Circus in Russia—had for their finishing stunt a complete blackout of the lights, and worked with luminous paint on their tights in a design representing jagged streaks of lightning. As their bodies shot through the air from trapeze to trapeze, there were drum rolls for thunder, and the effect was most thrilling, especially when they purposely missed a trick and dropped into the net. All they used as guides for their spacing and to avoid knocking into each other were balls (used to give weight and balance to the long bars) painted with the luminous paint on each end of their trapeze. Many acts have since copied the idea, but I have never seen any of them do it as the Zimgannos did. Ograinsky used to watch these great performers every show and got so much inspiration from their work that he nearly killed us trying to copy them. Both grandmama and Ograinsky felt that we were reaching the zenith of their hopes and that the Olympia Circus with such a galaxy of big acts was the taking-off point for a fabulous career.

I worked so hard those weeks that practising became a nightmare and I went about in a daze. The strain of the Christmas matinées did me still more harm, and I really felt ill but did not dare to complain about it. So I neglected to take care of myself according to the rules laid down by Ograinsky. It was partly my fault that I fell. Children do not have the subconscious reflexes of older people, especially when fatigued or not well.

I have often been asked to train children for aërial work and have always refused, because it is one of the hardest and most dangerous professions. I have never wanted to be instrumental in helping them go through what I did, or suffer the hardships and accidents which are inevitable. Of course, good aërial acrobats made large salaries if they had a sensational act—and the work does become fascinating after the preliminary hard training is accomplished—but to-day, these acts are not so much in demand, for it is an impossibility for acts

52

of physical strength to work four or five times a day in vaudeville without a speedy breakdown. Many parents, even old performers, think twice nowadays before they put their children through the severe training and all the nervous strain which must be suffered before an aërial act can be any good at all—especially when they know that sooner or later a sensational act will get some bad falls, and any money saved will have to be used to pay doctor and hospital bills.

And yet it would indeed be a tragedy if the graceful trapeze acts should become a lost art, for they form one of the most important parts of the circus entertainment; together with the clowns, elephants, horses, and wild beasts—the five great factors. I personally think that the circus is like Christmas and will be with us always and that our billing in the Olympia rightly described the show as an entertainment "Appealing to All Children from 8 to 80." So, as long as somebody else takes the responsibility of breaking in an aërial act, I am always happy to give any help I can (from a considerable stock of experience) to avoid accidents and teach scrupulous care in the changing of old material—frayed and worn ropes and shackles—and avoidance of a hundred and one causes of falls.

People have often asked me what it feels like to fall from a great height and what I have thought about at the time. I have been able to tell them only that the whole thing happens so quickly that there is not much time for thinking about anything except a moment of wild panic, a frenzied grab for a rope or anything handy, and then, as one's body goes hurtling toward the ground, a feeling of resignation with the one hopeless thought, "This is IT." Before the final grinding crash and, with any luck, merciful oblivion, I have on two or three occasions been perfectly conscious when I hit the ground—only to pass out later, generally in the middle of trying to smoke a cigarette, which was the first thing it occurred to me to ask for.

To return to my first fall in the Olympia: I was working off time and could not get into the correct beat of the swing.

While I was doing a difficult crossing pass, the bar twisted somehow and I lost my grip. It all happened in an instant, but I kept my head as I felt myself falling and tried desperately to "tuck," as I had been taught to do, for the fall in the net. But the twist of the trapeze bar must have thrown me sidewise so that I struck the side of the net where an iron hook was fastened to guy it out. This broke my fall but fractured my skull, and my body fell outside the net on to the tanbark of the ring below.

I was unconscious and terribly smashed up, and when they got me to St. George's Hospital, the doctors did not think there was any hope for me. In fact, they did not even trouble to clean the dirt out of a wound on my wrist, and this caused an infection a few days later that very nearly cost me my left arm.

Mother was sent for, and grandmama cabled my father to come at once. As soon as he arrived, he made arrangements to have me removed to a private hospital in Sloane Street, one of the best in London, where I had every care and attention money could buy. My father was never a rich man, and I can imagine what sacrifices he had to make to pull me through, for many times the doctors thought I would not recover.

When I got to be a little better and could take in what was going on around me, I found the numerous incidents that occurred between my grandmother and the nurses a source of welcome diversion, even though I was nearly always in pain. In a way they did me good, for I managed to have some laughs, especially one day when grandmama arrived at the hospital with a quantity of thick brown paper bags, purloined from the nearest grocery store. She had soaked them in olive oil to form an unpleasant-looking compress which she had liberally sprinkled with red pepper. This compress, held in place with a hot iron, she maintained was an infallible Spanish remedy to relieve pain. Needless to say, the efficiency of this treatment was never tried out on me.

The nurses were always on the watch, to be sure grandmama did not get in when I was alone. However, one day when the nurse had gone out for a few minutes, she slipped into my room, bringing with her a large brass brazier which she had smuggled in somehow; she filled it with charcoal and lighted it. When the coals began to glow, she sprinkled some dried herbs on them which sent out a terrible black smoke and the most weird smell. Then she opened the window and waved the smoke out with her arms, chanting, "*Que salga el Mal, y que entre el Bien*" ("That the Evil go out and the Good enter"). Soot from the smoke floated down on the bedding and pillows. The nurse rushed in thinking the place was on fire. Grandmama had caused quite a commotion, and I thoroughly enjoyed myself.

My fall had been a bad shock to my father, for he had not known anything about my working at Olympia. Relations were very unhappy between my parents, who never lived together and seldom wrote letters. The only thing that made father happy was a positive statement from the doctor when I got better, that I could never work again because my left shoulder had been too badly smashed. I spent eighteen months in the hospital, and for the first few months went through operation after operation, till at last they pulled me through the worst of it.

My left shoulder was completely stiff and helpless, and at one time there was talk of amputating my arm. Only my mother's firm refusal prevented this—and the wonderful care I had from Dr. Abercrombie, a little Scotch surgeon who saved my life. Poor man! What he went through at times with grandmama was unbelievable. Mother was extremely nervous and constantly worried about my brother, who had run away from school and joined the Foreign Legion, claiming to be twenty-one when he was only eighteen. She could get little news from him, only the army postcards with three or four lines of stereotyped news. I realize now that she went through a terrible time between the two of us.

During the latter part of my illness, I read avidly—especially English literature. Father, before returning to America, had made a list of English classics for me to read, and I studied and absorbed English writing from *Piers Plowman* down to contemporary writers. In addition to the list of books, I managed to get another concession from father which had taken quite a lot of persuasion: he finally did smuggle in a cage of white "waltzing mice." All animals, of course, inspire horror in hospitals, and the scene that occurred when the mice were discovered was very stirring. They insisted on taking the cage out of the room at night, and then some of the mice got out. The result was that in the course of the weeks that followed, the elegant nursing home was overrun with gray and white mice. After a lot of pressure had been brought to bear, I agreed to let the remainder be returned whence they came—but only upon condition that they be replaced with a dog which I was to have as soon as I left the hospital.

When at last I was able to get out of bed and tried to walk again, a difference in the length of my legs became terribly noticeable. The left one, which had been most badly fractured, was one and a half inches shorter than the right. Despite hours spent in hanging bags of sand on it and pulling and twisting, they could not get it stretched. So it was decided that when my father left for Canada again, my mother would take me to Switzerland, regardless of war conditions and traveling difficulties, for there was just a glimmer of hope that perhaps Doctor Neumann of Lausanne could help me. He was a famous orthopedic specialist and very expensive but considered an authority in such cases as mine.

He advised mother to send me to a convalescent home near Lausanne where I would receive treatments. When I saw the chart showing all the injuries I had got through that fall in Olympia, I realized with some feeling of pride that I must have put up a pretty good fight to be alive at all. Nearly all my left side had been shattered, including internal injuries and what not. Under the circumstances, it was almost impossible for the doctors who had to set my legs and arm to have done a better job than they did.

We arrived at the sanitarium by car with my Irish terrier, Lady Drogheda, who, after much argument, was permitted to come along with me. The Swiss-German doctor who received us was stupefied at the sight of the dog: she had been carsick and had deposited her lunch on a new brown leather suitcase. As soon as we got to my room, the doctor looked at her and said, "She shall not stay. She shall go. She shall be sick—it is a nonsense." I have never forgotten this speech. After a heated altercation with my mother, who wanted to get rid of me and return to Paris (she had hopes my brother might get leave), a compromise was arrived at. They did not want to upset me too much, and because I refused to be separated from Lady Drogheda, they moved me to a little wooden pavilion in the beautiful grounds away from everybody, so that the dog and I could keep our germs together in peace. From our quarters we could see wounded men in wheel-chairs and in beds on wheels everywhere.

For the three months I stayed in the sanitarium in the spring of 1915, I had a French governess—Mademoiselle Solange something-or-other, who had a mustache and was very intelligent, and I liked her because she took my dog for walks. We spoke French together, and she also taught me the usual subjects. It was she who put an idea into my head of studying English literature for a Girton Scholarship. She had coached a girl for it in England, and the subject fascinated me so much that when I proceeded to make unusual progress, she was astonished.

I am often told, especially in the United States, that I have an English accent. Personally I don't think I have any specific accent at all, unless I acquired something of the English way of speaking and pronouncing certain words while in the hospital in London, where I could speak nothing but English except with mother or grandmama. I have always retained the habit of thinking in Spanish or French, then translating my thoughts into English or any other language I am not familiar with, which may account for many discrepancies in my speech or writings. At any rate, my eighteen months in

57

a hospital gained for me a better command of the English language and a great love for its authors.

I knew that as far as a stage career was concerned, I was through—and so I reflected that there were three roads open for me in which I had ability. First came music, but I would be handicapped on account of my broken shoulder for some time to come. Then there was painting, for which I had some talent but not enough experience to be sure of my ground. The third course that seemed logical to me was to take up a subject for which I had ability and which I could teach later on.

When the time came for me to leave Lausanne, mother was preparing another concert tournée and was too busy to come to Switzerland for me. It was with mixed emotions I found myself traveling with grandmama. However, she was rather nice to me and never mentioned the subject of what I was going to do to help the family budget along, till I finally broached the matter myself.

When I explained to her all my ideas on what I could do and wanted to study, she just stared at me blankly and then relapsed into silence. Grandmama had plainly shown that she was disgusted with me for my careless stupidity in wrecking a promising circus career just when I was showing the ability to carry on where she left off. For she had made up her mind that after the Olympia Circus, she would retire and devote her time to my professional future.

She often quoted a French proverb, *"Il faut mourir en beauté,"* or, in unpoetical language, "Get out while you're still good." She felt that she wanted to leave the stage while there were still top bookings being offered to her and before she was relegated to a sideshow, which to her would be a *déchéance* more bitter than death. Both she and mother had an almost morbid fear of freaks and avoided their booths like the plague.

While we were with the Hagenbeck show in Hamburg, some Indian pals of our musicians had appeared with a "pin-head Indian boy" from Simla, who was more ape than anything else. European circuses as a rule do not go in for freaks as the

58

American ones do, but this boy was taken on as an exhibit called the "Missing Link."

One Saturday afternoon the boy got excited about the immense crowds that stood around gaping at him, and the men could do nothing with him. Grandmama's Indians were getting the snakes ready for the matinée; she had just left them and was passing the exhibit, trying not to look at it, when a big fat German woman began to laugh and make fun of the wretched boy, with true Teutonic brutality and coarseness. This woman, like the majority of German *hausfrauen*, was generously endowed by nature with a pair of *nichons* that looked like captive balloons. They were too big a temptation for the boy, who apparently was not so dumb after all, for he leaped on the woman and sank his teeth into her right breast. They had a terrible fight to get the boy off and had to take the woman to a hospital. The scene so upset grandmama that she was deathly ill and could hardly get through her act. When we were at the Olympia there was a selection of "Queer People" imported from Coney Island that disgusted grandmama so that she often walked the whole length of the immense building to avoid seeing them.

Among these freaks was one of the most unusual I have ever seen, a colored woman from New Orleans billed as the "Two-Headed Nightingale." She had two separate and distinct heads, one a little smaller than the other and with a wall eye. They were joined to her body at the shoulders, where they merged into the single spine. She, or they, sang duets, and her star number was a song sung by the soprano head in French and the mezzo-soprano head in English. This woman— or should I make it plural—was intelligent and very ambitious. Somebody must have told her that mother was a noted opera singer, for she came to our dressing-room one day and introduced herself. The expression of grandmama's face defied description—I thought she was going to have apoplexy. I had to get the woman out in a hurry as best I could, but she was not to be outmaneuvered and haunted the corridors and ring seats till she finally found mother watching a rehearsal and then insisted on singing "The Last Rose of Summer" for her, and wanted some pointers on the rendering of that classic. Mother became hysterical and ran to my dressing-room, where she had such a fit of crying that I thought we would have to send for the doctor.

So with such decided ideas on the subject of sideshows and freak exhibits, it is understandable why grandmama, when she felt she was growing too old to dance any more, preferred to donate her big snakes, including Rajah, to the Regent's Park Zoo in London.

Most of her musicians had returned to India to join the British forces, and thus the last curtain was rung down on "A Night in India."

I knew it must have been hard for grandmama to give up the sawdust trail, for when I was in Switzerland she wrote me that she had again gone wandering off by herself, visiting all the places and theaters where she had worked. As she grew older, this habit got worse: she positively hated to stay for more than a few days in one place. Mother tried several times to bottle her up with her sisters (the widowed ones with the large families) in Seville, since they had to stay put principally for financial reasons. They always said, referring to my grandmother, *"Ella es tan gitana"*—meaning, she is such a gipsy—as if they never had anything to do with such people.

IV

I N LONDON, mother was too busy to listen to my request for the course of English literature but said she would write to my father about it (which she completely forgot to do), and in the meantime she would let me go to all the schools and classes I wanted, provided I left her alone with her concerts.

I started studying piano at the Guildhall School of Music and attended classes in drawing from the nude three days a week, at the Frank Brangwyn School of Art in Kensington. The rest of the time I divided between the evening classes at the Chelsea Art School and the Whitmore School for Women. The Whitmore School (one of the oldest in England) takes pupils from quite small girls to students of eighteen and twenty and prepares them for Girton College in Cambridge. The English course has a very high standard and is, I believe, only for girls over sixteen, but for some reason I had grown quite tall for my age during my illness and appeared much older than eleven years, so I got in everywhere without comment (after, of course, they looked grandmother over and talked to me to see whether I knew anything, and how advanced I was in these subjects).

Despite all Dr. Neumann's expensive treatments, I limped badly and could not even put a hat on or brush my hair with my left arm. Mother was bitterly disappointed about this, and I think this was the reason I threw myself into my studies with fervor and worked hard to please her, so that the money that had been spent on me in Switzerland should not be wasted. The old inferiority complex returned with interest, but I battled it through, passed the Girton exams with honors, and won a gold medal for piano and theory of music at the Guildhall, in spite of my arm and the tortures I went through practising with it. My fingers were uninjured then, but in another fall in later years I broke two of them in my left hand and have since practically abandoned the piano except for composition, orchestration, and as an accompanist.

While I was at the Brangwyn Art School, I met Nina Hamnett and we formed a warm friendship which has lasted through the years. She became a brilliant painter and author of a famous book, *Laughing Torso,* which was the sensation of the Paris season of 1924. Nina, a tall gangling girl of seventeen when we first met, was of Irish descent and had a keen sense of humor and a brilliant talent. Most of the students of Brangwyn were of the *bourgeoisie* and very prissy: they thought painting from the nude was the height of depravity, and they were very "arty" and extremely boring.

To me it was a tremendous compliment that Nina should even notice me, and I took good care she should not discover my age and perhaps drop me in consequence. She, too, had been brought up by her grandmother—her mother was dead, and her father, a retired naval officer, was one of the most depressing men I have ever met. I went to studio parties with Nina, met the famous Augustus John, the sculptor Jacob Epstein (adored by students for the scandal over his monument to Oscar Wilde), and the brilliant young sculptor De Brescha who did a statue of Nina later on, which he called "Laughing Torso" and exhibited in the Salon at the Grand Palais in Paris.

All this new phase of life fascinated me—I had never known clever people outside the operatic world, and then I was too young to be taken much notice of. But of course it was too good to last. Grandmother started to agitate mother about my being so much out of the house—and I was foolish enough to tell them that I had committed the crime of going to the Café Royal with Nina to see Augustus John and had drunk *one* crème de menthe. This famous café had been the hangout of Oscar Wilde and his friend Lord Alfred Douglas in the Gay Nineties and was now one of the favorite meeting-places of artists and writers.

Somebody must have given mother the idea that it was a sink of iniquity, for she made a terrible scene, calling up Nina's father, who could not understand a word she was saying and imagined that both his daughter and I had been raped in the middle of the Café Royal. As a result of all this, I was not allowed to profit by any scholarship at Girton, and it was decided that I must be removed from the immoral atmosphere of the world of Art and Letters and go to work again in some capacity in the theater, where they could keep their eyes on me.

The discussions about my future continued daily, and unfortunately mother suddenly conceived the idea that I should be made to sing—which would simplify matters no end. I opposed this idea, for I had a small contralto voice which I felt instinctively would never come to anything more than a mediocre ballad voice. I had absolutely no ambition to become a singer and never could understand why mother got this idea into her head—for she was such a fine musician herself and also a very good teacher, although not overly patient. I knew what I would be in for if I did not respond to her hopes as a singer. But in the end, grandmama got her way, as she generally did, and we consulted the doctor about my trying to regain my flexibility for dancing.

He said that my physical condition had improved very much and that in his opinion I could have massage and stretching exercises, especially on my arm, which was the worst of all my troubles. If I had the will to take a good deal of punishment, he saw no reason why I could not start dancing exercises very gradually.

I started training at the Pavlova School at Ivy House, Hampstead, and was really surprised to find that I could dance perfectly on my toes again and hide completely the shortness in my left leg. For this, I had in all justice to thank Ograinsky, for he had worked me so hard in the ballet we danced with his troupe that my legs were far stronger than I had ever realized. In addition to this, my early training in Russia had been so complete and the teachers in the Nelidova

School had formed my feet and legs to such perfect positions, that together with all the acrobatic work I had done with Ograinsky, I had a physical basis to depend on, even with all the broken bones.

The teachers at the Pavlova School were amazed, knowing my background, for my body became limber in about three weeks, and it was impossible to tell there was anything the matter with me except for my left arm. This remained weak and awkward. I tried to stand on my hands, throw walk-overs and somersaults, but it was impossible, for I got severe pain and my hand would swell up at once. As for trying to hang from a trapeze bar, it was out of the question.

To say that grandmama was happy about my dancing would be putting it mildly: she simply radiated joy and worked me for hours with castanets—called *palillos* in Spanish dancing.

I had started working at the Pavlova School directly after Christmas, and at the end of February, mother returned from another tour. She was worried about finances again, and she could not afford to keep up my classes at Ivy House. However, I was getting along splendidly in my dancing, and it was decided that we would accept some engagements in opera and concert that had been offered by cable from Gatti-Casazza, the impresario of the Metropolitan in New York. I would have corps de ballet work in the operas, which would of course help out financially.

Grandmama went to Granada for some sun after the London winter, and mother and I made a hastily planned trip to New York. The work helped her peace of mind considerably, and I danced well enough to get in on a few of the last functions of the Diaghilev company at the Shubert-Murat Theater. Diaghilev had never had other than Russian dancers, with a few exceptions, in contrast to Anna Pavlova, who preferred English girls. Happily, when I appeared on the scene, everybody thought I was fifteen and an authentic Russian, because of my speech and the background of the Nelidova School. I acquired the nickname of "Miçka," which means a little black animal in Russian slang, and it stuck to me through my ballet career.

Once again, after six weeks in America, we met grandmama in Paris and found she had not been idle while we were in the States. She had arranged for me to work immediately in vaudeville with an act which had been cooked up by Mr. Braff of Sherek and Braff, grandmama's exagents. Mr. Braff was the husband of Tortola Valencia, the exotic Spanish dancer, and was considered one of the best agents in London—but not a producer. This balletomane had spent all his savings promoting crazy companies that never got anywhere. It finally sent him mad, for a few years later he went completely out of his mind in Paris. One morning he rushed down from his office in the Rue de la Paix to the middle of the street and started directing the traffic, telling the astounded passers-by that the cars and buses were ballet girls and waving his arms at them in waltz time. They finally had to bottle him up, and he died very soon afterward.

The act Mr. Braff had cooked up was entitled "Señor Ghirardy and His Drawing-room Dancers." It was a lulu and consisted of an enormous Dresden china clock in a scene supposed to represent a drawing-room in an old French château—but it looked more like the parlor of a theatrical boarding-house in Bloomsbury. Two girl dancers dressed as shepherdesses simpered on either side of the clock. Ghirardy, who was a foul dancer and knew it, contented himself with doing the part of the clockmaker who had come to wind the clock. Of course he fell asleep, and we were his dream. We got down from the clock and fiddled about on our toes. I did a solo and got my name billed. (It was then I started to use the name of Davis, a family name and easy to remember.) The show was so corny that I did not think it would last a week, but it had a nice success, and we played every music-hall around London. It helped me a lot to get back into shape, working before an audience again—but I left it after a few weeks to dance in the corps de ballet at the Palace Theater, in the *Sniegurotschka* (Snow Maiden Ballet).

During this engagement the biggest of the Zeppelin raids over London occurred, about eleven o'clock at night. Thirty-five Taube planes preceded the Zeppelin, which soared over London at a low altitude. Some bombs were dropped over the center of the city and Piccadilly Circus. The top floor of the theater, where we dressed, was plunged into darkness and partially damaged. The management rushed us downstairs in our long white costumes and ballet shoes, giving us time only to grab our coats, and grouped us all together in the foyer of the theater. A few members of the elegant English audience left, but the orchestra kept on playing, and some of the acts went on the stage and sang "Tipperary," so everybody sat down in the stalls and joined in the chorus with them.

The raid was a severe one, and the police would not allow any one to leave the theater while it continued. I was worried about my mother, who was in the Savoy Hotel where we were living, for I heard people say it was in a bad position: the Germans were guiding the Zeppelin by the light of the moon on the Thames, which flows by the Embankment just behind the Savoy. Another girl and myself managed to slip out with raincoats over our costumes and with the ballet slippers still on our feet. We got to Piccadilly Circus, but there we could go no farther. Bombs had fallen, and the police were keeping the crowds away from a huge crater in the middle of the square. As we stood there we saw the Zeppelin, which had been hit by an English plane, float slowly earthward in flames. It looked like a piece of burning cotton batting and gave off a red glare that lit up the city for miles. The crowds in the streets, many of them half-dressed, cheered and laughed and cried: some of them even fell on their knees, an extraordinary display of emotion for the English. Then they pulled themselves together and sang "God Save the King."

My friend and I did not feel any particular emotion about all this, and we were not at all afraid. We decided to make our way to the Strand, where the Savoy Hotel has its entrance. A policeman got a load of our costumes and grabbed us, saying it was no place for little girls, especially ones with make-up on, and took us to the Vine Street Police Station. To verify our story they immediately called mother, who was so terribly frightened she was quite unable to be of any practical use, but finally the excitement subsided and we were able to go home. I have often laughed over the incident of that memorable night which demonstrated my grandmother's superb disregard for her personal safety.

It seems that when the raid was at its height, one of the staff of the Hotel Savoy had gone up to the apartment about the lights. There they found grandmama crouched in front of an open window, the bag of jewelry in one hand, shaking her other clenched fist at the raiders and shouting, *"Cobardes—a que no se atrevan de bajar,"* meaning, ''Cowards, you don't have the nerve to come down here.'' She was absolutely indifferent to the scene mother was making behind her. When they tactfully suggested that an open window was not the safest place, and that the crew of the Zeppelin was a long way off, she pushed them away and cried, *"Dejarme sola,"* the cry of the bullfighter when the bull charges him for the kill.

The effects of this raid were disastrous for mother's nerves, and besides, she was fretting continually about my brother. We knew he had been in action and that his division had sustained heavy casualties. Mother thought she should go with grandmother to Paris and endeavor to get my brother back on leave, or see if there was any way to get him transferred from the Legion. (This was, of course, impossible, but she insisted on trying it.) It was eventually decided, on advice from my father, that until the end of the Palace engagement I should board at the Sacred Heart Convent, Portman Square, where a relative of his, Mother Maria Agnese, was Mother Superior.

The convent was a wonderful experience for me: I loved it and for the first time in my life realized the full meaning of the words ''peace'' and ''quiet.'' On my arrival, the sweet and wise old Mother talked to me for a long time in her office, asked me not to tell the nuns anything about the theater or any worldly topics, and said I was to be in the convent by ten-thirty every night. Our ballet finished at nine-thirty, so she had calculated to a fraction of a second, the time for me to return on the bus.

Mother Maria Agnese was a wealthy woman, but she had given everything she had to the poor. When I had to leave the convent to join mother, she was very sad and as a mark of special favor decided we should spend the last days together. She wanted to give me a Missal (I have always kept it), and so she took me on foot all across London, God knows how many miles, to buy it at some very special shop. She was a very old woman, and I could see that she was tired out. I suggested taking a taxi, because the leg I limped on was giving me hell (although I did not say so) but there was nothing doing—she said that the money for the taxi would buy a meal for a poor man and the bus fare a glass of milk for a starving child, so we walked all the way back.

By the time I had got into the swing of living in a convent, a telegram came from mother in Paris, stating that she had been notified Bunnie was missing, and she wanted me to come to Paris at once to be with her. Mother, of course, had never thought of getting a passport for me (it had not been necessary up to this time) or even had me put on her own passport which she had got before leaving England. Therefore I could not leave and she had to come back to fetch me.

Upon arriving in London, mother was so upset and excited that she had a row with Mother Maria Agnese because she thought the convent should have had enough authority to oblige the passport office to give me one immediately. We had to go to Caxton Hall in Westminster, the foreign passport office, which was crowded with people and harassed officials. There were endless complications over names, and mother's habit of speaking a mixture of Spanish, French, German, and Italian whenever she got excited took up a lot of time. She had no birth certificate for me and had to cable father. She then proceeded to get the date of my birth and all my names

68

wrong (I had been christened Esmeralda Consuelo Maria Holland), until the desk we were sitting at got littered up with useless forms and officials were convinced we were spies. This went on for a week, until at last the American Embassy was reached.

I went to see Ambassador Walter Hines Page with a letter of introduction from a friend of father's. I had left mother behind with the object of avoiding any further complications, preferring to tackle the matter on my own. Mr. Page was visibly startled at my youth and called in Mrs. Page to have a look at me. He was very courteous and sent an official down to straighten out the muddle, and we got the passport. I had told him my reason for leaving, and about my brother, and the help he gave us was instrumental in obtaining the necessary document called "Permit to Visit within the Zone of the Armies" and issued under the "Defense of the Realm Act." Without this it would have been impossible to visit field hospitals and dressing-stations behind the lines.

When mother had received notification from the Ministère de Guerre that Bunnie was missing, she rounded up every one of influence in Paris who might be able to help her trace him. She felt positive he was not missing or dead, but wounded, and this eventually proved correct. He had been with the 126th Division of the Fifteenth Corps de l'Armée at Bois Clausair, where there were several divisions of North African troops, Foreign Legion, and Special Corps, so that official information took weeks to filter through. Unfortunately she did not explain clearly to her friends that my brother had enlisted under his second name, Lewison, and this naturally muddled up their efforts to assist her.

At last, through a friend in the Red Cross, we met Captain Hendry, director of "Pour les Blessés," an Orthopedic Institution for French wounded on the Avenue Breteuil. Principally through his kind efforts, mother received information that Bunnie was, or had recently been, at the field hospital at Bois Clausair but that he was badly wounded and would be transferred.

69

My grandmother was in Spain for an urgent family matter and the day mother received this news I had gone by train to the base hospital at Amiens and had been delayed getting back to Paris. Trains were filled with wounded, and I had to wait for the last train, in which there were soldiers on leave sleeping on the floors of the corridors and nurses stepping over them to get into the compartments where the sick men were crowded together. I did not arrive at our hotel till nearly two in the morning, and found mother so ill from shock I was afraid she would lose her mind. The next morning, on the advice of Captain Hendry, I called a doctor, and was told that mother would have a complete nervous breakdown if she were not made to rest and stay away from the hospitals, and that there was nothing for us to do but wait for official confirmation of Bunnie's condition and information about where he could be visited.

The recollection of those days has acquired a nightmarish quality with the years, but I suppose I was too young then to realize the tragedy of those hospital wards and should have been kept out of them, yet all I could do was continue making daily rounds in the hope of finding Bunnie. Those expeditions included a horror of a plane trip to the Bois Clausair district, which Captain Guérin, a friend of Captain Hendry's, arranged for mother but which she was too ill to undertake. Since we had the British military permit from London and there was no action on the Allied front at that particular point, it was decided that it would be all right for me to go instead.

When we left for the Coublaye Airport at daybreak, Captain Guérin seemed to get a terrific kick out of my youth and calm acceptance of a flight in an open observation plane. It was one of the tiny old-fashioned kind, with the pilot in front and the passenger strapped in a seat behind him, wrapped in furs, goggles, and anything else handy. After the boarding of the plane and the business of strapping me in were accomplished, the crew wound up the motor, ran back from the propeller, and shouted, *"Vive la France!"*

A terrific noise from the engine resulted, and after three leaps forward, the thing stopped with a back-breaking lurch. They tried it again, with the accompaniment of more cheers, waving, and terrific explosions—and again the same thing happened. At last we got off the ground, swayed, and wobbled upward.

Once in the air, I could not see or breathe and was too frightened to move; besides, on climbing into the plane I had noticed two flasks of oxygen which the pilot had placed in front of him, and I kept wondering if he contemplated using them en route. Afterward I found out that he had been gassed and frequently required a stimulant while flying. Fortunately, he did not need any when I was with him.

There had been fighting all over the district where we were going, and civilian traffic was at a standstill. After landing I was given a seat in a commissariat truck going from the airfield to Bois Clausair over roads that were almost impassable. Long lines of trucks and French and British ambulances were plowing through the mud, and as we neared the village, I saw wounded everywhere: some coming in on stretchers, some leaving with minor wounds, and some wearing the blue linen suits of the Canadian and British wounded, with their uniform caps on heads that were swathed in bandages, singing as they hobbled along.

With a letter from Captain Hendry as my identification paper, I waited patiently in the Bureau de Réception, a wooden shed built on the grounds of a ruined school-house and crowded with civilians, harassed officials, and soldiers. Nobody had time to listen to my story, and the nurses and doctors looked at me with dead eyes. I suppose they were too tired even to wonder what a child could possibly be doing there. I wandered around from one building to another, on the verge of tears, for I had only two hours before the truck returning to the airport would pick me up again.

At last a Canadian nurse advised me to talk to a French surgeon with a beard who was standing in the doorway of one of the buildings, a burned-out cigarette hanging from his

71

lips, his white coat bloodstained, and an enormous rubber apron in similar condition around his middle. He did not even seem to hear me when I started to explain my mission but called a sister in the blue habit of St. Vincent de Paul. She told me that the doctor had been operating for thirty-six hours without a rest, and gave me a list of names of wounded that had come in that morning. I found nothing, so she sent me to one or two other departments, but nobody had any information that would help me, and I had to return to Paris and face mother again without news.

Three days later Colonel Pricardin, who had been reached by Captain Hendry, wrote a personal letter at the request of my brother from a hospital at Côte Soixante, to which he had been removed from Bois Clausair the night before my visit. Presumably the list of men sent back to base depots had not been ready when I was there looking for him.

Of my brother's arrival in Paris and the discovery of his blindness I do not want to write. All my life I have tried to forget it. Fortunately father arrived and took charge of everything, and the fact that Bunnie was at least alive, though in a very serious condition, saved my mother's reason. She behaved splendidly and threw herself into the fight to save his life in a way I never thought she had the strength of character to do.

Father took entire charge of my brother's hospitalization, preferring to place him under doctors of his own choosing rather than depend on military hospitals. When Bunnie could be moved, he was placed in the American hospital in Neuilly and later in a convalescent home in Fontainebleau, where we took a furnished house.

It was while we were living in Fontainebleau that mother gave very definite proof of her psychic qualities. The house was an old one with a rather large garden full of old-fashioned flowers. Mother used to sit alone in the drawing-room at twilight, gazing out into the garden. She told us that ever since she had begun sitting there at that hour, she had kept seeing

72

a little gray-haired woman with a sweet face, who passed through the French windows, bowed to her apologetically, and went out through the other door. She wore, mother said, a gray dress of an early Victorian period and always carried a basket of flowers from the garden.

Mother spoke about her once or twice rather diffidently, till one day she came across an old daguerreotype of a woman which she immediately recognized as her visitor. Upon inquiry, we learned that it was the picture of an aunt of the owner of the house, who had died abroad many years before.

I have inherited some of this power myself: it is a quality that I can describe only by the Irish word "fey." I sense unseen things but seldom mention them, for I feel people would not believe me, although I instinctively know these things are true, and I have dreams which tell me more than I could possibly foresee. A particularly vivid one I had was just before leaving Paris for Rotterdam in 1937.

At the time I was very unsettled about coming to America. I loved Paris: it had been my home for nearly twenty years. Although there was a good deal of international dissension going on, few of my friends thought there could ever be a war. About two nights before I sailed, I had a dream in which I saw a cluster of huge white buildings bathed in brilliant sunlight, with the sea foaming around them, and closer at hand a strip of land surmounted by a high tower on which stood French officers in full uniform. I awoke shivering, got up, and started to pack. I knew at once I was leaving a state of war and feared I would not see Paris again for a long time.

During this early fall of 1917, I joined the autumn classes of the Delacroix Cours de Croquis, in the Rue du Bac on the Left Bank, and attended the École des Beaux Arts in the same quarter of Paris. I had had for some time the idea of trying for the Chase Medal, which provides a scholarship of six months in the American School in Rome. Nina Hamnett, who was also working for the medal, encouraged me to go in for it while I was dancing at the Palace. I studied piano and theory of music at the American Academy in Fontainebleau and commuted every day to school.

Paris was so beautiful that year—there seemed to be nothing but beauty and color in the world, and it was bitter to think that my brother, who loved such things, would never be able to see them again.

I worked extremely hard, for I knew father was having a trying time with finances. It was about this time I began to want nice clothes and stole mother's make-up. But both my mother and father were much too worried over my brother and balancing the budget to give me any attention.

I spent all my spare time in the galleries of the Louvre, the Luxembourg, and the Cluny Museum in the Boulevard St.-Germain. I studied and worked hard, spending any spare moments in the studio of a Russian friend, Olga Gougout-chieff, painting the miniatures which were afterward exhibited in the Royal Water Color Society and the Royal Academy in London. We shared the models and had a lot of fun.

When the term ended in December, I won the Chase Medal for a large study of a woman in the nude. What they did not know was my age. I looked much older and told most people I was sixteen, which was young enough, for although there were students of all ages, the majority were from twenty to thirty.

Although my father was very proud of my having won the Chase Medal and scholarship, my mother took it as a perfectly natural consequence of my studies. I think she would have been much more surprised if I had not won it. Anyway, it had the effect of drawing their attention to my existence, and my father, observing one day that I was using lipstick, tackled mother about her allowing me to use make-up—but she hadn't even noticed it. I could see my father was upset about this, so I didn't use it again till after he had left for Canada.

We all spent Christmas together in Fontainebleau, and it was the only occasion that I had ever lived with both my parents under the same roof, and also grandmama, back from Spain. After the New Year, mother and I accompanied my brother to the Orthopedic Sanitarium at Berck, Paris-Plage. In addition to his head wounds and loss of sight, he had a shattered hip which had been operated on and had a platinum or silver head fitted to the hip-bone. As a result of the operation, he could stand but not walk: his spine had become affected and he was very ill. Father and mother had received two decorations for him, as he was too crippled to appear at any ceremonies.

Most of the hotels in Paris-Plage had been taken over by the Military—principally British—and the hotel we stayed in was full of the most enterprising ladies of the Parisian demi-monde. They lay in wait in the lobbies for the American officers, who presumably had better pay than the other Allies. As we came through the revolving doors, one of these hetæræ was displaying her charms in the lobby in the company of a small dog, in tow for introductory purposes. Mother managed somehow to get herself mixed up with the dog. We were talking voluble Spanish, so probably the animal thought we were fighting and bit mother in the ankle. I pounced on the dog and removed it. The owner, the manager, my mother, and several guests all started talking at once. The manager, who was eying mother's diamonds with affection, took her part and naturally asked her if she was sure she was hurt. Mother with great emphasis replied, "Of course—the dog—he rush at me and fix his leg in my teeth." The confusion that followed this statement was remarkable and the only bright moment in the visit to Paris-Plage.

V

BEFORE MY FATHER left for Canada he promised me that this time nothing would interfere with my course at the American Schools in Rome, but I could see that he was aging from the strain of my brother's illness and the hospital bills, and I felt selfish about spending six months for study and not sharing the financial burden with him to the best of my ability.

Mother and I set off for Rome (grandmama had returned to Spain, for she was having her own monetary problems), and it was not until we got settled in the train that mother told me vaguely about some sort of difficulty which had arisen about the records she had made in America. She was very casual about it, and at the time I did not realize what it was all about. Not till I was in South America with the Pavlova company, did I know that she had sung the same music (which had been specially arranged for her to make the recordings) for more than one company—and that the result was a lawsuit of overwhelming proportions being brought against her. She had never meant to do anything wrong but must have needed the money and I suppose she didn't realize the seriousness of what she was doing. She had not told my father anything about this, for she knew this sort of thing drove him frantic. Another thing she revealed as we traveled to Italy was that she had a contract for the Costanzi Opera in Rome which would coincide with my term at the American Schools and she had telegraphed to obtain a contract for me to appear in the corps de ballet as well. I did not want to upset her and start any arguments, but when I saw the veritable orgy of work she had planned for me, I wished I had never heard of the Chase Medal. She overlooked the fact that I had worked very hard to

76

win it in Paris and that I needed some relaxation in order to profit from the teaching of my art classes. Unfortunately, she had again thought of the possibility of my acquiring a voice and felt that the air of Italy—land of operatic stars—would perform the miracle required to make a singer out of me. And so she had also arranged for me to study voice production and elocution with a Maestro Sabatini in the mornings before my classes started in the art school.

The schedule she had planned ran like this: singing lesson 8 to 9 A.M.; 10:30 to 12, painting class; 12:30 to 1:30, lunch; 2 to 5, drawing and decorative art; 5:30 to 9:30, ballet school, and the Costanzi performance 9 to 12 P.M. when the Opera gave a performance with ballet—which was nearly every night. If they had a Sunday matinée without ballet, I was supposed to devote that day of rest to visiting museums and the wonders of Rome.

By the middle of April, I was pretty well sick of the daily routine and bored stiff with dancing the Italian operas, after the Russian Ballet technique I had been trained in. I had to pass a roller-skating rink on my way to and from the Hotel Excelsior on the Pincio, and this was my undoing. It tempted me morning after morning. I craved some sort of diversion, and I could hear the strains of a fairly good band as I passed the building. One day after lunch I saw a group of girls about my own age entering and followed them in. I had never had time to roller-skate, and it fascinated me. I went back a few times and learned very rapidly to dance on skates—the worst thing in the world for a dancer's legs. The *pattinagio* (skating rink) was perfectly respectable as far as I could see. Instead of attending my classes at the American Schools I used to sign the roll book at the door, spend half an hour pretending to paint so that people would see me, then slip out and go skating.

Of course the inevitable happened. Somebody in the office of the Art Schools wrote mother and told her I was playing truant. Mother went to the skating rink with a private detective she had hired, and flew at the wretched Mr. Hook, the manager. The detective was of course determined to get all he could out of mother while the going was good and so filled her up with lurid tales about where I had been seen, and so forth. The climax was reached when Curly, a little American boy I had been dancing with, sent me a note asking why I did not come to the rink any more. Since I was not allowed to leave my room, mother got the note and read it. She told me nothing but went directly to the *pattinagio*, unearthed Curly, and frightened the poor kid out of his wits.

All her friends were called in consultation, as well as the great poet Gabriele d'Annunzio, who admired mother and wrote poems about her which nobody could understand. The door of my room was locked on the outside, but I found it was quite simple to get out of the window and climb on to the ledge of a small hall window that was generally kept open. I did this a few times until a big Swiss porter saw me leave the main door of the hotel and of course told mother. More drama ensued.

I had only gone to the skating rink to tell Mr. Hook how sorry I was for all the unpleasantness. He told me about the detective, and also that he thought my mother was the most beautiful woman he had ever seen, but he begged me, almost with tears in his eyes, never to come to the rink again, for mother had terrified him so that the mere thought of another visit from her made him break out in a cold sweat.

Cables flew across the Atlantic to my father in Canada, and across Europe to grandmama somewhere in Spain. Needless to say she got funds from mother and arrived with such speed that she seemed to have flown on the magic carpet of the Arabian Nights.

Upon hearing the whole story, her natural comment was that she had always said art schools were the cause of all the trouble—as in London—and that they were a waste of money because when people eventually became painters they always starved to death anyway and died in garrets with everything in hock, no heat, and the snow falling outside. This dreary picture was of course the only thing she had ever heard about artists and was based entirely on the libretto of *La Bohême*.

Secretly she was delighted about my escapade which was an excuse for her to travel again. I used to observe that after a lengthy stay somewhere, every few days grandmama would pack and unpack a little Spanish leather trunk she had owned for years, to give herself the illusion she was going on a trip. It was rather pathetic.

Father had cabled that he was writing instructions as to what he thought had better be done with me, and mother by this time definitely decided that I was to wind up my studies the best way I could. I was bitterly disappointed and felt sure that the American Schools would have allowed me to continue my classes, but mother positively forbade this. I continued to fulfil my contract at the Costanzi Opera, while mother, grandmama, and the maid took turns guarding my movements. Spring was just around the corner, and Rome was very lovely. I spent hours wandering around Keats' house and the Coliseum.

Some of the ridiculous people mother had surrounded herself with, who were probably getting something out of it (it takes arranging, introductions, and a lot of rigmarole with embassies, I believe), led her to imagine she had to see the Pope—and drag me along with her. Women must dress in black with a sort of mantilla arrangement on their heads. Merry del Val, brother of the famous cardinal, was Spanish Ambassador, and I think he was the one who fixed up the affair for grandmama to accompany us. Anyway, I could not see the point of the whole business, but mother said it was an experience for me to remember all my life. I told her I did not need that, for after the episode of the skating rink I was never likely to forget the Eternal City, and I was not going to be badgered into the thing unless I got five pounds for myself.

Mother had bought me some clothes before leaving Paris, and I looked awful in them. For a change I wanted to buy a few little things myself, but mother simply would not

79

realize I was growing up. However, on this particular occasion, grandmama agreed with me for the first time in her life and borrowed the money from mother to give to me. I think the idea of a snake-charmer interviewing the Pope of Rome tickled her. Anyway, it was all arranged and we went.

We followed the ushers past Papal guards to an antesala where the women were separated from the men. I was very sleepy and have not retained a very clear memory of that morning. It was cold, and we had to take a small elevator, like the one that ascends to the Dome of St. Peter's. The man who ran it was old and smelled of garlic but spoke excellent English. He gave mother's fanny a dexterous pinch as we left the elevator—they always do that in Latin countries, even to American school-teachers on Cook's tours, and especially to pretty women who are not too thin—but I must say it was rather disconcerting in the Vatican. Two dilapidated countesses who had come with us, and were I believe the ones who had originated the idea (of the visit, I mean, not the pinch), were deeply shocked.

The audience was very brief. I think the men filed in first through the magnificent gallery, knelt to kiss the Pope's ring and receive the blessing; the women followed them. I was so nervous I dared not look about me but could just catch a floating impression of superb color and beauty, contrasting with the kneeling black-veiled women. It was extraordinarily impressive. Never had I seen my grandmother so subdued as when we walked out after mother, who was trying to look like Sœur Angelica in Puccini's opera.

My father had written suggesting that I should have a different sort of life for a while and very justly pointed out that a young girl must have companions of her own age to work off high spirits in games; that he thought I should attend a good English school and he was willing to make a sacrifice financially to send me to one—which is the normal idea of any man brought up in Great Britain, where the school life is traditional. It seemed he had carried a list of schools about with him for months: he had investigated them when we were in Paris.

By this time, mother was due to sing in Milan, so grandmama and I dropped her off there and continued to Paris. I went at once to see my brother at Berck and found him terribly changed. The worst of his illness was over, and he had had time to take stock of his condition. He had been a strikingly handsome boy—tall and slender, but powerfully built, with a very dark skin and the most beautiful eyes I have ever seen in a man, a strange blue-gray with long black lashes that would have made any woman beautiful. He had always had a strange disposition, sometimes very lovable and sometimes so violent that he used to go off by himself when he got mad about anything. Women were crazy about him.

He had a great gift for music, played the piano, organ, violin, and guitar, and had a tenor voice of rare beauty and power. He was very lazy but had studied a little with Jean de Reszke, who was enthusiastic about his voice. Mother had wanted him to train for opera, but he was not keen about it, and father thought he should be a doctor on account of his sensitive hands and delicate fingers. He himself would have preferred the navy. His enlistment had of course put a stop to any of these projects, and his wounds and blindness lost to the world a great singer.

His illness had made him bitter and warped—all the more because he had been unofficially engaged to a young American girl. I knew he had had several affairs with married women, but I think he really loved this girl. When we were in Fontainebleau, he had told mother about it and asked her to write for him and release the girl from any promises she had ever made him. He was only twenty-two and the girl about the same age, I think. Anyway, she came to see him while he was in the American Hospital and according to mother had carried on like mad—said she would marry him regardless of his blindness and crippled legs. Apparently she thought better of it after she left and wrote him a letter at the sanitarium in Berck—which his nurse should never have read to him—

telling him she thought she could not face a marriage with a blind cripple and saying good-by. This had happened while we were in Rome, so of course we knew nothing of the tragic end of his romance.

It was early in April when grandmama and I got to London to learn that the school father had chosen was at Reading on the Thames, advertised in the best magazines as "a school for the daughters of gentlemen." It was also one of the most expensive places, and father cabled quite a lot of money for the term.

Mother had asked a friend of hers, a Mrs. Duffus, whom I particularly disliked, to see about my clothes and take me to the school. It was a beautiful place in a big park with old trees. We were received by two spinsters, a thin washed-out one whose name I don't remember and a short-haired female who talked in a deep booming voice and dressed as much like a man as possible. Her name was Miss Charlesworth—Charlie Charlesworth, the servants called her. She adopted a rolling sea-going gait, and I sensed at once it was she who handled the tough pupils, if there were any, and I mentally named her, for myself, "Old Ironpants." She was so hale and hearty that I thought at any moment she would slap Mrs. Duffus on the back. I was to have a room to myself, father had said, and study the subjects I preferred—continue painting and piano, also riding three times a week, plus any games I wanted, the more the better.

After Mrs. Duffus had gone home, I had a short interview with the nameless spinster about the ethics of English school life. I was told that above all I was to avoid any mention of theatrical experiences. This was bad enough, but when she started telling me I would have to have riding "lessons," I laughed in her face. I was the best rider Ograinsky ever had in the troupe and could not imagine how anybody could possibly teach me anything more when he couldn't.

The next day I discovered that, apart from the usual school classes in arithmetic, algebra, geography, and history, the teachers were much inferior to the nuns in the Sacred Heart.

82

Their languages were pathetic. They knew about the Whitmore School where I had passed English Literature with honors, and the woman who held the class in this subject was both spiteful and stupid about it. The French teacher was a rather nice little girl but came from Bordeaux, where they speak an ugly French and add an ''e'' to the end of everything. I knew I had a pure Parisian accent and was not going to have it messed up for anybody—and said so.

Of the art classes I know nothing, because I took one look at the horrors the teacher had concocted and walked out on her. Things went from bad to worse: I saw I was wasting my time and father's money as well, but I did want to give the place a fair trial for his sake, even if it was a disappointment. I had had very little to say to the other girls, for I still had a slight foreign accent and had seen them giggling over some of my remarks. One of them I particularly disliked, a pasty-faced creature with money and a big opinion of herself. She was anemic and had hands like a dead fish, but was the favorite of Charlesworth. One good thing she did have, however—a nice little sorrel mare, her own property (all the others had mounts from a local livery stable) and she was extremely proud of it and her ability as a horsewoman. On my second afternoon we were to go riding. An old beery-looking man turned up with a cluster of rather seedy horses and proceeded to show me what to do with mine. Of course, I told him I was a professional rider—had been at Olympia, and so on. This created such a stir among the girls, who crowded around me to listen open-mouthed, that it took him half an hour to get started. I was not as a rule inclined to show off, but when we got to a stretch of land they called the ''common,'' I got the mediocre horse I was riding to gallop and left the entire party behind. The sorrel mare belonging to the girl I disliked had some ginger in her and started to cut up: the girl couldn't hold her, and the old man had his hands full. I left them at it and had a good ride for some miles till I realized I had no idea where I was or how to get back. It was quite late when I did arrive, and there was a scene. They were convinced I had been thrown off and was lying dead in some ditch, and they had phoned the police to send motorcycle patrols to scour the country. The riding master, who had had a tough afternoon, was upset and very sore about the horse being lathered.

Three or four of the older girls were still in their riding-clothes, eagerly awaiting the "bawling out" they hoped I would get: they probably listened outside the door of the office while I was in there talking to the Heads—Ironpants was the one who did the talking and really told me all she had on her mind. We had what is described in the English classics as "high words." I was not to come down for supper, they would write to my mother, I was utterly incorrigible....

When I started upstairs, the Heads shooed the girls after me—and as I walked up the wide polished staircase I heard my *bête noire* make a very insulting remark to her pal, Miss Charlesworth, about "gipsies" and "circus tramps." I don't remember exactly what it was—but it was enough. I turned as they came up and handed her a beautiful right to the jaw—I had had considerable experience with the Ograinsky kids and knew how to hold my own. The blow sent the girl backwards down the polished stairs; screams rent the air and they picked her up with a tooth knocked out and some bruises. I was locked in my room, and a stony-faced maid shoved a tray with some dinner on it through the door and fled as if I were the incarnation of Evil. It was about eight o'clock—I had heard the gong go for the dinner at seven-thirty and knew they were all in the dining-room, except Miss Charlesworth, who was waiting for the doctor to come and diagnose her pet in the school infirmary.

I changed my clothes rapidly, got out of the window, crawled through the next window into a dormitory, and tiptoed down a small service staircase which led to the back of the school. All I had was a few shillings, but I knew it was just about enough to get me to London.

Not a soul saw me as I skirted the house and made my way through the trees. I climbed the wall and walked calmly

84

along the road in the direction of Reading. It was nice and dark, and I did not meet any one for quite some way. Then I heard a car coming behind me and decided I would save time and get a ride to the station. The man driving the car was middle-aged but rather nice. I told him I had been visiting people in the neighborhood and was going back to London. He became so curious and nosy that I had quite a time thinking of lies to tell him, and as soon as we were in Reading I managed to get out of the car and walk to the station. I caught the train for London without a wait, which was very lucky.

I took a taxi to the hotel and walked in on grandmama who, to my surprise, was charmed to see me. I started my story by mentioning my reason for hitting the girl on the stairs—stressing the insult to the gipsies and the circus. In the middle of this the telephone rang, and Miss Charlesworth on the other end poured out the story of my misdeeds. As soon as grandmama told her I was safe at home, she said I was incorrigible, and of course *persona non grata* at the school; that the parents of the young lady I had injured were arriving post-haste, to bring action for assault and battery, etc., etc.... Grandmama got so bored with it after a while, she did not even listen.

It seems that the police had been notified, for when Miss Charlesworth finally stopped for breath and grandmama had hung up on her, the police station in Reading called us up. They must have had a busy day, having been sent out twice after me.

Father had to lose most of the money he had paid for me, in the end—between the ladies claiming I had ruined the reputation of their school, and the parents of the wretched girl declaring her looks had been spoiled by the loss of a front tooth and wanting to prosecute. It was all finally settled out of court by a lawyer.

The next day I learned the reason for grandmama's strangely gracious behavior. Being very bored alone in London, she had gone to see all her theatrical friends and had heard that Pavlova, then playing New York, was looking for dancers for a six-month tournée, taking in the winter season in South America and returning via Mexico. Grandmama had also seen Diaghilev in Seville just before she came to Rome. He had talked with her and met all the dancers in the gipsy quarter, through Vincente Escuderos, the great flamenco dancer. Both Pavlova and Diaghilev knew and respected grandmama as a great artist when she was in her prime, and had seen her work in Russia. She felt that either of these companies would engage me for the corps de ballet upon her recommendation.

Whether she had seen it in the *baraja* (cards) or not, she evidently knew I was not going to last long in the "finishing" school and had been weighing carefully the matter of getting me in one of these companies—investigating the question of visas for South America and the matter of my age on the contract. She had it all fixed and announced that, whichever engagement we got, she meant to travel with me.

Mother was cabled to give her consent for grandmama to take the situation in hand—and replied that nothing would please her better than to lose sight of me for a while—provided Pavlova or Diaghilev had the strength of character to cope with me. I wrote to my father after this and was fortunate in getting my letter to him first. He wrote me a rather chilly reply but said that if I honestly felt I would not make progress in my studies at the school perhaps it was all for the best, but I was never to strike anybody again.

Grandmama ran about sending cables to Pavlova and Diaghilev, with a gleam in her eye at the prospect of all the traveling we would do. Just before I left the ballet school in Hampstead in 1916, Pavlova had seen me dance and had watched me carefully. She very rarely attended the children's classes, but when she did, she was very critical, and later when I knew her better I used to get a kick out of all the charming things she would say to some eager mother who had brought her daughter in the hope of an engagement. Madame would rave about the child and unfailingly give an appointment to see her dance. When they arrived, generally at a most inconvenient hour, all dressed up and ready to show what the child could do, Pavlova would fly into a temper and refuse to see them, saying she would have a nervous breakdown if people continued to bother her with their stupid, clumsy children. And they would have to be got rid of immediately, with orders that they were never to be allowed near her again.

After she saw me dance, she told grandmama I was exceedingly graceful and she would like to use me for a character dance later on; she said I had the toes of a classic dancer but that I must learn to get more expression in my face. This was very true: I did have a cold expression then. She would often tell us to watch her every night when I worked with her company—to study her truly marvelous facial expressions. She often danced a matinée on her mimic work alone—she was a mistress of showmanship, in addition to her wonderful technique, which, like all great artists, she was never satisfied with: she would shut herself up in the studio of her house in Hampstead and dance before a mirror, losing all idea of time. Victor Dandré, her husband, used to be afraid they would find her in a faint on the floor, and I understand they did a few times.

It was decided we were to go to Madrid first and see what was "cookin'" with Diaghilev, who had never seen me. If that did not work out, we could clinch the affair with Pavlova for South America by cable and leave on a neutral Spanish ship, which was the best way to travel in wartime. Grandmama was itching to be off—I think because she was so anxious to get in on the *Tricornio* ballet of Manuel de Falla, which Diaghilev was creating at the time.

Before we left, I took the miniatures I had painted in Paris to Alfred Praga, a teacher of miniature painting I had known since the Chelsea days and one of the best of critics and teachers. He liked my work and was happy to hear about the Chase Medal but thought it a crime that I had not been allowed to finish my term. He particularly liked two of my

things and said I should enter them for the Royal Water Color
Society and the Royal Academy during the month of June.
He was a Fellow and on the judging committee of the Society
and thought I had a good chance because I had received a
notification from Paris that one of the watercolors I had
done there had been accepted by the "Independents" exhibition. Both the miniatures he entered for me were accepted for the London exhibitions, but as they were held late
in June I did not get a chance to see them, nor did my father,
though it made him very proud. I know that mother, who
sang the season in Covent Garden, saw them and took all
her friends—which was always a good sign in mother. Nina
also wrote me that they were good and very well hung "on
the line."

The day grandmama and I left London, I watched the
flower women outside Victoria station throw the contents of
their baskets of spring flowers under the muddy boots of the
soldiers arriving from France. The English are a wonderful
people.

Upon our arrival in Madrid, we discovered that the tournée
of Diaghilev at the Teatro Real had gone through a lot of
difficulties. Diaghilev had no money; Nijinsky had made a
financial flop in the United States and was fighting about his
contract for South America, where Diaghilev had intended
sending a company without his personal supervision. He had
had Nijinsky arrested for something or other—it was one of
those complications that only Russians can cook up.

The Diaghilev company was scattered all over Madrid. My
old friend, Natascha Mikulina, and the two Chableska girls
had to work in a cabaret run by Jack Johnson, the Negro
prizefighter, who went everywhere with his white wife. Picasso
was there and Manuel de Falla, the great composer—it was a
mad mélange of everybody and everything.

Diaghilev was bound for Italy, where he hoped to get
money and then to play the season in London—which he
did the following year—at the Coliseum, the Empire, and
the Alhambra, where he gave the magnificent *Tricornio*. In

Madrid he offered grandmama the contract for South America, but after what she had heard about the tournée in the United States and all the fights, she wasn't having any. She was disappointed but not daunted. She refused his South American offer but got a promise out of him for London. We were staying at the same hotel, of course, for just this purpose.

How she got all the fast action that followed—at her age—I don't know, but she immediately cabled Pavlova's managers in New York and got a cabled contract for me to dance in the Pavlova company in the South American tournée, which was to be a six-month engagement. She had passages booked for Montevideo on the S.S. *Infanta Isabella de Bourbon,* which would get us there at exactly the right time to coincide with the arrival of the company from the United States.

At the last minute grandmama had to go to Granada for family and financial juggling, and had arranged to take the boat when it stopped at Cadiz. But whatever finagling it was that grandmama was doing it resulted in her having to postpone her sailing until a later ship. She put me in charge of the captain, cabling Pavlova's manager to be responsible for me and to meet the ship at Montevideo.

The trip, although interesting to me—especially since I was on my own for the first time—was not a very agreeable one. The food was terrible, and some of the older people and children died from ptomaine poisoning. There were all sorts of odd, mysterious people on board, and the only cheerful place was the steerage, where the Galician emigrants danced and sang all day and most of the night.

Every Spanish passenger ship carries two or three priests who watch over everything. On the *Infanta Isabella,* they stopped women from smoking or dancing the tango (which was then forbidden by the Pope), and the captain put sailors on campstools to sit outside the cabins of single women at night. I never discovered who watched the sailors.

A long detour was made around Fernando Noronha Island (the Brazilian penal island) to let the German submarines search the ship. The English had already stopped us outside Tenerife for the same purpose and had taken off two men. They were probably British subjects or deserters.

I was just beginning to wake up to the beautiful things in life and will never forget the Rock of Tenerife at dawn, or the first time I saw a flying fish sail over the water while we were crossing the equator. The captain, in whose charge grandmama had placed me, was so worried about running out of coal, what with all the detours he had been obliged to make to comply with orders and counter-orders he'd received from Germany and Brazil (one of the Allies), that I don't think he spoke to me once during the twenty-eight days of the trip.

I was considerably happier when I saw at last the monotonous flat coastline of Montevideo and as I crossed the gangplank to meet the agent from the Pavlova company who had come to meet me, I felt I had left my childhood behind with the captain of the S.S. *Infanta Isabella,* and was really starting to be a responsible grown-up person with my career before me.

PART II

VI

THE PAVLOVA COMPANY opened in Buenos Aires at the Teatro Coliseo, an opera house second in importance to the government's Municipal Opera, the Teatro Colón, where the Diaghilev company was scheduled to appear under the direction of Nijinsky.

Anna Pavlova had been having some difficulties with her group of dancers, for a few of them did not have their papers in order, and one of her first figures, the brilliant character dancer Richard Nemanoff, had to remain in Rio till he could get his passport ironed out. These complications made it necessary to rehearse a week with intensive study and application in order to get new-comers and understudies ready. We all knew the Temporada (official season) meant excessively hard work, in keen competition with the Colón.

We were to dance a month in Buenos Aires and then go by way of the cities of Rosario and Mendoza across the Andes to Santiago, Valparaiso, Panama, Havana, Vera Cruz, and Mexico City, where the tournée would end.

Pavlova had quite a number of Russians in the company, all of them good artists, but wherever there are Russian dancers there are squabbles and plots—either because they are dissatisfied with their publicity or because they think they are not getting enough salary. The only company where things rolled along more or less smoothly with them was Diaghilev's. As a rule Anna Pavlova preferred English girls, for although they are undoubtedly not such good dancers, they are "stickers" and never complain: they will go through fire and water to keep the show going. I like to work with Russians and admire their great talent and temperament, but they are impossible to handle in a company, and I have never yet known one that did not have some sort of trouble.

93

With Pavlova, the upset originated among a little group of Russians that stuck together and met in cafés to sit around tables in an atmosphere of gloomy discontent and discuss their grievances. The whole thing was a question of money with them. It is true that they were not getting big salaries and had all joined the company from different parts of the world where the changes in currency in which their contracts had been signed were against them. They felt that the business managers were to blame for the fluctuating money and the fact that they were not receiving enough to meet their expenses or put anything aside for emergencies. Victor Dandré, Anna Pavlova's husband, was a charming man and did all he could to straighten out their difficulties, but there was not much to be done, for Pavlova could not increase salaries. Buenos Aires was expensive during the period of the war, and she insisted upon the corps de ballet girls and men having immaculate shoes and tights at all times. These were costly items, and led to one of the principal complaints of the Russian group.

Pavlova was fanatical on the subject of shoes, both in the theater and in her private life, and had quantities of ballet shoes and slippers made for her by Nicolini of Milan. She gave many of them away as souvenirs and sometimes autographed them.

Pavlova was so careful of her feet that she would not dance unless the stage was immaculately clean, and everywhere we went stage managers had to mobilize extra stage hands to wash it before rehearsals and every show. Naturally she wanted all her dancers to have the same spotless footwear and had kicked up a fuss with several of them because their shoes were stained and worn. One thing led to another, and the storm finally broke, with Jakobleff, his wife Maria, Gala Chableska, Katy de Galanta and several others leaving Pavlova in Buenos Aires, with the intention of forming their own company— which they had a terrible time doing, almost starving to death. They tried all sorts of arguments to get me to join them, but I didn't want to get mixed up with their messes and had enough sense to stay in Pavlova's good graces and mind my own business.

I was not too affluent myself, but grandmama had cabled me money from mother which I had received the week of my arrival, so I tried to help them as much as I could, but when my own funds dwindled, I used to sneak rolls, bread, and pieces of ham for them when I had my dinner and take them up to their room in my bag. The girls stayed in bed all day, being afraid to go out in case the hotel locked the door of their room because of the overdue rent.

Argentines are crazy about young girls, dancers especially, and I received many invitations in the cafeteria under the theater—which I accepted mainly to get more sandwiches and cookies for my hungry Russian pals. The English girls in the company spoke no Spanish and were scared to go with me, for they were terrified that Madame Pavlova would find out. She was very strict with her girls and would not stand for any nonsense or promiscuous love affairs that might reflect on the reputation of the company. She knew all about what everybody did, and if any girl was out with a man and came in late, there was always some one who would run tattling to her or Dandré about it. Since I was the youngest dancer in the company, I got away with murder on account of my youth and my knowledge of Spanish, and also because I never got too friendly with any of them (I had learned to keep my own counsel while I was in the circus), and so they never really knew much about me.

The loss of the eight dancers made the work all the harder, and I think they would have been glad to come back to the company before we left Buenos Aires, but both Madame Pavlova and her husband were too angry ever to consider such a thing; therefore some members of the corps de ballet got chances to dance more advanced rôles than they had ever dreamed of.

Pavlova could be very hard when she was sore at anybody. She left those eight artists behind in Buenos Aires and obtained from the court an injunction preventing them from working anywhere. They were weeks trying to get it lifted by the authorities before they could work again.

We were in Rosario when grandmama arrived from Spain and my little adventures and invitations had to cease—which meant nothing to me either way. I wanted to get ahead and learn, and worked so hard that Pavlova gave me two solos in the "Divertissement" part of the program.

Pavlova always claimed she had lost money on the tournée, but her success throughout the South American countries was tremendous—and she worked hard for it. She was an absolutely tireless person, and sometimes the girls could not stand the strain of continuous rehearsals and fainted during the performance. In many ways she had a character not unlike my mother's, except that she was a better business woman, but she differed widely from mother in the musical branch of her art, for she had no technical knowledge of music, and after every show there would be arguments with the orchestra about nothing. She was very temperamental and given to overwork and consequent fits of despondency.

She took dislikes to people on sight and could be very rude when she wanted to, could never understand why anybody ever wanted to rest, and had a mystical side to her character that was melodramatic at times. I shall always remember the frequent spectacle of her standing on the steps of a train leaving the station of some town we had been playing—her arms full of flowers, saying good-by to a deputation of fat, elderly, South American officials who were seeing her off and crowding around so that they would be in the pictures the press were taking. Some portly retired banker who was an Art Patron, or the head of an Artistic Commission, would be gushing over her, and she would say, "Ah, my dear friend, you have such an appreciation of the Russian Ballet, you are so kind—I love your country—and when the war is over, you will come to Russia and I will take your hand and we will kiss the Russian earth—and we will weep." Of course, the fat man would be enraptured at the prospect and agree with enthusiasm, being convinced that she and all Russians were raving mad.

Pavlova had a side to her character that was very humane, and most of the money she cleared from the South American tournée went toward the Home for Russian Orphans, which she founded during the year 1920 in Paris. She was always ready to give benefits for charity, even when she was nearly dead with fatigue. She was very fond of animals, particularly birds, and this was capitalized on by every one as an outstanding trait in her character—especially in reference to her swans, who were extremely bad-tempered and hissed at everybody but her. One of them once chased a distinguished society matron clear across the lawn in the middle of a garden party.

In South America she bought a lot of tropical birds that died immediately they were on board ship, principally because they were kept in the butchers' quarters or somewhere near the cold storage. (Butchers have no imagination, I have noticed.) This made Pavlova unhappy for days.

With her I progressed in the study of the relation of color to music and their application to rhythm, which had fascinated me in my early days with Diaghilev. I was anxious to study stagecraft and scenic design and felt that I had developed mentally as well as physically. I was, and am still, most grateful to her—may she rest in peace—for she was the greatest technician I have ever seen, and a fine teacher. I owe her a lot, for I made tremendous progress on her tournée. When she took me, I was an unformed child with much to learn.

The Pavlova tournée continued on through the scheduled route, and we were in Panama when the Armistice was declared. To celebrate it, I bought a little brown snake and called him Pushkin. He made a real trouper and was the one who came in so handy at the customs. Although the last weeks of the tournée had been complicated by transportation difficulties and strikes, we had a brilliant success in

97

Mexico, where they adored Pavlova, who some years previously had given popular functions in the bullring.

Before leaving Mexico, she told grandmama that she expected to open in the Drury Lane Theater for the London season of 1919 and that she wanted me to be with her. Then she spoke about a projected world tour through Canada, Japan, China, India, and Egypt. Grandmama cabled mother about my accepting but received a reply from her that it would be too long for me to be away and that grandmama was too old to attempt traveling with me. For a change my grandmother agreed with mother. We arrived in Cherbourg, France, via New York, in December. Mother met us at the boat, and we returned to Paris to spend Christmas.

Mother was in the financial "dumps," she told me, although she had had a successful season at Covent Garden. My brother had required a costly operation which had been a terrific sacrifice for both my parents and unfortunately was not successful. He was suffering from neuritis of the eyes, which is incurable, and had attacks of severe pain. I could see mother had been having a hard time with him. In his bitterness about his blindness, he would not try to learn Braille or interest himself in anything and was so helpless that he had to have a nurse with him constantly. However, during the last days of October, he decided he wanted to go to Ireland, and mother accompanied him, leaving him near our relatives in Antrim. This was the solution of his greatest problem, for he again started to write and did some of his best work there. He got much better for a while, was in higher spirits, and began to show interest in meeting people again and in his old literary friends, Joyce, Lord Dunsany, and Moira O'Neill, who wrote *Songs of the Glens of Antrim*.

All our Russian friends were arriving in Paris, many of them destitute, with terrible tales of hardship and separation from their families and of the Bolshevik Revolution. Princess Soltikoff was among them. She had been separated from her two daughters; her old mother had been shot in the dining-room of their home in Moscow by the Bolsheviks, who, according to Princess Soltikoff, wanted to know what the old lady had done with the gold plate and killed her when she refused to tell them. With friends and relatives who could get away, the princess had fled to the Caucasus, and when the Bolshevik menace caught up with them there, they continued on foot into Turkey.

Mother thought, as father had done, that I had been through too much hard work and that it was spoiling my looks. She wanted me to have some concert repertoire in the form of recitations on music, in different languages, that I could use as a side-line in her concerts to save my overworking in too frequent ballet engagements. This had been the motive for my taking elocution together with piano.

I have since studied with many brilliant teachers of elocution and dramatic recitation but have never met one to touch mother in this type of work. One of her principal talents was her dramatic ability, and in many of her operatic rôles she made very realistic interpretations of the part. She was one of the first singers to use speech in such scenes. For example, in playing the death of Manon in Massenet's opera, she spoke, almost sighed, her last words, instead of lying on the ground dying and singing at the top of her voice in the old traditional style.

I did not mind studying recitations, for they did not interfere with my dancing practice, but I would have much preferred to study decorative art and stagecraft although I never mentioned it because I knew we did not have any money to spend on art classes. Mother was even meditating on how to get grandmama back to Spain so as to economize, and had broached the subject with determination. Grand-mama, however, had her own way of circumventing any plans she did not want to have materialize. On this occasion, she gave me an astounding proof of the efficiency of her spells.

One afternoon when mother had told her that she had arranged for all the details concerning her return to Spain, grandmama called me into her room and asked me to go out and buy a small sharp knife with a wooden handle. I was somewhat startled at this request and wondered if she contemplated murdering mother, but she explained very earnestly that it was for a *brujería* (witchcraft) to cut her impending voyage—she definitely did not want to go. I felt rather sorry for her, and when I was certain there would be no bloodshed, I went out and bought the knife. She took it to the window of her room, where there were some window boxes of frozen earth that had contained plants. She stood at the open window and stabbed the earth with the knife, to the north, the south, the east and the west, saying at every stab, *"Que se corta mi viaje,"* meaning, "May the plans for my voyage be cut."

It was about six o'clock in the evening, and the following day at the same hour mother came home all excited. Her agents had offered her a contract for concerts in Greece and Turkey, together with an engagement for me to dance at another establishment, so grandmama would have to come along to look after me if mother accepted.

I never told mother what we had done with the *brujería,* and could hardly keep a straight face when grandmama craftily started making objections about her rheumatism— while all the time, at the thought of getting into more traveling, she was like a war horse scenting battle.

Grandmother was a good business woman, but the contracts for Constantinople were not a very clear-cut proposition, so mother was hesitant about signing them. However, the more we heard about all the refugees and all our friends in Turkey, the more grandmama wanted to be on the move again.

I had no experience in reciting before an audience, so mother thought if the numbers were not so hot in Turkey it wouldn't matter very much and anyway it would be a good place to try them out. I also had a contract to dance once a night at the Grand Cercle Muscovite—which sounded swell when we read the contract, but turned out to be a dump.

It was to be something in the nature of a paid holiday, we decided, and at the same time, we would see who was in Constantinople and whether we could help Princess Soltikoff about her family, supposed to be in the Caucasus.

The three fantastic weeks we spent in Turkey are difficult to describe and so, I am afraid, still more difficult to believe. Of course, when we got there, it was nothing like what we expected to find—except for the refugees. The political situation was unsettled, and Kemal Pasha was reported to be mapping out all the unpleasant things that could be done to strangers of all nationalities, Russians in particular.

We had not had an agreeable voyage getting there, principally because mother got one of her "yens" for the sea, and nothing would satisfy her but a train across Italy to take a boat described as a "pleasure steamer" through the Greek Archipelago to Salonica and Constantinople. Erico Zipilli, mother's accompanist, upon hearing that we intended passing through Italy, had decided he would meet us at Corfu, which he did, but nearly missed the boat—a habit inborn in all musicians. This got mother in a state of nerves bordering on homicidal mania.

The train through Italy was unheated and full of priests and pilgrims going somewhere or other and demobilized troops and officers going home. At the Italian frontier, Domo d'Ossola, mother, of course, had a row with the customs, and her bill for excess baggage (a specialty of the Italian railroads) was brutal. She had really spent money in Paris for clothes for both of us, and her baggage was devastating. I had to use Pushkin to get through the customs and on to the train before they closed the frontier. This is a common occurrence in Italy, and I can't imagine why they do it, it flusters people so.

Mother was too obstinate to admit that it would have been wiser to take the overland route via Vienna than to atttempt the trip by sea so soon after the war, when nothing was organized. The boat was an impossible old tub which smelled of sardines from one end to the other and had a galley on

101

the deck whence the cook used to spit on to the deck railing as he prepared the meals.

From the word go, we had storm after storm. There were a few Armenians who sold carpets, some mad monks, and a few sinister Greek nuns and priests, and as the ship wallowed and pitched through a heavy sea, everybody, including Zipilli and Marie, mother's maid, vanished from the scene almost immediately.

The beauties of Greece were shrouded in fog, sleet, and rain, and it was bitterly cold. I spent most of the time in my cabin with the *Life of Byron*, which was depressing, and the *Chansons de Bilitis* of Pierre Louÿs, which helped a great deal. The few times poor Zipilli came up for air, he heroically tried to start a flirtation with me. This spelled disaster if mother noticed anything; however, he never could stay at it very long on account of the ship's rolling—he would turn green in the face and dash back to his cabin before he could really get started. He was not particularly attractive but very clever and had strange black eyes that were always somber.

When the mad trip was nearly over—we were at it the best part of a week—the captain, a messy little Italian with dirty fingernails, told mother he had been obliged to refuse passengers coming from Greece because they had every sort of epidemic raging there—typhoid, cholera, Spanish grippe, and diphtheria. I think he rather exaggerated the situation—it did not seem possible for any country to have such a conglomeration of diseases—but it got mother in a frightful state, for she dreaded contagion of any sort.

When we got to Constantinople, she checked the captain's information and found that it was not possible to drink the water in Greece, only mineral water, and that they did have influenza and diphtheria plus a certain amount of typhoid. This came from all the ships carrying wounded back after the Armistice: they appeared to have distributed loads of germs as they sailed by. Mother's throat was very weak, and as soon as she heard of the health situation in Greece, she made up her mind that she would not sing there.

102

All the good hotels in Pera and Constantinople were full, so we finally had to end up in a sort of glorified pension in the Mustafa Superior. We located a cousin who was employed by Standard Oil, Turkish branch. He had a villa on the Bosphorus but was unable to put us up there because it had been mysteriously burned down: it seemed the Turkish had taken a dislike to everybody who was a foreigner. He was as much good as a sick headache as far as being at all useful to us. Grandmama seemed to terrify him for some reason, and anyway he was leaving at once for the London office.

Our next shock came the morning following our arrival, when a Mr. Negretti, representative of the impresarios who had made the engagements for mother, arrived at our hotel and announced that the concerts had been arranged by a Society for the Cultivation of Music and that they had failed to get the theater they had counted on leasing, with its orchestra, but had arranged for her to sing in the German Club instead.

This turned out to be a drafty barracks with bad acoustics. Big fat women kept arriving at the hotel from the Society, telling mother how they would like the program arranged; they seemed to want nothing but German Lieder. Germans were mixed up in everything, and a man with a monocle and saber cuts all over his face in the approved Heidelberg fashion was fussing about and telling everybody what to do, which infuriated mother. Then they wanted her to sing three programs at their club, go to Greece, and return for the balance of the functions, at which time they hoped to get hold of a theater.

This, mother said, she had no intention of doing: even grandmama's assurance that an ear of garlic sewn in a little bag and worn in the brassière would positively ward off an infectious disease of even the most virulent character would not move her. She had also made up her mind that she would not sing anything in the German language, but only French repertoire and Russian Lieder, and in this Zipilli backed her

103

up. The Comité Artistique held out for German repertoire, of course, and the battle raged.

I was to recite Verlaine's "Cortège" and Rostand's "Posthumous Tribute to Sarah Bernhardt" in the first part of mother's program, a Russian poem of the sixteenth century and one of Pushkin's (the poet, not the snake) in the second.

While mother battled with her first program, grandmama and I rushed like mad to the Grand Cercle Muscovite to get there for band rehearsal at one o'clock as my contract stipulated. We arrived about 12:30 and found the doors of the place hermetically closed. After we had done a lot of ringing of door-bells, telephones, and so on, a sleepy Russian porter emerged and informed us that the man who ran the place lived above it and never got up before six, when it was opened for cocktails. He then shut the door in our faces. As we stood contemplating the ornate façade of the building, a big fat man put in an appearance and introduced himself as the chef, Mr. Koubeloff.

He was most polite and expansive about his personal history and told us he had been chef to Grand Duke Michael and had fled from Petrograd and the Revolution; also that the proprietor of the Cercle Muscovite, a Prince Gagine (this was not his real name, we found out) was ill and that he, Koubeloff, looked after everything—with the assistance of a floor manager and the personnel of the gambling salons. He showed us these, which were rather sinister-looking and smelled of sin and stale tobacco smoke. The ballroom where I was to dance was magnificent and overlooked the bay. The whole place was very grand, with wonderful rugs and great silver-framed mirrors laden with Russian double eagles, but when he showed us my dressing-room, grandma began to look upset.

It was like an illustration I had once seen in *Madame Bovary*—full of artificial flowers and reeking of patchouli. He wanted me to work at 1:30 A.M., but grandmama put her foot down at that—11:30 P.M. was the very latest, she told him. He was very gallant and replied with a quaint little bow, "Oh, Madame, she is so young and fresh—you are right,"

104

and immediately changed my name to an earlier place on the bill.

While I rested before the 4:30 band call, grandmama did a bit of sleuthing and discovered that the "Prince" (the proprietor) was a morphine maniac who never got up, and that Koubeloff loaned money on jewelry which the Russian refugees pawned to gamble with—they always lost, so he generally stayed with the jewels and was reported to be rich. The place was run as a club—was well frequented and had political pull. Of course it was no place for a girl of my age to be working, but we needed the money, and grandmama said she would stick to me closer than adhesive plaster.

She attributed all the bad breaks we were getting to the Greek monks who had traveled on the ship with us. They were a wild-looking lot and so fanatical, they crossed themselves every time they saw either mother or me on the deck: one of them used to turn away his head and spit when he saw a woman. I have seen monks do this in Rome. Grandmama said the holier they got the goofier they got.

Mother and I got our respective débuts over fairly well, considering the adverse circumstances. I opened first, and fortunately mother was too tired to attend, for it would have upset her even more than the German Club had done. When I think of my youth (I was thirteen) and the naïveté of my dances—the Kreisler arrangement of Ferraud's "Jeunesse" and "La Nuit" of Rubinstein—in that decadent atmosphere, it all seems fantastic. I danced a purely technical classic style which must have seemed out of place to the crowd of blasé men and hard-faced women, but they gave me a wonderful hand after they got over the first shock. When I came out to take my bows, they looked at me with the same sloppy expression some people get when they see a new-born infant. Everybody was very kind and complimentary, but grandmama rushed me out of the place as if it were on fire.

Mother had a tremendous success the following night, and I did quite well—especially with the Russian poems. One thing I could not quite understand was why a lot of the people from the Cercle turned up. I worked at 9:30, in the first part of mother's program, which gave me time to get to the Cercle to dance at 11:30, so how anybody would want to see me twice in one evening, in different places, was mystifying to me. When I drew grandmama's attention to it, she looked grim and told me that Koubeloff had asked her, after they had seen me dance the first night, if she would consider prolonging my engagement. She told him she would do no such thing, and as soon as we got our three weeks over we would leave immediately.

Mother did not get paid after her first concert, which was most unusual, but she decided not to say anything after all the bickering that had been going on, but to wait for the second one and in the meantime turn her attention to the Russian refugees we intended to look for. There seemed to be nothing else in Constantinople.

First we found Madame Filipovitch, who had been one of the most beautiful society brides when we were in Russia and had lost everything in the Revolution. She was gambling, drinking, and three days after we met her was taken to the hospital with typhus. Her husband and all her relatives were killed: she had no one left. Another was the Countess Shouvalova, a beautiful woman and very talented, who sang well enough for a professional career but was doing the same thing as Elena Filipovitch—only she had some money, fortunately.

And so went on the long saga of tragedy. There was little anybody could say to them in such a hopeless situation. Some of them had money and were spending it like water in a desperate effort to have some happiness and forget.

One boy, a relative of the Galitzine's, said, "I want to spend all I have left, then I will see how it feels, perhaps I will kill myself." They steeped themselves in that luxury of grief dear to the Russian heart. Apropos of Russian temperament, I will never forget one girl, a niece of Princess Soltikoff, who told me about her fiancé. They were driving back from a reception (before the Revolution) in a sleigh on a beautiful moonlight winter night. When he got out to say good night to her and her mother, he gazed at her with rapture and said, "You are so beautiful, the world is so beautiful in this moonlight, I can bear it no longer"—and he shot himself. She seemed to think it was wonderful and said she would never again be able to find a man with such a sensitive soul.

As the days went by, we did not find any of the people we were most anxious to trace, and it was impossible to get accurate information about the Soltikoff girls. People arrived on foot and in rags; there was a great deal of illness, and the hospitals were full of typhus and smallpox.

After the second concert, mother developed a sore throat and became terribly alarmed for fear it would turn into something serious. In addition to this, there was still no *cachet* forthcoming from the Society—so Negretti was sent for. He was a funny little wizened man who had been stranded in Constantinople by a third-rate opera company. He was deeply impressed by mother as an artist, but at the same time his allegiance was divided between her and his meal ticket with the Society. After a lot of excuses, he finally said they were holding out on the salary because they could not cancel the concerts arranged in Greece. Publicity had been paid for and they were out of pocket, etc....

Mother was having a considerable success: the press raved about her and every concert had been sold out, so the excuse for not paying her seemed extremely feeble. She gave him one

107

hour to dig up the money for the two concerts, or, she said, she positively would not sing another note.

While Negretti was trying to find the money for her, she called a doctor and had a certificate made stating that her throat was badly inflamed and she should not sing for at least three weeks. When Negretti eventually returned with the money for one concert only, mother was furious and talked so much that both grandmama and I felt she would not be able to sing for considerably longer than three weeks. She gave him the doctor's certificate, shut herself up in her room, and let nature take its course. Negretti waved his arms about and shouted outside her door, but to no avail, and he finally left to break the news to the Society for the Cultivation of Music to the best of his ability.

They were at fault in a sense, as mother's contract read that she would be paid by function—but on the other hand, she had flatly refused to sing in Greece. Grandmama was very cross about the whole business, but she was practical and said that obviously we had to get some money from somewhere, so I would have to finish my engagement at the Cercle.

Mother was so disgusted with everything that she wanted us all just to walk out and take the next train back to Paris. The end of it was, she left early the next morning with Zipilli and Marie, before the Society had time to get a *saisie foraine* on her baggage. This is a "stop" under the French law, preventing a defaulting artist from embarking, and permits the theater or impresario to seize trunks and personal effects at the railway station or docks. It is generally employed where artists have received an advance on their salaries. I am not at all sure they could have done this to mother in the face of her doctor's certificate and in view of the fact they owed her money.

The newspapers announced that she was ill, which should not have surprised anybody who knew the German Club, but the worst side to the matter was that mother had been able to leave us only very little money. The salary I was getting, although much more than I had received from Pavlova, was just about enough for our hotel expenses.

Before the disaster of the concerts we had offered so much financial help to friends from Russia who kept arriving at our hotel daily, bringing their friends with them, that grandmama had already given away practically all the money she had. Everywhere we met people we knew, some of them working as porters, chauffeurs, and cabaret singers. Most of the waiters at the Cercle were ex-officers and magnificent looking men.

One little English girl we met in Constantinople had come to Russia with a troupe of Tiller girls—the famous English precision dancers, like the Rockettes and Gae Foster girls— and had become the mistress of one of the Grand Dukes. She stayed on in Moscow after her troupe left, when the city was in the hands of the Bolsheviks and her Grand Duke expected they would come after him at any moment. He got out the little cheap tin trunk she had arrived with, that contained her theatrical finery, and filled it with thousands of roubles' worth of jewels, and gave her a letter, which she sewed into her clothes, to his bankers in London saying that if she got through with the jewels, they were to sell them for her and invest the money. The Bolsheviks arrived just as he had completed these arrangements, and arrested him. They glanced at her trunk and saw a big pile of what they supposed was old junk—rhinestones, tinsel, old tights, etc., and let her go. They never stopped to go through it.

She arrived in Turkey with everything intact, and said that her ambition was to buy a theatrical boarding-house in London but that first she would try and find any of the Duke's heirs who needed help. She was a decent little thing, and as cool as a cucumber about her escape. How she ever got over the mountain roads with that trunk is something fantastic under the circumstances.

Some of the women who got across on foot had babies by the side of the road; their feet were cut and infected from frostbite, and their clothes were full of lice since they had slept in shepherds' huts and abandoned shacks. We tried to give all the help we could to these poor people, and grandmama's fame as a Mæcenas spread abroad and everybody thought we were Russians.

One evening the man who paid the artists and ran the floor show at the Cercle, Monsieur Albert, a Greek, suddenly disappeared. It was nearly the end of the third week, and we naturally noticed it and asked for him. From one of the Russian doormen, we discovered that all sorts of trouble was brewing. The general belief was that all foreigners not employed in diplomatic work or business necessary to the Turkish government would be requested to leave at once—especially Russians.

For some reason, the authorities had suspended the licenses of the Cercle and other establishments, and when the artists got wind of the situation, they besieged the office and apartment of the owner, Prince Gagine—but he could not be found. The next day the Cercle Muscovite was closed.

Grandmama held a council of war! There was no use wasting time trying to get paid—that we could clearly see. Every train and boat leaving the town was jammed, so we got our visas and cabled mother—but got no answer. Then we really started to worry a little, since we did not have enough to pay the hotel and our fares to Paris as well. It was the end of a perfect trip.

When, the following day, there was still nothing from mother, I sent a cable to my brother in Ireland, but received no reply from him, either. Grandmother interviewed the Spanish Consul, and he advised us to leave but had no suggestions as to what we could use for money; his office was jammed with people who could not get out for lack of funds. Grandmama began to get very worried, so I decided to play our last card.

I scouted around and got hold of Koubeloff, the chef. I knew where he lived and caught him just in time. He was leaving that night for Paris. I knew he liked me, and after some reluctance on his part I got him not only to lend us the fares, but to go and battle with the crowds besieging the ticket offices and get our tickets for Paris. I had explained to him that we would repay the loan and give him a present when we arrived there and that I did not want to have to wait for a cable from my father as we had only enough money to pay the hotel now.

I waited in his office while he went for the tickets, and when he returned he showed me a paper bag he had in a valise, in which he kept the jewelry he had loaned money on. It was a magnificent collection of gems and pearls. He told me he always kept it in the dirty old grocery bag, so nobody would think of robbing him with such a disreputable piece of luggage. He traveled with us and was helpful and charming.

When we arrived in Paris, we found out the reason why we had received no answer to our cables. Mother had simply left for the Riviera without any thought of our possibly having difficulties in Turkey, although the papers were full of the situation there for foreigners and she knew we had very little money. It was typical of her. She did not mean to be selfish, but she had received a telegram from my brother asking her if she would accompany him to Monte Carlo, as he could not travel alone. He had taken it into his head that he wanted to write a book there, so she went over to Ireland to get him. She never thought of letting us know a thing. She said she had intended writing from Monte Carlo but had been too busy. Grandmama had an awful row with her about it, for if it had not been for Koubeloff, God knows what we would have done.

VII

WHILE I HAD BEEN DANCING in Turkey, I came to realize more and more the truth of what I had been told when I worked in the Diaghilev company in those few functions in New York. Diaghilev said: "Ballet is a fusion of three perfect things, Décor, Music, and Dance—and none of the three can triumph without the others." I had seen all the great figures of the Russian ballet when I was at school in Moscow. At the Bolshoi and the Marinsky theaters, when Fokine was one of the choreographers, I had seen Nijinsky dance with Pavlova as his partner, also the great Keschinka who had Mischa Elman as first violinist at Covent Garden. For me, the ballet had many more possibilities which had not been exploited—I kept that thought with me for years. I think perhaps it was born in Constantinople while I watched that great Italian acrobatic dancer, Faraboni, who worked as the star act at the Cercle Muscovite.

I was not old enough to be able to formulate definite plans for what I wanted to do, except for the one thought—to study music, color, and décor as a base for creative work. I began to think that such ballets as *Walpurgis Night,* which were given with dancers strapped in harnesses and flown from arm booms over the stage, could be done in a marvelous way with aërialists trained as dancers, with the requisite ballet movements, and working in harmony with dancers on the ground in a spectacular ballet. Russian technique not only is artificial in theory but borders on the acrobatic, yet Russian choreographers will not recognize this and are almost fanatical in their hate for anything savoring of acrobacy: "circus," they call it with contempt.

The greatest of all of them to me was Fokine. I had worked

under him several times—but not till we met in Buenos Aires in the Colón season of 1930 did I dare talk to him about such a combination. He would not even comment on it, so I never mentioned it again. The last time I ever saw him was in New York in his school at Carnegie Hall—I had gone to see him about some posters for a presentation I was doing for a perfume called "Ballet," in which he kindly took an interest. He loved the idea of a Byzantine case for the perfume, with the Bakst drawing of Nijinsky in *L'Après-midi d'un Faune* as a decoration for it. When I told him I had been working for some years in my own aërial act, using an almost complete ballet technique in the work, he looked at me as if he thought I were to be more pitied than blamed.

On my return to Paris from Turkey with all these thoughts in my head, I started a book in which I made notes of combinations of décor, musical themes, and movements of every type—not dance alone, but acrobatic movements in rhythm, both on the ground and in the air, with the idea that they should not be done as feats but in the same manner as a dancer uses her technique. All this material I had collected was out of the reach of any amateur, thus preserving a professional ability and perfection. This book has been a continuous source of choreographic material which I have used both in my own act and in production work, much as a chemist uses his formulas.

So in my small way, I battled along with my studies and dreams, hoping to realize some day a new conception of dancing. Perhaps the nearest I ever came to this realization was in 1937 at the Salle Pleyel in Paris, where I had the nerve to try my aërial act in a "Festival of the Dance" organized by Felix Rosan and Rolf de Maré, producer of the Swedish ballet.

It was purely a classical dance recital in a concert hall where such things as acrobats had never been seen. Serge Lifar danced with the ballet of the Opéra; there were a group of Japanese dancers, Boris Knaisieff and many others. The orchestra was the "Pas de Loup" symphony orchestra of

113

Paris, under Saulnier of the Opéra. His face, when I handed him the music of "Cortège" and the "Plus que Lente" of Debussy, was a study. He looked as if he were going to be sick. While the men lowered my ropes for me to show him my timings and run through my routine, he muttered and gesticulated with the musicians. I thought he was never going to start and waited patiently for him—my hands damp and clammy with nerves, which is not a pleasant sensation when one has to do difficult tricks in the air. Rolf de Maré and Rosan were in the stalls giggling with joy at the whole thing, and the dancers were grouped together looking at me as if I were poison ivy. When Maître Saulnier finally got his men together, he shouted, *"Eh bien! Mademoiselle l'Acrobat—commençons."* I was both nervous and angry, and between the two emotions, I really did a good act. When I got through, I walked down to the orchestra pit to talk to the drummer about some details I thought could be improved—although it was the best interpretation of Debussy I had worked to in France. I completely ignored the Maître, since I supposed he did not want to conduct for an aërial act and the less I had to say to him, the better. When I finished talking to the drummer, the Maître looked up at me and said, "I have never seen anything like this in my life. Why, it is ballet in the air. *Mademoiselle, mes félicitations."* I took five calls that night before a crowded house and did a repeat performance the following week—so I proved my idea was not so far wrong.

Another artist whose performance taught me a great deal in my early days was Loïe Fuller. Her company was in Paris when I got back from Turkey, and it was a spectacle of originality and color. She had a great deal of what I wanted to do, but it was not quite modern enough, and too much depended on her lights. Still, she had always been a success in Europe, and nobody has ever done anything like her since.

I started studying decorative art and the usual piano classes again, but now with a more definite purpose. In the early spring of 1919, mother had a lot of trouble over that old lawsuit of the records. I don't know what father had done about it, but she was fretting herself to death over it, and her throat was not in any too good a condition after she came back from Monte Carlo. My brother had returned to Ireland, for he did not like Paris or any other large city—and between one thing and another, our home life was not very gay. So when a telegram came from Pavlova in London, saying that she was arriving for a short tournée to be held during the months of March and April in Belgium, I joined her company again with great joy.

After a gala performance in Brussels for the Russian refugees in the Théâtre de la Monnaie before the King and Queen of Belgium, the short tour was over and she mentioned her opening in Drury Lane, London. Rehearsals were starting almost immediately, and she naturally expected me to go on with the company, although grandmama had previously explained to her that I would not be able to accept the world tour which was planned to follow the Drury Lane engagement.

I returned from Belgium to find mother still in a whirl with legal complications. She had got nothing settled (I could never get her to explain exactly what she was up against), but I knew that she was obliged to work despite the delicate condition of her throat. I presumed poor father had not been able to send money to get her out of the lawsuit mess, and it was up to me to help and get working as soon as possible, wherever I could get the most money.

There was a series of long and heated discussions with grandmama, who wanted me to go with Diaghilev, opening in the Alhambra at the end of April. He had promised her in Madrid that I was to work in the *Tricornio*, and his word was the same as a contract. Besides, he wanted her to give him Spanish details for the dances. They got on famously and were always in a huddle with cards and incantations. Diaghilev was extremely superstitious and loved all the things grandmama did and said to bring good luck.

Pavlova had engaged nearly all English girls for this season; Diaghilev had all the Russian dancers with him. He was far more technical and held a higher standard than Pavlova;

also, he paid his dancers much better. On the other hand, he was often broke in consequence, but he never failed to pay anybody as soon as he got another backer to finance him.

Pavlova expected me to work for her in London in June, since we had accepted her terms verbally, but mother would not sign any contract with her, and the situation became very involved. In the end, grandmama got her way about my joining Diaghilev, and we went to the Alhambra at the last minute. God knows how I ever got in at all, with all the fiddling about that mother and grandmama had done between the two companies, but I was a good Spanish technician, and Diaghilev wanted all the Spanish and gipsy dancers he could get and had already brought several from Spain.

It was not a nice thing to have done to Pavlova, for she had been very correct with us. I have always hoped that she understood I was not to blame. Nevertheless, for any dancer to go from her company to Diaghilev was unforgivable, and I knew she disliked mother from then on.

The ballet season of that year was marvelous. The triumphs of the *Boutique Fantasque* and *El Tricornio* are too well known for me to give a dissertation on them, but undoubtedly they were two of the most brilliant representations Diaghilev ever produced. I had special lessons with Maestro Diaghilev's ballet master and technical aide, Cecchetti, who was perhaps the world's greatest teacher of dancing and worked his pupils relentlessly. As soon as he got hold of me, he started after my left arm, which was still stiff and often difficult to work with.

Up to the time I started with Cecchetti's intensive training, I had been able to hide any deficiencies very successfully: even Pavlova had seldom criticized them. Cecchetti had no patience with people who had anything wrong with them, and when I began to have pain in my leg, I was terrified he would find out about that, too. As I have said before, I am able to hide the shortness in my left leg so well that it is impossible for anybody to detect the difference in length

116

while I dance or do aërial work—but in my fear of Cecchetti's noticing there was something wrong with the leg, I strained my muscles and made the pain worse in an effort to hide the limp. Cecchetti never said anything about it, and I never told anybody that I was suffering, but the pain in my arm was another story, for it ached continually and kept me from sleeping at night, till I began to lose weight. Finally I went by myself to see Doctor Abercrombie, who had taken care of me after Olympia. He told me I needed an operation to have the shoulder opened so the bone could be scraped, and that if I didn't have it, the arm would give me serious trouble in later years. Of course I said I would think it over, but I never went back to him or told my grandmother or mother about it. Fortunately, after a while it got less painful.

When the first rehearsals were over, I had a little more time in the mornings before my lesson with Cecchetti and took classes at the Academy of Dramatic Art in Gower Street. I wanted to study facial expression, acting, and above all, stagecraft. It was not a bad idea, for I learned a lot there.

London was simply wonderful that year. I will always remember the summer mornings with the smell of the hot asphalt along Piccadilly, the flower-sellers on the corners, and the big pink Malmaison carnations I used to buy for mother. Often I have thought how every country has its own peculiar smell: Paris smells of gasoline and L'Origan of Coty; Seville smells of oranges, frying oil, and incense; Moscow smells of wet umbrellas and burning wood. I could go on describing smells from all the world capitals I have visited, although some of the Oriental combinations are hardly fit for print.

Nina was back from Paris for the opening of the *Tricornio* and was making a name for herself as a painter. She had made an unfortunate marriage to somebody who had long hair, no chin and did woodcuts. But it did not last long, and the experience seemed to have helped her talent considerably. I saw a great deal of her, for she adored the ballet, and

117

grandmama was too busy with the Spanish artists and all the excitement of the *Tricornio* début to keep such a strict eye on me. Besides, I was growing older, and so was she.

I managed to get away from her quite often after the show, and went to the Chelsea Art Ball and lots of parties with Nina. She knew crowds of interesting people—José María Sert, Picasso, Manuel de Falla, Georges Auric who wrote *Les Matelots* for Diaghilev, based on old sea chanteys which Nina collected and sang very well. That famous patron of artists, Lady (Bubbles) Mitchelham, was another person who gave grand parties, with Teddy Gerard, the American revue artist, Lee White, Glyn Phillpots, the painter, and lots of clever charming people.

Mother had improved a little in health with the advent of spring and sang at some Sunday concerts at the Queen's Hall. She could have accepted a contract at Covent Garden but for the question of the records: she feared they would garnishee her salary; in fact, they did try something of the sort. So she went to Italy partly on account of this and sang at Rimini with Puccini for a few weeks. In addition to her legal troubles, she had another experience which upset her and everybody else.

Some one had introduced her to a young man who was making a name for himself as a poet: she was always getting mixed up with mad people who wrote poems for her to have set to music. We had christened him "Bunions" after Bunyan of *Pilgrim's Progress* fame, and this boy, young enough to be her son, fell madly in love with her and nobody could do anything with him. We were then staying in a funny little hotel just beside the Royal Albert Hall in Kensington, where singers often stayed because it was possible for them to practice all day and half the night. It was not exactly a restful place at the best of times, and when grandmama invited one of her nieces from Seville, with a tribe of kids, in addition to the complication with mother's poet, life became unbearable.

With the advent of this set-up from Spain, I spent more

118

and more time in Nina's studio to get away from it, and in my absence, Bunions hung about the street corner day and night until mother could not get in or out. She was very much upset about it, for she had no idea of flirting with anybody. I had told this pest of a poet several times that he was making a nuisance of himself, but it did no good, and he managed to get letters put in mother's room by those wretched little gitana cousins, who would do anything for what they called a *perra gorda* (fat dog—Spanish slang for a large silver coin) or five shillings in English money.

One evening when I was in the theater, they took Bunions into the hotel, and he waited for mother in the hall of our apartment. When she returned and found him there, she had to get the manager of the hotel to throw him out. It was an unpleasant scandal, and the next morning he sent a letter saying if he did not hear from her by a certain hour, she would never see him again, etc., etc., hinting suicide. Mother showed it to me and I advised her to ignore it, as we were trying our darnedest to get rid of him, and above all not to reply and compromise herself by writing letters to lunatics.

The next morning, the papers were full of what the boy had done. When he got no reply from mother, he went to his cottage in the New Forest, sent his Arab servant to the village to post farewell letters to mother and his family, and then set the place on fire with kerosene and shot himself. The police found his half-charred body and, what was much worse, about ten letters written to mother that had not been entirely destroyed, lying about on the floor.

Naturally, the affair upset mother terribly. She unjustly blamed herself for the whole thing, and to make matters worse, the boy's father, a retired colonel, came to London and made a terrible scene, after she had been kind enough to receive him. I had to show him the door, and mother got it into her head that he would do her harm as an artist. This unnerved her so much that nothing would induce her to stay in London. She left immediately for Italy. Soon I had orders to join her, at the end of the Diaghilev engagement for a

119

tournée in South Africa with the opera company of Camillo Bonetti.

I felt very depressed when I went with grandmama to say good-by to Diaghilev. He more or less told me that I was leaving an atmosphere of art which I would not find elsewhere and that when I returned I would have lost ground by his standards. Diaghilev was to all dancers a personage whose word was law and' who could not possibly be wrong about anything. They practically groveled at his feet whenever he spoke to them, which he seldom did unless it was to flatten them out with criticism—but he watched everybody and knew how much progress every young ballerina made. He had never paid much attention to me one way or the other, but what he said when I left made me feel very unhappy. Maestro Cecchetti, too, was disappointed, although he was very sweet and kindly and wished me all sorts of success.

Mother had told me nothing in her letters about the formation of the ballet with the Bonetti company which I was now to join, or who was ballet master. I did not want to dance under an Italian, because they are always fighting about Russian technique. Cecchetti was of course an Italian and had been originally brought from Italy for the Russian ballet, but he was exceptional and had nothing of the antiquated operatic methods that most ordinary Italian teachers use. Although I knew that any pupil of his would not be found much fault with, I was still afraid Diaghilev's words might come true.

I was all packed and ready to start for Italy when a cable came from mother saying she was coming to London for twenty-four hours and that I was to wait for her and get her grand piano out of storage to take with us. Between the piano and mother's changing her mind several times, we got started on our trip late in July, sailing for Cape Town. Once on board the ship I began to feel a little happier, for the ballet master was a dear old man I had studied under at the Costanzi in Rome. He knew all about my skating-rink episode and had thought it was a perfectly normal incident. His name was Vitulli.

On the boat there was the usual conglomeration of dull people, rather common in general, but there was one most interesting person, a Mrs. Louth, champion big-game shot and explorer. She was an extremely plain woman and on the eccentric side, for her back and arms were entirely tattooed with snakes and lizards writhing in complicated patterns of blue and green. When she wore an evening dress (which was always a green one) the tattooed designs on her arms looked like peacock-blue lace.

The first night she came to the captain's table dressed in a low-cut dinner-gown, the effect on the passengers was terrific. She was reported to be enormously rich and owned a ranch near Nairobi, Kenya Colony. She was going to meet a scientific expedition of some sort in Cape Town, give some lectures for them, and then leave for Mombasa to take a safari up country. Traveling with her was a tall handsome Austrian with flaming red hair, called Fritz Schindler. He was a professional shot and guide, and it was quite evident that she was madly in love with him. After the first few days on board, Mrs. Louth took a real fancy to me, probably because I had been extremely rude to Schindler, who had started chasing mother as soon as he saw her, and I had at her request succeeded in stopping his bothering us with his attentions. This incident cemented a friendship between Alice Louth and my mother that lasted for years.

The Bonetti company was coming from Durban, and mother and I spent a week in Cape Town preparing publicity, repertoire, and so on, and as usual, flying from one rehearsal hall or newspaper office to another, without ever getting time to look at the country we were in. Among the things I remember best about our South African trip was an old house overlooking the sea: we had seen it one day when Mrs. Louth had insisted upon driving us about Cape Town. It was an immense property and one could just see the top of the low roof, for it was shut behind high walls surrounding a magnificent garden. The

121

whole road beside the walls was perfumed with Cape jasmine.

Houses have always fascinated me, and the brooding sadness that hung about this one, despite its beauty, was so strong I simply could not tear myself away from it. Mrs. Louth told us that it belonged to a very rich young boy. His parents were dead of leprosy and he also was infected with the disease. The English are very strict about such cases and send them to the Leper Colony on Fire Island, but I suppose the wealth and influence of this boy permitted him to live on his estate with a doctor. He never went out, nor had he been seen for two or three years. His house haunted me for weeks because it was so tragic and so much like a place I had seen in Toledo. I had walked with my friends through the town after visiting the Church of the Miraculous Virgin, and we had passed a great red stone building with barred windows which overlooked the cliffs around Toledo and a park where there were benches. Suddenly we heard the most wonderful tenor voice singing an old Spanish love song: the voice came from one of the barred windows in the red stone building above us. We listened fascinated, thinking it was a professional singer; then we asked a man who was passing what the building was. There was infinite sadness in his voice as he replied, *"Es la Casa de los Locos, y un loco que canta todos los dias."* (It is the madhouse, and a madman sings there every day.)

The sea air and the rest of the voyage had done wonders for mother's voice, and when the tournée got under way she sang better than I had ever heard her sing before. The success she obtained made her so happy that she was a different person and expanded like a flower in the rays of the footlights. I often thought of the day when she would have to retire and wondered if she would take it as courageously as grandmama had done. I asked her that question once, after a matinée when she had received a particularly brilliant reception. She told me she wanted to die before she got wrinkled and passée and unable to sing any more, for music was the only thing she cared to live for.

As our tournée in South Africa proceeded, Maestro Vitulli gave me the place of first character dancer, much to the fury of the other girls. We spent long hours working out choreographic combinations, and when Massenet's opera *Thaïs* was given in Durban, I got Bonetti to give the prelude before the ballet, as Pavlova did, and to let me dance it. I had watched her night after night and knew every step and gesture that she used: she always danced it with a white veil over her face and glided like a vision across the stage, in blue lights, to the music of the famous "Meditation," which is generally played as an orchestra solo. It is an exquisite effect, and I had a great success with it. Mario Carelli, Bonetti's business manager, was so pleased that he spoke to mother at once and told her he was negotiating for the Teatro Colón in Buenos Aires for the coming season and that he wanted to engage me for it. He showed us a cable from the Municipal Art Commission of the Colón, saying that they had engaged the ballet company of Alexandro Jakobleff with the dancers Pavlova had left behind the previous year. Mother finally gave her consent for me to go to Buenos Aires under the care of Mario Carelli and his wife.

Before we left Cape Town, Mrs. Louth had invited us to visit her when our tournée ended. She suggested we take the boat from Natal or Durban to Mombasa, and from there we could take the river boat to Nairobi where she would meet us. We received a cable from her telling us that she had arranged two concerts for mother at the Kenya Club, one for the Governor, and also a big reception that she intended giving upon her return from her safari.

Our opera company had a tremendous reception on its tour and we played all the important towns. Mother had a good personal success with her concerts as well: she had always sung the simple old Scotch and Irish ballads perfectly, and this created an enormous sympathy for her. When the tournée was drawing to its close, mother received a belated letter from grandmama telling her that there were some distant cousins living on a farm near Pietermaritzburg, in some

123

unget-at-able place—I forget the name of it. Mother wrote to them and received a deluge of letters and telegrams in reply, insisting we visit them and of course give a concert at their local Town Hall. I knew how mother hated that sort of function. Like Pavlova, she would always demonstrate delight at such invitations, and half an hour later—after she had already accepted them—decide she would not go and that they bored her ... which was exactly what she did with these cousins. In a weak moment, mother had accepted their invitation and had promised to sing at a concert for them. She tried to get out of it and kept postponing the date, until it was too late to draw back, and we finally had to go.

We started for the Godforsaken place with Zipilli and the grand piano: I was obliged to go along to fill out the program with recitations. Mother managed to have some mix-up about the trains, or perhaps they did not think she was really coming, because when we arrived there was no manager or agent on hand to arrange about delivering the piano, and it had to stand for about two hours on the station platform in the hot sun while the local transport company tried to fit it into a small truck. Naturally, it was of prime importance to get it to the hall somehow, for without it mother was capable of refusing to sing.

She did not seem to realize what we were up against and drove off in a car with three of our cousins with the greatest serenity, leaving Zipilli and me to wrestle with the situation. Abandoning the truck, we finally got the thing into a bullock cart and rattled off along a dusty road, with a crowd of what they called Hottentots pushing the end of the cart in which the piano banged around. When we finally got the instrument hoisted up on the platform of the hall, it was really in bad shape.

On taking the piano out of the case, we found that strings had snapped and twisted, and hammers had sprung. The fat Dutch piano tuner we had sent for decided there was nothing he could do about it and suggested brightly that mother sing with a brassy upright affair that was used for local dances.

124

It was a disaster of an instrument and out of the question, so Zipilli took his coat off and tried to show the fat man what had to be done with the replacements we carried, getting him into such a dither that we finally had to send him away.

By this time people connected with the concert committee began arriving by the dozens, and they all proceeded to give us useless advice and kept carrying in pots of plants and red carpets: they cluttered up the stage so much that we had to ask them kindly to go away, too. Zipilli wrestled with the piano the whole day, and we were both still working on it when the audience started arriving. As there was no curtain, they sat in their seats watching Zipilli and the piano as if they were part of the performance. Then mother appeared, all dressed and ready to sing. She found us on the stage, filthy dirty and struggling in a maze of wire, and she became hysterical, especially when she heard the pitch of the piano.

I don't know why she should have been upset, because the audience looked as if they would never know the difference. About fifteen minutes before we were scheduled to begin, Zipilli by some miracle succeeded in getting the piano tuned to suit mother. I shall never know how he did it, and of course, as is always the case when something goes wrong before a performance to stir up the nerves, we had a grand success and our cousins were delirious with pride and joy.

They were well meaning, but so uninteresting I don't even remember their names. Their mother was Spanish and grandmama's relative. There seemed to be a great many of them, and they were not particularly well mannered: they asked me and Zipilli, who by this time looked like a Zombie, so many idiotic questions that I was rude to them. However, the drive out to their fruit farm over the moonlit veldt was lovely, and I shall always remember the African night sky, the low-swung stars, and the noise the insects made. I can understand why it is said that people who have lived in any part of Africa always go back again, for there is a haunting fascination about it, and I know of no other country, except perhaps Brazil, where one feels that curious tension and expectation that comes after sunset, when it seems almost possible to hear the minutes and seconds of time throbbing like native drums.

The next morning they routed us out at 8:30 for breakfast and had a lot of people present who wanted autographs. Mother, who never got up before twelve under any circumstances, was so cross that she told them we had to leave by the next train. Everybody was disappointed and upset, and I don't know how we ever got that piano out of the concert hall and to the station.

VIII

Mother and I spent New Year's Eve on the boat going to Mombasa. Everybody on board seemed to know us and wanted to buy us champagne, but mother was not in the mood for festivities and spent most of the time in her cabin writing special piano parts for her songs, for Zipilli did not come with us. She had the habit of working herself up to a terrific state of nerves whenever she did not have her own accompanist with her and always had visions of getting hold of some moron who would mess up her concerts. I generally played all her Irish and Scotch ballads, as well as a few of her Russian and Spanish songs, but she had a disconcerting habit of changing her mind about what she would sing in the middle of a program—for she said she could sense the mood of an audience as to what they were receptive to as soon as she had sung her first song.

Mrs. Louth's *homme d'affaires,* Captain Prendergast, sent us several letters regarding the concert arrangments and the publicity that had been done. He told us that Mrs. Louth had arranged "everything" when she was in Nairobi, before she went off again upcountry for a two-week safari, but apparently the all-important matter of the accompanist had been left in abeyance until our arrival: hence mother's preoccupation.

I sat on the deck and watched the shores and the gray-green jungle going down to the water's edge, till sunset, when the night came down so suddenly it seemed like a scene on the stage. Above the chugging of the boat's engines, I could hear the jungle noises and sometimes the bubbling cry that the lemurs make when they hunt their insect prey at night.

127

We arrived the next morning and were somewhat disturbed to receive a note from Captain Prendergast, brought by a colored chauffeur, telling us that he had reserved rooms for us at the Norfolk Hotel in Nairobi and would get in touch with us as soon as possible after our arrival. As his last letter before we sailed had notified us that he would meet the boat in Nairobi and drive us to Mrs. Louth's ranch, we felt sure that something must have happened to her, for she was such a correct person that it did not seem possible that she would not make arrangements to carry out her invitation in the most punctilious fashion.

When we got to the hotel, our worst fears were realized, for the Italian manager told us that Mrs. Louth's party had met with a terrible accident somewhere out in the wilderness. It was not until Captain Prendergast turned up later in the afternoon that we learned what had happened.

It seemed that Fritz Schindler, who was in charge of the party, was more of a European playboy than a safari guide, and that he was a heavy drinker. He had invited some cronies of his on the trip, including a Portuguese guide. There had been a quarrel between them, and the Portuguese had decamped one night with most of the bearers and the stores. The party had started back, and one evening nearly at the end of the trip they stopped to make camp in a part of the country that is infested with leopards. It is the custom, Captain Prendergast explained, when there is a shortage of stores, to suspend the game killed for food in between rocks, to form a kind of open-air larder whenever possible. They had found a suitable spot, and Schindler had had this done, covering the top of the rocks with branches to protect the game.

Later that night, after Mrs. Louth had gone to bed, the men of the party were doing some heavy drinking in Schindler's tent when the bearer came running in to tell them that there were leopards trying to get at the meat. Schindler, who was very drunk, made a bet that he could shoot them with an automatic pistol belonging to Mrs. Louth, and said he would go after them alone. He staggered in between the rocks and flashed an electric torch to try and see where the leopards were: there were three of them crouched on the branches above him. They dropped on him and clawed him to death before he could fire a shot.

His cries brought the rest of the party running, but by the time they got him out his body looked like a heap of red knitting yarn. There was a Belgian doctor with the party, who tried to keep Mrs. Louth from seeing Schindler's body, but she fought him off. The shock of what she saw was so terrible that it sent her out of her mind. They had a terrible time with her, for in addition, she had developed fever. In spite of her condition, she ordered Schindler's body placed in a litter, and when the party started back for her ranch, she insisted on walking beside the body and positively refused to have it buried. The doctor told her several times that, as they had a four-day march ahead of them, it was impossible to keep Schindler's remains in the heat and without any embalming work, but she carried on like a wild animal every time they tried to get her away from the side of the litter, till at last she collapsed, and the doctor kept her under morphine so they could get poor Schindler buried. The party had got back two days previously and taken Mrs. Louth to a friend's ranch, as the nearest possible place, because she was too weak to support the journey by car to the hospital in Nairobi.

Here indeed was an unfortunate situation, and I expected mother to get all excited and upset over it, but again I was surprised by her splendid common sense and strength of character in an emergency. She knew from Captain Prendergast's conversation that Mrs. Louth was severely criticized by the more strait-laced English society of Kenya Colony about her love for Schindler, whom Prendergast described in no uncertain terms as a notorious adventurer with a reputation for ruining wealthy women all over Europe. As a rule, mother hated all such irregularities in people's lives, but when she found out that the ranch where Mrs. Louth had been taken was owned by two men and there were no women there except natives, she said that Mrs. Louth could not remain there alone without more scandal and gossip, and obviously needed some one to nurse her till she could be moved.

As it was, the whole story had appeared in the local papers and was a theme for mud-slinging everywhere—but mother did not give this a moment's thought, or weigh the consequences and possible prejudice against her concerts if she went to the assistance of Mrs. Louth. She said that she would leave me in the hotel and start at once. Prendergast was sent to get a car and, if possible, a nurse. Mother threw some changes of clothing in a suit-case and was all ready to leave in half an hour, forgetting her throat, the dust and the possibility of tsetse flies that she dreaded. Since her first concert was not for a week, she hoped to be back in time; meanwhile, I was to behave myself and hunt up a suitable pianist, get my own repertoire ready, and see that everything was set for the concert at the club.

When Prendergast, a very stately old bachelor, arrived with a car, she asked him to look after me and left immediately for the six-hour drive out to the ranch. It had been impossible to get a nurse in the short time, and I tried every way I knew to persuade her not to take on such a strenuous job alone—but when she got anything into her head, nothing would stop her.

There was one bright spot in the picture, and that was the consolation of my not having to cope with any grand pianos this time. The club, where I went to practise the next morning, had a good one. Of course the inevitable musical lunatics turned up, including a violinist protégé of Mrs. Louth's who had some talent and was angling for the opportunity to play obbligatos to mother's songs. I could not get rid of him or get any work done—he haunted me constantly.

The hotel was full of seedy-looking English remittance men who hung over the bar and around the entrance all day, talking about things they had shot. The manager, Mr. Gabuzzi, was quite a character and very kind (he turned up years later in Buenos Aires as manager of the Plaza Hotel there) and I think was rather concerned about my being alone in his hotel. He knew everybody from everywhere, and his office was a museum of trophies of the chase, presented to him with autographed photos of all the crowned heads of Europe that had stayed in the hotel for their hunting trips.

He certainly had some queer specimens hanging around, especially the women. I have never seen so many odd-looking females anywhere as in the Norfolk Hotel. They were of all different nationalities and ages, some of them hard-boiled and over made-up, others intensely sporting and semi-masculine. The hotel also appeared to be noted for the number of divorces that came off within its precincts, and mixed up with all the human flotsam and jetsam were the usual type of English, American, Dutch missionaries coming and going to vacations and missions.

Captain Prendergast called for me the next afternoon: he said he had come to show me around and inquired where would I like to go first. I asked him to take me to see some of the animal camps. He was really most upset when in one of them we visited I bought a lovely little gray-and-yellow snake for grandmama, to send back to her by mother as a playmate for Pushkin, whom I had given her when we left for South Africa, and a big gray female monkey for myself. I called her Jiminy Christmas because that was the first thing Prendergast said when he saw her. She was silver gray and had a lovely face, but mad eyes, and turned out to be rather hard to handle when we got her in the car. The next day, I found a better camp and would have bought a civet cat, too, only I knew Gabuzzi would not let me bring it into the hotel; there had been enough stir over the monkey.

Mother had sent me word that she had managed to get Mrs. Louth back to her own house, where she was progressing fairly well under the care of the Belgian doctor and a native nurse. So mother expected to be back well on time for her concert, and I started interviewing the local talent for a pianist. I found a good Italian musician and felt I had done all that was required of me and might just as well have a good time. Mrs. Louth's violinist had introduced me to a pompous young man with an Oxford accent—he was the son of people called Lidstone who owned a chain of butcher shops in London and were apparently very wealthy. This young man took a terrific fancy to me and bought me a lovely cage for Jiminy Christmas, who had been raising hell in my bedroom.

Ronnie Lidstone was perfectly harmless and spent most of his time playing polo and looking for an estate to plant tea on or something. He took me riding and was at least better company than some of the dilapidated bar-flies that had started pursuing me, much to the fury of their lady friends, who seemed to think my youth was unfair competition.

Mother came back in nice time for her concert—she had done a splendid job, got Mrs. Louth back to her home with a nurse, over impossible roads that were under construction. She had been delirious most of the time, but before mother left had fallen into an apathy and was easier to handle. Then the Belgian doctor had been taken ill and had to be transported to the hospital, while a German woman doctor had been found to take care of Mrs. Louth, who wanted to stay in her own house till she was well enough to go back to England.

Mother was very cross with me for having gone riding with the Lidstone boy. Captain Prendergast had told her about it, with, I gathered, a certain amount of spite—partly because he envied the string of polo ponies that Lidstone owned, and partly because the men in the Club said he was a "rank outsider" and sneered at his plebeian background. It was impossible to convince mother that the only attraction was the horses.

For several reasons, mother's first concert was not a brilliant success. The accompanist I had engaged for her, although the best obtainable in Nairobi, was not up to rendering certain songs well enough to satisfy her. She managed to terrify him to such an extent that he played with mechanical precision and absolutely no feeling—in addition to sitting at

132

the piano with a glassy stare which was no asset to the general effect.

The violinist finally wore down our objections and was let loose with a beautiful violin arrangement of "The Last Hour." He was violently nervous and scratched and squeaked his way through it till I couldn't help thinking the performance would probably be his "last hour" and that mother would hit him over the head at any minute with one of the potted palms decorating the stage.

Just before the concert I began to feel ill with a racking headache and fever and could hardly get through my recitations. I got gradually worse during the next few days. Although I managed to make myself get up for the last concert, I was obliged to leave before it was over, and when mother returned from the Governor's reception, she called the doctor who said that I had a bad case of dysentery and fever. A Dutch missionary's officious wife, with a face like rice pudding, got wind of my being ill, and there was no way of keeping her out of my room. Mother thought she was a wonderful person, but Jiminy Christmas, who thought differently, bit her on the arm. Both she and her husband made such a frightful fuss over it that Gabuzzi got mixed into the matter, with the result that I had to send my monkey back to the animal camp where I bought her, until I left Nairobi.

It was arranged that I would meet Mrs. Carelli at Port Natal a few days before our ship for South America made that port. Two days before leaving Nairobi, I was able to get out a little and visited several animal camps with Mrs. Louth's Indian butler. He knew animals like nobody's business, had been a gun bearer all his life, and was a most amazing person. He told me how many of his fellow countrymen had settled in Nairobi and worked at their native crafts as silversmiths, weavers, and so on, and I thoroughly enjoyed seeing the different sections of the native quarters with him instead of with old Captain Prendergast, who always wanted to get back to some club or bar to drink "gin and tonic."

Ronnie Lidstone, who had been moping about like a de-

133

jected robin all the time I was ill, sent me a lovely leopard skin rug the night before we left, which I hid in my trunk so that mother would not see it and make me give it back. She always said that young girls should not accept presents from men unless they meant to marry them—so with this teaching in mind, I went to meet Ronnie in the hotel gardens and was extremely embarrassed to receive my first proposal of marriage. Before I had time to say a word about the present, he blurted it out in the most unexpected manner—something like this: "Oh, hullo, how are you—I say, will you marry me?"

I managed to conserve enough presence of mind to confess that I was a little too young, being fourteen instead of seventeen as I had originally told him. I said I would write him and perhaps we could meet again on my return from South America, and I did write to him for a while, for he was a nice boy although a trifle on the unromantic side. Before we said good-by that evening, I offered to return the leopard skin in the approved manner, but he felt so hurt, begging me to keep it, that I could not insist.

Buenos Aires was plastered with announcements of the début of the great company for the Colón, and the *abonnements* were completely sold out already. The opening was a sensational triumph for Camillo Bonetti: the opera chosen was *Le Roi de Lahore,* a work not often given. The décors were superb, with Natalino of Milan, a great stage craftsman, in charge, and the Maestro Tullio Serafin conducting.

The ballet took place in a scene representing an oriental palace with an enormous blue fountain in the center of the stage. Jakobleff was painted silver from head to foot, with all his veins traced in blue paint, and he danced with a big silver ball around the tall fountain. It was a very startling effect and established his company firmly with the Argentine public.

This was the first time I had danced in a performance for the President, and none of us knew that the custom in Argen-

134

tina is to leave all the lights on in the house, so that the society occupying the stalls and boxes can see one another and bow and whisper and the ladies can discuss their toilettes and jewels. It is very disconcerting until one becomes used to it.

I danced a solo in the opera which was on rather quiet violin music, with a rain of rose petals floating down and around me. The effect must have been beautiful for as I danced I could distinctly hear the murmur of that great audience above the music, and with the lights on in the house, it did not seem like the familiar separation from the auditorium which is perceptible when there is normal lighting—for the spotlight had no effect. I received marvelous applause and began to have newspaper interviews and more success than I had ever dreamed of, during the next few days.

My mother wrote from Spain that she had conveyed Mrs. Louth to her relatives, where for some months she was very ill. Grandmother had been delighted with the snake; father wrote me a good letter, and so for the moment everything was *couleur de rose*. The only fly in the ointment was the behavior of Jiminy Christmas: she had been very good while I was ill, but I had considerable trouble with her on the boat which was a Japanese one. That boat bothered me, too, for I found out that all Jap ships have pens filled with dogs which they use for food, even in the Navy. Dogs are considered a delicacy, although they claimed they did not serve them to the passengers except by special request. They also carried women down in the hold somewhere—I don't mean, of course, that they kept them to eat, but for the diversion of the crew so they would not require shore leave. They were little Jap girls hired for the trip and only allowed on deck for air, at night— with an older woman who had charge of them. This seemed to me less revolting than the dogs, but the tourists on the ship thought it was inhuman and immoral and wrote long letters to the directors of the steamship line on the subject.

Jiminy was a great problem in Buenos Aires, and I had a hard time getting into a hotel with her. The Plaza, where the Bonettis and the Carellis stayed, was far too expensive for me, but mother had not thought of this and expected me to live in the same place they did. Mrs. Bonetti thought I should stop with Luce de Alba and the Italian dancers who had come over with Vitulli, but the hotel management did not want anything to do with monkeys. Finally I got a room in the old-fashioned Avenida Palace on the Avenida de Mayo, where most of the married singers were living, and there Jiminy raised all sorts of trouble, finally reaching her peak of destruction by turning on the water in my bathroom to amuse herself while I was out.

The tub rapidly overflowed and the water ran under the door to form a pool in the middle of the bedroom floor. It gradually seeped through the floor of the room, and the crimson drops from the dye in the red carpet dripped from the ceiling into a bed in the room below. The woman who lived there started screaming that there was a murder in the room above. The manager and entire hotel staff rushed to my room and found Jiminy Christmas sitting on the foot of the bed, chattering with terror. She was unchained and so frightened that she ran out on the balcony and all around the hotel.

In Argentina, the older buildings have a connecting balcony outside the rooms on each floor. This in turn opens on an inner hall called a patio, where people can sit. It is generally filled with chairs and plants and has an open or sliding roof.

Jiminy tore through all this, and when I got home from rehearsal the place was in an uproar. The manager, waving a revolver, was trying to shoot her, and she had bitten three bellhops in her flight. There was nothing to do but take her to the Zoo to board. The damage she had done in the hotel—to the ceiling and the carpet and the bellhops—cost me nearly three hundred pesos (seventy-five dollars), a lot of money for me in those days, which my modest dress allowance from father certainly did not cover.

I learned a great deal in Buenos Aires that year of 1920, for I had an opportunity to study stagecraft with the Natalinos, father and son. These two men produced most beautiful scenic effects, and stayed on at the Colón after Bonetti left. Their settings for *Walküre,* Strauss's *Salomé,* and the old war horse *Aïda* made history in South America. I have rarely seen productions put on with such care and attention to details, or such perfect harmony backstage, with the tremendous crew that was necessary to work the revolving stage. The place was so immense that it took a part of a second for the music from the orchestra to reach the backstage entrance, and there were four to six maestros who stood in the wings and watched the director's wand in mirrors which reflected the podium, so that they could give the exact cues to singers and members of the ballet when they couldn't see the director and might make a late entrance if they depended on the music.

The Colón was like a world in itself, and has been the scene of many strange incidents that can happen only to artists— from the hopeless fight of the unfortunate Nijinsky against the creeping madness that tracked him down in the midst of his triumphs, to the tragic-comic incident that occurred in the first Bonetti season.

In the cast of artists was the brilliant and beautiful soprano, Claudia Muzio, who died a few years ago while still very young. Her mother was always with her, a most remarkable old Italian lady, as fat and peasant-looking as her daughter was distinguished and elegant. Of course the old lady worshiped Claudia and never left the dressing-room. The Colón has, among other things, most luxurious star dressing-rooms, with bathrooms, reception rooms, walls hung with brocade, and beautiful rugs on the floors. The Signora insisted on cooking spaghetti over a small stove in their dressing-room at all hours, and even during the functions a potent smell of frying oil and garlic permeated the passage and stairways. It was the despair of the firemen who haunted the corridors of the immense building looking for signs of fire and a chance to jump on any one sneaking in with alcohol, which was strictly forbidden.

The odor of spaghetti and meat balls that met the nostrils

of pressmen and distinguished visitors as they approached the stars' dressing-rooms was really something, but nobody could get the Signora to forego this habit—any more than they could manage to get her to stop drenching the stage with holy water every time her daughter sang. Before the evening performance, there were as a rule only a few firemen and a watchman left in the theater—all the stagehands and company being out eating. The stage was left set for the first act, lighted only by a small pilot light placed near the orchestra pit. One evening they were giving *La Forza del Destino,* an opera which has the reputation of being a *jettatore* or jinx to all Italian singers, and old Mother Muzio went down from her daughter's dressing-room all by herself to give the stage a good dose of holy water in order to cut the bad luck.

She wandered about muttering prayers to herself all over the vast expanse of the darkened stage, and straight off it into the deep drop of the orchestra pit—landing on the violin section of the instruments. Now the Colón orchestra had about one hundred and twenty musicians, and I don't recall how many bass fiddles and violins, but mama Muzio flattened out most of them. Nobody heard her cries for help until the stage manager arrived and got her out. She was not badly hurt, only shaken and frightened, but the cries and lamentations of Claudia Muzio about her mother's accident were nothing compared to the fuss the musicians made when they arrived and discovered what had happened to their instruments. *La Forza del Destino* had lived up to its reputation.

Still another diverting incident of the famous Colón stage was the occasion when the Comisión Artistico—composed of strait-laced society matrons and all the most important government officials who support the Colón—were gathered in the stalls for an audition of singers recommended for entrance to the Government schools, with the corresponding engagement for the opera season. Achilles Leietti, the orchestra leader appointed to hear the audition, was seated with Maestro Gandolfi, a well-beloved singing master of the Colón Conservatory of Music and a quaint old bird who had a most disconcerting habit of speaking his own mind in no uncertain terms. A very nervous young tenor had just finished singing an aria—rather badly—and was standing in agony on the stage

awaiting the verdict. Leietti was whispering to some personage seated behind him, and in the immense echoing auditorium, Maestro Gandolfi yelled out: *"Si éste es un tenor, mi culo es un Capitano de Bomberos,"* which translated literally means, "If this is a tenor, my posterior is a Captain in the Fire Brigade." This speech was like a bombshell bursting among the distinguished audience, whose facial expressions were something to be remembered with joy. I never knew what happened to the unfortunate tenor.

In the first days of October, I sailed for England, cabling mother to meet me at Southampton. The boat took eighteen days for the trip across and had the usual rather dull crowd of English small-time officials and their families, going home for Christmas, and rich Argentines in a state of advanced boredom. I had left Jiminy Christmas at the Zoo with my friend Mr. Onelli: she was too wild to travel, and besides, the gardens were so lovely it seemed a shame to subject her to the possibility of an English quarantine. But I could not resist a little lion monkey that I saw in Pernambuco. This species of tiny monkey is beautiful and quite rare but very delicate as a rule and hard to keep in a cold climate. However, I took a chance and bought little Dempsey just before we sailed out of

Pernambuco Harbor, relying on an idea of mine to put him inside a fox fur so as to get him off the boat and into England without having to give him up to the quarantine. I was particularly careful that nobody, except the stewardess whom I had bribed heavily, would know I had him—on account of the hundred-pound fine to any captain or purser not declaring a passenger disembarking with an animal at an English port.

I had managed to keep him out of sight very well until one fatal day when I took him up to the top deck, where there were seldom any people. However, this time there was one lady asleep in a deck chair with a red air cushion behind her head, and an old deck hand, whom I always called the Ancient Mariner, sitting in the shade of a lifeboat gazing out to sea with bleary eyes. They were both unaware of my presence, so I settled down in my chair to read while Dempsey, who was never chained because he was just as tiny as a marmoset, played around on my shoulder.

After a while the lady's air cushion slipped out of her chair and rolled along the deck, and Dempsey was on it before I could stop him. He bit it, and the air rushing out with a hissing noise scared him to death. He made one bound for the top of the radio cabin and from there up an iron ladder leading to one of the big funnels of the ship. I started after him up the ladder, but as soon as I got near him he jumped to one of the ratlines they used for the deck winches, and there he clung, screaming desperately, for he could not hang on in the strong wind. I glanced below and could see a conglomeration of excited people looking up at me. Somehow I managed to get hold of the ratline, swing on to it, and grab the poor little monkey. I stuffed him into the front of my sweater and started down with him, but it was impossible to get back to the ladder, so I had to use the ratlines. I have never felt anything so hard as the ropes they were made of: they tore my hands even though I was climbing down with my legs wrapped around them; my stockings were ripped to shreds and my clothes black with soot from the funnel smoke.

The ratline led to the top of a cabin, and by the time I

140

reached it an officer had arrived, plus a tribe of nosy passengers with time on their hands. The whole incident had been clearly visible from the bridge, where the captain was on duty.

The officer who met me as I gained the deck was young, very red-faced, and extremely embarrassed. He stuttered and stammered something about "They couldn't have this sort of thing going on," that "I might have been killed"; besides, they did not like monkeys. The end of it was that I interviewed the purser, paid five pounds for Dempsey's passage, and before dinner that night, made it my business to corral the captain in the bar after his third drink and make my apologies to him. He read me a lecture but turned out to be one of the nicest men I have ever known.

My experience with Dempsey on the boat gave me a real thrill, because I realized that my broken shoulder had done a very good job on those ratlines, considering that I had no muscles in my shoulders and had not done even a "chin up" for six years. Also, my legs must still have had an extraordinarily good grip, for without that, I would have had a bad time getting down against the force of the wind at that high altitude. I went immediately to the ship's gymnasium, worked at handstands and horizontal bars, and tried swimming in the canvas tank rigged up on the deck, but the last was not so easy for me. I could, after a while, manage to swim a little on my right side, but only a few strokes, for my shoulder would "lock," and I could not free it to use any force.

The trip ended in an unforgettable dawn over Southampton Water on one of those misty late autumn mornings, rare in England, but perfectly beautiful. The sky was like an opal, with a pale sun just lighting the mist, and one could see the great ships at anchor all up the water.

Mother had come to meet me, and I was shocked at her appearance. She looked ill and white and started crying at once. Then she told me that five days before I had sailed from Buenos Aires, my grandmother had died.

141

The news stunned me. I had been looking forward to having her with us at Christmastime, and the thought that I would never see her again seemed unbelievable. She loved life so intensely, had been a magnificent artist and a great character. I knew my mother depended on her even more than she cared to admit.

Grandmama had gone up to Aberdeen, Scotland—of all places—to visit her sister Sofía who lived there with a daughter married to a man in the shipbuilding business. Grandmama was always very fond of this sister and had named mother after her. I surmised that grandmama and my mother had been having some disagreement and had not seen much of each other for some time. She had taken a severe chill in the cold climate of Scotland, refused to go to bed, and developed pneumonia. Mother had been telegraphed to come at once. She nursed grandmama night and day, but it was no use. Before she died, she was perfectly lucid and wanted to see my brother, who managed to make the train from London just in time to say good-by to her.

I found mother very nervous and difficult, and she upset me a great deal by saying that my traveling around so much alone had made her ill with worry. Apparently she had had visions of my getting raped or kidnapped. Although we were in mourning, she did more social flying around than I had ever known her to care about before. I could not understand it and was bored stiff, but went everywhere she wanted me to just to please her.

Dear old grandmama had left me her best Spanish shawl, one that had been given to her by the Dowager Queen of Spain many years ago after a command performance in San Sebastian. It is one of my most cherished possessions, as is a very old and beautiful cameo brooch that she always wore when she danced, and a gipsy scarf that I have been told is over one hundred and fifty years old—for it is not embroidered with the Chinese flowers, as are most Spanish *mantones*, but has a Moorish design on it that is very rare.

142

Fortunately all these things are safe in New York, and not stored with my other things in France, or they might now be adorning the plump shoulders of some German soldier's girl friend. I would pity her if they were, because I am sure grandmama would find some way to get back from beyond the grave and haunt her.

IX

I HAD TAKEN it for granted that mother would have no objection to my returning to Buenos Aires for the next season but discovered that she had never sent a formal acceptance of my contract to the Bonettis. It was impossible to get her to discuss the matter at all. I was genuinely unhappy and upset but never mentioned this to mother and kept trying to please her, although she did not seem to like anything I did or said. At last I made her tell me frankly what was the matter.

After some hesitation, she explained that all the social running about she had been doing was because she wanted me to meet people and get married, her reason for this being her serious preoccupation about her health. Now that my grandmother was dead I would be alone in the world were she to die too—except for my father and brother, neither of whom was in a position to look after me. Mother said she would not hear of my traveling by myself, and she could not accompany me. She felt too ill to travel at present, but if her health improved she would want to continue her own career as a singer. Therefore, she explained, she had not signed my contract for the Colón.

I tried to reason with her and make her understand that I loved my work and had no desire to get married to any one, that although I was only fifteen, I was more than able to take care of myself. I wanted to make money and make it fast, for I used to watch fat comfortable dowagers riding about in limousines, wrapped in sables and looking the last word in comfort, and sometimes I walked for miles through the streets of London, thinking out plans for the future that would enable me to make enough money to give my mother those things and keep her out of the struggle and overwork she had known all her life. But the idea of marrying somebody who had money was another story, and one that had absolutely no appeal for me. The situation began to worry me terribly, especially the question of the Colón. More than anything in the world I hoped to play that contract, but there was no way to do it without mother's consent, since I was under age. When I tried to argue her into it, she would always get upset and angry and say I was making her ill and she "wished to God I was married and off her hands."

These scenes hurt. I have never been able to stand arguments and quarrels, for, like my father, I am inclined to be easy-going. At the time I did not realize that all mother's condition was pure nerves and that it would pass. I longed for my father to talk to about it, but I knew he was worried enough without letters about my own troubles, so at last I decided to do something definite to end the impossible situation.

When I had arrived in England in October, I had met a grenadier guardsman, Captain Leslie Strudwick, at the house of some mutual friends. As a matter of fact, he had shown a very definite interest in mother to start with, but he liked horses, which was a bond of sympathy with me. He hunted, knew the right sort of people, and we became friends. He had taken me riding a few times in Hyde Park and had wanted me to visit some relatives of his, to hunt with the Woodland Pytchley (a marvelous pack in the midlands) with two horses a day and timber-jumping. He had been most disappointed when we went away for Christmas, and after we returned I accidentally ran into him one day on Bond Street. The mild "affair" started all over again.

I had several boy friends in the offing, including a midshipman who had given me a turquoise ring in the form of a forget-me-not, but mother disliked all of them and made a scene when anybody called me up—except Captain Strudwick, whom she described as *un hombre serio* (a serious man). He was only twenty-six, but to my fifteen years this description made him appear almost senile. I knew therefore that

145

mother approved of him, so when he asked me to marry him, I accepted.

I don't know why he ever did ask me, for I don't believe he was really in love with me when we were married, although I amused him and was more or less of a novelty and completely different from the English girls he knew. He did not realize till later that the theater and dancing could mean anything more to me than a hard and tiring way of earning a livelihood. I am sure he honestly felt that once I became accustomed to his way of life I would be happy and enchanted with the social position he could give me. I had told him very often that I was not happy at home, and I think he felt rather sorry for me.

For my part, I had never given much thought to love, but I liked him and thought it would be the most practical thing to do, since there seemed to be no other way out for me. I realized that I was doing this only for selfish motives and because I was convinced mother was really ill and I felt that I would have to come to marriage sooner or later. However, I did not dare let myself think about giving up my dancing career, after all my success in South America, and could not bring myself to write to the Bonettis telling them I was leaving the stage to be married.

What upset me more than anything else was my father's reaction to the news. He was furious with mother and wrote her that he could not come over to England for the moment, but that I was far too young to be married and must wait several years before taking such a step. Mother disagreed and insisted it was the best thing I could do. My brother wrote that he, too, felt I was too young; however, he had not been asked what he thought about it and as long as mother and I were satisfied, that was all that mattered.

One January morning I walked out of the hotel and quietly got married at a registry office. Leslie had given my age as eighteen to avoid having to get my parents' consent when he applied for the license. A few days after the civil ceremony, mother arranged a church wedding at the Brompton Oratory, the Catholic church in the Brompton Road—with a wedding breakfast at Prince's Hotel, given by Leslie's brother officers. Mother sat beside my father-in-law, Colonel James Strudwick, whom I had never met before and who seemed very unenthusiastic about the whole thing. He and my mother did not get on at all well together. I thought he was a rather nice old man, though inclined to be tactless.

At first he had behaved as though he were doing us a favor and had told mother some long and complicated story about

guard officers' having to leave their regiment if they married chorus girls, which drove her to the verge of frenzy, for I was not a chorus girl. It was all most unpleasant. When we arrived at the church, mother suddenly felt she had no right to give her consent to the marriage without father's: this unfortunately had occurred to her a bit late in the day, and at the last moment, when everything was settled, she did not want to sign the register, got all the names and dates mixed up, forgot her English, and cried till she was on the edge of collapse. I did not know whom to be sorry for more—mother or myself—for both wedding ceremonies had been nightmares,

147

in which I was filled with an insane desire to rush out into the street, take the first taxicab that passed, and tell the driver to go anywhere he liked and never come back.

I had been married in a black dress with a white bouquet, which is considered very unlucky in Spain, but at the time I never gave it a thought. The first days of my married life were spent at the Carlton Hotel in London, a place full of memories of the Diaghilev company, for most of the great figures made the grill room their rendezvous, and Diaghilev, Nijinsky, and Stravinsky used to have supper there after the ballet.

I was soon plunged up to my eyebrows in a very different milieu, that of English society, in which I felt like the proverbial fish out of water. But hunting and the English country were another story, for I had the love of horses and hunting in my blood from my father's side of the house and knew no joy greater than the English meadows on a hunting morning.

My husband took me for a charming visit to the country estate of Sir Charles and Lady Bunbury—delightful people who, with their family, were exactly like personages from the *Pickwick Papers.* Their house reminded me of my father's home in Ireland—four-poster beds, fireplaces that always smoked, and a monks' refectory (the house had been a priory) with an ancient mechanical chair that galloped when you wound it up, originally used by monks who had overeaten.

The first hunt meet I ever attended took place on the drive of the Bunburys' house, and everybody drank cherry brandy before starting. I rode well, managed to attract quite a lot of attention, and was awarded the fox's brush for being in at the kill. This is a somewhat barbarous custom, for the hunt servants drag the fox away from the hounds who have run it down, cut off the tail, the paws, and the head, and smear the blood on the face of the person who has arrived first at the scene of action. This is called "being blooded," and the honor is only for some one hunting for the first time.

I had been well coached by my husband in the rules of the hunting field and was told I had comported myself very well and had not forgotten the important rule of letting a man pass me at a jump; this had involved a lot of self-control on my part, for I rode considerably better than most of them. My handling of a horse began to cause such comment that my husband was in a cold sweat for fear somebody might find out that I had been a professional rider in a circus.

I soon found out that he placed his career above everything else. He had a splendid record from the World War and intended entering the diplomatic or intelligence service, since his left arm had been badly shattered when he was wounded in France. He had had several unsuccessful operations on it which eventually led to his being invalided out of the army. He had many fine qualities, but when I married him, he seemed far older than his twenty-six years, and his nerves had suffered, like those of many other men who had been in war. He was a stickler for punctuality and decorum, and an excellent officer, but he wanted everything done with military precision, and I don't think he could possibly have found anybody less adaptable than I was to his way of life. Although I did my best, I could not possibly remember all the things I was supposed not to do or say in order to keep from putting my foot in it and prejudicing his career. I just could not get into the swing of society, which has always bored me to tears. As long as the hunting went on, it was fine, but this came to rather an abrupt end for him—and in a way I was to blame for it. We had gone down to the New Forest by ourselves for a fortnight's hunting.

One day we went out in what is called "soft going," and at the top of a steep bank the hounds gave out the "View Halloo!" and the whole field charged madly after them. I was riding a smart little mare, and she went down the bank like the wind. My husband's horse, an officer's charger, far too heavy and unsuitable for hunting, started causing trouble for him at the top of the bank and threw him badly, right on his wounded arm, making a terrible mess of it. I knew it was largely my fault for going off at the pace I did, not realizing that a man will not let a woman ride better than himself. As a

149

result of the fall, his wrist was broken and ligaments were torn in the arm. He was in great pain, and the doctors who set his wrist wanted him to stay quietly where he was for a few days.

We were staying at an old-fashioned inn, where most of the better-class people stayed for the hunting season. One morning I saw an old gentleman dressed in what looked like brown-paper sacks being hoisted up on a pony in the middle of the drive. An old lady fluttered around him, and I heard her say, "Now, dear, do be careful." It was the great Rudyard Kipling and his wife. He was very taciturn and glared at anybody who looked at him, but his wife was very sweet, and as I timidly bowed to her, she asked me something about the hunt. I managed to stammer out that my father and grandfather had known her husband in India, and that I knew most of his books by heart.

At last I managed to meet him one evening. He loved to talk about Ireland and all things Irish. He remembered my grandfather, whom he had known in Simla many years before. It was wonderful listening to the immortal Kipling: he had a great sense of humor but was also a mystic and deeply interested in the occult. I think he must have been staying in the New Forest for his health, for he never put in a whole day hunting, and sometimes I met him riding back alone from the meet with his head on his chest, smoking a short black pipe and almost leaning on the horse's neck.

My husband was very reasonable about his accident and let me do all the hunting he could possibly afford, but the horses that were for hire from the local livery stable were poor beasts with hard mouths and no stamina. I found out from some people in the hotel how it was quite easy to get two mounts a day and four hunt days a week: all that was necessary was to be a good rider who could show a horse's paces off to advantage at a meet and possibly sell him on a commission. This was especially easy for a girl.

It did not take long to get at a man who sold horses, a terrible, loud-mouthed person called Captain Fred, known among the horsy crowd as "Major Chutney." The second day

I rode for him, somebody told my husband, who, of course, had not known what I was doing. He was so furious about it that he got out of bed and dragged me back to London at once. That was the beginning of a series of what he called "escapades" which reminded me of Rome and the *pattinagio*. I felt as though I had got back to school and would never get out.

We moved to a beautiful apartment in Buckingham Gate, just in front of the guards' barracks, which Leslie had rented furnished from Lady Mary Burton, a relative of his late mother's. They were Burton's Beer heiresses, and from her photograph, Leslie's mama must have looked something like an amiable Pekingese in a diamond tiara. My husband took after his old man and was rather good-looking.

I used to cross the road from the apartment to the guards' riding-school and talk to the old sergeant major about dogs and horses. He was a nice old soul and taught me a lot about horses and their care. In the course of these visits, I told him about the circus and showed him some tricks I could do on a horse. This got back to my husband and was the cause of one hell of a row, in which he told me I was ruining his career. He got mother into the argument and she took his part, which did not help matters, for all she would do was to keep saying, "You made your bed and must lie in it," or words to that effect. It was ridiculous, because I had only got married in the first place to please her.

My father-in-law was much more sensible and firmly refused to take either of our parts in any domestic squabbles. He was nearly blind and lived alone with a butler and valet in Queen's Gate. I used to dine with him very often and tell him all about the circus and theater, which fascinated him, although he pretended to be scandalized.

As the weeks went by, I saw less and less of my husband. He was a club man and liked the society of other men. Unfortunately we had nothing at all in common besides hunting, and it was very dull for me. I missed my work and did not know what to do with myself. Nina was in London off and on, but he would not let me see her because she had said something that shocked him; besides, he detested all artists and thought they were mad. I thought his friends, the females especially, were a disaster. They played bridge all day, ran about with other people's husbands all night, and loathed everybody who was not in their set.

So what with one thing and another, I began to suspect our marriage had been a mistake but tried to put up with it all to the best of my ability. Then one day my old friend, Sergeant Major Carruthers from the guards' barracks, gave me a female bull puppy. I had lost my little monkey Dempsey from pneumonia and was happy to have another pet. To avoid arguments, I told Leslie I had bought the dog.

She was a big awkward creature and not house-broken, which was an unfortunate combination with the pearl-gray carpets of Lady Mary Burton's apartment. The gallant captain (as I sometimes called my husband) simply could not be patient about her shortcomings and hit her brutally several times. We had a nasty row, and I told him that the best way to get on the wrong side of me was to interfere with my dog. He stormed and sulked and that evening got all dressed up in tails and went out somewhere, not returning till after I had been asleep for hours.

The puppy, who was sleeping on my bed, heard him come in, and remembering the blow he had given her, she flew at him and bit him through the wrist. Of course it had to be the one that had been injured and had just come out of the cast. The next morning he said she had to go, and insisted upon knowing where I had bought her—so I told him frankly that she was a present from Sergeant Carruthers and that I had no intention of giving her back. That really started something, for he raved at me for my lack of respect for his position in accepting a present from a sergeant.

That afternoon I took my puppy and my belongings and went to a hotel near mother. This was one of many bad rows, and in the end I had to go back, for both my mother and my father-in-law pleaded and carried on to such an extent that there was nothing else to do. I kept my puppy, and all might have been well had I not found out that my husband had destroyed a letter from Mr. Bonetti inquiring why I had not answered several letters he had written me about the Colón. Leslie's excuse was that mother had told him I was so unhappy about giving up my dancing (and of course he could not allow me to work) that he had torn up Bonetti's letters because he thought they would only make me feel worse.

He went on to say that he had been appointed to a military mission in Cairo and that he expected me to accompany him and stay with some God-awful friends of his while he went out in Faiyum as aide-de-camp to a general. As an alternative, if I did not want to go to Egypt, he would send me to a good finishing school to learn ''deportment,'' so that when he came back I would be a credit to him and could be presented at Court and prepare to take my place in society.

I get hot under the collar every time I think of it, it was so humiliating, but I suppose in all fairness to him he was right in his way, for I was very shy and felt and looked miserable at all the functions I had been dragged to. I loved art and music and the life I had been brought up in, and had kept silence about missing all these things, for I felt I would have played a dirty trick to marry him if I did not intend to do my part and try to be of some use to him in his career.

I told him I could not consider either of the alternatives he proposed. I suppose he felt that if he was nice enough to me, he would eventually get me to accept one or the other of them, so he arranged for us to go to the Vale of Aylesbury for the last few days of the hunting season (it was already March), and suggested that I could think over my decision there.

We went to a place called Tring, where Lord Rothschild's stag hounds hunted till late in the season. There we stayed with some friends of his at the hotel, for the last meet. My husband intended to follow the hunt from point to point in the friends' car. We were having breakfast in the coffee-room with them, when I happened to look out of the window at the stable yard and saw a drunken groom, who was holding a horse by the bridle, close under its mouth, striking the animal again and again with his clenched fist, full on the muzzle —the most sensitive part of a horse. The animal was rearing and bleeding, and this was too much for me. I was out of the door like a shot before any of them knew what was happening, picked up an empty bucket, and whanged the groom over the head with it. The narrow rim of the bucket cut his head open, and he started yelling blue murder.

Everybody ran out of the hotel and stood gaping at me open-mouthed. My husband was horrified, and the groom brought an action for damages for "assault and battery," which of course had to be paid. For some strange reason, I had to go to court and be bound over "to keep the peace," under an antiquated English law about things called "grievous bodily wrongs." It was a bad mess, for my husband's name was dragged into the scandal and the newspapers got hold of it— all just before he was officially appointed for the mission to Egypt. There was considerable gossip about the petty, stupid affair, and some of my husband's friends said—I quote Leslie —"What can you expect from a gipsy?"

This decided me, for with all the unpleasantness I'd had more than enough and honestly felt I would be doing him a favor to leave him at once. In addition to everything else, I knew he was often worried about finances and my total ignorance on the subject of housekeeping, which had let him in for a certain amount of unnecessary expense. I told him very nicely about this, and exactly how I felt about our situation; also that, as a married woman, I was legally of age and therefore intended leaving at once for Buenos Aires to fulfil my contract with Camillo Bonetti (I had already sent them a telegram and received my fare to Argentina) but that I would like to remain friends with him—and that was that.

He finally had to agree but was naturally hurt and resentful and gave me the impression that he was indifferent emotionally. This proved later to be far from the truth.

Fortunately, mother was in Spain, winding up some legal

matters of grandmama's, and I did not write anything to her about what I had done till I sailed from Le Havre with some other artists bound for the 1921 Colón tournée.

Before leaving London, I had seen, for the last time, dear Mother Maria Agnese. I had never told her how unhappily my marriage had turned out, but I think she knew. When I went to see her at the Convent, the day I said good-by to her, she gave me a lot of sound advice but naturally said all she could as a nun to persuade me not to go to South America or break up my marital life. Most of her advice was impossible for me to follow and still work out my own destiny; besides, girls of that age are selfish creatures and not easily persuaded to make sacrifices. However, what she told me lingered in my ears for a long time: in fact, I never did really forget, and it made me feel guilty about Leslie.

The Colón season opened with a really fantastic bill—far more important and costly than the previous year. The Argentines had made so much money on the World War, they did not care what anything cost them. The début was early in May with a sumptuous production of Verdi's *Aïda*—heavy and boring, but delighting the public. Nemanoff as choreographic director had his troubles with all the female dancers, especially in the ballet of *Aïda*, which is an important one and had been hotly contested.

An Italian star who had one of the principal parts in it created a heated argument with the Comisión Artistico by insisting on dancing on her toes in the classic Italian fashion, despite the logical argument that in oriental countries and the epoch of *Aïda*, ballet shoes were completely unknown and therefore out of character. Her début in the ballet was outstanding in a way which had nothing to do with her talent as a dancer but with one of her well-developed breasts bouncing out of her corsage in the middle of a circle of pirouettes. The "élite" public of Buenos Aires are not renowned for their good manners, and the row they kicked up when this happened sounded more like a Saturday night

155

audience at a prize-fight. Fortunately, she was dancing alone (Nemanoff had seen to that) and had to weather the storm as best she could by herself.

I had one success after another from the very first night and was treading on air. All the teamwork I had done the previous year at the Colón and during a short engagement with Nemanoff at the Empire was a perfect base for us to work on. He was just a little taller than I, and though not handsome made a magnificent appearance on the stage. He was powerfully built and as fair as I was dark—always an interesting contrast for dancers. I was also having a personal success, with all the admirers I could possibly want and a lot I did not want. When I looked in retrospect at the last six months of my life, I could not believe that I had ever been so weak and stupid as to have got myself involved in a marital tangle. Not only had I upset another person's life, but I had wasted time and lost ground on my own training. Nemanoff, one of the best friends and teachers I have ever had, told me seriously he was afraid I would not do so well on account of this. I came through all right, but at the cost of my working so hard that I became terribly thin and could not sleep.

Because I could find no hotel both good and inexpensive, I found a tiny house on a quiet street close to a shady park where I could have all the animals I wanted without interference and a large studio where I could install a piano and practise. Number 1420 Juncal was the address of this house which was very lucky for me and became quite famous in Buenos Aires.

I did not dare to write mother that I was actually living all alone in my own house and did not think it was diplomatic to tell father either, but of course I wrote the entire story about Leslie to him. He replied saying that the subject of my marriage was very painful and that he would prefer not to hear or write any more about it.

I had a wonderful time in that little house and often think of it. I can remember many details of the interior, and sometimes at night, I still dream of the place. I had never been able to run the apartment in Buckingham Gate successfully, or handle the drunken red-faced cook recommended by one of Leslie's aunts, whom I always suspected of unloading the woman on us from some sinister motive, or Leslie's browbeaten "batman" who played the races and had innumerable schemes for procuring extra cash from butchers, wine merchants, and so on, at our expense.

So it was with certain misgivings that I engaged an old Spanish cook called "Remedios" (Remedies). She in turn brought a most extraordinary man called José for my inspection. Remedios explained that two women alone in a house in Buenos Aires, even in a residential section, were in danger of being robbed; besides, it was impossible for a *señorita distinguida* not to have a manservant to polish the front doorknob, wash the steps, etc. Anyway, they were both very inexpensive and the house was rather large, with a big "patio" to be kept clean, so I took both of them.

I have never had more faithful servants, especially José, whose devotion to me became positively oppressive. He was really a character who had been a picador in the Seville bull-ring and had been badly gored in a fight. For that reason he had been dropped from his *cuadrilla* and had emigrated to South America. He was from Andalusia, talked a blue streak, and had wild black eyes and sideburns. Every morning I was awakened by his sticking his head out of the window of his room—which opened on to the patio—to call Remedios on the other side. *"Olé, purgantes,"* José would shout—meaning literally, "Hullo, purge!" Remedios would reply at the top of her voice, *"Poco vergüenza, no sabes que la señorita duerme, la pobre, que tiene los pies cansadas de ganarse la' vida."*—"Shameless one, the señorita sleeps, poor girl—she has to wear out her feet to earn her living."

This picturesque couple looked after me to such an extent that it became embarrassing. When I would come in wearily from rehearsal, Remedios would tell José. Then if any one telephoned or came to see me, he would say, *"Dice la señorita que no esta."*—"The señorita says she is not in." This caused

157

quite an amount of ill-feeling with people who had no sense of humor.

Having taken a house with a patio, I proceeded to stock up on all kinds of pets. Before I left London, I had given my bull puppy, Belle du Jour, to a friend, Captain Shepherd, as a mascot for the barracks in Aldershot, and she was very happy there, so of course I had to buy another dog. I found an Irish bartender who bred bulldogs and was also a veterinary and from him bought a big raking English bulldog called Jonnie. He was very sweet with people but turned out to be a holy terror with other dogs.

One day I was down near the docks sending a parcel to Nina when I saw an Italian truck-driver with a most marvelous young lady chimpanzee sitting beside him on the truck. Her name was Jeannette, and he said he got her off a ship from Africa, having won her in a crap game or something of the sort. I saw he had no idea of what she was worth and evidently thought she was just a big monkey, so I managed to buy her for relatively little.

Jeannette and Jonnie fought like fiends at first, but she generally got the better of him. She was three years old, had never been trained, and had some unfortunate habits: one was a passion for sitting on the balcony railings of my room in the front of the house and calling to all the truck-drivers that passed. Although she was good with me, she hated all other women, and Remedios could not come into my room when she was there. I practically had to give my bedroom over to her, for when she could not look out of the window she was miserable and would cry just like a child. She had never been shut up in a cage, and when I tried it by decoying her into one, she worked herself up to such a pitch of fury that I never attempted it again.

It was impossible to whip her whenever she did anything wrong, she was so powerful. I tried one day with a rolled-up newspaper, and she tore it out of my hands and hit me over the head with it. Whenever I scolded her, she used to sit and make faces at me; then she would come and hang around

158

my neck and croon to me. It was impossible to be angry with her. Nevertheless, life became very complicated, and every one was talking about the "monkey" in my house. I did not want to attract too much attention to my pets for fear the landlord might take exception to them.

Jonnie was an enormous dog, really too big for his breed. Twice I landed in the police court because he had got loose and killed pet dogs. The second one he eliminated belonged to the wife of a judge who insisted that he be destroyed. After a long struggle with the court, Gabuzzi of the Plaza came to my aid and invited Jonnie to his hotel in the country. There Jonnie amused himself by killing sheep, so he was hastily removed to a tennis club in Palermo. A few days later he killed a tramp who had tried to break into the clubhouse, probably to make off with the silver trophies. Of course, the dog was protecting the club's property, but the Argentine law says that an animal who has killed a human being must be killed in turn.

At the precinct I begged for his life and offered them anything they wanted to give him back to me, promising I would send him away to a friend's ranch, miles from Buenos Aires, but while I was pleading with them they shot him in the courtyard of the station-house.

I heard the shots, and when I realized what they had done, I fairly lost my temper. My dog had done his duty: if he had not killed that tramp, the watchman would have been murdered, for he was an old man. I will never know why they did not arrest me in that precinct. I was beside myself with rage, for I loved that dog, and must have made a scene that was unequaled in the annals of the Argentine police force. For years afterward, officers of the mounted police regiment told me they had heard about it. Argentine women are like subdued sheep and never say anything to men. I had thrown the inkwells and all the papers they had on their desks into their faces and told them what their ancestors were for generations back, before I finally went out. They had just sat and stared at me—in horror, I suppose. They never did anything about it, which was really very nice of them, but perhaps they were sorry for me. I think they were ashamed of killing the dog.

Jeannette had been getting more and more unruly as time went on. Mr. Onelli of the Zoo (who still had Jiminy Christmas, the monkey from Nairobi), had looked over the chimpanzee and advised me to send her out to the Zoo to be bred. I did not know her exact age and was undecided what to do with her, when she decided it for me.

A man called one afternoon to see me about insurance. I told Remedios to show him into the little library on the first floor, which had a door communicating with my bedroom. I did not think about the chimpanzee at the moment; she was behind me, and I did not notice her as I turned to receive my visitor. He was more or less a friend of mine and very well connected in Buenos Aires. Also, he was impeccably dressed, as are most young Argentinos. Jeannette ran up to him and proceeded to try to kiss him, as she was in the habit of doing with Mr. Onelli. This man was different—he got such a shock that he struck her with his fist and must have hurt her, for she turned on him and tore the clothes off his back.

The man had a weak heart, which of course I did not know, and fell on the ground in a sort of syncope. José was out, unfortunately, and poor old Remedios was of no earthly use. I yelled to her to call a doctor and then the Zoo for them to send a truck and men at once. Jeannette did not bite the man once while he was unconscious, but she did keep tearing at his clothes, and I could do nothing with her. I tried to get hold of her arms, but she threw me off like a feather and kept dancing around her prostrate victim, chattering and tearing at his few remaining garments. I tried to drag him into the passage in the hope of shutting Jeannette into the library, but it was no good, for she held on to him and screamed like a fury and looked so savage that I was afraid she would injure him. She bit me through the hand so severely that I was unable to work for a week. Finally the men arrived from the Zoo, but they had a difficult time with

160

her: whatever she thought I had done to her I don't know, but she came at me like a devil. Finally I left the room, and she quieted down for one of the keepers and was quite sweet and docile with him.

They managed to get her into the truck, which of course she loved, and took her to the Zoo. "Purgantes," the cook, who had been running up and down the stairs like one possessed, calling on the saints to come and protect us, finally produced a doctor for the young man. He had had a shock to his heart but beyond a few bad scratches was not seriously hurt. However, he lay on the couch like a wilted lettuce and insisted I send for his brother to come at once and bring him some clothes: he made a frightful fuss about himself, although the doctor told him he was all right.

Naturally, the exaggerated accounts of what had occurred at my house caused a lot of gossip. People used to stare up at the windows as they passed by, to see if they could catch sight of any more strange animals looking out. So among all my pets I began to get the reputation of being a rather eccentric person in the eyes of my Argentine friends, who, except Mr. Onelli, had a hard time trying to understand anybody's having an unusual love of animals.

After the episode of the chimpanzee, another animal came into my life in an unexpected way, and this is a very treasured memory for me. In Buenos Aires that year there was one of the political upsets which occur inevitably from time to time in most South American countries. The one I refer to was known for years afterward as the "Semana Tragica" (tragic week) and was the result of some internal upheaval credited principally to communistic activities. People shot at each other in the streets, and all traffic was paralyzed. We had the greatest difficulty getting to the Colón performances on foot across the city. Dead horses of the mounted police troop rotted in the sun under the usual swarms of flies, and the bodies of the dead combatants were carried away only after the population had had time to get a good look at them and learn a lesson. Some of the more bloodthirsty malcontents sat behind the railings of their balconies and took pot shots at the passers-by, regardless of who they were. For a week the theater was empty, and the Saturday matinée had to be postponed.

That afternoon I was driving with a friend of mine, the wonderful dancer Peer Gynt, in an outlying district of the city where things were quieting down, when we saw a group of soldiers and workmen taking turns firing their revolvers at a little white dog who was running up and down trying to get into a doorway to hide. It was too much for either of us to stand. Both my friend and I decided to get the dog if it meant being shot at to do it.

I grabbed her first and had a hard time holding her, for she fought me off. The men shouted that she was mad. (They always think this about frightened animals in Buenos Aires.) But finally Peer and I got the poor little terrified thing into his car and back to my house where we looked her over.

She was a nice female fox terrier, and Peer said to me, "Why, Esmé, look—she has a black cat on her back. She will bring you luck—you must call her Mascotte." One of the black markings on her back was exactly the shape of a cat sitting, with its head just below the shoulders, and the tail running down into hers. For two days she hid under the piano in my studio and would touch neither food nor water, but just lie and stare at me and show her teeth, till I began to despair of ever getting her to come to me.

The third evening, when I got back from the Colón early so I could try and get her to eat, she refused as usual. As I sat watching her, she crawled slowly out from under the piano, so weak she could hardly stand, but she came toward me without my calling her and laid her head on my knees. Her large brown eyes were so human that she almost spoke. Anybody who loves dogs will understand that this was a great moment for me. I knew she would be a wonderful dog, and she certainly repaid me for saving her life by saving mine a year later in Rio. Of all the dogs I have owned, she was the dearest to me, and all my life I shall remember her. I often think of her little grave under the willows in Palermo.

She loved the warm Argentine earth with the odor of *biscachos* —the little, fierce beavers that dogs love to hunt. It is the right place for her to rest after her travels all over the world with me.

Just before I found Mascotte, somebody made me a present of a baby skunk. He had been operated on and had his glands removed, and he really did not smell very nasty except when it rained. I had put him in the dining-room, which was on the ground floor of the house (it was a nice parquet floor and there was inlaid furniture), before I discovered that he was very destructive. He had a little box in which he slept all day, but at night he enjoyed himself enormously by eating holes in the middle of the floor under the dining-table, so that he could get in and hide when anybody came into the room. In short, he made a terrible mess of the dining-room.

I had been having lots of fun with some Spanish naval officers from the gunboat *Reina Regente,* which was paying a good-will visit to Buenos Aires. All the girls in the ballet had been receiving a good deal of attention from these officers, and I had been indulging in an innocent affair with the Duque de Santos Mauro—known to all of us as "Ratty"—who, to-gether with another officer, Espinosa de los Monteros, repre-sented the Spanish Court.

Ratty had asked me to give a little dinner party in my house with the girls from the Colón and four or five officers from the ship. I was happy to do it, so the girls were invited and everything arranged—but I had no idea he intended to do things on such a grand scale. Early in the morning, the flowers started arriving—great boxes of regal red roses, till poor José, who was to wait on the table, nearly had a nervous breakdown.

We were rehearsing all day, and I got back from the theater just in time to dress and receive my guests. Stupidly, I did not go into the dining-room, merely glanced through the door at the dining table loaded with flowers and silverware. When the guests had all arrived, with the girls in a dither at such grandeur (for the men were all in full-dress uniform

—a charming compliment to my house), we filed into the dining-room after copious cocktails in the library.

Into the hole gnawed in the floor by Peter the skunk stepped no less a person than His Excellency the Marqués de Amposta, Spanish Ambassador to Argentina, who had invited himself at the last minute. He nearly broke his ankle, but laughed heartily and took it in good part. Few men would have been so gallant. Poor José was petrified. This was his big moment, for never in his wildest flights of fancy had he dreamed of serving such distinguished countrymen. Anyway, the little mishap was soon forgotten, and the dinner was a great success. The next day Ratty sent me a beautiful diamond pin with a card saying, "Please use this to skin the skunk with."

One night not long after the dinner-party, poor Peter ate his way out of the dining-room and was drowned in a rain barrel in the patio.

So with my animals, my success in my work, and the wonderful feeling of independence through my own efforts, life was very pleasant in Buenos Aires that year—I don't remember a dull moment. I also found time, once the hardest part of the rehearsal work was over, to give some dancing lessons. In fact, I had as many pupils as I could handle—for not only were a good many girls studying to be professional dancers, but the craze for ballet dancing had spread to the college and society girls as well.

I was making and saving money. My only extravagance was the parties I gave in Juncal for my fellow-dancers. I got on well with all of them and we had some riotous times on beer and sandwiches, generally after the show—for we were all too serious to think of letting any amusements interfere with our work. We danced and sang and played the piano. There was nothing wrong or vicious about any of it.

I made many friends in Buenos Aires whose esteem I valued and from whom I received a great deal of kindness and help. The people of Argentina are loyal friends if they like you. If they don't, they just ignore you, which is a very

164

simple and satisfactory way of doing things. I liked the older men best, for they were generally more understanding and past creating scenes of jealousy over nothing, as the younger Latin men are inclined to do upon the slightest provocation.

Many of the girls in the ballet had got themselves tangled up in sentimental complications, but I always steered clear of anything of the sort. Although I never used my husband's name except for business purposes or told any one except my best friends about my marriage, I felt I owed him at least enough respect to keep myself to myself and concentrate on the work I had left him for.

I gained more confidence in myself as the season went on and began to think seriously about trying out an idea I had for a ballet. I made a plan of it and showed it to a good friend of mine, Auguste Maurage, a composer and concert violinist of outstanding merit. He had come to the Colón, first as first violinist with Saint-Saëns and then with the Pavlova company. He liked my idea so much that, after studying it, he said he would write the music and we would produce it together if it was successful. We worked on the ballet *Harlequin Noir* in my studio, and I designed the décor and costumes and planned out the choreography with Nemanoff.

The season of the Colón was crowded with opportunities for me. I danced as first dancer for the command performance for the President and scored a big success in *Swan Lake*. Then I danced for an enormous charity benefit at the Coliseo. That night as I took my applause I could not help feeling I had done rather well, to be standing as first dancer on the boards of a theater where three years before I had danced in the corps de ballet of Anna Pavlova's company.

X

I HAD SEEN enough of life to know that when things are going unusually well, it is best to be prepared for a swift kick in the pants from Lady Luck pretty soon. Sure enough, I got several of them on my return to Buenos Aires after the usual six weeks in Montevideo and Rio with the Colón company.

One day I missed a diamond ring that I treasured because I had just bought it with money laboriously saved in Rio. It was nothing very special, but it was a souvenir of a lot of hard work and my first jewel. All Spanish women have a weakness for jewelry, and I inherited the trait from mother. I was proud of my ring and showed it to a young Turkish girl whom I had given a job of taking care of numerous details connected with my teaching. When the ring disappeared, there was good reason to think that she had something to do with it, for she came and went in the Juncal house very much as she pleased. I was heartbroken about the loss.

One of my most influential friends gave me a letter of introduction to the chief of police, and upon my arrival at headquarters, I was taken at once to the chief's office. It was an odd experience that I shall never forget. The man I was going to see had the reputation of being one of the ablest chiefs of police Argentina had ever had, and a charming man. When I entered his office, he was sitting in his shirt-sleeves with a cup of black coffee before him. Through the patio windows came the most deafening noises of the police band playing the march from *Aïda*, with all the force of their lungs. As any conversation was an impossibility, the chief pressed a button, and the row stopped.

He was a short, dark, fat man, and he stared at me with the shrewdest pair of eyes I had ever seen. He struggled into his tunic and, after reading my letter, asked me what he could do for me. I explained what had happened about my ring—while he sat and looked me over from head to foot. After I had finished my story, to my surprise he merely said, "Señorita, I have heard that you speak Russian. Is this the case?" I could not imagine what this had to do with the theft of my ring; however, I said I did. He immediately pressed some more buttons, doors flew open as if by magic, and officers appeared. He told them to "bring in the prisoners."

The officers reappeared, pushing before them some dilapidated-looking men who were obviously Russian and very dirty. Apparently I was supposed to ask them the questions the chief gave me in Spanish on a piece of paper. I felt most uncomfortable, and there was nothing to be got out of any of them. They were extremely suspicious of me and as far as I could gather were political prisoners connected with the recent communist upset of the Semana Tragica. All they would say to me was that they didn't know anything about anything, and that they were being unmercifully beaten in their cells downstairs.

When they were finally removed, much to my relief, the chief explained to me that he had ordered the band to play, as loudly as they could, the only two pieces of music they knew—the Argentine National Anthem and the march from *Aïda*—to drown out the screams of the men who were being beaten into giving information, which he found very annoying. He went on to say that he had been getting no satisfaction from his Russian interpreters, whom he suspected of getting twenty pesos a day to come to the police station and misinterpret everything on purpose in order to draw out the job. So I had come into the picture at the precise moment to do a bit of interpreting gratis.

I was extremely annoyed and asked what he thought about my ring. With a twinkle in his eye he replied that, personally, he thought I would never see it again; nevertheless, he would have an investigation made and do what he could to

167

help me. I could have cried with disappointment. He did a lot of fiddling about the next two weeks and arrested the Turkish girl on suspicion, then had to let her go. I never did see my ring again. He became a good friend of mine, however, and was very useful to me later on.

When mother finally wrote she ignored most of the questions I had been asking her for months and made the principal theme of her letter my beautiful little cousin Pepita. She had made her first appearance with the Diaghilev company in the *Cuadro e Flamenco* at the Coliseum in London, under the name of María d'Albaïcin. She received bad criticism, and Hayden, in his book on Diaghilev, wrote that she had nothing to offer but her beauty. Mother agreed but said that no one could reasonably expect anybody with such a perfect face and figure to have brains as well.

Mother went on to say that Diaghilev had a contract for me as soloist for his winter season if I cared to accept. This she begged me not to do, on the grounds that my appearance on the London stage would only reopen the gossip there had been when I left my husband. As mother also reported that she had sung a short concert tour in Scandinavia, I was encouraged to think her neurasthenia was beginning to subside. But in her next letter she was beside herself again.

My brother had announced that he had decided to follow the example of a cousin of father's and enter the Trappist Monastery at Lismore, Ireland. I immediately wrote and tried to get mother to understand that my brother would probably not remain in a monastery for any length of time or take the ultimate vows—I knew his character too well. The monks of the Trappist order are hard-working, self-sustaining men who toil on the land to feed the poor, the sort of manual work that was out of the question for my brother. I knew his pride would not let him stay with a band of men who worked, even if they would admit him into the Order, when he could do nothing to help them except perhaps play the organ in their chapel.

At this point, also, Leslie began to send me a series of epistles, all more or less the same. He had switched from a state of apparent indifference to one of deluging me with appeals to "have another try," as he naïvely put it, after I had had my way and got my "dancing whims satisfied." These letters worried me and made me feel selfish, but I had firmly decided that nothing would induce me to return to England and that when I could get away from my work, I would devote a vacation to visiting my father.

The season of the Colón was to finish in Buenos Aires with some "farewell" popular functions, and rumors had been flying about ever since Rio that, in spite of the colossal success, everything was not well and that Bonetti had been losing money. It seemed incredible, for the Colón had been packed for every show—with the exception of the "tragic week." Bonetti undoubtedly had a terrific salary sheet to cover, and I suppose the general intake was not up to his expectations. We continued working unusually late in the season, giving command performances for the Presidents of Argentina, Uruguay, and Brazil. Both Mr. and Mrs. Bonetti were worried about something, I could tell, and I felt terribly sorry for them—they were such a grand couple. Some of the big stars who had earned thousands of dollars sulked and muttered in corners about the Bonettis' being broke.

The climax came when the season in Buenos Aires was nearly over. I was up in the wardrobe room with Madame Bonetti one afternoon, checking ballet costumes that were to be sent back to Italy, when her son came running upstairs looking for her. After talking to him she turned white and asked me to accompany her. We hurried down to Mr. Bonetti's private office. Stagehands and the office personnel were standing about looking scared. I felt a chill creep over me when Madame Bonetti tried to open the office door and found it locked. She could get no answer from within, so young Bonetti, nearly beside himself, broke down the door. Mr. Bonetti was unconscious in his chair, with a loaded revolver

169

clenched in his hand. He had suffered a stroke at the precise moment he was about to pull the trigger.

The Bonettis were ruined, and there was nothing for poor Madame to do but take her sick husband and, together with her son, return to Italy. Mario Carelli remained to close the Colón. I never heard what happened to the Bonettis except that they sold their home to pay up everything they owed, and that Mr. Bonetti was an invalid.

The next thing for me to do was to get at my ballet project. I knew that I could form a company with Richard Nemanoff and make a success with it. We had offers from the Mar del Plata Club, one of the biggest Municipal Casinos and theaters which open for the summer season, and from many other places that were anxious to have a company of ballet proceeding from the Colón. I approached Don Faustino da Rosa, the theatrical tycoon and capitalist, and through him obtained a contract with the Teatro Cervantes. This theater was the property of the Dias de Mendozas, a famous old couple of dramatic artists whose company had been coming to Argentina for years and always played to a full house. They had made a fortune there and, in tribute to the Argentine public, had built a magnificent theater. It was pure Spanish in architecture, with an interior of extraordinary beauty, and had cost a fortune. It was just finished and the most expensive and smartest place in Buenos Aires.

For Don Faustino to offer me such a spot to open in was a compliment that left me gasping, and when I talked it over with Nemanoff and Maître Maurage, they were so enthusiastic that they gave me courage to sign the contract.

The theater was a big house, and when I started to get the company together and put my décors and costumes into execution, I had no idea of what I was getting into or what expenses I would be confronted with. It was my first venture, and both Nemanoff and Maurage were so bohemian they had absolutely no idea of business—any more than I had. I reflected that Don Faustino was far too foxy to get himself

170

involved with a company in such an important house unless he was pretty sure they would not flop on him. Ballet was at the height of its popularity, so I set my teeth and plunged into the struggle for all I was worth.

Richard Nemanoff and Maurage were working on a percentage basis with me. Nemanoff had some costumes, and Maurage did all the orchestrations, but musicians and artists were on salaries, as was the corps de ballet. It was indeed a gamble, and I spent nearly all the money I had, to have the black-and-white décor of the *Harlequin Noir* properly painted by Peralta, the best scenograph in Buenos Aires, as well as a garden set for the *Sylphides* in the second part of the program. I also had a painted closing curtain and the cyclorama for the divertissements, which was very costly. So by the time we opened, I found myself confronted by an impressive list of debts.

The night before our début, the evening papers were full of the news that Anna Pavlova had cabled, announcing that she would give some functions almost immediately in the Coliseo. This scared us nearly out of our wits, for there was no possible chance of our company's surviving in competition with hers. However, the contract had been signed, publicity released on the company of "Ballet Intime Moderne"—as I called it in preference to opening under my name, though I did this later on when success was assured. The show was ready and I was up to my ears in debts, so there was nothing to do but put on the best performances we could before she arrived. Newspapermen, to whom I talked on the afternoon of our opening, were so wonderfully kind and understood so perfectly what it meant to me if Pavlova came to Argentina, that they caught the evening editions of their papers and boosted the company to the skies.

When we opened that night to a full house, the show went over with a bang. Every critic in Buenos Aires gave us good notices, and both Faustino da Rosa and Dias de Mendoza were delighted with the entire production. Fortunately, we had done so well that it was not necessary to change anything

171

for two weeks, but it was not long before Don Faustino tackled me about the question of a second program, and I was obliged to give him the names of the ballets we would present —which he immediately announced in the newspapers.

We had to retrench on sums expended for advance salaries to the company, and had just enough, when this was more or less adjusted, to buy canvas. Nemanoff and I hauled it to the roof of the theater, and there I proceeded to cut and paint the scenery for the ballet *Orange et Vert,* on music by Debussy, and a Viennese potpourri, *Le Beau Danube Bleu.* It was a hectic job, and Peer Gynt and another boy helped as much as they could with the filling in of the designs in color.

Don Faustino began to look very old-fashioned when he discovered I was painting my own decorations on the roof of the most expensive and luxurious theater in all Argentina. Pressmen began to flock there—which was most embarrassing. I could not imagine what they wanted, or why they insisted on climbing up to the hot, stuffy room on the roof to look at the mess we were making. Several newspapermen told me that when they had first heard about the ballet and that the décors and costumes were of my own design, they had been skeptical. They knew me as a dancer and had never really believed that I was capable of doing anything else, but when they saw me actually working on the scenery, they were tickled to death and turned something I was ashamed to have known into tremendous publicity for me.

When the décor was completed, they took photographs and wrote articles about what I had done. I can never be sufficiently grateful for the support and help they gave me, for my name as a designer of stage sets was made in Argentina.

The morning before we put on the second program, Nemanoff and I had arranged for the stagehands to come at 6 A.M., before either Da Rosa or the old Señora Mendoza were up and snooping about the theater, so that we could hang the décor and see what it looked like. I had been obliged to paint it on the canvas, which had been stretched flat on the floor. The two boys and I had walked up and down, painting with

172

brushes fastened to sticks—it had been an exhausting job and we must have walked miles.

When the first décor—which was for the Debussy number —was hung, it looked surprisingly good in color, but there was a very badly painted space in the center of the backdrop. It was impossible to do anything about it before the show, and Nemanoff and I were in despair. Suddenly I recalled having seen a most lovely terra-cotta bowl in the window of an expensive garden-sculpture house downtown, which would be just what we needed to fill up the back of the stage—thus hiding the unsightly spot. With a lighting effect inside the bowl, I felt that the defect would be invisible.

As soon as the store opened, we rushed there and measured the bowl, which was designed for a terrace ornament. It was four and a half feet in diameter—just what we needed, but it cost one hundred forty pesos, and we did not have enough money. There was no way to get the salesman to deliver the bowl to the theater without a full payment, for apparently he had a deep-rooted distrust of artists. Precious time was passing, and Richard Nemanoff, after having counted our combined funds for the third time, told me to wait and with a set jaw dashed out of the shop. Twenty minutes later he returned with enough cash to complete the price of the bowl. As we hurried back to the theater he told me that he got it by hocking his watch.

I painted the bowl blue and had the theater electrician light it with rose- and heliotrope-colored bulbs. The effect against the blues. and greens of the scenery was beautiful. We grouped the girls around the wide lip of the bowl, and as the curtain rose on the soft adagio music of Debussy's "En Bateau," they opened their arms in a plastic pose and the orange veils of their costumes caught the different lights from the lamps. The tableau took a tremendous hand from the audience that afternoon, and Da Rosa was the first to come flying to my dressing-room with congratulations.

This ballet was one of our best successes, together with my first effort, the *Harlequin Noir*, which had also been a considerable triumph for Maurage, the composer. The work involved in this production had been intense for all of us, Nemanoff with the choreography and rehearsals, Maurage with the musicians and their unions.

I feel sick whenever I think of the entire partitura and orchestration of the *Harlequin*, which is in a trunk containing my music in Paris, and which may be lost forever. It was really a marvelous composition and perhaps the best thing Maurage ever wrote. He gave it to me and, as far as I know, never published it. He was a strange, unhappy person and never looked after his own business interests, and though he was a magnificent violinist, he was always thinking of committing suicide and did attempt to do so twice while traveling with my company.

For my part, I had, in addition to my own dancing and painting the décors, the supervision of costumes, their designing and making, and the checking and rechecking of the light rehearsals, beside all the financial worries. However, all the shows were good, and contracts rained in on us.

There was still nothing concrete about the Pavlova company's coming to South America, so we engaged a manager to line up future work we had in prospect. Old Señora María Dias de Mendoza, who had the last word in what was to go on in the theater, offered to hold us over for another three weeks. She was a great character and sat all day long in the foyer of the theater with a priest who continually blessed the house and whose opinion of the morality of the performances she valued highly. She was as happy as could be about our success, even when we played to bigger audiences than she ever had. The only thing she did not like was one of our male dancers called "Bubbles." He was a very lady-like young man who insisted upon resting in his dressing-room most of the day except for intervals when he would come tripping down the stage with his hair in curl-papers and cold cream on his face, dressed in a gaudy silk kimono—to ask the manliest of the stagehands to go out and buy him a chocolate bar.

174

He managed to upset Señora María no end, and when she offered me the three weeks' prolongation, she made one of her conditions the immediate dismissal of Bubbles. He was a good dancer, and we had to hold on to everybody—in case the Pavlova company did arrive and needed corps de ballet. Besides, I was too busy to worry about all these little details which can be so disturbing in a company. I had enough to do trying to get our debts paid off and keep the show going.

Our new manager, Mr. Evar Mendez, settled the matter. He had been controlling the box-office entries and came to me with the disturbing information that, up to the moment, we had been getting a good gypping at every performance on our percentage, so, if the management wanted to hold us over, it would be on a fixed salary with no nonsense about whom we were to fire. He handled the matter so successfully that we got everything we wanted on his terms, and for the first time I could breathe freely about the payment of our debts.

The season at the Cervantes ended to the satisfaction of all parties concerned, and I have a photograph of the table of honor at the Plaza Hotel where a gala dinner was given by the French Comité des Fêtes for the best ballet performance of the year. I was invited for my production of the *Harlequin Noir;* all the Colón stars and directors were there under the auspices of Monsieur Clausse, the Ambassador of France, who was a great art patron.

Evar Mendez had lined up work for us for several months ahead as soon as we finished the three-week hold-over at the Cervantes, where Franz Lehar and his company of operettas were to replace us when we started on our South American tour. We played several towns in the Argentine and finally got the contract for the Prado in Montevideo, Uruguay, that Anna Pavlova was supposed to play. It was an open air theater in the Prado Park and had a terrace of concrete instead of a stage. The reason Pavlova did not appear there was supposed to be that she had found out that the Uruguayan Commission of Fiestas, who were sponsoring her engagement, could not build a wooden floor over the concrete to

175

suit her, and so she had turned down the engagement. I don't know why she never came to Buenos Aires that year, but she didn't, and I am sure this was our salvation.

The show at the Prado was a terrific success, despite the unquestionable difficulties of the concrete floor, which wrecked our feet and ballet shoes. I was not carrying very many stagehands, and only one carpenter and electrician, but Evar Mendez was more than equal to the task of decorating the enormous stage with natural plants for the *Sylphides* ballet. The men worked all night to do it and had to build the podium and stands for the orchestra, as well as everything else except the seats—which the Municipality undertook to do. How they did it I don't know, but it was a rotten job.

Such a tremendous crowd arrived that they filled every available seat and overflowed into the gardens around the theater. For some reason, everybody thought the Pavlova company was appearing, in spite of the publicity that had been done and that I had received personally as head of the company. Additional ticket booths had to be hastily thrown up to cope with the crowds, and the manager said that gauchos rode in from miles around, tethered their horses at the park gate, and offered gold dollars (which they must have inherited from their grandfathers) to get in.

It was a beautiful warm night, but with a light wind that blew the dancers' dresses about a little—resulting in such wild enthusiasm among the masculine portion of the audience that the mounted police were summoned by the management. During the interval, crowds of wild-looking camp men from the Uruguayan ranches swarmed at the backstage entrance and could not understand why they were not enthusiastically received by the girls—whom they imagined to be like the cabaret and small theater troupes (generally Polish and French of the worst type) they were accustomed to see.

The four ticket booths were unable to manage the crowds in the cheaper seats, and far back in the amphitheater, people were standing and crowding to such an extent that in the

176

middle of the second ballet, the "Rondo Capriccioso" of Saint-Saëns, various rows of seats collapsed. They were so far back that we did not realize what was happening. Maurage was conducting sixty-three men in the orchestra, and the music was so loud we could not hear the screams and shouts. The mounted police came in handy, for they rode in among the crowd and prevented a panic, but many people were hurt.

We gave, in all, three of these shows—though only two had been originally contracted for—in conjunction with the opera-house in town. They were such a success that we were booked for a month the following year, and the Government Art Commission promised that they would have a wooden stage specially built for us. I had been obliged to accept most of the dates we played on a percentage basis, which in South America, as a rule, is the wildest gamble anybody could possibly take. The majority of impresarios were past masters in the art of cooking up the box-office receipts to make it appear that there was much less money in the house than actually came in. But somehow or other, we were making good profits just the same, and the shows were so packed that the impresarios could rob us to their entire satisfaction without our suffering in the least. Nevertheless, when we played some of the smaller Argentine towns, I began to sit up and take notice.

Upon the advice of some old timers I had talked to about this situation, I engaged an enormous Italian stagehand called Hermingildo, who looked a lot like Primo Carnera, for the express purpose of sitting on the side of the stage beside the fire-curtain during the performance. This metal curtain, by Argentine law, must be lowered for five minutes during the intermission. I had Hermingildo put a steel chain and padlock around the lock of the curtain as soon as it was lowered by the firemen, and he held interferers at bay with the biggest sledge-hammer we could buy. During the fifteen-minute interval, Evar Mendez would bring me the monies corresponding to my percentage of the ticket sales for the performance, and at the same time, another employee—generally José the ex-

177

toreador—would bring me the check he had made of the seats on my behalf. If we found, after careful scrutiny, that the box-office money did not coincide with José's figures, I would simply send for the manager and inform him that until he made good the deficiency, the fire-curtain would not go up. If the manager tried to bluster and refused to see reason, Hermingildo would brandish the hammer in his face. This generally obtained immediate results.

Sometimes the manager would protest or create a scene and waste time—which was worse in the end, for the public in South America are not easily handled if made to wait too long. They stamp their feet and shout insults at the management and the artists. If this fails, they will invariably tear up the seats and throw them at each other until the police intervene.

This actually happened to us at La Plata near Buenos Aires. All the workers from the great frozen meat plants of Swift and Armour came to the show on a Saturday night, a rough crowd indeed. The theater manager was an impossible little man who made a lot of noise when Hermingildo went into his act with the fire-curtain, and refused to recognize the obvious theft of about six hundred pesos which we had proved to him were wanting in the pay envelop.

He screamed and threatened to send for the police, but while he was shouting, the public was also shouting—only much louder. As the curtain remained down, pandemonium broke loose in the auditorium. Backstage, we could hear heavy missiles being thrown against the fire-curtain. The excited ushers came flying back and forth from the house to the stage to report the progress of the damage that was being done to the stalls and the orchestra. I would not let Maurage take his place on the conductor's stand, so finally the manager had to give in and pay me. We ran up the curtain and continued the show.

The theater was packed, so there was quite a sum of money to take back to town. I was playing this date out of Buenos Aires, for La Plata is only two hours by car, and had bought a ramshackle Peerless automobile for the tournée. I did not know how to drive a car in those days and had no time to learn, so I had engaged an Italian chauffeur who knew as much about cars as I did. After the show, we started back to town with the usual crowd of autograph hunters milling about the stage door and hindering our departure. The infuriated manager was still hurling abuse at me—to which I light-heartedly replied with interest.

Two Russian girls, who could never forgive me for having worked like a dog and got a company together—which they were totally incapable of doing—usually rode back with me, but this night they refused, giving some vague story about having met some friends. I gave it very little thought at the time and invited in their place Peer Gynt and Maurage, who accepted. We started off, and when we were about three miles on our way, the chauffeur suddenly turned around and told me that he had overheard one of the girls telling the other in Spanish, for the benefit of the rest of the company, something about the theater manager's having said that I would never live to spend the money I had made him disgorge that night.

We were discussing this piece of news when suddenly the car came to a dead stop on a very dark part of the road (it was not a lighted highway). Steam poured out of the engine— there was no oil, no water, no gas: the machine had been drained dry. Our only hope was that a passing car would assist us—but not a soul drove by, and to top it off it began to rain. The Italian chauffeur got out and tinkered with the carbureter for no earthly reason, and eventually we decided to settle down as best we could and wait for morning. Luckily, it was a roomy, closed limousine and very comfortable.

Shortly afterward, in the stillness of the night, we heard the throb of a car engine far down the road but could see no lights. I suggested that the chauffeur go and investigate, to see if perhaps the driver would help us, but Peer Gynt said it was better not to, for possibly they were the hold-up men sent by the manager of the theater. Presently we saw flash-lights bobbing about, still a long way off, but apparently heading toward us. It was an eerie feeling, for by this time we were pretty sure there was something wrong.

We kept as still as we could. Peer Gynt was wonderful: he laughed and joked in whispers, but poor Maurage was incoherent, and the chauffeur trembled like a leaf. We had no gun, and I asked him to open the tool kit and find a jack or hammer so we could at least have something to defend ourselves with. The lights came no nearer, and when dawn began to lighten the sky, the hidden cars started their engines, and we could hear them drive away in the opposite direction.

About two hours later—it was broad daylight—a truck from Armour's passed and took Peer Gynt and the chauffeur to the traffic police station, which was about five miles away. They returned with a car and a motor-cycle cop who said that there had been an anonymous telephone call from La Plata the previous night, telling them to be on the look-out for my car, as there were rumors that it was to be held up somewhere on the road between La Plata and Buenos Aires. The police thought that the thieves who had drilled holes in the gas and oil tanks had calculated that we would be much nearer Buenos Aires when we ran out of gas, and they were waiting nearer town for us.

The police had been scouring the road all night and had finally decided that we were not coming, so they had given up their vigil. Evidently the car we heard belonged to the thieves, who had no idea how near we were to them all night. It was really a lucky escape, and I immediately obtained a police permit to carry a revolver—I was not having any more upsets with that helpless idiot of a chauffeur, who practically collapsed from fright when we arrived home. I decided to take José on all similar trips, for I knew he had plenty of courage. It was interesting to see the expression of keen disappointment on the faces of the Russian girls when they beheld me alive and perfectly well the following day. There was no proof against the manager, so we finished our engagements around Buenos Aires and left for the Mar del Plata Club.

I had been getting letters from mother on every boat, asking what on earth I was doing and why I had not returned as soon as the Colón closed: I had not dared write to either of my parents that I had put on my own company without any money or experience. I also received a letter from father, telling me that he would be with my mother for Christmas, and as she complained dramatically that the selfish behavior of both my brother and myself was driving her into her grave, he begged me to get leave from the manager of the company (which made me feel very guilty) and come to London to spend Christmas with them. There was nothing I would refuse my father, but it was an impossibility to leave for Europe before the end of December, when the Mar del Plata engagement terminated. I decided to give the management of the company to Nemanoff and Evar Mendez (who had proved so capable a business manager), and leave about the first week of January for Europe, returning late in April for the opening of the Colón in May, for which I had already received my contract as "Primera Ballerina Absoluta," the star rôle in the ballet.

What I wanted more than anything else in the world was to see my father again and to be with him in the Paris I loved so well—to tell him all about my work and the company, for I hated to deceive him about anything I was doing. He always wrote me wise, kind letters and continued to send me an allowance regularly, although I had written to tell him, after Montevideo, that I was making money and did not require anything from him for the present.

After the show closed in Mar del Plata, the papers announced my forthcoming trip to Europe, and I was given a wonderful send-off at the station despite the early hour my train left. They literally swamped me in bouquets of flowers until I felt like Pavlova, facing a barrage of cameramen and reporters. My schedule had been calculated so that I would arrive in Buenos Aires with exactly enough time

181

to make the S.S. *Arlanza* for Cherbourg. I had always taken Mascotte in my compartment, for we generally traveled on night trains, but this time there was no way I could induce the guard to allow me to have her in the pullman—so I was obliged to put her in the baggage-car.

As soon as the train left, I went to the dining salon, where all the company were having breakfast. While I was drinking my coffee, a woman came rushing in and told me she had seen a white dog leap from a window in the rear of the train and that she believed it was mine. I ran to the baggage-car and sure enough, Mascotte was gone. She had broken her lead and jumped through an open window. The baggage man told me that the train would stop a mile farther on, at a small junction, the last stop of the express. As soon as the train started to slow down, I jumped from the baggage-car doorway and ran as fast as I could back down the tracks.

Officials shouted after me that there were live wires and God knows what other complications, that I would be electrocuted for sure—but I ran on. I had my bag with all the tickets for the company, plus their baggage checks—which was unfortunate for them, but I did not think of this till later. I ran and ran over the ties in the burning sun till I was ready to drop. At last I saw a little white speck running like Billy-Be-Damned in the direction of Mar del Plata. It was Mascotte.

When I caught up with her, I saw that she was covered with sand and luckily must have leaped on to a sand-pile beside the tracks. One of her legs was slightly hurt, but she was wild with joy to see me. I am sure she thought I had left her in the baggage car and gone back to Mar del Plata, so she was on her way to find me. I had to carry her all the way to the outskirts of the town, where I discovered there was no train leaving until nine in the evening, which meant that I would miss the boat for Europe, since it was scheduled to sail at midnight. I could picture Nemanoff and Mendez having an awful time without the company's tickets and baggage checks—it was some mess!

I cabled the resourceful José to get on the job and try to find a combination that would enable me to catch the *Arlanza* in Rio or Santos. On my arrival in Buenos Aires the next morning, he told me that the only boat leaving was a French ship, *L'Ouessant*.

It was a tub. The crew were all Bretons and wonderful seamen, but the captain, who looked like a dyspeptic walrus, was a riot. He sat in his cabin without taking the slightest interest in the ship and drank yellow chartreuse.

I discovered that the ship's principal cargo was French pimps and white slave traffickers traveling with their merchandise for Argentina and Brazil. Several samples were pretty and quite young, but others looked as if they had seen a good deal of the tough side of life. Their "managers," as the pimps called themselves, were very strict with them, not permitting any nonsense on board except with the captain. The whole set-up reminded me more and more of our Turkish trip, for a terrific storm came up off the Brazilian coast. There were no adequate lifeboats on the ship and none that were provisioned, but the captain's.

I began to foresee that with all this, we would be overdue—for the *L'Ouessant* was hardly moving against the heavy sea, and it was inevitable that I miss the *Arlanza* at Santos. The morning we were supposed to get in, we were still many miles from port. I lay on the bunk of my deck cabin, cursing my luck while Mascotte, the reason for it all, sat there and admired me.

In the end I had to wait three days in Rio, lose my passage on the *Arlanza,* and change from *L'Ouessant* to another third-rate boat. I managed to get one of the few decent cabins on the ship, which I occupied with Mascotte and a snake I had picked up in Rio.

He was really very pretty—about a yard long, brown with yellow stripes (the same color as the captain's chartreuse on *L'Ouessant*)—and had a beautiful little arrow-shaped head. He was quickly tamed and used to watch me with a pair of sparkling eyes, like black diamonds. The man I bought him from said he used him as a watch-dog. This was certainly a contradiction to the argument about snakes being deaf, for this little snake knew in a marvelous manner when any strange noises went on and would hiss and strike if somebody he did not know came into my cabin.

I kept him in the pocket of the linen hold-all that hangs beside the bunks of English ships. He had found this place for himself and coiled into it to sleep. Nobody saw me bring him on board, except the butcher, a long-suffering man who passed his time in the frozen-meat department of the ship in an atmosphere of raw beef and beer. I sought him out and assured him that he would get his tip ever so much more easily if he left me and my animals in peace and minded his own business. He collaborated handsomely, and all would have been peace and quiet but for an idiotic stewardess who was one of the officious kind and inclined to be overbearing.

I had told her never to come into the cabin when I was not present, or at hours when she did not have her usual duties to perform. I suppose her curiosity got the better of her, and one evening while I was watching the sunset from the top deck, she went into my cabin and proceeded to stick her face into the pockets of the linen hold-all. Little Dandy, the snake, asleep in one of the pockets as usual, got scared, uncoiled himself, and hissed for all he was worth.

I suppose it was a bit startling for the stewardess, who rushed screaming up and down the corridors of the ship till all the passengers and crew were set agog, including the purser, a pot-bellied personage with a bad breath and no sense of humor—as I discovered when making excuses to him. The butcher's comment was, "We haven't had so much fun since mother caught her tit in the mangle," and it seemed to close the incident very nicely.

However long and dull the day seems on the South American run, there is something so magical about the tropical nights that it makes me long to take the trip again. Those evenings and the ones on the little boat going to Mombasa, as well as the trip up the Tana River to Nairobi, are memories that I often dig up and dream over. I can still hear the whirring sound the night insects made in Africa, the queer bubbly sound of the lemurs hunting insects along the bank of the Tana River, and the cry of the mopokes from the jungle —those bewitching little creatures, with immense luminous eyes, like Disney drawings.

I radioed mother from the ship and to my delight received a reply from father, saying he would join me in Paris at the Hotel Meurice on the Rue de la Paix, where he always stayed, so I gathered that mother was not coming over. Of course I wanted to see her but felt glad that I would have an opportunity to discuss many things with my father alone and on a more equal mental footing, for I had been sixteen in January and felt very mature.

I wanted to tell him about the company and the situation with regard to Leslie, and, if I had the chance, to try to help him adjust his life with mother. They were both getting old, mother was in poor health, and young as I had been at the times I had seen them together, I knew how much he loved her and how he made sacrifice after sacrifice for her happiness. Their drifting apart seemed unnecessary and cruel. I understood their situation perfectly, for I, too, had been married and knew something about the bitterness of making a mistake that involves another person's happiness.

I thought about these things the night before we reached Cherbourg and will always have the memory of that ship racing its engines past Ushant Lighthouse on the French coast in a scudding sea, with the spray whipping my face. I was the only person on deck, and it was bitterly cold. I have passed that point of Ushant many times since and have always felt a queer tightening of the throat and a sense of expectancy. It makes me wonder if it could possibly have something to do with my father's seafaring ancestors, who had fought and died in battles off that very coast and whose spirits moved in me.

PART III

XI

I SPENT TEN of the happiest days I can remember with my father in Paris and wanted very much to stay there longer, but he had brought me a rather incoherent letter from mother and explained that he had found her not well at all and had stayed with her longer than he could afford, while waiting to talk things over with me. He had aged considerably; his hair was turning gray, and I thought he looked very tired. He told me that mother had taken a house at Godalming in Surrey for her health, with some woman writer—who I gathered from my father's description, was another of those meddlesome old witches she was always collecting as friends.

Mother, as far as I could make out, spent her time traveling between Godalming and London, for she did not like the house after she moved in, and they could not get any servants. Miss Effie Robertson, mother's friend, wrote poems which, according to father, all started more or less like this: "What is this thing that men call Love?"—the type of thing common in frustrated spinsters. She and mother knew nothing about how to run a house, and neither of them wanted father there. I really flew off the handle when he told me that, and it gave me an opportunity to get down to an open discussion of what we could do to straighten out our tangles. I told him everything I had in my heart and am always thankful that I offered him my company anywhere he wanted me and at any time. I felt that the recital of my theatrical success hurt him, but swallowed my disappointment and never told him that I had started my own company without capital and was still running it. I only let him think the venture was Nemanoff's and that I had not much responsibility in connection with it. I did not want to spoil one moment of those few days in Paris, for they were a great joy to him. We went everywhere together: he came with me to choose the hats and dresses I needed; we went to shows and museums and took long walks on the *quais* where father loved to pore over old books and prints. When the time came for us to rejoin mother in London I felt we would never again be so happy together if we left Paris. I talked to him about this and the future, and also told him that I had no intention of returning to married life. I could sense in him a wistful yearning to stay with me and take a little house, but when I begged him to do this, he would change the topic. I offered to teach and work at the opera if it would help him and said I was sure we could find some way of getting mother to stay with us—it would be like old times in Fontainebleau.

But he told me at last that he definitely had to go back to Canada and the States to continue work on some of his investments that were worrying him. He felt that mother did not want to be tied down with housekeeping that would hamper her singing engagements.

About my own situation he was very kind and gentle. I knew he understood my feelings but at the same time feared I had inherited mother's restlessness and would never settle down with a home and a husband, which, to my father's old-fashioned viewpoint, was the sum total of every woman's prospect in life. I knew that he longed for grandchildren and believed the ancient curse on his family would never permit this hope to be realized. He did not know my husband as yet, having waited till I arrived before meeting him—a very loyal and sweet gesture.

I had planned on leaving Mascotte with my old friend Olga Gougoutchieff while I went to London, but a pilot I met was sporting enough to offer to take the dog over for me in his plane. This was not a simple undertaking, but we took the risk rather than have her held in quarantine, for I intended to stay in England no longer than I could help, after father left for Canada.

Father and I took the boat from Boulogne and smuggled

the snake Dandy through the customs successfully by the simple and well-tried expedient of cutting a seam in my silver fox scarf and slipping him inside. I then wore the scarf around my throat. Father tried to look disapproving but in reality got a great kick out of this and behaved like a small boy who has done something naughty. He worried constantly about Mascotte and the disgrace that would befall us if she were discovered in the basket where the aviator kept his uniform changes.

The next morning we met the pilot in a bar near the Croydon Airport. He was as white as a sheet and told us he'd been through a terrible experience and had nearly been discovered in his attempt at canine smuggling. In fact, he was so upset that we had to buy him several double whiskies before he became normal again.

Mother looked as beautiful as ever but was pale and seemed more nervous than she had when I left England. She was not strong enough to sing in opera, but was nevertheless busily preparing a more modern type of repertoire for ballad concerts—songs with words supplied by the female Byron, who was all my father had said and then some. Mother always made it a point never to have good-looking women friends, but in the case of Miss Robertson she had surpassed herself.

This Scottish Sappho came from Aberdeen and had stuck to mother like a leech ever since my grandmother's death there. She had a face that resembled a slab of the granite for which her native town is famed, and her skin was so rough and weatherbeaten that one felt sure any fly who had the temerity to walk over it would break its leg immediately. In addition to writing poems she was a Yogi, and claimed she was so sensitive to beauty that she could thrive only in Greece where she had a villa. When father and I impressed upon her that she should, for God's sake, go to her villa and stay there, she replied that mother needed her and both father and I were materialists, incapable of giving poetic nourishment to her sensitive soul.

191

Mother told me that some months previously they had gone to the south of France together and had stayed at a little village inn. Miss Robertson was practising Yogi culture in her room one morning when one of the valets, thinking she was out, opened the door with his pass-key and beheld her standing on her head in a corner with nothing on. This spectacle upset the poor boy so much that the proprietress wanted to send for a couple of keepers from the nearest lunatic asylum to come quickly with a strait jacket for Miss Robertson—whom she referred to as *"cette espèce d'hysterique."* Nevertheless mother thought she was wonderful and was so completely under her influence that it made my father miserable.

A few days after my arrival, who should turn up but the "gallant captain," my husband, laden with flowers and as nonchalant as if I had only been away for the week-end. He suggested we start on a round of theaters and restaurants that very evening, but I managed to get out of it gracefully, for Mascotte was so sick and feverish as a result of her plane ride that I simply would not hear of going out and leaving her. So he stayed and helped me nurse her, which was very nice of him, but I was not at all blind to the fact that he was doing it just to get into my good graces and make an impression upon father—who I could see did not like him, although he asked him to dinner that night. He told me afterward that he thought Leslie a "snob." Father was such a simple sweet person himself that he hated people who talked about Society with a capital S and all the important personages they knew. Poor Leslie had tactlessly done this to impress father with his social standing. When I left them alone for a few minutes after dinner, to give father a chance to talk more frankly, Leslie had taken that opportunity to pour out a long muddled account of my conjugal shortcomings. This annoyed and embarrassed father who in the end cut the conversation short by saying he had no intention of taking me to task about private matters, that were entirely my own concern. He also said that, in his opinion, mother was to blame for the whole thing and should have minded her own business to begin with. As far as giving me advice in any way about the future, father simply would not discuss it and merely said that I must act according to my own feelings and conscience, adding that if I felt I could never be happy with Leslie, I should tell him so frankly and go my own way without interference from mother or any third party.

Partly to please mother and partly to make things easier for my father by doing so, I went everywhere she wanted me to. So for the next two weeks I was plunged into a whirl of invitations and functions with all mother's old friends, some of whom, I was certain, were the ones who had egged her on to try and get me settled down again with Leslie and London society. Every time she started on this theme, I would tell her about my contract with Da Rosa for the coming Colón season and about the successes I had had in Argentina.

She would listen with apparent enthusiasm, read all my press clippings with pride, and then suddenly commence another rehash of the old story about her health, begging me not to go away again but to try and live once more with my husband. Yet she knew I could never be happy with him and would be only an impediment to his career. I decided to wait until father returned to Canada before telling her plainly and emphatically that I intended to live my own life.

All of a sudden, a chain of circumstances cropped up that obliged me to give way partially in my decisions. Mother's doctor wanted her to get away to Italy or the south of France for the good of her throat. Father agreed to take her to Capri, and I was going along to be with him. We tried in vain to induce my brother to join us. (As I had predicted, he had not entered the Trappist Order, but had written a book about it instead.)

The gallant captain arrived to see me the afternoon the matter of the Capri trip was settled. He looked ill and said he was having trouble with the old wound in his arm, which had flared up badly during the past few days. The doctor declared that an emergency operation was necessary. Like all Englishmen, Leslie was morbidly ashamed of talking about his health and made light of it, but he looked so unhappy when he heard we were going away that father invited him to visit us for his convalescence.

Leslie was very casual about the gravity of his operation, and we had been in Capri about a week when I received telegrams from his father and Reginald Greir, his doctor and personal friend, that they had been obliged to amputate his arm at the elbow and he was very ill. Of course I left immediately for London, and from the day I arrived there his condition improved. My parents came back shortly afterward, and mother saw my father off to Canada from Southampton.

Leslie's illness had upset everything, but I felt the least I could do was to stay with him as long as possible. It was a clear case of *noblesse oblige,* and as soon as he was able to leave the hospital I took him down to the house in Godalming with a nurse. I had managed to get rid of the Robertson menace by paying her share of a month's rent on the house, which with true Scotch thrift she had been delighted to receive, and, for the time being, had betaken herself to parts unknown.

Mother came down to Godalming for week-ends; she had been rehearsing and studying again for Covent Garden. Her throat had improved under a new doctor's care, but she should have stayed in Capri, for Leslie's sickness upset her. London was certainly not the best thing for her, either, but she was so happy at the prospect of getting back to opera that I had not the heart to criticize her.

When we returned to London, mother and I went to Claridge's, and Leslie, still very helpless about dressing and in need of a valet, stayed at my father-in-law's apartment. It was now the middle of April, and I felt the time had come for me to leave. I knew Leslie cared a great deal more for me now, and I was trying to make up my mind how to announce

194

my departure tactfully, when I received a letter from Nemanoff.

He had decided, with the approval of Evar Mendez, to close the show and store the décors, costumes, and so on, in my house in Buenos Aires. The principal reason for this, it seemed, was that in Tucumán there had been a fuss with both the newspapers and the management because I was not appearing in person.

Nemanoff now definitely knew he was not being engaged for the Colón and felt that his prestige had been hurt. Da Rosa had engaged a Russian called Paul Michailovitch from the Paris opera, as first dancer and choreograph, and he was to head the ballet with Galanta and myself. Nemanoff had been offered a tour through Havana to the United States with an American dancer named Loubovska and her company, and cabled me to ask if it was all right for him to accept.

Evar Mendez also wrote, giving me facts and figures regarding the tournée of my troupe. Fortunately, there were no debts. As a matter of fact, there was even a small profit waiting for me.

I had cabled Da Rosa regarding the date for rehearsals and received a reply asking me to get in touch with the dancer Michailovitch in Paris. I went at once to mother with Da Rosa's cable and announced my departure, bracing myself to meet the storm which I felt to be inevitable. To my surprise she did not seem to mind my leaving and was so absorbed in her own work that she merely said she felt sorry for Leslie and hoped I would treat him with as much consideration as possible.

Before speaking to him I had to talk with my father-in-law, and was glad to hear that he had been wire-pulling and thought it very probable that Leslie would be appointed to the Intelligence Service attached to the Sudan government. Leslie began to feel much better and spent considerable time at his club again (a very healthy sign). He asked me to see as much of his relatives as I could possibly bear, for they meant a great deal to him, all of them being extremely influential in military circles. He was so reasonable about my leaving that I decided if it would make him happy, I could curtail my visit to Paris to a few days and devote the time to coping with his family, thereby endeavoring to eliminate as much as possible any bad impression I had made upon them when we were first married.

Something else was giving me no small amount of preoccupation, apart from my work and the prospect of forcing myself to be agreeable to my in-laws. Before leaving London the previous year I had met somebody I liked very much, and we had gone out once or twice while I lived in Buckingham Gate. He was a handsome Irish boy named Geoffrey, and our friendship had been limited to a few innocent meetings and a couple of drives in mother's car. He was an automobile salesman and I had met him through some visits I made for mother to his place of business. He had sold a car for her and had been so nice about it that she sent me out to lunch with him because she couldn't be bothered to go herself.

While Leslie was in the hospital, I ran into Geoffrey again and went out to the 400 and Murray's Club several times. He was a wonderful dancer.

During the days that followed our return from Godalming, I saw him often, and the inevitable happened. I began to feel all the symptoms I had heard and read so much about, and knew that I was on the verge of falling in love—with a terrific crash. Mother met us one night when he had brought me back to Claridge's rather late. She sensed immediately what had happened. Of course the usual scene took place, and she told me that if I saw him again she would go straight to my husband and tell him about it.

I had never questioned Leslie about his "affairs" and knew he had several of them always on hand—they simply didn't interest me. But I knew that if *I* tried anything of the sort, there would be fireworks. So I decided that to take mother's advice was the best way out of the whole situation. Telling Geoffrey I could not see him again was a lot harder than I had imagined it would be. He was so unhappy—it made me feel that at sixteen, I was already a *femme fatale* going about breaking up people's lives. Finally he went down to his family's place in Bognor and wrote some heartbreaking letters which worried me so much that I hardly knew what to do.

To please Leslie, I agreed to a ridiculous whim he had always bothered me about—a formal presentation at one of the Court Balls in Buckingham Palace. For some reason, he felt that this would firmly establish the fact that he had not made a mésalliance in marrying me. He had filled out all sorts of complicated documents at the Lord Chamberlain's office about mother's having been an opera singer exclusively and did not mention the fact that I had ever been on the stage. At the bottom of the whole silly business was Lady Mildred, a formidable dowager, a relative on his father's side, who attempted to cross-examine me as soon as I met her. She had a deep-rooted conviction that foreigners must be made to understand their inferiority in her eyes to all members of the Anglo-Saxon race.

The ceremony of being presented at Court has a fatal fascination for some women, but for me it was as unpleasant an ordeal to look forward to as a major operation without anesthetic. It was also an expensive business, and I told Leslie I would not contribute one cent of my rapidly diminishing funds, earned through much hard work, on such extravagance. Lady Mildred certainly turned an honest penny every year, for together with another titled dowager who gave classes in "court protocol," she turned up débutantes from the United States and daughters of wealthy English tradesmen who had been knighted, and sponsored their invitations. She then sent them to her friend's "court classes" in deportment where they were taught how to curtsy before Royalty and handle their long trains. In addition to this, the candidates were referred to the Court dressmakers, who, under Royal Command, had the distinction of making the Court gowns in whatever colors the Queen decreed for that season. If somebody wanted to wear pink and looked like hell in anything else,

197

she could not have it unless this happened to be the "color of the season."

Lady Mildred used all her powers of persuasion to entice me into one of the most expensive houses in London, but I was not having any and went to a Frenchwoman called Mighele, who had extremely good taste, and let her cook up a creation in the requisite color, a light blue, the shade of a star sapphire, which suited me and was perfectly lovely when she got through with it. There was the added charm of its being much cheaper than anything purchased at the other house. I was supposed to get into the gown and attend the "class" at the house of the expert in deportment, the Honorable Mrs. Something-or-Other. She coached women in court etiquette and bred Yorkshire terriers in her spare time.

I went there with mother and witnessed the astounding spectacle of a line of rather hefty young women, crouching on their haunches with their skirts spread around them, striving to rise to an upright position with approximately the same amount of grace as a pack camel getting on its feet in heavy sand. Mother's eyes shone with joy when I dropped a sweeping curtsy and rose again in one movement. Nobody knew, of course, that I was a professional dancer and had made grace my business, so this was rather an unfair advantage really. It annoyed all the other women, Lady Mildred in particular, and this delighted mother. She lent me some of her jewelry for the ball of the First Court in May, so between that and Mighele's dress, I looked and felt like something out of the Paris Revue des Folies-Bergère, compared to the rest of our party.

I was in no mood for festivities when the night of the ball came, for that afternoon I had received a telegram from Geoffrey telling me he was going to a nursing home with appendicitis and was obliged to have an emergency operation the next morning.

We set off in the pouring rain, and I was amazed at the crowds blocking the sidewalks around the Palace, while the police formed a cordon to hold them back. Inside the immense vestibules and antesalas I found myself jammed by crowds of excited women and impeccably groomed men. Court officials in tail-coats and black satin knee-breeches dived in and out with invitation cards, and small boys dressed as pages in black velvet suits, some with kilts, were struggling with yards of satin and brocade forming the trains they were to carry for the peeresses. In the crush I managed to get separated from my party and on looking around could not see Leslie anywhere. Clutching my train, I made for a small salon where there was a chair to sit on; I was extremely nervous about losing some of mother's diamonds in the jam.

I sat and thought about Geoffrey and counted the days that would elapse before I could get away from everything and forget about him by burying myself in my work. I felt guilty for having let myself care about him and knew that if mother heard anything more of it she would not only create a terrible upset with Leslie but was capable of writing my father, too. Such a piece of information would both shock and hurt him.

While sitting there, oblivious to everything going on around me and thoroughly miserable, I became aware of a tiny, dapper old man dressed in the court costume of a foreign diplomat—tail-coat, decorations, and skinny legs in black silk stockings—who was bowing before me, speaking in French and asking my permission to sit down. He introduced himself as an attaché of the Belgian legation, but he looked like a personage from a fairy tale and made me think of the mice in Cinderella's pumpkin. He was perfectly charming and such a man of the world that for the first time that evening, I began to feel better. We discussed Paris, and it came to light that he knew mother and admired her greatly. He told me about the doings at Buckingham Palace for the last twenty years. It seemed that the present dull proceedings were like a Harlem hotspot in comparison to Queen Victoria's day, when he had first come to England.

He was perfectly delightful and paid me compliments with such old-world grace that they were not in the least boring. When nobody was looking, he said, "Mademoiselle, will you permit an old man one moment of intense joy?'' and kissed my arm just above my elbow at the top of my long white kid gloves. It was precisely at this moment that I heard the strident voice of Lady Mildred and beheld her quivering with indignation, accompanied by Leslie and an usher with a notebook.

I introduced my aged acquaintance, who made one of his charming bows and attempted to kiss her ladyship's hand, but she drew it away as if he were going to bite her, snorting loudly. Leslie, red and perspiring, dragged me off by the arm, and the last I saw of my little old friend as I was hustled toward a line of flustered débutantes was his whimsical pixie's face laughing back at me around the plump shoulders of a woman in a blue taffeta dress.

The rest of the evening was a confused nightmare of long galleries, immense chandeliers, red carpets, busts of Queen Victoria, and a group of nervous women curtsying before Their Majesties, who somehow gave me the fantastic illusion that they were sitting miles away on the top of red and gold clouds. They bowed and smiled straight through everybody with the most exquisite indifference. Meanwhile, the ushers and court chamberlains bellowed out the name of every one who entered the enormous gallery. Leslie, Lady Mildred, and her honorable friend (of the Yorkshire terriers) fussed, whispered, and glared at me as if they thought I might decide at any moment to kick off my shoes, burst into the middle of the audience chamber with a tambourine like the operatic gipsies, and start shaking it in the faces of Their Britannic Majesties.

The presentation took only a minute; then I was out of the line and being carried along toward the ballrooms with the stream of excited giggling girls. There a most frightful altercation took place with Leslie. He raved on and on about my scandalous behavior and what his aunt had said and thought, while every two minutes our conversation was interrupted by some man who wanted to be introduced and have a dance with me when the ball opened.

I managed to get Leslie down a corridor and told him I was sick and tired of being badgered and insulted, since I had come only to please him, sacrificing my own holiday and work in Paris for his sake. When I had got this across, I turned on my heel and left him standing there, found my wraps and a most obliging functionary who led me through a side door and called a car to drive me back to the hotel.

The next morning I started to pack my things, intending to leave for Paris on the two o'clock boat train, but decided to put through a long distance call to the nursing home in Bognor before leaving. Geoffrey's mother answered. She told me he was very ill and that complications had arisen from the operation. He had been asking for me constantly, and she wanted to know if I could possibly come down to Bognor at once. I left as soon as I could, after taking all my things to the luggage depot in Victoria station. I felt panic-stricken, as if the world were falling to pieces around me.

The second day after my arrival, at one o'clock in the afternoon, Geoffrey died. It was all swift and horrible—I had never before understood what death meant. His family were sweet simple people, but they were strangers to me, and I felt I could not bear to stay for the funeral, so returned to London. Geoffrey's mother had lost five sons in the war, and I had lost the first love I had ever known. The pitiful tragedy of it overwhelmed me.

I called mother up from the station and told her what had happened, and also that if she felt like making a scene, I could not stand it and would rather send for Mascotte and leave at once for Paris. She was not unkind, but when I joined her at the hotel she was so cold and indifferent that I 'phoned for tickets and left the next morning.

The stop in Paris and the crossing to Buenos Aires were uneventful and depressing. On a blue and gold morning on the River Plate, the voyage ended, and as the ship docked, the clear light that always seems to prevail in Argentina made everybody feel old and somewhat bedraggled after the crossing. The press and reporters were there in full force, and I got a flattering reception from all my old friends that raised my spirits at once. Da Rosa and his partner, Walter Mocchi, had given me vast publicity on all their announcements, and the bill of directors and artists who opened the late opera season was one well worth waiting for.

Both Faustino da Rosa and Mocchi were priceless zanies and didn't know it—for had they made a comedy team, they would certainly have ended up in Hollywood. Don Faustino had the habit of locking himself in a small private "toilet" adjoining his office, in moments of stress and turmoil. He took with him upon these occasions a bottle of sherry and a box of his favorite black cigars. Only his private secretary, the prim and dignified Señorita Carmen, knew where to find him and would tap timidly on the door when some insistent caller (usually a bill collector) could not be got rid of. Don Faustino would converse with her through the locked door.

His partner, Walter Mocchi, had something mysterious the matter with his throat. He was an excitable person and used to scream and yell about anything and everything that annoyed him, till he had no voice left for two or three days. He would then be obliged to confine his means of expression to "biting his thumb" in true Italian fashion and eventually would put it to his nose in the gesture of a street Arab—after everything else had failed. Had I not been so blue, I would have got a lot of laughs out of the whole business, but I was very unhappy and my only comfort was getting away from the theater and being alone in my own little house.

Life took up its routine as before, and I found a very dear friend in the person of a little English cockney girl called Mollie Heywood. She was a pretty little thing and had been working as a line dancer with a Tiller troupe at the Casino but was now in need of a job and had come to see me with a letter from Evar Mendez. She had three other English companions from the same troupe, and one by one they all drifted into the corps de ballet through my recommendation. They were a pleasure to have around the company, for they never mixed themselves in any of the fights, were hard workers, and used to sit quietly in a corner during rehearsals, knitting. They dressed with all the Argentine, Italian, and Russian girls of the corps de ballet in long rooms on the top floor of the theater. I often went up there about some last-minute details before a performance and heard their fresh young voices harmonizing cockney music-hall songs—generally unfit for publication. Their favorite one was called "Dan the Lavatory Man," and this unprintable ditty echoed down the lofty corridors of the majestic Colón, while in the dressing-room the other girls sat staring at them as if they thought they were mad. I knew Grabinska, the Italian dancer who accompanied us from Paris, understood a little English, and complained to Michailovitch about the lack of respect in their choice of songs, and that he disliked them for it.

This year the Argentine police had decided to become very strict on the subject of disorderly houses and put a stop to the promiscuous street-walkers that haunted every corner of the city whooping up trade for their establishments. They had published this news in the papers, with an order that no women were allowed to walk through the streets unescorted after eleven o'clock at night. If they did, they were subject to arrest. The English girls, who never read any newspapers, knew nothing about this new order and continued their habit of walking back to their pension after the show without waiting to remove their make-up. The other dancers were too mean to warn them that they were likely to get into trouble.

One night I was called by a downtown police precinct near the Colón and told that one of our *baillerinas* had been arrested on a "disorderly conduct" charge and had given my name as a reference. I immediately called a friend of mine, Dr. Juan Fitzsimon, an elderly and very influential lawyer who was playing bridge at the Jocky Club. He came right over and together we set out for the precinct.

When we arrived, there were Black Marias blocking the entire street and disgorging crowds of women of all nationalities,

herded together by embarrassed policemen. In the small
station-house there was no room for them to move, and in
the middle of that unholy gathering, who were screaming and
protesting in the foulest possible language, was little Mollie,
calmly sitting on a bench—knitting! My elegant friend in
white tie and tails came in for a good share of abuse from
the women as he fought his way through the mêlée to speak
to the comisario in charge. In five minutes, Mollie was free to
leave with us: otherwise, she would have had to spend the
night in jail and appear before a judge the next morning.
She told me that when they brought her to the precinct, she
had requested the officer to call up Michailovitch, who, as
director of the ballet, was naturally the proper person to do
something to get her out. He had refused to help and had
been very nasty, so she called me. This information made me
so angry, remembering how careful both Monsieur Dandré
and Anna Pavlova were of their girls, also Gregoriev, the
ballet director of the Diaghilev company, that the very next
morning I had the pleasure of telling Michailovitch just what
I thought of him in front of the entire company.

A few nights after this, we gave the *Sylphides* ballet for
the second half of the performance, after the short opera,
Cavalleria Rusticana. I wanted to dance alone but an order
came from Da Rosa stating that we were to follow the arrangement by Nemanoff—particularly in the exquisite "Grande
Valse Brillante" as the finale, danced with two men and
two girls. I purposely ceded to Galanta the honor of dancing
with Michailovitch and took Peer Gynt as my partner. The
number has a fast, stirring tempo and we had all danced it
many times. But Michailovitch was at a bad disadvantage on
account of his near blindness: he floundered and muddled
through it with Galanta during rehearsals until she flew at
him and made him so nervous he got worse and worse.

It was to be the first really important representation the
ballet had made under his direction, and of course both Da
Rosa and Mocchi were watching everything he did very
closely. The décor was a garden scene with an enormous tree

backed by heavy wooden supports in the upper left corner of the stage. Michailovitch narrowly missed running into it several times at the dress rehearsal, and the night of the performance Galanta was in a fever of nerves. Whether Michailovitch was preoccupied in avoiding the tree, or whether he did not see her clearly, I don't know: anyway, when the moment came, at the end of the number, for us to run forward and leap from an arabesque into our partners' arms, Michailovitch was not there when Miss Galanta leaped! Peer caught me perfectly, and from his shoulder I was able to catch a fleeting glimpse of her lying flat on her stomach in the middle of the stage while Michailovitch peered at her from beneath a coy blond wig with a pageboy bob. It was quite a finale!

Mr. Mocchi sent for Michailovitch as soon as the curtain fell and called him everything under the sun. But he had no reproaches to make to Galanta, for she was a fine dancer and not to blame. From then on, Michailovitch lost his nerve completely and was so terrified when he danced that he shook like a leaf and seemed to have no strength to lift any of us.

Peer Gynt was essentially a character dancer and could not work in many classical ballets, so there was nothing left to do but utilize some of the line dancers who had strength and ability. Among these was a Russian boy, Ivan Brodsky, who was tall and very strong. He was really a Cossack dancer but an excellent lifter. I used him several times in preference to Michailovitch, who, though a good technician as a classical dancer, had me thoroughly scared after the incident in *Sylphides*.

One night I was dancing with three men in the ballet of *Africana*, an antediluvian musical relic in which the music is tricky and the dance is supposed to be abandoned African frenzy, with drums and a lot of showy lifting. Michailovitch had a series of altercations with the maestro, who didn't think much of the ballet anyway and was only interested in the singer—as are most great conductors—and so did nothing to help us with the intricate tempos.

This rattled Brodsky, and somehow he lifted me too high in an adagio movement and, instead of lowering me slowly, practically dropped me. I managed to land on the toe of my ballet shoe and felt something crack under me. I didn't wait to take stock of what had happened and just made the wings without the public's being aware that anything had gone wrong. I nearly fainted when I finally got to a chair and tried to take off my shoe: the little toe on my right foot was broken. It was not Brodsky's fault, and he was most upset, but there was nothing for me to do but rest at home for three weeks.

During my absence there were all sorts of fights between Galanta and Grabinska as to which of them would replace me. Unable to arbitrate the dispute, Da Rosa sent a noted specialist to examine my foot and see if I could not possibly manage to dance the ballet of *Marouf,* an oriental opera in which I could wear sandals. I arranged a number which was practically all done on one spot and which I danced with an enormous sword. This was one of those freak things which took the public's fancy and became one of my greatest successes.

XII

I BEGAN TO FEEL a little more like myself and ashamed of my inertia since arriving from England, so I took courses in piano, theory of music, and orchestration, at the Colón Academia, read a great deal, and started getting my notes together to plan out a few ideas.

I became very interested in building a "Chauve-Souris" show, something on the style of the delightful company of Nikita Balieff which I had seen in Paris, and wanted to get away completely from the old ballet repertoire which was getting passé for the time being in Buenos Aires. Also, Leonide Massine was coming to the Coliseum with a small ensemble that he had formed with the dancer Jan Kaweski, after leaving Diaghilev in Europe.

Da Rosa had told me confidentially that, after Rio, the Comisión Artistico of the Colón intended putting on a series of functions with Argentine national authors and composers whose works would be chosen by vote. I immediately got down to sorting ideas on ballets for this and received from the Comisión a month's contract as first dancer. Happily they decided to book Nemanoff as choreographer—if he wanted to come. I felt sure of a success with him, so when he cabled his acceptance, I was overjoyed and began writing three modern ballets. The first was a mimioplastic on *La Maison de la Courtesan,* by Oscar Wilde, with the music of the *Treues Liebes Herz,* by Strauss, which runs through the poem. I also built a more elaborate ballet in three tableaux which was to be called *Three Silent Things*—"The Hour before Dawn," "The Wings of a White Moth," and "The Mouth of One Recently Dead." Of course, it was an ambitious theme, but Emeric Stefani, the modern Czech composer, liked it so much he began to write the music for it. For the third, Maurage, whom I wanted to collaborate with me in another style of ballet, wrote the exquisite music called "Brume." This, I am happy to say, later became one of the favorite pieces of the Paris symphony orchestra. It was his swan song, for he never wrote anything much thereafter and died a few years later.

On this music of nostalgic beauty, I had designed a scene to be played behind tulle curtains giving the effect of mist. The scene was the side of a wharf with a watchman dreaming beneath an oil lantern. The prow of an enormous old-fashioned ship almost filled the background and towered over the form of the man. The figurehead on the ship, a woman with long fair hair, came to life gradually, and from the sea beyond she called groups of dancers with veiled faces. On the deck of the ship and from the sea, sailors with drowned white faces and seaweed dripping from their clothes gathered to watch the veiled girls as they danced around the sleeping watchman like a vision. When dawn came up behind the ship's bow, they gradually disappeared—all except the figurehead. The dancer who took this rôle returned to her place and wooden pose as the day broke.

It is a difficult thing to describe and could have been dull and morbid but for the music Maurage wrote, which portrayed the scene so perfectly—I believe it would have been impossible to do anything more suitable for it. All these compositions were of a completely different type from anything I had ever done, and all in a nocturne mood—probably the result of the depressed frame of mind I had been in for the last few months. I was aware that this might strike a blue note but could not seem to get into a different form of composition till I met a Spanish writer and newspaper correspondent, recently arrived from Paris, the Vizconde de Lascanotegui, whose name is well known in Europe, where he is considered a master of whimsy. He was (and may still be) one of the Paris correspondents of the Argentine newspaper, *La Nación*.

Friends to whom I can never be sufficiently grateful brought him to my house. He was an accomplished pianist, knew stacks

208

of obscure Russian folksongs and tales, and was an enthusiastic admirer of Balieff. I told him a lot about the company I was hoping to present after the Colón, and one night he brought the Uruguayan composer Alfonso Broqua to see me. This fabulous old man, who was past seventy, had been all his life a conductor on the railroad running through the Argentine and Paraná interiors. He was a genius and had eventually been discovered by some wealthy art patrons who had brought him out as a composer. His knowledge of the Guaraní Indian songs and Inca music was astonishing. I saw at once that a series of folk-tales done in crude modern tableaux with brilliant color and presented in the same way that Balieff gave his show, with the explanation of each tableau cleverly delivered before the curtain by a *criollo* actor in gaucho costume, was what I had been looking for.

These tableaux were gay and candid and gave me the chance to get away from my morbid complex. I spent hours in the Incaica Museum in Buenos Aires, and night after night with Broqua, Maurage, and Stefani, working on these tableaux.

All the work I had done in the museums on Incaican art came in very useful, as we were to open in Rio with the opera *O Guarany* by a Brazilian composer, and the Colón archives had neither costumes nor props for it. Da Rosa and Mocchi had me designing like mad to get together the vast amount of detail for the presentation, in combination with the Colón scenographs who were painting the décors. We even had to rehearse on the boat, which was crowded with delegates from Argentina and Uruguay, bound for the Centenario (the hundred-year anniversary in Rio). This trip is one of the memories I cherish because of its gaiety and fun: I had not enjoyed myself so much for a long time.

When we arrived in Rio, we found every hotel and pension full, and in most of them there were no elevators. My foot, which never had a chance to rest properly, was giving me a good deal of trouble, and I could not risk straining it further by walking up and down flights of stairs two or three times a day. Eventually Natascha and I found rooms in the Hotel

209

St. George on the Praio do Russel out of the center of town on the sea road. Gabriella Benzenzoni and the two Cattaneo sisters (both singers and understudies) were on the same floor with us, and we all used to go to the Gloria for meals with the rest of the company.

When the Brazilians are out to have a good time, they really do a job of it, and Rio was in full fête. Crowds of laughing, excited people jostled each other on the main thoroughfares, there were cabarets and restaurants everywhere, and the streets were filled with music day and night. We were behind in our rehearsals and with all the extra work this entailed, were so exhausted we had just about enough strength at night to fall into a taxi and go to our hotels.

We did manage to attend one dance at the Nevada and enjoyed ourselves so much we didn't get home till four in the morning. The next day we received notice from Mocchi that all such festivities were to be curtailed until the show was in better shape. The row he kicked up with Gabriella Benzenzoni about going to cabarets and jeopardizing her voice was considerable, but as a great artist she could afford to ignore such orders, so continued to dance and enjoy herself every night and was never in the hotel.

She was famed for her magnificent collection of jewelry which she wore everywhere and left in a valise in her room whenever she was out, instead of depositing it with the hotel manager. This habit led to one of the most terrible experiences I have ever gone through.

The night it happened, I had returned absolutely worn out after a gala performance of *Carmen* where Michailovitch managed to get in one of his most unfortunate mistakes. Maestro Mascagni had decided to play a part of Bizet's opera seldom used, called "La Bella Fanchula"—a ballet of gitanos which takes place in the last act outside the Plaza de' Toros. The entrance for the dancers was a small doorway which opened directly in the center of the stage. It was a very awkward place to get through, with the enormous crowd of chorus people standing in lines before it to sing the opening chorus.

210

I had to enter first and, after some solo dancing, wait for Michailovitch, who was supposed to be a bold bad bandit and burst through the crowd, seize me by the wrist, and go into a wild dance.

On the night of the performance the house was packed. We had been obliged to await the President's arrival, then stand on the stage while the Brazilian National Anthem was played. This had delayed the show, and we were waiting around for the last act. Michailovitch had retired to his dressing-room until his cue to dance, and I could not see him anywhere when I was called so a boy was sent to tell him to hurry.

Upon entering the stage, I was obliged to push my way through the chorus men who, dressed as toreadors, consisted mostly of the elderly Italians that had been picked for their voices rather than their appearance, the majority looking like Mussolini with spectacles. As they brandished their capes and long lances trying to look fierce, it was all I could do not to burst out laughing in their faces. I went into my dance after a very cordial applause from the audience—but no sign of my partner! The time came for his entrance: still no Michailovitch. I became nervous and had to improvise as best I could. Only at almost the very end of the ballet, when I was positively frantic, did I see the gentleman groping his way through the chorus singers as if he were playing blind-man's buff. It was ghastly!

He could not get into the dance routine at all, and missed me in several pirouettes. How we ever got off that stage without being booed off, I shall never know. When it was over I was utterly exhausted and dripping with cold perspiration. The first person I saw was Mocchi, shaking his fist in Michailovitch's face and emitting hissing sounds combined with staccato explosions that sounded like ''Old Faithful.'' Michailovitch fled to his dressing-room, and I felt like bursting into tears from sheer nerves—although Mocchi had been very sympathetic, patting my shoulder.

I took an open taxi back to the hotel along the beautiful

Beira Mar road that runs beside the sea to Copacabana. It was a hot night, and when I got to my room I opened the two windows overlooking the terrace and gardens to let in all the air possible and literally fell into bed. I must have been in a dead sleep for an hour or more when I was awakened by a shrill bark from Mascotte, who was sleeping in an armchair between my bed and the window. In the moonlight streaming into the room, I saw the dark crouching outline of a man creeping toward the window with my valise in his arms.

Being half-asleep, I did a foolish thing which normally I never would have: I leaped from the bed on to the intruder, and at the same time Mascotte attacked him, biting his arm as he struck at me. The blow hit me in the chest and threw me to the floor against one of my trunks. Scrambling to my feet, I saw the man drop my valise, grab the long window curtains, and swing by them out of the window bringing down the curtain pole behind him—which broke his fall. But through the window with him went Mascotte, still hanging on to his arm! From the window, which was about eight feet from the ground, I could see the man limping but running fairly fast toward the gate of the hotel, leading to a path up the mountain.

I got the revolver I had carried ever since that night on the La Plata road, and because of the moonlight and an electric lamp above the gate, I saw him clearly and Mascotte's white body leaping at his legs and hips. I wanted to bring him down with a shot in the legs, but feared I would hit the dog, so aimed for his shoulders. Two bullets missed, but the third and fourth got him. I saw him stagger and reel through the gate, where he was covered by the wall. Once more I had reason to be grateful to Ograinsky for the training in fancy shooting he had given me while with his troupe.

I rushed to the door of my room. It was locked and the key gone. I could hear excited voices shouting on the outside as I threw my weight against it—for by this time I was fighting mad and wanted to get out after Mascotte. While one of the hotel staff went to get a pass-key, the precious minutes dragged by. When he returned and opened the door, I grabbed a raincoat and ran through the crowd out of the hotel, across the gardens. As I reached the gate, I saw two armed marines, guards from the near-by naval camp. I told them what had happened, and they came with me up the mountain. The thief had evidently got into an automobile, held for him behind the hotel grounds, and in the darkest part of the bushes we found Mascotte. She had been kicked so brutally that blood was oozing out of her mouth, and she lay in a pool of it. After we carried her back to the hotel, I realized she had saved my life, for as she had bitten the man's arm when he struck at me she had evidently knocked a long, white-handled razor from his hand. Coated with half-dried blood, it lay in the middle of my bedroom floor.

The police had already arrived, and a colored police sergeant was taking notes in a book, while the night manager, porter, and a crowd of half-dressed guests were pressing closely around, all talking at once in half a dozen languages. My friend Natascha was there with her hair streaming down her back, and as she came toward me, I did another foolish thing—the second one that night—which was to let go a string of rather high-colored remarks about not having been lucky enough to kill the man who had hurt my dog. I instinctively spoke in Spanish, and my words horrified an old lady in curl-papers who bleated out something about "using such dreadful language in the face of death." I brushed her aside and made for the telephone to call a vet for Mascotte.

The police sergeant stopped me to ask if the gun I still held belonged to me. I showed him my permit, and as he made a note of the number, a police captain arrived and asked me if I knew the two Cattaneo sisters who slept in the room next to mine. I said, "Yes," and he requested me to accompany him. As we crossed the hall, I noticed for the first time that there were no lights on the floor, with the exception of two portable lamps held by the manager and the police sergeant. The officer told me that every light on the entire floor had been put out of action at the main switch, obviously by the thieves, and that the hotel was repairing it at the moment. Then the full horror of the night's work broke over me.

We entered the darkened bedroom; an electric torch flashed on the bed. I don't think I could ever find words to describe adequately what I saw. Those two poor girls were lying with their throats slashed and practically covered in their own blood, which soaked through the sheets and clotted in an ever-widening stain on the floor. I managed to tell the officer that I recognized them and stumbled out. He wanted to take Natascha in, too, but I begged him not to. There seemed to be no need for her to see such an awful thing!

When the lights went on, the police, who had questioned everybody, came to the conclusion that there had been more than one thief roaming the hotel. It was evident that they were looking for Gabriella Benzenzoni's jewels. She was out, and they had gone to the Cattaneos' room first. The police thought that these poor girls had been killed to prevent their screaming and waking the hotel. After this, one of the thieves had entered my room, and Mascotte's barking and brave attack had undoubtedly saved me from the same fate.

There was an awful to-do about it the next day, for the police accused the management of having accomplices in the hotel who had tampered with the lights and given information about there being an artist with valuable jewels on that floor. They insisted I move to the floor above, for the rooms overlooking the terrace were without any bars on the windows—a very dangerous thing in Rio, where it is a well-known fact that hoodlums haunt the residential districts in murderous bands, looking for an opportunity to get in through a window and rob. They also said the thieves might return and do me some damage as a reprisal for having wounded their pal, since the police had found a distinct trail of blood up the mountain path and beyond the spot where we found Mascotte.

Early in the morning I received a cable from mother which had been sent at approximately the same hour that I was in such danger. She asked me to cable a reply if I was all right. There was no reason why she should have cabled me, for I

214

had written regularly, but later on she wrote that she had a presentiment for a couple of days before sending the cable that something very serious was about to happen to me. I was most anxious that my father know nothing regarding this episode and wrote no details to mother until two or three months later.

I had a desperate fight to save Mascotte and was fortunate enough to procure a good vet. The police demanded I go to the precinct at all hours and produce references of all sorts, and a "Cédula de Buena Conducta," a document issued by the Argentine police vouching for the bearer's respectability. I inquired the reason for all this investigation, and they told me it was because the old lady in the curl-papers, who had got herself very much in evidence as a witness, had told them about my having returned to the hotel brandishing a gun and voicing my regrets at not having managed to kill the thief. This seemed, after all, to be a very reasonable remark for anybody to make under the circumstances, but Brazilian law states that any foreigner who has drawn blood from a citizen of Brazil with a weapon of any description can be indicted for a crime and held under arrest if it is so desired. They had merely told me that until further notice I would not be allowed to leave Rio.

With the police, the criminal court, Mascotte, and the theater, I was running about like mad in all the heat. I finally got hold of a lawyer, Dr. Cavalcanti, through friends of mine who advised me to have some protection. He wrote to Buenos Aires for my credentials and received a most helpful letter from my old friend, the chief of police for whom I had acted as Russian interpreter. He sent all sorts of recommendations and told several of my friends in Buenos Aires, with the result that they in turn wrote friends in Rio, and I began to meet many influential people. They were most kind, and everything was going along nicely when the thief was arrested.

Just as the police had suspected, he was one of a band of young Negro hoodlums, profiting from the influx of visitors for the fiestas by robbing as many as possible. He admitted

215

to the crime in the Hotel St. George and gave a detailed account not only of the murder of the Cattaneo sisters but also of two or three other women he had killed in various rooming houses. I had to identify him, which was ridiculous, since I had not had time to see his face and had only been able to notice when I fired at him that he was very short, had extremely broad shoulders, and wore a gray suit. When he was well enough to be brought to court from the prison hospital, he sat slumped in a chair, sulky and defiant till he faced me. Then he turned the color of bilge water and would not look in my direction. He was only nineteen, with an obscene mouth and unwinking red-rimmed eyes that looked sidewise like a cobra's.

By this time the Argentine papers were full of the shooting in Rio, and I received telegrams from Nemanoff and the Colón Commission regarding the approaching rehearsals. I sent my lawyer to get necessary formalities arranged, as I wanted to leave at once: there was such an amount of red tape to go through, it began to appear as if *I* had broken into the hotel and committed the crime, instead of the Negro. They claimed that until the man was out of danger from the effects of his wound, I was technically charged with manslaughter and therefore, under Brazilian law, was not free to leave the country.

After all sorts of guarantees and references had been sent from Buenos Aires, Natascha and I got away on a German liner, the next ship leaving for the Argentine. The next day I received a radio from Dr. Cavalcanti telling me that the night I sailed the thief had died in the prison hospital. If he had done so before I managed to get on the boat, it would have been a nasty situation for me.

The Commission of Arts and the Consejo de Deliberantes had notified me after I arrived that they had chosen two of my ballets, *Three Silent Things* and *Brume*. Also they wanted a few representations of the *Harlequin Noir* during the season. It was a short temporada but a very successful one,

216

and although both my ballets, especially *Brume,* had fine notices, it was clear from the reaction of the public that they had been through enough ballet to last them for some time.

The Commission had decided to run the opera by themselves the following year, without any outside impresarios, and were kind enough to offer me a contract as first dancer again. This meant I would be dancing four temporadas in succession at the Colón, something nobody had ever done before, which was of course extremely gratifying, and naturally I accepted.

My plans were carefully set and worked well for the Empire, the Mar del Plata, and Montevideo, and thence back to Buenos Aires to liquidate the company and close my house, after which I was ready to accept a cabled offer from Mocchi for the Costanzi in Rome.

The engagement at the Empire was enlivened with one of those backstage incidents that half-wreck a company, while the audience is completely unaware of what is going on. It was an inconvenient house, and the women's dressing-rooms were crowded together on the ground floor behind the orchestra pit. I dressed in a tiny one next to Raquel Meller, who nearly always rested in her room between the three performances a day: her husband, Gomez Carillo, the Spanish newspaper columnist, used to bring in lunch and refreshments for her. She was a quiet, frail person who very seldom spoke to anybody, and one of the greatest artists I have ever had the pleasure of working with. People said her husband was a sort of Svengali and practically hynotized her whenever she worked. I don't know of course how true this was, but he was undoubtedly a brilliant man and never left the wings when she sang. Until the afternoon of our début I had never met Raquel Meller, and our first meeting was under very trying circumstances.

I had been as usual occupied till the last minute with a hundred and one things, and arrived in my own dressing-room with just enough time to dress hurriedly. There was not an inch of space that was not occupied by my costumes: they

217

were stacked up everywhere, particularly the enormous, brand-new tarlatan ballet skirts that covered every available chair. Boxes of new shoes littered the floor, and sitting in the middle of all this was my dresser—a placid Indian girl with the good old Scottish name of Flora. I had brought her from the Colón, where there had been sufficient space for everything, and she was totally incapable of adapting herself to any change in circumstances. This annoyed me so much that I sent for a hammer and nails to make some additional hooks on the walls so that she could hang some of the dresses up out of my way.

In my haste, I drove an enormous hole straight through the plaster and into a water-pipe. A stream of cold water gushed forth, soaking me in an instant. I was half-dressed and could not call for help from the stage until I found a robe to wear—during which time the water literally burst from the pipe and was flooding the room. Loud screams and shrieks came from the adjoining dressing-rooms as the girls climbed on chairs to get out of reach of the water, which was running under the wooden partition, while Flora, the pride of the Highlands, dived for my shoes in the rising flood like a cormorant after fish. When I opened the door to call for help, the first person I saw was beautiful Raquel Meller in a gorgeous gray taffeta gown with a crinoline skirt, standing in a pool of water. She asked me in the most polite musical voice with a Catalan pronunciation if there was anything wrong! I hastily introduced myself and made what excuses I could for the disaster.

They turned the water off at the main, eventually, and somehow or other we managed to get dressed, and the show went on—though how we did it was a miracle. The men were all impeccable, for they dressed on the top floor, but the women, including myself, were damp and clammy—and had the giggles in consequence. Fortunately it had happened in the first afternoon house, giving us time to mobilize an army of dry cleaners and valets, so by the evening and the gala for the Consejo de Deliberantes, all was in order again.

The evening newspapers had head-lines in the theater news

saying, *"La Davis he acertada otra vez"*—meaning I had scored another success, which was not exaggeration, for the entire program had been enthusiastically received—especially the Incaica tableaux. For weeks afterward, restaurants and bars blossomed forth with "Incaica Rooms" inspired by my décors, of which they were practically exact copies.

Just before I left Buenos Aires for Italy, the drama that took place with José was the only upset I had to contend with. He could not understand why, when the company had met with such success, I wanted to close down. The principal reason for his grief was that I had employed him as baggage man during all the tournée, and he had been very proud of his work. It really hurt me to have to tell him it was over.

I sublet the Juncal house to a friend of mine and his wife, an American couple who were perfectly willing to take José on as valet together with the house, but he would have none of it. The afternoon they came to sign the lease and interview him about working for them, he refused not only to talk to them but also to serve them coffee which I had ordered in the library. Very naturally, they said he appeared to be a little deranged and they thought it would not be possible for them to engage him. After they had gone, I gave him his salary plus an additional month's wages and told him he must leave at once. He refused to accept my money and barricaded the door to his room.

Remedios and I both thought he had gone insane and called Dr. Fitzsimon. (I always called him whenever I had any exceptional difficulties to overcome.) When he arrived, I let him in myself, and as we crossed the hall, a knife flew from the door of the patio and narrowly missed the doctor's head: it had been thrown by José. We had a hectic time getting him out of the house, for he appeared to have an endless collection of knives in his trunk, and he kept flourishing them in our faces. But the whole matter ended in his calming down finally and begging the doctor's pardon in a wild jargon of explanations of how I tried to get rid of him by hiring him

219

out to some *extranjeros* (strangers), to whom he seemed to have taken a violent dislike. He was a good boy and honest, if slightly mad, so Dr. Fitzsimon got him a job as porter on the country estate of a friend, where he was very happy and attached himself with the same enthusiasm to his new patron.

The opening at the Costanzi was very successful for me, and I received a series of flattering press notices—all beginning with *"Il grandioso sucesso de la Bellissima Baillerina Assoluta...."* I had managed to dance all the repertoire Mocchi had engaged me for, alone, although there were several good first dancers including Cia Fornarolli and Di Vincenti who had been with the Bonetti tournée in South Africa.

The day after we closed at the Costanzi, I left for Paris and on the train ran into Matto Erazuriz Alvear, son of the Chilean Minister to Argentina—a charming but eccentric young millionaire who had always been a great friend of mine. He was escorting the fascinating and exotic Princess Paula de Medici, famous in three capitals for the parties she gave for the Diaghilev company, modeled on the Arabian Nights, in which she herself danced in a leopard skin and her best emeralds. She was always seen with the richest and handsomest men in Europe. Antonio de Portajo, a magnificent-looking person whose love affairs were the talk of Paris, was with the party. We spent the best part of the night drinking champagne in Matto's drawing-room, and I was very tired when I finally went to my compartment to get a couple of hours' sleep before reaching Paris and mother's inspection.

The de luxe express for Paris has a habit of swerving around corners with abandoned recklessness, and somehow as I struggled down the corridor, I managed to wrench my foot, which was still weak from the accident in Buenos Aires. I did not think anything much of it at the time, but the next day it was so stiff and painful I could hardly walk.

Mother was delighted to see me and seemed to be happy that I was planning to dance in Paris where she was working so we could be together. I naturally did not want to spoil

220

her pleasure, so said nothing about my having hurt my foot but hobbled around for three days instead of resting it.

Mother told me that my brother had moved to the Channel Islands where he had always been happy and was living in Jersey—writing with success and singing again. His voice had improved so much that mother said that, in her opinion and also that of other professionals who had heard him, he was undoubtedly one of the greatest living tenors. Yet nothing would induce him to accept concert appearances or even make recordings, for he was morbidly sensitive about his blindness and imagined the scars on his face to be much worse than they really were. He had sung some months previously (after a great deal of insistence from mother and friends) at a charity concert at the Royal Albert Hall in London, given for the blind veterans of St. Dunstan's Hospital. Mother said it was something marvelous, and offers for engagements poured in. The newspapers raved about the beauty of his voice, but he had been so emotionally upset after the concert that he refused to receive anybody for days, and she had not dared to mention the matter again.

I was expecting the advent of Diaghilev at any moment and wanted to polish my technique before he saw me dance, but I was having all sorts of trouble with my foot. It was weak and numb at times, and I could not hide this, but following the tradition that exists among all dancers and acrobats, that "hard work is the best remedy," I forced myself to dance on my toes till the day Diaghilev came.

I chose an extremely difficult and technical number on my points, and at his request danced a Spanish *Seguidilla* which involved a good many heel taps. He was pleased, I could see, and from the way he talked I felt sure he meant to do something quite important with me—telling me of his plans for the company and that he was taking on some new dancers, also about the proposed "Grand Fête de Versailles." He had never been so cordial to me before.

I walked down the hill from Montmartre, treading on air for about three blocks, and suddenly the pain in my foot

221

became so intense I had to take a taxi back to the hotel. I went to a doctor with mother, and after X-rays and various examinations, the verdict was that I must rest the foot completely. A nerve was affected, probably from my having danced too soon after the toe had been fractured, and the wrench I had given it on the train had resulted in a tiny sac of water forming under the ankle bone, which had to be removed with a needle. After this, I had a long series of diathermic treatments to undergo if I wanted to avoid an operation, which might leave my foot permanently stiff and useless for dancing.

I was bitterly disappointed, and mother was so sweet and sympathetic about it that for the first time I realized how she felt when she desperately needed to work and the weakness of her throat did not permit her to do so. However, there it was and nothing could be done but accept the situation, devote the interim before leaving for Buenos Aires to studying as much as possible, and do everything the doctor prescribed. Mother went to see Diaghilev about me, and some of the things he said regarding my dancing did much to help my frame of mind. He had been very agreeably surprised, he told her, and was most disappointed that I could not join his company.

Pepita and her mother were living at a boarding-house in Montparnasse, and the first time they came to see us her beauty made a deep impression on me. I had not seen her for three years and although she was still very young, she was so breathtakingly lovely, all I could do was stare at her and think of Byron's lines, ''She walks in beauty like the night.'' She created a sensation wherever she went and although not a good dancer, had been given an important rôle in the *Cuadro Flamenco* by Diaghilev because of her beauty. I went to some of the rehearsals and, at Cecchetti's request, did all I could to improve her work. She was a sweet child but rather lazy, indifferent to the ballet and always complaining about her salary which was undoubtedly a small one.

Paris was wonderful and filled with talented people whose only aim in life seemed to be giving each other as good a time as possible. Money flowed, and I have never seen the Parisian women more exquisitely dressed and attractive. I often wonder if those days so full of *joie de vivre* can ever return.

I went to all the theaters, studied and made notes, but with the exception of Pitoyev's productions and the Théâtre d'Atelier, I was more fascinated with the Cirque d'Hiver and the three Fratellini brothers than anything I had yet seen. I had known them for years but never had a chance to watch their wonderful performances from the audience. I went back to their dressing-room nearly every night and found I knew most of the artists in the company—the trainer Herman Paats from the Hagenbeck circus, with their No. 3 company of polar bears, and the great juggler Rastelli who died insane a few years later.

While watching the show, I remembered that when I set the Chauve-Souris program, I had arranged a number Ograinsky once gave—a ballet of clowns with a jack-in-the-box set in the center of the stage. When the lid was opened, a man dressed as a golliwog was shot from a spring up to a trapeze hanging directly above it. Nemanoff had done this number, and the few tricks I taught him on the trapeze, though simple, had been beautifully mimicked and far surpassed any of his dances in the applause he got.

Remembering the effect it had on the public, I began to imagine a number on a long climbing rope in which the performer would open the act dancing, following the same ballet movements on the rope in the air. I told the Fratellinis about it, for they were masters in production and in arranging all sorts of acts for the Cirque, which they owned. They thought such a number had great possibilities and kindly offered me the use of the ring in the mornings if I wanted to work on the idea.

They were an enormous family, and although I knew every one by sight from the various circuses where they had worked with the Ograinsky troupe, I was never really able to disentangle their family tree. They had a community dressing-room on the ground floor of the Cirque d'Hiver, in which their

223

respective wives arranged their many props and costumes, cooked "snacks" on electric stoves at frequent intervals, and received an almost constant stream of visitors. Their sons, daughters, nephews, nieces, and grandchildren went in and out from their own acts, carrying props and materials of all descriptions. The whole family worked together and allowed no outsider to handle or examine their trick props, presumably so that they might never be in danger of being copied. The three brothers, who had made a large fortune from the Cirque d'Hiver which they ran during the World War, were of Italian origin and had been decorated by the French Government for their services at charity functions and for their generous donations to the hospitals. Despite their money, they preferred to live the same simple existence as always, and owned modest houses near Paris where they all lived side by side.

I did not avail myself of their offer of the ring, but went to the old Gymnase Pons on the Rue Lepic on the Butte of Montmartre, where Ograinsky used to take us to practise. It was a most picturesque place and belonged to another ex-wrestler named Armand Saulnier, who gave lessons in acrobacy between bouts of wrestling on a carpet in the middle of the gymnasium, for which he charged admittance. Acts of all sorts practised in corners while this was going on, and some of the best performers I have ever seen worked and sweated in perfect harmony on the deep and extremely dirty tanbark that covered the floor. At one end of the gym was a bar lined with photographs of performers—featuring Monsieur and Madame Saulnier in their heyday, he with a handlebar mustache, lifting incredible weights, and Madame in tights, high laced boots, and holding a rose.

As I could not use my foot very much, I felt that to work off the ground was obviously the practical way to keep in condition, and to remain supple, I did a good amount of contortion work. While I played around with the rope to see what I could get out of it, I received enough advice and suggestions from the other performers to make a dozen acts. They nearly all knew I had been with Ograinsky and were for some reason deeply interested in my getting up in the air again, all except Saulnier, who had heard about my fall from many sources—mostly exaggerated and full of harrowing details. Whenever I practised at any height at all on the rope, he would stop whatever he was doing at the time and shout in pure Montmartre argot, interspersed with a prolific flow of bad language: *"Dis donc toi! Je ne veux pas que tu viennes ici pour casser la gueule!"*—"I don't want you to come here to break your puss!" It was lots of fun.

XIII

THE STUDIO OF Ignacio Zuloaga was not far from the Gymnase Pons and near the Sacré Cœur. He was now painting Pepita, as he had painted her aunts and grandmama, and sometimes I would call there for my cousin. All the Spanish colony gathered at the studio to drink manzanilla and listen to the great musician Malaga Cuencas, who always played his guitar while Zuloaga painted. I had never seen him without his guitar and imagined he took it to bed with him at night.

Zuloaga, greatest of the Spanish contemporary painters, was a peculiar man, and when he was in a bad mood, he could be abominably rude to his guests. He painted most of the time from an ordinary dentist's chair which he could wind up and down as he wished. He flattered and spoiled Pepita, who was only too well aware of her beauty. During this time, she was having a violent flirtation with the Argentine painter, Roberto Ranaugé, who also painted her for the Paris Salon, much to Zuloaga's annoyance, since he intensely disliked having any one else use his models.

Carlos Reyles, author of *El Embrujo de Sevilla* (one of the most fascinating historical novels about Spain), and Blasco Ibañez, the still better-known author, would come to these afternoons. They brought Rex Ingram and his wife, Alice Terry, who happened to be in Paris prior to leaving for Algiers to film Hichens' novel, *The Garden of Allah*. Ingram had noticed Pepita in our hotel and was crazy to use her in a picture. He had talked to Ibañez about producing *Blood and Sand*, starring Rudolph Valentino, the maquettes to be done by Zuloaga, and suggested writing in a small part for her. It was little wonder, when she was attracting so much interest among the movie folk, that it began to go to her head. Her

226

mother, already worried enough about the rest of her prodigious family in Spain, could do nothing with her. She would not rehearse properly, and I had visions of Diaghilev throwing her out at any moment.

Fortunately, he was too occupied with the extensive preparations for the "Grand Fête" at the Palace of Versailles for French charity. This was indeed a superb production, and Diaghilev had costumes made after originals in the museums—even down to such details as the jewelry and shoe buckles. The great crystal chandeliers were wired for electricity—a tremendous and costly job—and the dancers were carried into the historic Galerie des Glaces, where the ballet took place, in sedan chairs. Every musician was in the correct costume of the court of Louis XV.

Tickets cost a fortune, and Matto Alvear invited a large party, among them Roland Toutain, Theresa Wilms (the Chilean writer), Madame Chanel (the famous couturière), Spinelly, the French comédienne, mother, myself, and one of the most entertaining people in Paris—the Vizconde Jaime de Zulueta. After the fête, we took Pepita along with us for the party he was giving at his house in the Rue Pauquet. Jaime de Zulueta was very popular with men for his caustic wit and was also attractive to women although he was short and ugly: he had a big head and a pair of small humorous eyes that were his only charm. His manners were almost too perfect for modern times, and he gave the impression of being a person from another century who had stepped out of the pages of St.-Simon or Le Nôtre.

Son of one of the oldest families in Spain, he had no personal fortune but made his extravagant livelihood by selling antiques (on commission) for ruined aristocrats, which he also copied with such consummate art that even the owners could not tell the difference. The walls of his house were hung with magnificent tapestries and so overcrowded with furniture, statues, and bibelots, that it was difficult for any large assembly of guests to circulate. However, that night, all Paris seemed to have managed to squeeze in somehow.

227

His reputation of being irresistible to women was undoubtedly true, for beautiful young society matrons, movie stars, and bejeweled dowagers with exuberant bosoms, gazed at him with the rapture of school-girls. And their antics to distract his attention from any possible rival were positively indecent.

Zulueta sold quantities of antiques to Matto, but I think theirs must have been a sincere friendship, for he never tried to unload any "phonies" on anybody he liked, and said so very honestly. Matto had gone to see José María Sert one afternoon, asking his fee for coming out to Buenos Aires to decorate two rooms for him in his parents' house. Sert, a great painter and true bohemian, was not at all interested, and to get rid of the offer, he asked the fantastic sum of sixty thousand pesos. To his astonishment, young Matto (then about twenty-two) calmly wrote a check for the full amount, adding the price of a de luxe suite on any ship he preferred. All Paris gossiped about this, and Zulueta basked in the reflected light of Matto's riches.

My foot had improved considerably by this time, and I was able to practise a little, very carefully, and also scout around Paris buying all the material I could afford for the company I intended to build for my farewell tour after the Colón. I had made up my mind that the 1923 season at the Colón would be my last, since I wanted for many reasons to stay in Paris and work.

I loved Buenos Aires and was grateful to its public for my success and the money I had earned, but I knew there was such a thing as "outstaying one's welcome" in every artist's career. I felt that if I could have a good success at the Colón, and a farewell tournée with an improved Chauve-Souris company, it would always assure me an open door at any time I wanted to return.

For some time I tried to get sensible instructions from the Colón about how I was supposed to get there. A new man, Dias Grassi, was in charge of the artists and their traveling arrangements. He had managed to produce the utmost confusion for all of us. Finally I had to book my own passage

228

and barely caught an English ship that got me to Buenos Aires on the twentieth of June, the day rehearsals were to start. Mother was going to Portugal and Spain to sing, so we were able to travel together until she saw me off from Lisbon.

I told her then that I hoped to make enough money to take an apartment in Paris upon my return, and wanted her to settle down there and take life a little easier. She looked so worn out after the long stretches of operatic singing that I was worried about her. She said it would make her happy, and during the entire trip I worked on plans to make and save as much money as possible, with this object in view.

At the last minute, Matto gave me a long list of things to do for him in Rio, the principal one being to see all the best horticulturalists and the Botanical Gardens, to make a collection of tropical orchids which he wanted to plant around a swimming-pool he was building as a surprise for his mother's birthday. I promised to do what I could about it, for I spoke Portuguese and he did not.

When we docked in Rio, I drove out to the Botanical Gardens to see about Matto's orchids. It was worth while, for I had never visited them and it proved to be one of the most fantastically beautiful places in the world. The Vanderveld expedition had brought orchids from the tropical Amazon Delta that were as beautiful as the seven deadly sins. I was hypnotized by their beauty and dreamed of a ballet inspired by them and Baudelaire's *Fleurs du Mal*. However, the curator of the Gardens told me there was no possible way for orchids to be grown in the open air of Argentina, so I cabled Matto that he would have to find some other idea for his mother's swimming-pool. He did. The week after I arrived in Buenos Aires, in the midst of rehearsals and other complications, I received a cable from him asking me to take charge of a shipment of parrots and macaws he had ordered from Rio.

My old friend Natascha, who was staying with me (she had got the house ready after my American tenants vacated at the end of May), was the only person who could possibly find time to go to the docks and receive Matto's parrots. The poor girl started out with the best will in the world but found that the English freighter that had accepted the cargo was in all sorts of difficulties regarding the Board of Health laws on parrots. There had been an epidemic of psittacosis in Argentina, and all parrots had been confiscated in a house-to-house canvass and removed to the Zoölogical Gardens in quarantine. In fact, parrots were positively taboo in Buenos Aires.

Natascha was frantic and 'phoned me from the dock that there were literally dozens of crates of the screaming flustered birds cluttering up the isolation quays of the Ministry of Agriculture, and the place was in an uproar. I told her to call Onelli to send trucks and get them out to the zoo if possible. This was eventually managed, but I was pestered every day about what was to be done with them, for Matto had given my name as the person to deal with the situation.

From the very moment I had disembarked in Buenos Aires, everything had gone wrong, and the superfluous worry of having about two hundred contraband parrots on my hands was not helping matters. The first thing Natascha had told me when we met was that there had been an announcement in the newspaper *La Nación* about my having been engaged for the Diaghilev season in Paris. This had been followed by several articles lamenting the fact that I was not coming to the Colón as advertised. Then Di Vincenti had arrived to take over the corps de ballet and had found himself confronted with a Madame Dalenova who, as girl-friend of one of the musical directors, had been engaged at the last minute. The regular dancers that had always held their positions, like Natascha, Borisewa, and Ivanowa, found themselves relegated to the ranks of ordinary ballet dancers so as to make way for some young ladies whom Mr. Grassi had produced from his personal collection of friends and relatives.

The confusion and upset that I found at the theater, under these circumstances, was indescribable. Di Vincenti, though glad to see me, was unusually cold, and I finally got the reason for this out of him. It seemed that the papers were putting on a terrific campaign to get Nemanoff back in command and had been writing articles about Di Vincenti's inferiority, both artistic and physical. It is true that he was a little on the heavy side, especially in the rear end, and, as if for contrast, Dalenova was painfully thin. Articles written against the ballet were unpleasant enough, but when Dalenova grew convinced that I had something to do with it all and became my bitter enemy, and when the reporters who had interviewed me at the docks got their evening editions out, the situation was tense.

I have kept all these articles, and every paper without exception had my pictures, some with head-lines saying, "*La Davis he llegada por fin.*" ("At last Davis has arrived.") The *Ultima Hora,* a newspaper edited by the brilliant writer, Julio Escobar, whose criticisms were always irrefutable, had attacked the Colón Commission, and Mr. Grassi in particular, about what they termed the "disaster of the Colón ballet." They printed at the same time a large picture of me, under which was written: "The arrival of Esmé Davis will, we hope, do much to help the coming season, and we are thankful that the management has contrived to get her here—as the only possible solution to the present unfortunate state of affairs." It went on to give a long account of the work I had done with Nemanoff in previous temporadas, and ended by openly naming Galanta and Chableska as having telephoned the newspapers to inform them I was not appearing with the ballet that year. Neither of these girls had been reëngaged for the Colón season, so I could not see that it possibly mattered to them whether I danced there or not. "But," Escobar had added in his article, he supposed "they could not forgive any dancer whose qualities were such that she could afford to line her ballet shoes with hundred dollar bills."

Many of these articles had appeared in print while I was aboard ship, were dated the sixth of June, and were based on a cable *La Nación* had sent from Paris denying the first report that I was with Diaghilev, and announcing that I had sailed for Argentina. This of course was proof that I had not been instrumental in getting these notices printed. However, the consternation they caused in the small world of the Colón was monumental. Di Vincenti pouted and sulked, and Madame Dalenova grew thinner and thinner as the days went by.

With the arrival of Matto, the question of the parrots was cleared up. He told me that when he received my cable about the orchids, his mother was so disappointed that he had promised her she could plant parrots around the swimming-pool instead. In addition to this, he said he would buy her a camel to ride about the grounds on. I should explain that Matto's mama, although a sweet and charming old lady, was inclined to be a little eccentric and had gone for the idea of the parrots and the camel hook, line, and sinker. The next thing to do was to find a camel, for she insisted like a spoiled child that one must be produced immediately.

Fortunately, we were able to buy one from the great German circus financed by Hugo Stinnes. They had arrived in boats belonging to the Hugo Stinnes Lines and were to appear shortly in Buenos Aires. As soon as they pitched their canvas, I rushed there and of course found many of my old friends working with the show, which was a mammoth spectacle in the Hagenbeck style, with some of the finest acts of Europe. The entire show had been sent to Buenos Aires for publicity purposes and must have been working at a loss, for they gave endless charity performances, free shows for children, and other good-will attractions. Matto bought not only the camel but also a lion from a trainer friend of mine. This led to another saga of misfortunes which I fortunately was not mixed up in.

Both animals were sent to the estancia, where the lion broke out of its cage one night, roamed the countryside, killing valuable livestock, and terrorized the farmers for miles around. Matto's father was furious about it and, according to reports, not too pleased about the camel, which the Señora de Erazuriz adored and wanted to keep in the Renaissance entrance hall of their country house.

In the meantime, Richard Strauss had arrived at the Colón for the production of *Salomé*. The other two directors were

232

Gino Marinuzzi and Hector Panizza, both hard-working young maestros who gave us plenty of tiring work-outs, but with the arrival of Strauss, anything they might have thought up in the way of long rehearsals was insignificant by comparison.

Di Vincenti was incapable of handling all the choreography alone, and everything he did was complicated by the interference of Madame Dalenova. To settle the arguments, I advised some of the harassed Commission to engage Stanislas Statkeweick as assistant choreograph. This they did just in time. He was the husband of one of the girls and a good all-round dancer and mimic, but he had a most extraordinary habit of introducing his young wife to people with the words, "Permit me to present my wife, Madame Statkeweick—she's a virgin!" When they joined the company, the English girls made life miserable for the wife by asking her every time she came to rehearsals if she was still a virgin.

Strauss had a habit of rehearsing at night after the show, and sometimes we did not leave the theater until three or four in the morning. On these occasions he always ordered coffee and sandwiches for the entire company, orchestra, and stage-hands. During one of these long sessions I had drawn a silly caricature of a rehearsal with the corps de ballet, depicting Dalenova massaging her ankle after having received a kick in the shins from Di Vincenti, whom I drew light-heartedly gamboling by himself in the middle of the stage. Statkeweick had his arm in a sling (having recently sprained his wrist lifting one of Mr. Grassi's protégées, aptly named Miss del Grande—she weighed 180 pounds), and he appeared in the front of the picture conducting operations, while a group of machinists and stage help looked on in bewilderment.

I did this for the amusement of Mollie and the English girls and had left it in a corner of my dressing-room. Some of the reporters I knew dropped in after rehearsals to see if there was anything new on the date of production. Unfortunately, they saw this caricature lying on top of some music and grabbed it, passing it from hand to hand. They could easily recognize the characters depicted and laughed their

233

heads off. They begged me to let them have it for publication, which I firmly refused to do, principally because I did not want to hurt Di Vincenti's feelings. One of them must have stolen it when they left, for the next day I could not find the sketch and did not know which of them might have taken it.

Upon arrival at the theater that evening, one of the stage managers showed me a copy of the evening paper *La Critica*. There in the middle of the theater news was my caricature. A short article beneath it described Di Vincenti first and in referring to him said, "In the country of the blind, the one-eyed man is king." Then it mentioned Miss Dalenova's kick in the shins and went on to comment on Statkeweick's arm being in a sling—presumably because he had worn it out trying to make the dancers keep time to the music. The last line said, "A group of stagehands are laughing in the corner, just as the public has done on a certain night, recalling the dancing of Nijinsky, Karsavina, and others on the Colón stage." The stage manager's face as he watched me read it was that of a man overwhelmed by a national catastrophe, and I could see in his eyes a growing suspicion as he asked me who I thought could possibly have perpetrated such an outrage.

I saw nothing of my colleagues until I went on stage to dance with Di Vincenti, who did not utter one word but looked at me all during the dance with the heart-rending expression of a wounded deer. He danced tensely, and his hands were damp like dead fish. Before I left the theater that night I was notified that my presence was required in the office of the Commission at once.

As soon as I entered the sanctum sanctorum of the Arts Commission, I saw from the expression on the face of Mr. Grassi and three other men that they knew who was the author of the sketch. When they asked me this question, I replied in the affirmative, giving them the brief story of how it came to be published, and requesting them to be kind enough to 'phone the editors of the newspapers concerned and check my story. This they agreed to do by letter, but said that, in the meantime, they had been unable to dig up any adequate punishment from the archives of the Colón which dealt with a similar misdemeanor. They did not think it would be correct to fine me, but instead they were not going to allow me the coveted opportunity to dance the "Seven Veils" in *Salomé*.

I said nothing to all this because I had already rehearsed it and felt that Maestro Richard Strauss might have something to say about their putting in another dancer at the last minute —especially since he had noted that Genevieve Vix and I were of the same height and somewhat alike. This was a very important detail, because in the opera the scene where the dance takes place was purposely built to permit the dancer at the end of her dance to slip behind an ornamental column, and the singer dressed in exactly the same costume, to glide from behind it in an almost simultaneous movement, thereby giving the illusion of their being one and the same person. Few singers can dance, or care to risk the possibility of coming on to the stage puffing and blowing to gasp out the opening notes of their ensuing recitative, although some have done it.

I knew, of course, that Dalenova had gone to the Commission with her friend the director and made a scene about having been ridiculed. In order to pacify her, Mr. Grassi (who owed her a good turn for her friendship with his protégées) had suggested they give her the dance in *Salomé,* for which she had been pining ever since the production started. I did not, of course, show up the following night for rehearsals, and Genevieve Vix looked everywhere for me. When the time came for Dalenova to make her appearance, the girls told me she was at least three inches shorter than La Vix and looked like a living skeleton by the side of her.

The maestro noticed it and stopped the rehearsal, demanding with much heat to know what the so-and-so had been going on, that a dancer should be changed without consulting him, thus holding up more important things. The next morning I received a notice by messenger, informing me that rehearsals for *Salomé* were to be resumed as before. I had been put back in the "Dance of the Seven Veils."

235

To say I was bored with the Colón ballet was putting it mildly, and when it was definitely decided they were not playing Rio that year, I started Nemanoff rehearsing on the revised and improved edition of the Chauve-Souris. I obtained an excellent offer from the Grande Splendide Music-Hall for three months, with the stage at my disposal for all rehearsals. This large theater gives movies and vaudeville in the style of New York's Radio City Music Hall, and it had a magnificent orchestra under the direction of the two brilliant Bolognini brothers, now playing in the N.B.C. Symphony of New York.

The owner of the theater, Don Max Glucksmann, was a sort of Argentine Billy Rose, who, from a modest employee in a company selling optical lenses and photographic equipment, had become one of the wealthiest men in Buenos Aires. With the assistance of his father-in-law, a quaint old Polish gentleman, he had become the owner of the company where he had been originally employed. He was a marvelous man to work for and gave me *carte blanche* to do whatever I liked in his theater. He was always present at the rehearsals and watched everything that went on. His father-in-law, Mr. Lerman, was kindly, too, but very old and getting to be what the French describe as "ga-ga."

A company headed by Mistinguette was playing at the Cervantes, which was now under new management, for the Mendozas had lost a lot of money with the theater and had been obliged to give it up. It seemed to be an unlucky house for everybody except myself who played there, for company after company went broke in it. Mistinguette was having a good success, principally on account of the beautiful girls she had brought with her, but nobody was unaware that if she lost them, the only thing for her to do would be to go back to Paris at once.

Papa Lerman spent every evening dozing in the stalls of the Cervantes and most of his waking hours taking the prettiest showgirls out to lunch and cocktails. He would then talk them into working at the Grande Splendide at a much higher salary and bring them over to see me. Gradually all of them

I could possibly use gravitated into the company—the rest found havens in duplex apartments with Packard automobiles at the doors—and life rolled merrily on!

Finally, Mistinguette left for Rio with the remnants of her troupe, and within a month those artists the Brazilians had not kept for themselves returned to Buenos Aires, heading directly for the Grande Splendide. This included a jazz band composed of eleven Negroes under a man who described himself as "Gordon Stretton, the Prince of Wales's Own." I had little or no use for an eleven-piece jazz band; nevertheless, Don Max thought they would be an extra attraction for the lounge and cocktail bar, and so they too were engaged.

Among the fair ladies that old Papa Lerman kept dragging in was a little Russian girl called Abramova, who said she was a "danseuse-chanteuse"—whatever that might be. He seemed quite keen on her entering the show, so I asked for an audition. She was, incidentally, the protégée of one of the wealthiest bachelors in Buenos Aires. If possible, I wanted to please everybody and thought I would stick her in a corner somewhere, but when I saw what she could do, and heard the unearthly wailing she let out while wriggling her body about to the music of Rimsky-Korsakov's "Song of India," I firmly said, "No!"

She then waylaid Nemanoff and offered to pay us one hundred pesos a day if I would let her do just one number. I thought of mother's apartment in Paris, and of all the money I needed for it, and told Richard we could split if he was willing. He agreed, so we engaged her. She paid for all her own advertising and plastered the city of Buenos Aires with posters announcing that the "Soul That Sings" was appearing at the Grande Splendide Theater.

The night she opened was what is called a "Noche de Moda," when all the débutantes sit in their boxes, flirt with their boy-friends and talk at the top of their voices. Evidently the gossips had been busy about the romance between Abramova and her wealthy protector, for the house was agog, and reporters besieged my dressing-room to get the dope on

237

her for their scandal columns. She had arrived in the theater about three in the afternoon and shut herself in the dressing-room with her maid. We wondered what she was doing all day, and when I returned to the theater about eight o'clock to dress for the evening show, the odor of banana oil that came from her dressing-room almost knocked me over. I sent Evar Mendez to find out what was going on, and if she was all set for her début.

He returned very flustered and told me that she had spent all day painting herself from head to foot with gold paint, using ordinary varnish made for gilding furniture. I nearly fainted, for when we used gold paint (which I often did in such ballets as *Sakuntala* and in Oriental operas) we applied the gold powder with oil, which makes it harmless to the skin and easy to remove afterward. There was no time to do anything about Abramova, and as she worked fairly early in the program, I went up to the side of the stage as soon as I could to catch her number.

She opened sitting on a gold throne made of wood, an enormous heavy contraption that I had borrowed from the Colón. The curtain went up, and she was there all right, but practically all she had on was the paint! I heard a distinct titter from the audience, who definitely did not like nudity. The tittering increased and began to worry me, when I beheld Abramova making desperate attempts to get on her feet and leave the throne (in order to come down stage to continue her wiggling and wailing), but to my horror, I realized she couldn't. She was firmly glued to the seat of the throne by the varnish from the gold paint and the heat of her body.

The audience realized it, too; also Ennio Bolognini, who was playing her accompaniment with the orchestra. He was standing under a spotlight and was the first to run for cover when the storm broke. I have already described what an Argentine audience can do upon such occasions. This one went a step further and shot wax matches rolled in little balls that burst into flame on the stage, in addition to shrieking and

238

screaming until they sounded like the Indians at Custer's last stand.

Above the tumult, I yelled to the stage manager to press the button that lowered the curtain and ran to call the English girls to hurry on stage and do a tap number or anything else that occurred to them to quiet the public. The stage manager lowered the curtain and sent a crew to remove the throne bodily, with Abramova on it. While they were dragging the thing out, some dope at the side of the stage accidentally pressed the button again and the curtain rose, disclosing six stage-hands in shirt sleeves and overalls hauling the heavy throne across the stage.

Once they were in the wings, there was nothing to do but literally rip Miss Abramova off it, despite her screams, for both she and the throne were blocking exits and entrances and the show could not go on. It was frightful, and she must have found it impossible to sit down for several weeks afterward. I don't know whether this was so or not, for I never saw her again.

My plans were maturing very nicely for the apartment I dreamed of in Paris. Letters from mother, who was singing at the Real in Madrid, were most encouraging for the future, so I promptly forwarded them to father, who I knew would feel happy about my idea. I seldom heard from Leslie, but he was apparently deeply interested in his work in Egypt and in studying Arabic and the Swahili tongues.

Although my foot was practically well again, it got very tired at times. I needed a rest badly, and I should have gone to the country alone for my one free week instead of staying in town, for the following seven days were filled with action and not relaxation. Jaime de Zulueta had arrived from Paris and chosen that particular time to open his display of antiques at the Plaza Hotel after traveling through Argentina since his arrival, selling "gems" from his collection. Every time he planted one of his best fakes for a good price, he sent me a telegram with full details and signed it "Mariposa" (Butterfly). This descriptive pseudonym was coined from

239

Benavente's play, *El Mariposa que volo sobre el Mar* (*The Butterfly That Flew over the Sea*).

All that remained from Zulueta's original collection was placed in an empty suite at the Plaza and invitations sent to likely candidates to come and see it. Within three days, there was nothing left except the carpet, which belonged to the hotel.

On the last evening of the exhibit, I had dropped into the Plaza with some friends of mine for a cocktail in Zulueta's apartment. We found him engaged in counting up the proceeds from his three-day sales. It was about seven in the evening when a lady arrived who said she had come all the way from Cordoba to visit the exhibition and had been delayed in getting there. She was a fussy little provincial person with a well-lined purse, from the looks of her, and was very disconsolate upon learning that everything had already been purchased. "But I must have something," she wailed. And when Zulueta repeated that there was nothing left but the carpet, she brightened up and asked the price of that, evidently believing that it was part of the original collection and probably a priceless Aubusson.

Like a flash, Jaime de Zulueta took her up on the idea and said, "Well, Señora, this carpet is a rare piece which I had reserved for myself and intended taking back to Paris—but, since you are so charming and have come all the way from Cordoba, I feel I should sell it to you. . . . If you will excuse me for a second, I will look up in my books exactly the price I paid for it." With that, he left the room, hurried downstairs to Gabuzzi's office, and asked him the price of the very ordinary and faded imitation Axminster. Gabuzzi, rather surprised at being asked the value of it and what he would take for it, gave at random the figure of four hundred pesos. Zulueta paid him immediately, rushed back to the lady and sold her the carpet for two thousand pesos. The parties he gave with the proceeds of the sale were almost imperial in their splendor.

That same week, I had an engagement to dine with Jimmy Petter, an old friend of mine, on the occasion of the Dempsey-

Firpo fight taking place in New York. After dinner, we went to the Richmond Bar in the Calle Florida, the fashionable thoroughfare of Buenos Aires, to hear the description of the match being announced through a primitive loud-speaker. When we arrived the place was jammed, and feeling appeared to be running high between Americans and Argentines, who, at tables and the bar, were loudly applauding the progress of the combatants. The bets on both fighters were enormous, and I knew that Jimmy had plunged heavily on Jack Dempsey.

Everybody in the place knew me by sight and that I was an American, for the papers frequently referred to me as the "Americanita." People were watching our table with ill-concealed dislike whenever Dempsey slugged Firpo, to see if we made any demonstrations. Jimmy had cautioned me to be calm and give no sign of enthusiasm for either fighter. Argentines are not only highly excitable on such occasions but inclined to be unsporting if the luck goes against their countryman.

I momentarily forgot Jimmy's prudent warning, and when Mr. Dempsey planted a "left hook to the jaw," or some such telling blow, I must have cheered wildly, because the next instant a glass whizzed past my face, thrown from a table of a young man near-by. Then everything became a kaleidoscopic hurricane of flying arms and legs, screaming women, broken glasses, and smashed chairs—while the result of the Firpo-Dempsey combat was lost in the commotion. The battling public practically wrecked the Richmond Bar, and I could not find a trace of Jimmy till the police arrived, and I saw them drag him off a man. The boy who had thrown the glass at me was lying very still on the floor. When they picked him up he was dead.

I could not get near Jimmy, for the police were pushing everybody out of the bar and hustling him with some witnesses into a Black Maria while ambulances screamed madly down the block. I went home and 'phoned Dr. Fitzsimon at once. He went down to the precinct and telephoned me later that Jimmy was held for manslaughter, incommunicado. For several days I felt most upset, for it was partly my fault, but knowing

Jimmy I could not have expected him to do anything but hit the man who had thrown the glass at me.

This boy's death, it developed, had not been caused directly by the blow, but by a heart condition. He was not supposed to be out of bed that night, having been under a doctor's care for some months. This circumstance eventually saved Jimmy. The boy's father behaved very well, and the affair finally blew over after a lot of unpleasant weeks in the courts.

The Mar del Plata Club, where we had a month's engagement, was as elegant as ever, and my show was a triumph in spite of the fact that we were working to practically the same public that had seen us at the Grande Splendide. In order to vary the program a little, I conceived a tableau which I shall always wonder how I had the audacity to present before the prudish audience of the Odeón, where we played after the Club. Vladi Jakobleff, who had worked with Balieff's company in Paris, was stage manager, and I exchanged several ideas with him. He was clever but had a weakness for numbers with white doves, blue hydrangeas, and soft music. We had given a good many of these, so I wanted something of a more whimsical character in the section of the program that was given entirely in French. In a moment of fantasy, I had designed a comic ballet called the *Ballet du Pissoire*. This, I should explain, is not translatable, and deals with the public urinals for men which are a landmark of the Parisian boulevards. They are odd-looking affairs with iron screens having an "In" and "Out" arrangement at the ends, and generally decorated with posters advertising toothpaste, liver pills, and the latest revue at the Moulin Rouge. Only the feet and ankles of the occupants are visible from the street, and they are, at times, very full of character.

My ballet showed these feet dancing as the curtain rose, and a typical Parisian "flick" (cop) made his appearance. The dance that followed between the cop and the six pairs of feet in the *pissoire* was so funny, it brought screams of delight from members of the audience who were familiar with Paris and its street scenes. This ballet not only brought me a contract from Don Max for the month of February, but its fame preceded me to Paris, and I later did it for the *Revue de Rip* at the Théâtre de l'Avenue.

I began to feel a little disgusted with the type of show I had been doing for the past eight months—it had been "pot-boiling," and I knew it and now wanted to work at something for

my own satisfaction. The very fact that I suffered pain every day while trying to hang from my weak shoulder was an incentive to me, and I knew that if I could get the better of it, I would do something worth while.

I think everybody who has ever visited France has felt the thrill of arriving on French soil and the anticipation of seeing Paris, however he may have traveled to reach it—but the real emotion comes when one arrives by boat after a long sea voyage. This day of late March, liners were disgorging their passengers from all over the world, for the 1924 Exhibition of Decorative Arts was being held in Paris. The tourists stepped ashore with eager faces. To most of them, Paris was a city of pleasure—a city of smiles. But to me, Paris meant home, a *foyer*. I had always had that feeling of coming home, ever since my earliest childhood, and the smile Paris had for me that day was filled with the glow of the fireside and the warmth of an old friendship. God willing, Paris will always smile, even through her tears.

I know of no place on earth where one can meet more acquaintances than in the *wagon* restaurant on the boat-train from Cherbourg. Friends from the ends of the earth meet again, sitting down to eat for the first time, perhaps, in many years, the unequaled French bread, the green almonds, eternal symbol of the French bill of fare, and the Normandy butter. Even the gloomy Gare du Nord was bubbling with laughter and gaiety the day I arrived, and the taciturn blue-bloused porters, with their odor of sweat, garlic, and vin ordinaire, were aglow with anticipation of the unprecedented influx of tourists and tips.

After two days in Paris I left for Jersey. My brother had taken a house in St. Clements at the far end of the island, and mother was visiting him. It was a beautiful place overlooking the cliffs and had been part of an old Elizabethan monastery. It had a study with French windows that opened on to a garden where he could sit all day in the sun and hear the sound of the sea on the rocks below. He had his books, piano, and all his Braille equipment for writing, and knew by the feeling of the room just where everything was. However, both he and mother were not well and had decided to go to Vienna, where there was a specialist for Bunnie that the doctor in Jersey had recommended.

I had a serious talk with mother about the question of the apartment and explained to her how I proposed to rent and keep it up—provided she would live there with me and share expenses, we could manage very nicely. She agreed to everything I suggested, and so, after ten days, I returned to Paris to find a suitable place.

For two weeks, I hunted for apartments. Nina was in London about her book, *Laughing Torso,* which had long been heralded as a sensational success and due to cause a considerable stir in the world of Art and Bohemia. Olga was in Salz-

244

burg studying stage decoration at the new Max Reinhardt School, which was drawing students from all parts of Europe. So there was nobody I knew who might be able to give me suggestions about an apartment.

In the end I seemed to have searched the entire city in the company of an impressive personage from "l'Agence d'Immeubles," with a silky black beard, a brief-case, and an umbrella. He bore a striking resemblance to the man on the advertisement for the "Dragées d'Hercules" in the Métros.

At last I found what I wanted in a *rez-de-chaussée* on the Avenue du Bois de Boulogne, now called the Avenue de Maréchal Foch, a stone's throw from the Bois and the Port-Dauphin. It was a large apartment opening on its own tiny garden with a gate leading into the street behind, and next to a garage. The garden had a laburnum tree and lilacs just in bud—the whole place was ideal. There was a delightful round room for mother and her piano, with another enormous salon for my own work, bedrooms, bathrooms, a big kitchen, storerooms, maid's room, and at the top of the building, a chauffeur's room with a private elevator from the apartment.

The day I visited it the rooms on the garden side were filled with sunlight, and big fat thrushes hopped about and squabbled with troupes of sparrows. It was perfect—all except the rent, which was far more than I had planned to pay. I interviewed the agents and made an offer of a five-year lease on the condition that they redecorated the whole place for me and made a few alterations.

Mother wrote from Vienna that the place sounded wonderful in every respect, and she would be looking forward to living there. I immediately signed the lease and started looking for furniture, little by little. This is a delightful occupation anywhere but particularly in Paris. I did not want to buy anything in a hurry but intended picking up objects I would want to keep. Studying the periods and character of furniture had always fascinated me, and I was thoroughly enjoying myself; when, without warning, came a letter from my brother that worried me very much.

245

He begged me to come at once to Austria, for he had received some disturbing news about mother's health from the doctor. In spite of this, she insisted on running about with some operatic people who were trying to promote a company of Swedish operas. It was, Bunnie wrote, the worst possible thing that could happen for mother to get herself mixed up with musical maniacs again.

I left for Salzburg at once and found mother at the Schweitzerhof Hotel, surrounded by a group of actors, singers, and musical phenomena. Salzburg was filled with all sorts of artists for the Festspiel spectacles, and mother was in her element. She was looking well, but I knew my brother would not have put me to the expense of going to Austria for nothing.

When I spoke to her about her health, contrary to other occasions when she had complained so bitterly about it, she would not discuss it or give me any idea of what the doctor had told her. I saw clearly that she suspected me of having come to Salzburg for the express purpose of preventing her from getting involved with any more engagements that might require traveling. I told her plainly that I expected her to take life quietly and live in the apartment I had worked so hard to acquire, where she could have proper rest and comfort and sing in concert or at the Opéra Comique—work that I felt would not harm her health. I even promised to recite in her concerts as we had done before, which was something I hated doing. This prospect seemed to please her.

She had spent all her time with a collection of freaks such as only she could have dug up. This group included a cadaverous-looking man with a monocle in one eye (the other one stared balefully at the world and was an opaque object like something fished up out of a well) : he was the moving spirit behind the Swedish opera. There was also a kittenish blonde woman who weighed about two hundred pounds, and who, according to mother, had knocked everybody cold with her rendition of Wagner in her native Sweden. Then there was the wife of a Swedish writer we had met at the famous "Cave of the Golden Calf" some years before in London; Benkt

246

Berenth, designer of some of the sets for the opera project, intense but very talented; and the sister of Paul Klingamen, a teacher of piano with knuckle-rapping propensities whom I had studied under in Düsseldorf. These, together with the inevitable "angel" in the person of a fat man who had made millions in potted fish and was in love with the Wagnerian Warbler, were the formidable contingent I had to deal with and, if possible, manage to keep as far away from mother as possible. They spent hours and hours talking about the revolution they were going to make with their operas in the United States. Mother listened to it all with such rapt attention that it gave me a cold feeling in the pit of my stomach.

The "merry month of May" dragged slowly to a close—and still no let-up in the whirl of artistic activities mother had planned. It was not until the fourth of June that I finally managed to get her started for Paris.

In the meantime, I had received a letter from Pepita. She was in Paris and broke, having got herself into a series of difficulties. She had been working at the Coliseum in London with the Diaghilev company but did not tell me how she came to be without a job. When we arrived in Paris, there she was—installed at our hotel without a cent, owing two weeks' rent, a bill at the hairdresser's, and cash drawn from the hotel desk on mother's credit.

She gave a long account of her troubles—none of which sounded true, and related that she had become entangled with a married man who had divorced his wife to marry her, and now the wife was hunting all over London for her with a revolver, so she had fled to Paris. This I was forced to believe because a couple of mornings after we arrived, and the day I intended to move myself to the apartment, a telephone call came through from a frantic female who threatened all sorts of violence to Pepita. I choked her off on the wire by saying that Pepita had left for Spain and that she had better pursue her search in the Albaïcin in Seville. I did not want mother upset by any such nonsensical scandal, so took Pepita with me to the half-empty apartment and made her understand that for once in her lazy young life she was going to earn her board bill and help me get the place finished so that mother could move in at the end of the week. This we did successfully, and the apartment looked lovely. I filled every corner with mother's favorite flowers—lilies of the valley and bowls of big pink roses. Then I went flying to the hotel to fetch her.

Everything was packed when I got there, and Marie was just closing her trunks—but not to come to the Avenue du Bois! Mother was leaving for London on the two o'clock plane from Le Bourget, to commence rehearsals with the Swedish Opera—for before leaving Salzburg she had signed a contract with them to tour the United States. The reasons she gave me were, primarily, that the salary in American dollars was far ahead of anything she could get from the Opéra Comique, and the fact that my brother had not sufficient funds to remain in Vienna for treatment which he badly needed had worried her to distraction. Second, the doctors had told her he might need an operation if he did not respond to their treatments, and this expense was out of the question for my father to afford at the moment. She talked hurriedly and nervously as she dressed, and I think she felt sorry for me but did not fully realize the situation she was leaving me in— with the enormous apartment and rental on my hands. I had bought furniture, made a three-months' deposit on the place, and after a hundred and one other expenses were paid I would not have a great deal of money left.

I felt stunned. All I could do was sit and stare at her. As if in a dream, I heard her say she was leaving her maid Marie to me for the apartment, since she was far too old to travel on the long tour. This was some legacy! Mother explained she had not told me anything about her change of plans while we were in Austria, for she was afraid I would tell Bunnie about it, and he would be angry with her. I knew her so well, and her habit of planning things on impulse. I also knew that she was capable of any sacrifice for his sake, and later I realized that she had been torn between letting me down and what she felt to be her duty to my brother, who unquestionably came first, and that she would far rather have settled in Paris and taken care of her own health. I knew she was very unhappy and noticed the big dark circles under her eyes as I helped her into the bus for the airport.

XIV

I WALKED SLOWLY back to the Avenue du Bois, trying to formulate plans. There was no clause in the lease I had signed permitting me to sublet, and anyway it was not completely furnished as yet, so that possibility was out of the question. But mother's room was finished, as well as her music room, so I decided to try and find a friend who might rent it, to keep expenses down while I was arranging to go back to work as soon as possible.

What I had seen in Paris since my arrival from Argentina was the great vogue for American acrobatic dancers. Nina Payne was having a big success; also the Ford sisters, Marion and Ethel, and the Hoffman girls were the sensation of Europe. I had not expected to be pitchforked into work before I had time to look around and build something new for myself, but now I had no time to lose and commenced practising at the studio of Staats of the opera.

I had a letter from the dancer Marcel Idzikowski, recommending that I get in touch with the agents Howell and Baud on the Rue de la Paix. They were reputed to be the best agents in Paris at the moment, taking only acts that they were satisfied could keep working steadily and that were up to their standards. I found them to be an interesting study in contrasts. Howell was a little English cockney who looked like a jockey, and Monsieur Georges Baud was a replica of the miniatures of the Cardinal de Rohan in the Hôtel de Sèvres. I have never seen such dignity and old-world courtesy: I very nearly expected him to whip out a lace handkerchief and take a pinch of snuff as we talked. Almost apologetically he asked for an audition, and after seeing me work, offered to procure my engagements if I would build some dances in the acrobatic style so much sought after at the moment.

A few nights after this, I went with a friend from Buenos Aires to the Grand Duc Cabaret on Montmartre, where Bricktop, the famous colored singer, entertained. Who should walk through the door, after we had been there half an hour, but Nina. I was so glad to see her, I could have cried with joy, for I had nobody in Paris to whom I could talk about my difficulties and worries. Her calm, level-headed summing-up of the situation helped me a lot. She told me the first thing to do was get around and meet the right people in Paris.

A day or so later, she took me to lunch on the *Péniche,* Paul Poiret's houseboat restaurant which was anchored in the Seine during the Exhibition of Decorative Arts recently inaugurated. Nina was very anxious that I be as charming as possible to Poiret, who was not only at the height of his popularity as the most famous designer of women's clothes in Paris, but had a great deal to do with the clubs, theaters, and restaurants, and was always happy to help in the launching of an artist if he thought she had talent. The houseboat was a very small one, with a dining-room so crowded there was hardly room to move. It was filled with smart Parisians, mostly women.

Poiret, when Nina introduced him, remembered me from the party he had given for Diaghilev the previous year and very kindly told me he would be only too glad to engage me if I thought there was sufficient space anywhere on deck where I could dance, but I saw at once it was not possible. Nina knew everybody and introduced me to lots of her friends.

I had left the house rather hurriedly that morning and in my anxiety not to be late for lunch had forgotten that in the pocket of a green linen suit I was wearing, I had left a little grass snake belonging to Pepita, which she invariably forgot to feed. In the middle of the lunch he crawled from my pocket and wriggled up the front of my coat. A waiter, bending over me in the act of serving some salad, saw him, let out a yell, dropped the bowl and its contents partly on me and partly on the table with a loud clatter. It frightened the

251

snake so much that he dived for the safety of my pocket but somehow missed and fell to the floor.

Chaos followed. Women screamed and jumped on chairs, while Nina and I crawled under the table but could not find the snake. I saw that Poiret, although the incident tickled him at first, was becoming a little peevish as Nina and I continued to search the place frantically—but, no snake! The party was disrupted, for nobody would sit down again until the snake was found. Most of the guests insisted upon having their desserts and coffee on the deck, but this didn't work out so well because it started to rain.

When the dining-room was empty, Poiret asked me rather stiffly to be good enough to find my snake before the cocktail hour. I feared I had made an enemy of him and regretted the incident for Nina's sake, but fortunately I was mistaken, for afterward we became good friends and he was very kind to me. We never found the snake, although I promised a reward to the waiters who caught him. I can not think what happened to the poor little fellow, unless he went down some hole or grating and got into the river.

I followed Mr. Baud's advice, arranged some acrobatic numbers and perfected the rope act on which I had worked tenaciously during the Colón season. With constant practice my troublesome shoulder was steadily improving, and I hoped in time to try trapeze again.

I obtained an engagement of two weeks at the Ambassador Theater Restaurant in the Avenue Montaigne, then under the management of Oscar Dufresne and Henri Varna of the Palace, Empire, and Mayol theaters. This house was attached to the restaurant of the same name and consisted of a stage built in the gardens facing the loges and terraces of the restaurant, from which the diners could witness the spectacle. There was a sort of vaudeville revue in the style of the old café chantant, which changed programs every two weeks.

On the opening night I was extremely nervous, for it was my first attempt at an aërial act since my fall in the Olympia. I had gone to considerable expense about costumes, designed

252

by the great artist, Max Weldy, and had plunged above my ears in the purchase of a lavender-blue presentation cape of ostrich feathers. The costume I wore below it was practically nothing but a brassière and abbreviated trunks made of rhinestones that glittered in the spotlight. I had another one of the same style in rose, for a fast tumbling number I used in the closing tableau. The thought of all I had paid for the launching of my act, and the mess I would be in if it flopped, was partly responsible for the nerves I suffered that first night.

Finishing my rope act I was so exhausted I could hardly hear the applause or keep track of the calls I took, and did not fully realize I had made good until Georges Baud, who was in the audience, came to my dressing-room to congratulate me. *"Mon enfant,"* he said, "I am very pleased with you. After to-night, you will never have to look back." Two days later he called me to his office to sign a contract with the big German Circus Busche playing a three-month route through Budapest, Vienna, Munich, Zurich, Frankfurt, Breslau, Hamburg, and Stockholm. It was at an excellent salary, with all expenses paid, and had in addition the unquestionable advantage of a unique opportunity for me to continue building my aërial work—for, on the advice of Baud, this was the line I would follow. He told me how difficult it was to find an artist with ability and training to do difficult acrobatic feats and combine them with the polish and finesse of a ballet dancer.

Apparently, the elegance of Max Weldy's costumes had done much to impress the directors of the Circus Busche, and loosened their purse-strings. The only thing I regretted, now my financial worries were at an end for a while, was leaving the apartment I had worked so hard to obtain and had so little time to enjoy. I had found nobody to share it with me and decided to leave Marie there with Pepita while I was on tour.

The Circus Busche was like all other great European circuses: crowds of Czechoslovakian ring personnel, perfect management of stock, horse acts of every description, and marvelous aërial performers. Their featured act was a sort of Tarzan sketch, in which a man with extraordinary acrobatic ability and strength, dressed as a gorilla, leaped from rope to rope at the highest point of the tent, tossing a young blonde girl about in mid-air. There was also the Sarrassani troupe of twenty-one elephants, as well as several good animal acts I knew from my old circus days. These elephants, some of which were males (seldom used for the circus ring), gave at the end of their act the Royal Salute used for the Viceroys of India. They reared on their hind legs in a circle and trumpeted, while their trainer, Sarrassani, a tall, splendid specimen of a man dressed as a Rajah with glittering jewels, stood in the center.

In Hamburg, we were playing on a ground near the Alster Park. On the last night of the show an electric storm came up about seven-thirty in the evening. For several days, the bull-men (elephants are called bulls in circus jargon) had been obliged to keep chains on some of the elephants that had been trumpeting and swaying from side to side—the unfailing signs of a restless complex and probable trouble. There was an old man, white-haired and bent, who trained nearly all of them and was said to be a wizard with elephants. He spent his entire time going from one to another of the nervous beasts that evening, and when their act came on, he stood in the entrance watching them.

The immense tent, seating about sixteen hundred people, was packed, and out in the animal trailers, the other acts were hastily boarding up their cages prior to moving on that night by special boat to Sweden. Every animal in the show seemed to have the jitters, and their roaring and howling was plainly audible to the audience. The elephant number closed the first part of the show. I had already worked and was nearly dressed when the storm reached the peak of its fury. Above the thunder and wind, I could hear shouting and people running—then women rushed into the dressing-tent screaming that the elephants had stampeded and were trampling the public to death in the jammed main exit.

254

Outside our tent, there was a mad scene of confusion. Stock hands and performers were trying to quiet the frightened animals, while riggers and barrier men fell over each other in the panic. It appeared that at the end of Sarrassani's act, two of the biggest male elephants had started trumpeting and balking—he could not get them into position. Men with bull hooks closed in to try and get them started through the exit, when quite suddenly an enormous bull wheeled, and as if on a given signal, the entire troupe followed him straight across the ring, squealing and jostling each other over stalls and boxes, in a blind rush for the main exit. There they headed through a line of taxis, turning them over with their trunks, and on over everything that got in their way. The panic that ensued was responsible for more deaths and injuries than the elephants themselves caused. Many women and children were hurt, and circus men and police were out all that night and part of the next day rounding up the bulls. After the worst of the panic had subsided, I got back to the Esplanade Hotel with some of the other acts living there, and we left the following night for Sweden. The directors of the circus and Sarrassani were detained a week in Hamburg because of this occurrence, but finally joined us.

All the performers were broken up over the news that the little old trainer had been trampled to death while hanging on to an enormous female elephant called Lottie. She had always obeyed him, and he evidently had hoped through her to get the herd turned—but she had been blind and deaf to his voice and held on her course till he lost his grip on her and fell. The rest of the herd thundered over him.

After the circus tour I could expect peace for a while. I had been able to save some money to clear up debts, and Baud's bookings for me worked out well: a week at the Olympia which led to an engagement at the Empire, one of the hardest publics in Paris to work for. These music-hall dates caused an excellent impression and in turn led to a three-month contract in the Folies-Bergère Revue, at not much salary but with excellent publicity and only two matinées a week.

Mother wrote seldom but I knew from theatrical news that the Swedish opera, if not a complete flop, was giving a very good imitation of one throughout the United States. I was prepared for the worst, which eventually came to my house in the form of the fat blonde singer, who, together with her friend, the potted fish magnate, had fought with the rest of the company and returned to Paris in high dudgeon. What on earth the woman wanted with me, I never found out, but she arrived one Saturday evening between shows. I had returned to the apartment for a short rest before the evening performance, and sent word to her by Marie that I was dressing to go to work, begging her to excuse me and come back some other time. She was so insistent about saying "just two words," that I began to think she might have a message from mother and so let her in. Not having even the courtesy to wait till I received her in the salon, she barged straight into my bedroom and let loose a torrent of conversation about the company and her personal troubles.

When she had plumped her entire two hundred pounds down on the side of my bed with a crash that shook the room, I had not noticed that under the coverlet, beneath her mountain of flesh, was poor little Dandy. Suddenly I saw his black head and about a foot of him strike at her as he writhed beneath her weight. I screamed at her to get up, and as she rose, Dandy was hanging on the back of her black seal coat, hooked into the fur by his two front fangs. I tried to make her keep still, so I could get him off her, but the way she carried on when she discovered that a snake was hanging on her was really disgusting.

She screamed and yelled and threw herself about the room, smashing Dandy against the bedroom furniture—even trying to climb out of the window in her terror. Finally, I got him off her and could see his body was limp—that he could not coil. I took him into the bathroom, putting him on the smooth tile floor, where he dragged himself under the bathtub to his favorite hiding place, a little crack in the woodwork that he had found. There he lay for three days until he died. There was no way to get him out of there; besides, nothing could have been done for him, as his back was broken.

Shortly after this tragic happening, I went out to supper with my old friend Ireneo Sampallo from Rio, who was a great lover of animals and had all sorts of rare ones on his estancia in the country. I told him about Dandy and how sad it had made me, so he promised to cable his brother to send me another snake from their estate. He did not say when it would arrive or what type it would be, so I didn't think he really meant it.

A month later, I received a telephone call from the office of the Chef du Gare of the Gare du Nord, saying that there was a crate containing a live snake waiting for me on the platform and that I must be good enough to come immediately and remove it. I got a taxi whose chauffeur I knew—a nice Breton boy called Marcel, who owned a big closed cab and often drove me to the theater. Away we went to collect the snake—and we didn't have much trouble finding it, for there, in the middle of a group of excited jabbering porters and officials, was a large crate covered with labels and instructions about its fragile contents.

It is always useless to argue with French railway officials on any subject, and nobody who has ever had any experience with them would dream of trying it. On this particular occasion, the argument they put up was about the snake's having been loaded on the baggage-car by some agent from the ship by which it had arrived. This was a breach of all French railway rules; besides, the cage was broken on one side, and about two feet of torpid reptile were hanging out.

A representative of the express company, who refused to move the snake, was adding to the confusion by waving a sheaf of documents in my face and breathing heavily through his nose, which was red and had a drop on the end of it. It was December and bitterly cold, so all I wanted to do was get the poor snake into some kind of shelter before it froze to death—if it had not already done so. I could not see what the argument was about anyway, for all charges had been paid. Finally I persuaded one of the more daring spirits in the group of porters to help Marcel get the crate on a hand truck and out to the taxi.

The drive across Paris was a nightmare. The crate, too big to fit inside the car, had to be covered with a tarpaulin and lashed on to the roof of the cab where it kept sliding and shifting about. I was terrified for fear the snake had somehow or other come to life and was breaking his way out. We drove to the back entrance of the garden, for I knew the concierge would not be easy to deal with once he found out what the crate contained. He was already greatly perturbed by the knowledge that I had a monkey in the apartment, and disapproved highly.

Finally, we got everything safely into the house and into a still unfurnished spare room. Marcel, who by this time was as excited as I, helped me open the crate. We beheld one of the finest diamond-backed boa constrictors I have ever seen— a splendid specimen, measuring about five feet from tip to tail and far too big for an apartment. I had no instructions from Sampallo's brother about him and did not know if he had been fed on the voyage over. We decided to leave him in the warmth of the room to thaw out—he was completely torpid but breathing.

As soon as we brought the snake into the house, Kimmie, the monkey, set up a most unearthly screaming. I began to have grim forebodings about what would eventually happen if this continued. One of the principal clauses in my lease read that the apartment was intended for people to live *bourgeoisement,* and I felt certain that the presence of a five-foot snake was not at all customary in a bourgeois establishment. Of course, the proprietor had the right to insist that either I or the snake leave at once, but I had become so attached to the apartment, it would have been heartbreaking to lose it. Besides, mother had cabled that she would be with me for Christmas—so, somehow or other, the snake would

258

have to remain until I could make some disposition of him in case of trouble.

When I returned from the Folies that night, Marie was waiting up for me and drew my attention to the weird rummagings and slitherings coming from the room where we had put the snake. Evidently he had "come to"—so all was well. Or was it? I had left a supply of eggs and a pan of water for him, which was about all I could do until I managed to get some guinea-pigs or rabbits, or make some kind of arrangement for his feeding in the morning. Marie was frankly terrified of him, for he had a peculiar way of raising his head and looking at anybody who came into the room, then slowly starting to uncoil himself.

I named him Botafogo (a Brazilian name) and decided I could make a kind of cage for him in a large linen closet with a window high on the wall to let in sun and air. I got Marcel to help me fit in a wrought-iron gate I had bought to serve the double purpose of a door and a front to the closet, so that the snake could see and be seen. I was not taking any chances of going into the room to feed or clean him without knowing exactly where he was beforehand. I also smuggled in a large branch of a tree for him to climb on, and gave Marcel the unpleasant job of bringing mice and guinea-pigs from the country where he lived.

Four days before mother was expected, I had in a cable from my friend, Dr. Fitzsimon of Buenos Aires, the most welcome piece of news I had received in a long time. A suit I had instituted there against a third-rate revue company over its misleading use of my name had at last been settled in my favor, and the doctor was sending me thirty-seven hundred and fifty dollars. This gave me the opportunity I had long dreamed of: I would get a car for mother with a chauffeur like the ones the old ladies had that I used to see in London. I bought the car the next morning and sent Marcel out after license plates. I wanted to engage him, but he said he was making money with his own cab; however, he promised to get me a reliable chauffeur as soon as possible.

In the meantime, Pepita, who knew the car was to be a surprise for mother, turned up at the apartment with a tall and very distinguished-looking Russian she had met through friends. He was, he said, an ex-naval officer, and of course an émigré from the revolutionary days. His name was Doubrowsky, he had a few references, had always driven his own car, and was in possession of a Paris license along with a *carte d'identité,* so we went around to the garage and I took out the car to watch him drive.

He drove all right and had most charming manners, so I offered him a month's trial, for I felt somehow rather sorry for him. I could see he had been having a rough time and was obviously a gentleman. The people whom he had worked for at various times were well-to-do refugees, and all spoke highly of him.

The following morning, he brought the car around for me (I wanted to learn to drive myself), and tied to the wheel was a bunch of Parma violets—one of the most costly flowers obtainable in the wintertime. This annoyed me, for I knew the man was broke and had probably not had any dinner the previous night in order to buy those violets.

The next day Pepita and I met mother at the station with the car. She was so delighted, I could not but feel happy about buying it, for she was drawn, pale, and very nervous, wanted to go everywhere and do everything at once, and started her Christmas shopping that very afternoon. I knew the car would be a comfort to her, as she dreaded the cold and that was one of the most bitter winters France had seen in a long time.

My brother arrived on Christmas Eve, and mother was loud in her praise of how carefully Doubrowsky had driven the car and helped Bunnie from the train. In fact, he seemed to be a pearl among chauffeurs. I gave him an advance on his salary for the holidays and Christmas Day off.

On Christmas morning there arrived two enormous bunches of expensive Parma violets for mother and me. This was becoming an embarrassing habit with Doubrowsky which mother thought was a nuisance but rather sweet of him. That night when he called for me after the show, I noticed he had been drinking. Mother and I told him in no uncertain terms that such a habit must stop. He was effusive in his excuses and promises and said rather pathetically that he had not been so happy for a long time—that was why he had taken some drinks, and they had bowled him over.

All went well until New Year's Eve. Mother was going to a dinner in Neuilly and had arranged to call for me with the car at the theater for another party. I was ready at eleven o'clock, the hour mother was supposed to arrive—but she did not come. Twelve o'clock came, then twelve-fifteen. The show ended, and I was just getting ready to 'phone the house where she had been dining, when the police precinct near the Place d'Étoile called the theater asking for me. They said mother and Doubrowsky were at the precinct and that my car was entangled in the chains around the Unknown Soldier's grave under the Arc de Triomphe. Doubrowsky, I gathered, was drunk as a lord, but mother was unhurt.

I grabbed a taxi and rushed to the precinct. There I found mother in her sable coat and all her diamonds, warming her feet and drinking cognac gallantly supplied by the commissaire. The story I pieced together was that Doubrowsky had spent the day with some pal of his, a Grand Duke in exile, and had succumbed to the temptation to get loaded again. He had driven mother at a reckless speed to the dinner-party, where the host had insisted that he imbibe some more alcohol in the hall while waiting till mother was ready to leave.

Of course when they started for the center of town again, he lost all sense of direction until finally when they were half-way down one of the exterior boulevards mother prevailed upon him to slacken speed and turn the car on to the proper street. His next move was to collide with a fire-alarm box on the corner of an intersection: it started ringing and eventually brought five engines rushing to the spot. He then proceeded to fly through the streets until he arrived at the Place de l'Étoile. There he headed straight for the Arch, ignoring the chains around it about a foot from the ground. The car crashed into a post, fortunately without overturning, the fenders locked in the chains. Naturally, the crowd of police always patrolling the monument had immediately surrounded and arrested him. The *amende* for the misdemeanor was so terrific that there was no mention of it in the police manuals. Moreover, as the car was my property, the Commissaire explained, manifestly the fines were all my responsibility; also the cost of removing the car from a public monument.

Doubrowsky was, they said, unhurt, and if he did not develop delirium tremens in the course of the next forty-eight hours, he would be brought into court on a drunken driving charge the second of January. I called up an old attorney friend of father's and through him got the question of fines and charges wound up as moderately as possible.

The car was insured, but the whole thing was an expensive mess. I refused to see Doubrowsky again, and he wrote every week for three months, tendering excuses and promises of sobriety if I would have him back. When the car was patched up, I got a little friend of Marcel's to teach me to drive it myself after mother left.

She stayed about a month with me in Paris and told me all about the misfortunes of the Swedish opera, which had got off to a bad start with the American public. The critics did not even have the kindness to pan the company: they did something much worse, which was to ignore it completely. This eloquent silence had been too much for the angel of the potted fish and his blonde bombshell who had killed my snake. However, the company had somewhat revived its drooping spirits, and the directors announced they were going ahead in England. Mother was very enthusiastic about the operas and felt that if she sang in several of those she personally liked, the show would pick up—so she intended leaving for Scandinavia in February, and from there she would go to London in the spring.

The fact that father had not been able to afford a trip over for Christmas and that mother was still obliged to work tormented me. I interviewed the bearded agent from whom I had rented the apartment, explaining that my mother found it impossible to remain in Paris and the apartment was too large for one person, and hinted tactfully that if he could think of any loophole whereby I could wriggle out of the lease, I would make it worth his while. My words fell on stony ground—that man was as hard as steel. He repeated with the monotony of a person using a familiar phrase, *"Madame, les affaires sont les affaires et un bail est un bail."* In other words, no dice.

I planned to accept a contract at the Opéra Comique for the month of February and asked Baud to obtain the best salary he could for me. There was not a great deal of rehearsal work involved, and since I did not have to dance every night I could employ my time in building numbers expressly for establishments where an aërial act was not feasible. I had received offers from many places to play the smart restaurants and clubs in Paris and had thought up a number that I could use where it was impossible for a rope to be hung, because the roof was made of glass or decorated panels, which of course didn't permit hooks to be drilled in. Then again, places of this kind often did not have enough height for the act to make any effect. With the monthly nightmare of the rent in Avenue du Bois facing me, I had to make as much money as possible to keep out of debt.

Acrobatic dancers were now flooding Paris, and I wanted to have a form of presentation that was a little different and more difficult than the average act. I had designed a staircase (collapsible for traveling) that could be mounted in almost any space, from a big stage to a restaurant floor. Each step had ground glass panels inserted, allowing the light from electric bulbs to shine through the glass and reflect the light on champagne bottles that were, of course, empty. They were placed upside down over a long steel pin screwed to the steps: this held them in place and allowed the bottles to pivot while I worked on them. The base of an ordinary champagne bottle is hollow and forms a perfect cup for the toes.

Standing in these with ballet shoes, I had power in my feet to turn pirouettes on the bottles, and their pin supports were strong enough to permit handstands and fast acrobatic tricks on them. It was a very effective idea but one of the hardest acts I have ever undertaken, requiring balance and stamina

as well as grace and acrobatic ability. Then there was also the difficulty of obtaining bottles without flaws.

It became necessary for me to practise with my toes bound in adhesive tape, in case a bottle broke, which happened frequently at first. There was enough room in the apartment to practise, and I did so off and on all day, but it was impossible to keep it up for a long stretch, as in dancing or tumbling. I am afraid I was a good deal more interested in the staircase than in what I was doing at the Opéra Comique, but I had a very good reception there with the gitanerias in *La Vida Breve*, and the fiery Jota in *Dolores*—which were what I had been engaged to do.

As soon as the engagement finished at the Comique, Baud booked me at the Apollo Music-Hall on Montmartre, almost next to the Casino de Paris. It was owned by the Impresario Lombard, who was also the proprietor of a very smart night-club next door. There was a crystal floor with changing lights, and the staircase placed in the center of it looked beautiful. I was giving the rope act in the theater and the staircase number in the club—and so required a man assistant for both these shows. Up to that moment, I had used a brother-in-law of Armand Saulnier, but he could not travel and had a bad appearance, so it became necessary for me to look around for a suitable person.

The agent André Meers called me one day, asking me to accompany him to Joe Zelli's cabaret that night—he had a person in mind for me. We sat in the balcony when the acts went on, and André pointed out the man in question. He was not very young but well-built and one of the finest tumblers I have ever had the luck to see. The idea André had in mind when he showed him to me was that I could probably use him not only in my act but also for stretching and timing when I practised.

His story was a strange one, for André told me he was half English, half Arab, and had at one time his own Arabian troupe with his brother. They then made a comedy act between them that was so outstanding it topped the bill all through England. The brother, who was even better than the man I was watching, did such fantastic falls and tricks that he injured his spine and became paralyzed. After the act split up, Albert Morgan (the one I saw) drifted to Paris. He had never been able to find a partner that could equal his paralyzed brother and had been obliged to earn his living as a single tumbling act anywhere he could secure a booking.

He was at Joe Zelli's place through the kindness of the owner, who had known Morgan for years and wanted to give him a break. Joe Zelli, incidentally, is one of the best-hearted people alive, and I know of many a kind and generous deed he's performed to assist broken-down acts in Paris. I asked

André Meers to call Morgan to the table after the act was finished, so that I could talk to him.

I had all I could do not to laugh out loud when he arrived, for he had the most terrific cockney accent, with all the dry humor so characteristic of London's East End. He took one look at me and said, " 'Ow are yer, Princess?" and from then on, that was what he generally called me. We had a long talk, and I discovered he neither drank nor smoked, was married to a French girl, and had two small children. I took an immediate liking to his straightforward manner and vast knowledge of show business. Joe Zelli stopped at our table that evening and gave him a splendid reference, so when he came to look at my equipment the next day, I engaged him. This was one of the best things I ever did, for he became a trustworthy, reliable person on whom I could always depend, and was also a real help in my work.

The first time we practised, I asked him how he liked the job. He said, "Not arf, Princess; you don't know what it means to me not to 'ave to tumble any more. I'm forty, and me bones is rattlin' about like a bleedin' skelington."

He had only one fault—that was his habit of using the most appalling language as though it were ordinary conversation. Personally I did not mind, for it was nearly always funny and never offensive, but it led to some rather quaint situations in the more distinguished places where I worked with him.

Both the Lombard engagements were decided triumphs, and I became known to the newspapermen and received good notices almost every week. The staircase number was particularly successful and well worth all the hard work I had put into it. But it was actually punishment every time I went on, for my toes used to bleed from beneath the nails because of the force required to maintain a balance on the bottles.

I was also acquiring a rather large crowd of admirers and beginning to see a lot of the night life in Paris. It was just at this time that Nina's eagerly awaited book *Laughing Torso* came out. If she had not sent me an autographed copy, I would not have been able to buy one anywhere, for Brentano's and all the large bookshops were sold out at once, so anxiously did people rush to buy it and scan the pages to see what she had written about them.

Nina became overnight the most sought after woman in Paris, and I do mean "sought after"—in more ways than one. For people who were not mentioned in her book wanted to be seen with her, and others who were pleased with what she wrote about them invited her to parties and dinners—while those who felt she had insulted or ridiculed them chased after her for less agreeable motives. She had been most charming and complimentary to me in a few pages dedicated to "Prudence," my nickname from our old student days. This tribute, together with my steadily increasing group of admirers, helped to fill the stalls of the Apollo Theater and the ringside seats of the other Lombard establishment.

When my contract was up, everything worked out very nicely. My friend, Olga Gougoutchieff, took over my apartment, and Morgan was in the seventh heaven of delight about our going on tour and opening at the Ambassadeurs of Cannes, the smartest place on the Riviera. I sent him to get dress clothes and tuxedos for the act, so that everything would be as elegant as possible.

I was about to leave on the night train for Cannes and the engagement for Poiret at the Ambassadeurs when who should turn up but Jimmy Petter from Argentina. He had never been to the Riviera, and when I told him I was on my way there, he said at once that he would travel down with me—reserving a compartment on the same train.

Marie had been given the day off after all the packing was accomplished, and I was anxiously waiting for her later that evening. I was not very well pleased about something she had allowed to occur during the last days of my engagement at the Opéra Comique. Only with the greatest difficulty had Marie summoned up the courage to tell me that one afternoon she had left the gate open in the garden while some tradesmen were bringing in packages. Mascotte, who was in season and should have been tied up, watched her opportunity and made a rush out through the gate. She was very crafty about these matters, obstinate on the subject of her love affairs, and had her eye on a disreputable dog that lived in a *bureau de tabac* at the end of the street. Before Marie, who was not the most agile of elderly maids, had got her second wind for the chase, Mascotte had collected her admirer and disappeared with him in the direction of the Bois de Boulogne. A trail of all sorts of dogs, who had joined in the elopement, greatly impeded Marie's progress, and she had been obliged to return to the apartment without Mascotte.

My feelings when I got back from a matinée and heard the story can be better imagined than described. I jumped in the car and scoured the drives of the Bois for miles—without success. However, when I arrived home to call the police, there was Mascotte, disgracefully dirty, with a lolling tongue and the most shameless grin on her face. Marie wept for two days without stopping, and her woebegone face got on my nerves to such an extent that I finally told her she would not be fired, that it was an unfortunate episode and would, of course, lead to many complications when the puppies arrived, but that was all there was to it.

This unnecessary problem had not increased my confidence in Marie's trustworthiness, so when she did not arrive that evening till half an hour before we left for the station, I felt very angry with her. When she came in through the servant's entrance I called her to my room at once. As she walked through the door I turned to speak to her, then got one of the most severe shocks I have ever experienced.

Marie, whose only charm was her impressive gray hair, had employed her afternoon off in getting it dyed a flaming red. The effect was devastating—I had never seen anything so awful in my life. Pepita, who was with me, nearly went into hysterics, while I groped for words to express my indignation. Perhaps the person who really got the most severe shock was Morgan, for when she opened the door for him a few minutes later, he stood stock still looking at her, then in a low voice vibrant with emotion said, "Gawd strike me bloody hooray." Volumes could not have said more. It was too late for me to get another maid for the trip, which I suspected Marie had very carefully calculated, so there was nothing to be done but leave for the Riviera with a *femme de chambre* who had all the earmarks of the procuress of a disorderly house, Mascotte in the first stage of pregnancy, and Jimmy Petter.

In the middle of the night, when the train had just left Lyons, there was a gentle tap on my door. Thinking it was either Jimmy or Morgan, I opened it. To my horror, I saw a man with a horribly scarred face and ragged cap standing in the doorway. Mascotte began to growl and would have flown at him had I not held her collar. When I asked what he wanted, he muttered something in a strange guttural accent about having been sent by the "gentleman" to give me a present. I gave him a push out through the sliding door, slammed it to, and tried to go back to sleep. All of a sudden, a piercing scream came from the compartment next door, and the sound of running feet down the corridor. I got up again, put a lead on Mascotte, who was barking frantically, and opened my door. All the guards on the train were crowded around an elderly woman from the adjoining compartment who kept saying that a man tried to murder her. They stopped the train, made a complete search for the scar-faced creature, and finally rounded him up in a lavatory. The train continued on to the next village, where the police were already waiting to take him off. It appeared he was a dangerous escaped convict from the prison at Lyons and they had been hunting for him all night.

I got hold of Jimmy, frolicking up and down the train, and he admitted seeing the man jump on at the Lyons station and talking to him. The man offered a piece of jewelry he had in a small package of gems, to help him hide until we reached Cannes. It had struck Jimmy as being an exquisitely funny joke to tell the man that he could give me the jewels to hide, since I was an international jewel thief myself and

269

would help him get away. By this time I was so sleepy, I could not see anything funny about it.

The next morning when we arrived, Jimmy, still in a playful mood, had somehow got hold of Marie's two sets of false teeth and fixed them with a wire to the tail of her fox fur. The poor woman searched the entire train for them, all upset at the loss, especially since it was practically impossible to understand a word she spoke without the teeth. This predicament was the last straw. As we proceeded down the platform at Cannes in search of the hotel bus, I noticed the oddest rattling and snapping noise coming from Marie as she walked past. It puzzled me, and then I saw the teeth, and, although this all sounds silly, it was one of the funniest sights imaginable.

I will never forget the first performance at the Ambassadeurs—I was so tired I could hardly move after the strenuous band rehearsal and a night without sufficient sleep. Fortunately, the show was good, and Poiret, who had gone to all sorts of trouble to have the lights properly adjusted for the staircase, was very happy and sent a telegram to Baud about it.

This was the first time since my childhood that I had visited Cannes. Only vaguely did I remember the Riviera and a visit I had payed with my mother to the villa of Lina Cavalieri, the beautiful Italian diva, who was at that time the wife of Robert Chanler, the American millionaire. I thoroughly enjoyed my present stay, and Poiret arranged a Russian evening under the auspices of the late Grand Duke Nikolas Nikolaivitch, in which I danced several classical numbers in addition to my acrobatical ones. This caused quite a stir and helped me considerably artistically.

Babe Barnato, my old friend from London and South Africa, was in Cannes and staying at my hotel. I introduced him to Jimmy, and the two of them hit it off perfectly, spending most of their time gambling in the Casino adjoining the restaurant. Occasionally after the show, I joined them. All the most interesting people in Europe gathered together in

270

those brilliant rooms: the Aga Khan, Basil Zaharoff, the Dolly sisters, and Madame Jean Nash, the beautiful American known as the best-dressed woman in Paris.

After a while I became seriously alarmed about Jimmy, for he would run from one table to another shouting "Banco" in the game of chemin de fer, no matter what limits the bank had reached among the world's millionaires gathered at the green tables covered with fortunes in thousand-franc notes. Nevertheless, it was a gay wonderful week, and the night before leaving for Nice I had supper with Babe and Jimmy—who, of course, returned to the Casino after seeing me home. About three in the morning, I was awakened by Jimmy, who 'phoned from Babe's apartment that he had lost all the money he had brought with him and was leaving by the next train for Paris—just as he was, in white tie and tails.

We opened on a Friday at the Rhul Hotel in Nice, and were scheduled to play the Fête des Armes on the following day as well as the shows at the Rhul. The United States cruiser *Pittsburgh* was in Villefranche Harbor for Easter, and the town was gay with flags and parades.

One afternoon Nina arrived at the hotel asking for me. I knew she had been invited to spend a week or so with Jean Cocteau at his villa in Villefranche, and when I went down to the lobby to greet her, I saw she was accompanied by a small slender man with sharply cut features and a bored expression. This was Jean Cocteau. He was nervous and fidgety, and Nina explained that with his house full of guests, he had in a moment of sympathetic *entente cordiale* invited a crowd of sailors from the *Pittsburgh* to spend the afternoon. Having fussed around all the morning to prepare for them, he had become so bored an hour after they arrived that he insisted upon leaving all his guests to look after themselves and told Nina to drive the car anywhere she liked—so she had come to see me.

They stayed for dinner and to see me dance—which was rather nerve-racking, for I had been told by Nina of the caustic criticisms Cocteau gave out if he did not like an act.

She had cautioned me not to ask his opinion or to appear anxious to know if he liked my work. I performed quite well that night and received more applause than usual, but all the time I was working, Cocteau sat and talked to Nina, his profile turned to the restaurant floor, so manifestly he had not seen anything I did. Feeling a little peeved, when Nina came to my dressing-room afterward, I told her so.

She laughed and said that Cocteau was a bundle of nerves, having recently left the famous Piccinnini Clinic in Paris, where he had undergone a cure for opium intoxication and written his book *J'ai fumée l'Opium* about sensations while experiencing all sorts of horrible torments. He also had a hectic interlude with a play he had produced in the Pitoyevs' little bandbox of a theater, on the Boulevard Rochechouart. There, Nina said, had taken place one of the most hilarious scandals ever seen in Paris.

The play had been a satire on the Trojan Horse theme, with death represented by a blonde woman in a priceless chinchilla coat (loaned to Cocteau by Coco Chanel, the couturière). The preview of the play had given rise to adverse criticisms, and the press, although recognizing it as a daring and brilliant satire, had spoken in strong terms of some of the ultra-modern scenes and the provocative political and social angles. In spite of this, Cocteau had insisted upon giving the first night as planned.

All smart Paris had crowded into the boxes and stalls, while in the gallery, students and political groups who resented some of the lines in the play as directed against their ideals, had bought seats with the purpose of making as historic a demonstration as they could think up. In order to gain their purpose of stopping the performance, they had brought sardine cans filled with unmentionable refuse, which they intended projecting on to the stage with catapults, accompanied by stink bombs. At a given moment, when the audience was rocking with excitement over one of the most thrilling scenes of the play, the hoodlums in the gallary let loose a barrage of sardine cans containing the malodorant filth—and the actors fled.

Coco Chanel had valiantly faced the deluge and gone on the stage to retrieve her chinchilla coat, while Lady Bubbles Mitchelham and some of her women friends climbed on their seats to shout at the demonstrators that they ought to be ashamed of themselves. But the barrage continued, and Cocteau with his friends had been obliged to beat a retreat, while the police cleared the house as best they might under the circumstances. Everybody, Nina said, had ended up in the police station, and the show had had to close so that the sanitary squads could disinfect the theater.

I began to appreciate the undoubted possibility of anybody's nerves being frayed after such experiences, but having always greatly admired Cocteau's work and his drawings, I felt a little crushed as I said good night to them. He gave me an elusive smile and muttered something I did not catch, then turning to Nina said, "Ask your friend to my villa for a few days." I was much surprised, after the events of the evening, but quickly replied that I was leaving for Monte Carlo when I finished in Nice and would not be back in France for some weeks. I was not taking any chances, even if I had been free to accept the invitation, after the effect produced on Cocteau by the sailors from the *Pittsburgh*. Of course, I did not know him, and it was not until some months later that I found out what an interesting and charming person he could be when in the mood.

We played Monte Carlo the following week when a telegram arrived from Matto saying he would meet me in Rome. I also received a letter from Olga saying that Botafogo had got out one night and spent his time romping about the kitchen. He must have wanted to get up the kitchen stairs but could not grip them with his scales, so he had spat up a lot of saliva on the bottom step that looked like whipped cream, presumably to slide on.

The unfortunate news in Olga's letter was that the maid, who came in to make her breakfast, slipped on the whipped

273

cream and slid across the kitchen floor, nearly knocking her brains out on the opposite wall. Olga managed to pacify her, but she left immediately, after catching a glimpse of Bota-fogo in his favorite spot—coiled affectionately around the toilet seat in the maid's lavatory. I had grave misgivings that the concierge might have got wind of his presence, and there would be the devil to pay, so I wrote Olga asking her to reply at once and let me know the worst. Her answer was reassuring: the concierge was still in ignorance of anything unusual in the apartment.

XV

I N ALL MY travels across international boundaries I thought I had seen just about every possible customs complication that even the Italians could produce. But I had yet to confront the Italians with empty bottles. After a good week in Monte Carlo we set out for Rome, and at the frontier, Domo d'Ossola, at five in the morning, Morgan took my keys to battle his way through the customs and immediately had difficulties over the theatrical baskets.

When I was called to the scene of action, I found a group of excited Italians peering into the basket containing the many bottles used for my staircase number. They regarded Morgan with deep distrust while he scanned the outrageous bill for excess baggage we were obliged to accept. They could not figure out why anybody would be willing to pay such a sum for empty bottles: it would have been bad enough had they been full. The officials spoke a little English but not enough to grasp completely the exact meaning of the language Morgan was using. *"Cosa dice?"* they inquired—"What do you say?"—and he would answer, *"Cosa dice* yourself, you blankety-blank sons of so-and-sos." Marie was scandalized. "Mademoiselle," she said, "this man is indecent—he will get us into trouble," and when we arrived in Rome and he discovered my keys had been mislaid after we got through the customs, they had a terrific fight, each blaming the other.

The managers of the Salone Margherita, the best music-hall in Rome, had gone to all sorts of expense to publicize my début, and the impresario, Signor Cavalotti, hovered about the stage with a beaming smile all the time we were rehearsing. But the opening performance was no fun for any of us. I had my first real view of what an Italian audience could do to artists on their first night, for it was an understood thing in Italy that the audience came to the initial show of a new bill for the express purpose of raising as much hell as possible with the unfortunate acts they did not happen to like.

The star act on the bill was the charming and talented Australian vedette, Jenny Golder. She had been held over at the theater, so was an established favorite. I came second in importance on the bill; then there was a good roller-skating act of eight people from the Gaumont Palace in Paris that closed the show. Third in importance was a French singer who worked in a blacked-out set with a spot and did ultra-dramatic work. There were also three musical clowns, a comedy tramp bicycle act in the style of the great Joe Jackson, and a Risley act, all more or less featured. The rest of the bill was like all other vaudeville programs, a mixture of this and that—some good, some bad. However, none of them deserved the heckling they received that night.

As I sat in my dressing-room, Morgan restlessly paced back and forth from the side of the stage to my door, reporting the progress of the show. I could pretty well imagine what was taking place from the comments of acts who got the bird —Cavalotti simply rang down the curtain on them when he considered things were going too far. Apparently the audience was in a very ugly mood. This was a charming prospect, and I became as nervous as Morgan was.

The applause for Jenny Golder in the middle of the bill was terrific, and she gave an encore at the close of her act. Then the trouble started. The poor clowns, who had been congratulating themselves that they could follow an artist who had put the audience in a good humor, were unfortunately sadly mistaken. Their act had barely got under way, when a roar of *"Ma, che cani! Basta! Basta!"* ("But what dogs' howling! Enough! Enough!") went up, the classic Italian cry of disapproval. The poor men quavered through their first number without any one's hearing it above the din.

Morgan told me Cavalotti signaled to the tenor, who sang rather well, to try his song and at the same time motioned for the next act to stand by: this was the French singer. As she stood there waiting to go on, she could hear a loud chorus of that international protest, the Bronx cheer, as it greeted the first notes of the tenor. That was enough for Cavalotti: he pressed the button on which he kept his hand during the entire show, and down came the curtain on the clowns. They had not even been given a chance to show what they could do.

Morgan came flying back to me, saying Cavalotti wanted us to stand by for our act in case the French singer got the works, too. I grabbed my resin bag and stood in the wings awaiting developments. The French girl used a rather long overture to open her act, and for that moment, the audience was perfectly quiet, listening to it. Then she stepped out on the stage as the curtain went up. The black velvet drop that draped the stage, her black dress and long black gloves, gave a most funereal, "the body is upstairs" effect, and the public was quick to react to it. *"Ma come bruta"* they yelled. ("How ugly she is!")

This was not strictly true, although undoubtedly she was no glamour girl. Her first song she announced in French, the title of which happened to be the lugubrious one of "Le Petit Bossu" ("The Little Hunchback"). This announcement was greeted with a storm of catcalls and ribald remarks. Then somebody threw a copper coin on the stage, several more followed, and it was literally impossible to hear whether she sang well or not. She had courage, though, and stood the heckling for about sixteen more bars of music, then walked down to the ramps and shouted, *"Salauds"* ("Swine") at the top of her voice. If the audience had not heard her song, they certainly did hear the insult, and as Cavalotti hastily brought down the curtain, walking-sticks, cigar butts, and empty match-boxes came raining on to the stage.

The riot continued. It was a bad situation for us following the Frenchwoman, and as Morgan lowered my ropes on the stage, I saw his face was white as a sheet. When I walked out, there was the usual moment of silence that had greeted each act. "The silence before the storm," I thought as I went into my dance. I used a rather soft opening in

277

those days, on the Spanish Dance of Granados, and as I whirled and pirouetted toward my rope, I could hear a confused murmur of voices—then a loud laugh. I lost my temper for a moment and stood with my hand on the rope looking straight out at the audience. For no earthly reason I got an applause—then I climbed up and started to work.

Morgan, anchoring the ropes on the stage, was trembling to such an extent that I felt the vibration under my hands as I held the rope and kept wondering just how long I could keep going before the audience got after me. I went from trick to trick, thinking each one would be the last, and decided if there was the slightest hostility from the spectators, I would slide down, walk off the stage and out of the theater. Finally the audience warmed up, and I began getting hands—good ones—so I breathed freely and started to sell the act. It ended in a frank and spontaneous applause. The situation was saved. When I went out before the curtain, I was greeted with the most outrageous and embarrassing compliments—an old Italian custom in any vaudeville house and a sign the act had been a success.

Out of the bill of twenty acts, seven were "canceled out," and Italian singers and orchestras replaced them. This happened every week, and it has always been a mystery to me why agents even bothered to send artists to Italy at all under the circumstances, for it was not a question of ability. Several of the acts, including the musical clowns, were definitely good and would have gone over anywhere else. The only ones that succeeded, apart from Jenny Golder, were the acrobatic and comedy acts—particularly the roller-skaters and myself.

Such goings-on were unheard of with the opera companies. When I worked at the Costanzi, there had been nights when some of the singers got booed and hissed, but the dancers were always fairly well treated and used to the shouts of *"Brava Baillerini!"* that occasionally disturbed the ballet—but that was the worst that ever happened. Some of the musicians told us that even the spoilt darling of Paris, Maurice Chevalier, did not escape a violent demonstration from the Roman public, who were, for some reason disappointed in his singing. Cries of *"Va via! Va en Francia, Putzolento!"* ("Go away! Go back to France—you big sissy!") greeted him on his opening night, and he had been obliged to wait in his dressing-room until the nitwits milling around the stage door had wearied of their vigil and gone home.

The first week in Rome passed peacefully after the opening night, and the audiences thereafter behaved normally. I began to feel happy about everything and formed a friendship with Jenny Golder, who was going on to Milan with us for the next engagement. She was a charming person whose tragic suicide several years later I could never fully understand. She had a great talent, was beautiful and always happy when she went with Morgan and myself on all sorts of amusing expeditions to the Vatican, the Catacombs and the other wonders of Rome. Morgan's remarks about some of these historic places were a scream. What he liked best was the Coliseum, because it stirred memories of his success in the London music-hall named after it. The imposing interior of the Vatican he described as being "a little bit of all right."

Matto arrived from Paris during my last week in Rome with the surprising news of his engagement to the beautiful Condesa Franca Antinori, daughter of an impoverished Italian duke with a dilapidated castle in Florence which Matto was busily planning to restore for the marriage ceremony. He had bought her a marvelous set of emeralds that must have cost a fortune and were just the color of her eyes. She was staying at the Excelsior Hotel, and the parties that Matto gave for her and the élite of Roman society were sensational. I was very fond of him and sincerely hoped he would be happy in his marriage.

Jenny Golder and I were the only acts continuing on to Milan, where, we were told, the public was even more demonstrative than in Rome. When we arrived at the theater, we stopped in the lobby to read the list of acts appearing with us. Suddenly I noticed that Jenny became deathly pale and seemed very perturbed. When I asked if there was anything

279

wrong, she pointed to the name of the act starring third on the bill after us: it was her husband, Joe Fallon. He was working with the woman for whom he had left her a few years previously in Australia. I felt terribly sorry for her, since it was evident she still loved him. The woman he worked with was a broken-down contortionist he had picked up somewhere, who threw her fanny over her head in the act a few times, but it was he who did all the work. Jenny was charming to both of them and continued with the same resounding success as always—but I knew she was suffering tortures all the time we were in Milan.

We opened with much the same scene as in Rome, reminiscent of the savage buffoonery displayed by pagan crowds watching the Christians being thrown to the lions. Acts came and went during the first few days, until finally they got a bill that pleased the public. My success with the rope number was repeated in this theater, as well as at the Pavillon Doré, a cabaret restaurant under the theater, where I danced with the staircase. The first night I mistook the wild cheers and yells that greeted my appearance as an unfriendly demonstration, till I could distinguish some of the words being shouted. They were flattering but, as in Rome, a little embarrassing.

During a back bend on the bottles, I felt a wad of paper hit me on the chest. I rose with all the dignity I could muster and threw the wad to the farthest corner of the floor. Waiters hurled themselves upon it, and after I finished, in a storm of applause, the house manager, a personage with the absurd name of Indelicato, came to my dressing-room to inform me that the wad of paper had been a five-hundred-lire note tossed by an enthusiastic admirer whose feelings had been hurt by my contemptuous gesture.

Mascotte was having a miserable time, for there was no park for her near the second rate hotel where I was obliged to stay, all the decent ones in the city being full for the spring Exhibition. She needed exercise, so one afternoon during the matinée I sent her out for a few minutes with Marie and gave strict orders that the dog was not to be allowed off the lead.

In case of emergency, Marie carried the muzzle Mascotte refused to wear. When we were due to work, Marie had still not returned, and just as I finished dressing, considerably worried at Mascotte's prolonged absence, Indelicato came to my dressing-room with a policeman from the local bureau of the Guardia Civile, who asked if Marie Serger, French citizen (who had been arrested for hustling), was my maid and if it was true that she worked for me in the theater. I called Morgan and together we accompanied the officer to the station house.

There we found Marie with Mascotte, sitting on a bench between two drunks and a pickpocket. Marie, who was nearly hysterical and spoke no Italian, had created such an uproar that the Commissario at the main desk had taken an immediate dislike to her, and this made things very difficult. He said that the town was full of French streetwalkers, arrived for the Exhibition, and that one of the policemen on point duty had observed Marie several times, tripping down the main street with an unmuzzled dog. She had, he said, gone into a café, sat at a table, and behaved generally in a suspicious manner. Her appearance, he continued with a glance at her flaming hair, was not what they would generally suppose to be that of a respectable woman.

In addition to all this, poor little Mascotte had done her duty valiantly by nipping one of the officials on the ankle. I had an awful three-quarters of an hour with the situation, and only when I suddenly spoke of invoking the aid of Indelicato did that magic name obtain for me the release of Marie and Mascotte—with a fine. Apparently Signor Indelicato was very much respected in the precinct and probably the source of unlimited passes and graft for the Milan police.

So that was the end of the episode as far as Marie was concerned, but not for Mascotte—for the shouting and excitement in the police station upset her so much that on the de luxe train for Paris four days later, she gave birth to eight bouncing nondescript puppies in my compartment at two in the morning.

281

I sent Marie to arouse Morgan, and by the time he arrived, disheveled and half asleep, there were three little squirming black and white puppies in the world. It was a nerve-racking job. Puppies kept arriving at intervals for the rest of the night, the last one about an hour before we got to Paris. This coincided with the taking of tickets by a couple of officials with gold-laced caps, who, blocking the door, expressed their disapproval of such things happening in their de luxe train. *"Porca Miseria! che cosa fare?"* they inquired. ("What are you doing?") As if they could not see for themselves what we were up against! Morgan's reply was unprintable.

I made a bed for the puppies in an open valise, so they could be carried to a taxi when we arrived at the station, and had forgotten, in all the excitement, that Georges Baud had wired to say he was meeting me with an extremely important manager from Egypt, who wanted to see me that day at any cost before he left Paris. The picture the three of us made trailing down the crowded platform of the station was anything but elegant, for I was juggling the open valise full of puppies and wearing a hastily applied make-up that would have handicapped Hedy La Marr. Morgan was white and haggard, his suit covered with dust and baggy at the knees, while Marie led Mascotte, who, in a frenzy of mother love, would not take her eyes off the valise containing her babies to look where she was going, so consequently managed to get her lead entangled in the legs of scurrying passengers at every few feet.

The expression on Georges Baud's amiable visage when he caught sight of us was that of a man who has just lost a deal for ten thousand dollars. He was accompanied by a dapper Egyptian, immaculately dressed, who most decidedly got a nasty shock, for I could just imagine the lyrical descriptions of me Baud had been filling him up with and the vision of grace and beauty he anticipated. He asked Baud in a weak voice, "Is this the dancer you told me about?" I don't know what Baud replied, for just at that moment Mascotte tripped up a fat man with a large umbrella, and the conversation was

282

lost in the torrent of mutual abuse that followed. Somehow or other, we finally got out of the station.

My next engagements were the Concert Mayol and a cabaret date at Le Jardin de ma Sœur. On my opening evening as I attempted to dress for the Mayol, Pepita, in a dither of excitement about a ball at the opera, got in my way and her own, spilled the face powder, and borrowed my stockings as was her wont, and to top it off, at the last minute I could not find Botafogo. While Marie and I searched everywhere, André Meers, impeccable in evening clothes, arrived and sat down on a divan in the hall to wait for Pepita. Little did he know that right above him, coiled on the top of the large wall cabinet, was my missing snake. I had to ask Meers to move in order to haul Botafogo down. When the poor man saw him for the first time, I thought he would have a syncope.

I had a complete success at the Mayol opening, and although terribly tired when arriving at the Jardin, I was so happy and excited that I worked particularly well. The *salle* had been packed, people were standing in the doorway waiting for tables, and when I got to my dressing-room I found it so full of people eager to congratulate me, I was afraid I would faint —having really overdone it that night.

The next morning Baud called up with the news that everybody was talking about my performance at the Jardin: the critics were unanimous in their praise of the Mayol revue. Although there were many well-known figures of French revues and the vaudeville stage in it, the honors had gone to another acrobat, Eddie Rogers, a young Californian, and to me. He was extraordinarily clever and performed the incredible feat of turning three pirouettes on his head, balancing himself with his hands in his pockets and smoking a cigar at the same time. The Parisian public had taken him to their hearts, but his performance was so strenuous he could not give an encore so had walked down to the footlights during a terrific burst of applause, and said, "*Merci beaucoup,*" in his quaint French, and this had caused almost as much enthusiasm as his act.

Every night at the Jardin I received invitations from people who wanted me to join them for champagne, which I continuously refused, being too tired to care about meeting anybody: besides, I never touched alcohol on account of my work.

Oscar Movet, the owner of the Jardin, used to tell me who everybody was and whom I should meet.

If I had success I felt sincerely that I earned it. Few people, even among my friends, realized that I had painful wounds on my hands and feet that wouldn't heal, caused by the work on the bottles in the staircase number, and an open sore on my ribs from rope burns sustained every night while sliding down from the top of the theater with the rope wrapped around my body. Only circus acts who have done this type of work can really understand what it means and the fatigue and nervous pain that bring insomnia in their wake, night after night.

One evening at the Jardin, I received a magnificent bouquet of pink roses from a table where I had noticed a large group of people applauding me. The card attached to the bouquet had a coronet on it and the name Princesse Eugène Murat. A few words of graceful congratulation accompanied it.

The next evening, almost as soon as I entered the restaurant to dance, I noticed the same party, sitting there and applauding me. I bowed to them and as I returned to my dressing-room I remembered I had discourteously forgotten to send a note of thanks to the Princesse Murat. Just as I was scribbling a memorandum about it, Oscar Movet arrived at the door with a message from the same lady, inviting me to join her party for supper. I told him I had an engagement, and he literally shouted, "What is the matter with you? Princesse Murat is one of the most important people in Paris for an artist! First you never thank her for the flowers, then you refuse an invitation to meet her—it is preposterous!"

I tried to make him understand that Nina was coming to fetch me for a quiet supper, and that I was wearing a tweed suit and therefore could not possibly appear in his restaurant among women in elaborate evening gowns. Fortunately, Nina arrived at the height of the discussion, and when I told her what it was all about, she said Violette Murat was one of her best and oldest friends and immediately sent a waiter with a note arranging for us to meet the party at the Bœuf sur le Toit, a more bohemian restaurant where evening dress was not enforced.

I was cross and tired, and Nina practically had to drag me to my car. As we drove to our rendezvous, she pounded into me the same thing Oscar Movet had said. Princesse Murat, it appeared, was a person who, if she wanted to make an artist famous, could do so almost overnight. She was very wealthy, very charitable, and considered eccentric, for she lived her own life with a superb disregard for the narrow conventions of the *vieille noblesse française*.

She sounded all right, but I was tired, sulky, and not the least bit receptive to meeting wealthy art patrons, yet when I rose to greet Violette Murat as she entered the restaurant, I forgot my fatigue under the great charm and gentleness of the most remarkable woman I have ever met. She was tall and in her late forties, with black hair going gray at the temples—not at all beautiful, but when she smiled, everything about her seemed to glow. She had deep-set hazel eyes, a frank sunny manner and one of those low-pitched musical voices that are a joy to listen to. Extremely intelligent, she had that rare gift of making people want to tell her about themselves when they interested her, and before I realized it, I had told her most of my past history—all about my youth and Nina, of whom I could see she was very fond.

The other guests in the party were the smart and brilliant Daisy Fellowes and her husband, and Princesse Hélène Murat, sister-in-law of Violette and an American by birth. Later on we were joined by Yvonne George, the singer, who was entertaining at the Bœuf, another friend and protégée of Violette's. She was a pallid, vibrant person who sang in a husky voice that had a tone of anguish to it, and undoubtedly she was very talented.

285

I had not stayed up so late for a long time, and when the party broke up, I offered to drive Violette and Nina home in my car. After we left Nina at her studio in Montparnasse, I drove slowly across Paris and the bridge over the moonlit Seine, to Violette's house on the Avenue d'Eylau. She talked about my work, said she thought I was overtired and would like me to come down to her country house any time I needed a rest—if necessary, to bring all my animals with me, adding that she would be happy to see me again very soon. She was so kind and sympathetic that I was almost ashamed of having talked so much and felt I must have given the impression of being very "hammy," theatrical people being invariably consumed with a mania for talking about themselves upon the slightest provocation.

Several days later, Oscar Movet was thrown into another paroxysm of indignation because I did not want to dance at a party given by Comtesse de la Béraudière. She had written him a note asking for me and a colored orchestra called the International Five, all excellent entertainers. The evening meant not only extra fatigue for me but very late hours, for we were supposed to work first at her house about one in the morning while another orchestra filled in at the Jardin, then come back there when we finished at two. The next day, Comtesse de la Béraudière called on me at the apartment and found me in the middle of rehearsing a new number with Morgan. She had brought with her two ultrasmart Frenchmen, the Comte de Morny and the Vicomte de Janzé, and while I was dressing, Morgan interviewed them. He came and told me that the "Marquis de Consommé Froid, and the Vicomte de Consommé Chaud" were both disposed to go fairly high in their fee, because, they said, the fête was for a very distinguished personage from England who was crazy about the Charleston and colored bands. I realized in a flash they meant His Royal Highness, the Prince of Wales, and thought I had better accept.

Madame de la Béraudière was simply enchanted with Morgan, and when she saw my monkey Kimmie and Botafogo, her ecstasy knew no bounds. I have never yet known a wealthy aristocrat who did not fall for anything to do with the circus and snakes. I can't imagine why this should be, unless it is a new slant on life for them—something different from their own elegant existences; like the lady in the song who "left with the raggle-taggle gipsies O." The fête at the Béraudière house was a brilliant social function and most uncomfortable to work in. The staff of servants had, with praiseworthy thoroughness, polished the floor of the ballroom until it was positively dangerous to dance and tumble. I was far too busy trying not to break my neck to take much stock of what was going on around me, until the moment when I could stand still and take my bows: then I saw that the room had been arranged like a cabaret restaurant with a floor show, and at one of the tables was the guest of honor, the center of a group of flattered guests, but like his royal parents, he seemed to be a long way off and not particularly interested in anything.

I was in error about this, however, for later that night he turned up at the Jardin, after an equerry had arrived to see who was there and arrange for a table next to the band, well separated from the vulgar herd, so that His Highness could play the drums all he wanted to if he felt so inclined.

It was already very late, and no amount of argument from the management would induce me to stay, but the next night the Prince of Wales turned up again, and the scene repeated itself. He liked the band and made them a handsome present together with a gallon of champagne for singing his favorite songs. Comtesse de la Béraudière's son, a nice boy, was with the party, and after I danced he came to my dressing-room and told me that I had achieved a great success, that some of my steps made a hit with the Prince, who was simply crazy about the Charleston.

After the show on Saturday Violette Murat called for me and we drove down to "Les Mées," her little château near Versailles, stopping en route at the Avenue du Bois to pick up Mascotte and Nina. This visit marked the commencement of the greatest friendship I have ever had with any woman, for Violette was one of the kindest and most loyal people I have ever met, in addition to being a very great lady.

The château of Les Mées was the most charming place imaginable and had originally been built by Marie Antoinette as a present to one of her favorite ladies-in-waiting, the Princesse de Polignac.

Not a very large house, it was set in the midst of an orchard and large park, with an artificial lake and magnificent old trees. There were small cottages with vegetable and flower gardens scattered throughout the grounds, and there lived the old retainers of the family to whom Violette gave a weekly stipend for living expenses and comforts. They were past working and spent their sunset years pottering about the grounds and looking after the white flowers and animals that Violette loved so much. She had white dogs and cats, birds and poultry, and the only other pet was an enormous kangaroo which was, of course, brown. All the flowers in the house and around the terraces were white, and her bedroom and boudoir were the same color.

It was a very quiet week-end, with just Nina, myself, Violette's eldest daughter Caroline, Princesse Hélène Murat, and Violette's secretary, Bubu Daschkaliani. This girl had a strange history, for she was a Caucasian princess, had gone through the World War dressed as a man, fighting with the Russian Army until the Bolsheviks entered her country. Her regiment was then forced to disband, so she had to fly to Paris with a brother and sister. They nearly starved to death until Violette met her and she was given the position of private secretary. Her benefactress had also financed a book she had written about her experiences.

Bubu adored Violette and told me a great deal about the wonderful things she did—how she had worked in gangrene wards of base hospitals and the Grand Palais as a nurse during the World War and had been wounded by shrapnel in her right leg when the Germans had shelled a first-line hos-

288

pital, neglecting the wound to nurse the casualties. The leg had become infected, causing her to go through months of torture, submitting to operation after operation. She still frequently suffered attacks of pain. After the war, she had given a large share of her personal fortune for the installation of a clinic that had the most modern artificial limbs for the veterans of the Invalides and the Val-de-Grâce hospitals, and had spent months in the United States studying scientific treatment for amputation cases. Her private charities were legion, Bubu told me, but added that Violette disliked any one's knowing or speaking about them, so asked me not to mention what she had told me.

Talking and listening to Violette on that first visit, I was able to sum up her character almost immediately and believe I understood her perhaps better than anybody else. She had a profoundly serious side to her nature but loved a good time—doing almost childish things that gave her an impish kick, because they were the cause for gossip in the strict, narrow-minded set of French aristocrats, who with a few exceptions were incredibly dull. Violette had traveled all over the world, knew human nature well, had a shrewd brain, and administered her large fortune alone. She adored her three children, the Princesses Caroline and Paule, her daughters, and her son, Prince Pierre. When I met her, Caroline and Pierre were both married and largely concerned with their own affairs, while Paule was still a very young and beautiful girl.

I quickly discovered that Violette liked people for their own worth and was not interested in any one unless he had some quality other than rank and riches. Many people bored her, and she liked to keep the same circle of friends, not caring particularly to add to it unless they held some special attraction for her. She had wealth and a position that permitted her to do as she liked—these two important factors were the reasons for much jealousy and spite— and I have heard many people whom she did not care to admit into her set malign her with the most bitter lies and slurs. In later years I was mixed up in more than one fight on her account.

After that summer, I paid a visit to the château at the time of a great taxi strike in Paris and with another girl drove to the country in Violette's car. When it was time to return to Paris she was afraid to allow her elderly chauffeur to drive the car back to town, for the strikers were over-turning private automobiles and generally making a nuisance of themselves. I had to get back, so we all started to walk to Versailles, some five miles distant, to take the train. Violette would not let us go alone, and I feared that with her bad leg she would never make it. In addition, it started to rain.

Just then a market truck loaded with vegetables for Les Halles passed us. We flagged the driver, and Violette asked if he would take us into town: he agreed. He was a colorful person, and Violette, sitting beside him, laughed and joked all the way. By the time we arrived it was pouring, so he gallantly drove us to the magnificent porte-cochère of Violette's town residence. There we descended, and she gave him a hundred-franc note, saying how much she enjoyed the drive and that she would like him to come and see her. The man inquired, "Whom shall I ask for?" and she answered, "I am Princesse Murat." He looked at her for a minute as she stood there in a simple tweed coat, dripping with rain, and replied, "If you are the Princesse Murat, I am the Duc de la Rochefoucauld," and roared with laughter.

This story got around somehow. The aristocracy pursed their lips and thought it disgraceful. I have heard a hundred exaggerated versions of this innocent escapade, and as it grew in proportion with the telling, it sounded as if we had all got drunk and rolled in the gutter with the truck driver, so eagerly did certain people calling themselves her friends grasp at the slightest chance to gossip about her.

After the engagement at the Mayol and the Jardin, I had to take it a little easy and accepted a short booking for the Perroquet, Léon Volterra's smart night-club built above the

Casino de Paris. I had more time to eat properly, and Violette 'phoned me almost every day to have dinner with her and then go to work. One night when I arrived at her house there was Jean Cocteau. He not only remembered me but was perfectly charming. I don't think I have ever heard a more brilliant conversation than the one that night carried on by Violette, Cocteau, and Toni Ganderillas, a very brilliant diplomat of the Chilean Embassy.

When I was not with Violette, I was with Nina, having a wonderful time and meeting the most interesting people in Paris. Their "sets" kept together, seldom going to any of the big glittering clubs or cabarets of Montmartre that delighted the tourists. Amongst the younger set, there were a few who had favorite cafés and restaurants, but as soon as people knew the celebrities frequented them, they became overcrowded and so were abandoned immediately.

Most of the more advanced writers and painters smoked opium, and there was a great deal of drugging going on. I must say, few of them really took it seriously but used it to create an atmosphere and because it was against the law and therefore considered "smart." Many tried to emulate such great authors as Paul de Cassagnac and Claude Farrère, whose marvelous books, *La Bataille, Fumée d'Opium,* and many others, caused such a sensation in literary circles in the twenties.

Then there was the foreign set, headed by my old friend Jaime de Zulueta and the Infante of Spain, Don Luis de Bourbon. They were even more exotic in their tastes, and when Matto and his money came to town the fun was fast and furious. Among other friends of those days in Paris were Gilbert Charles, the novelist, Henri Teppaz, Jean Guérin, the designer (now I believe in Hollywood), and the De Berthier boys. Those two were sons of the Duc de Sauvigny and a pair of charming mad young monkeys who had suddenly come into the Parisian limelight by shooting the tires off the wheels of an automobile belonging to the wife of the British Ambassador—while the lady was inside. In the Paris of those days, it was only necessary to do something crazy of this kind to become the fashion immediately.

I was due to play a two-week engagement at the Théâtre des Champs-Élysées for Rolf de Maré who had come with Georges Baud to see me dance. He was enthusiastic about the staircase and began to give me publicity before I opened. But whatever he intended to do became insignificant in comparison to the publicity that Botafogo obtained for me—which filled the Paris newspapers for three days.

The story begins with my letting him take the morning sun in the garden. He was becoming easier to handle as time went by and generally coiled himself around the laburnum tree to observe with sleepy eyes the doings of the sparrows. He was so well nourished by Marcel that, although he had a capricious appetite, we did not think at the time he had any interest in hunting, so both Marie and I grew a little careless about him.

The windows of the apartment directly above mine looked into the garden and had two fairly large balconies. The occupant of this apartment was nobody less than a foreign high commissioner who had two daughters and a nasty temper and never got up before noon. We always took Botafogo in before then, for he did not like the hot sun any too well, so I was certain he could not be seen beneath the tree. How the diplomat employed his evenings I didn't know, of course, but was pretty well certain he spent most of them getting plastered somewhere, judging by the stumbling and banging that took place whenever he came home late at night. Be that as it may, the fact remains that one sunny July morning Botafogo stayed later than usual in the garden and crawled, by way of the rain pipe and some vines, up to the balcony of my distinguished neighbor.

The window was open, and Botafogo, looking for some shade, decided to investigate. With half of him entwined around the railing of the balcony, and the other half sliding through the window, I am sure he must have been an impressive sight to any elderly gentleman with a hangover—at any rate it would seem so. All of a sudden, there was the most terrific commotion from the upstairs apartment—shouts, yells, and screams. Marie, attracted by the to-do, ran into the garden, convinced somebody was being murdered. There she spied Botafogo, like Romeo, on the balcony, and came tumbling into my bedroom with the news.

I flew as I was, in pajamas, to the rescue, while Marie ran to the concierge for a ladder. She returned with not only the ladder but also the concierge, his wife, and a pimply-faced son whom I cordially disliked and who stood there grinning like the village idiot. I scaled the wall and grabbed Botafogo with caution. He was thoroughly intrigued by the commotion inside and wanted to see more. Finally Pepita came to help me, bringing the long wire noose we used on such occasions, and between us we managed to drag him down—principally by the necessary, if unkind, expedient of rapping him over the head with the heel of one of Pepita's mules. I seldom hit an animal, but the precarious position of struggling with a five-foot boa in mid-air on a rickety ladder was not a pleasant one, especially as through the window, I could see the red-faced commissioner brandishing a revolver and naturally thought he might kill my snake if I did not get him down quickly. It was all very upsetting.

I dressed as rapidly as possible, preparing myself to meet the coming storm, and did not have to wait very long before it broke in full force, in the person of one of the plainclothes-men who guarded the building, accompanied by the precinct police captain waving a large blue paper. He demanded fiercely if I knew the French laws relating to anybody keeping in his apartment a live and dangerous wild animal to the jeopardy of the neighbors and general public.

I tried to wade through three paragraphs of fine print, looking for the extreme penalty, and noticed a clause that had been underlined which read, "The said animal shall be ejected, and if the owner refuses to remove it instantly, steps shall be taken, *au besoin avec les forces armées*" ("if necessary with the aid of armed forces"). I had visions of a detachment of Gardes Mobiles with shotguns marching into my apartment, so tactfully offered the captain and his pal a drink. Violette had given me a case of rare Napoleon cognac for just such an occasion. It worked marvels, for the captain sat down and became much more tractable under its mellowing influence.

We talked it over, and I promised to endeavor to get the zoo truck to come as soon as possible and take Botafogo to board there. He told me that the high commissioner was in a terrible state and threatened to leave the apartment, go to a hotel, and sue the owner of the building for permitting somebody who in his opinion ought to be in a lunatic asylum to keep a man-eating snake on the premises. I took the two officers, who, between the cognac and Pepita's beauty, were almost inclined to my side by this time, and showed them the iron door for Botafogo's cage, explaining that I would keep him shut up where he'd been safe enough all winter, but that they must give me time to find a suitable place for him. Finally they agreed to give me till morning, but not a moment later, and departed to interview the old fool upstairs who had kicked up all the fuss.

To my surprise, the zoo refused to have Botafogo, either as a gift or as a paying guest. They had, they said, too many boas as it was, and unless I had a rare snake, such as a nice Mamba or an Australian bushmaster, they were not interested. I then tried the smaller Jardin des Plantes Zoo, where the reply was even more unsatisfactory: they did not have a suitable cage and were not disposed to make one; besides, they had no steam heat for the winter.

I 'phoned Dr. Regnier, a veterinarian near the Avenue Malakoff, whom I knew slightly, and he came over to take a look at Botafogo. I knew he had one of the most distinguished clienteles in Paris but could see at once he knew nothing about snakes. The size and strength of Botafogo didn't mean a thing to him, and when I tried to impress upon him that a boa's head is like a battering ram, that one can break its way out of anything but steel netting, he was skeptical. I decided at last that as his office was quite near the apartment, I would send my snake there for a few days in spite of the outrageous cost, gaining time thereby to look around.

Violette was on her yacht in Toulon for a few days, but I knew when she came back I could get her to arrange something with the Jardin d'Acclimatation, the zoo I had first called. Marcel arrived and reported that the entire neighborhood knew about the incident with the high commissioner, for many people had witnessed the balcony scene from their windows. After a brief struggle, we got Botafogo into a big canvas sack and took him to the veterinarian establishment.

It was a nice place built over some old stables, with a sunny courtyard filled with cats and dogs of the smaller varieties. Dr. Regnier's assistants had made a temporary cage for Botafogo that was far too flimsy. When I told them this, they promised to put another layer of strong wire over the front and were sure that would hold.

When I returned from the vet's, Pepita said newspapermen from *Les Écoutes* had telephoned for details of the affair. I rang them up immediately and tried to make light of what had happened, for I did not want any more scandal about the matter than I could help. Early the next morning came another call. This time it was the establishment of Dr. Regnier.

"Madame," moaned the man on the other end of the wire, "your snake has broken out of his cage during the night and has eaten the Angora cat of Madame de Noailles, a distinguished client of the doctor's! What are we to do? You must come at once."

Pepita and I rushed over to the Avenue Malakoff. The doctor and his two assistants were sitting outside the *clinique* in the courtyard, afraid to enter. Inside, through the glass door, I could see Botafogo peacefully sleeping on the top of his cage with a considerable bulge in his body—which I concluded was the Angora cat of Madame de Noailles.

A group of excited women with small animals they had

brought for treatment were gathered outside the entrance to the stables, all discussing with volubility and gestures the horrible situation: nothing would induce them to enter while the snake was there. *"Quoi faire, Madame?"* wailed Dr. Regnier. *"C'est la ruine pour moi!"*—meaning that the behavior of Botafogo was ruining his business.

We found, after managing to get the man to pull himself together, that there was a small laboratory at the end of his apartment where we could easily put Botafogo for the moment. He would probably sleep anyhow while digesting the cat, and in the meantime I would manage in some way to get another place for him. I got Botafogo into the small room easily enough, for he was drugged with sleep and the Angora cat, and we locked him up. Then Dr. Regnier, who was shuddering at the prospect of breaking the news to his client about the loss of her pet (who had been in the family way, poor thing) revived sufficiently to tell me I would, of course, not only have to pay for the death of the cat and her unborn kittens, but also would have to arrive at some compensation for the loss of his clients, since no one would enter his place while Botafogo was there. I could see a fine bill for expenses looming and departed to send a telegram to Violette, begging her to reply if she could recommend me to some of the directors of the Jardin d'Acclimatation, so I could get them to accept my snake. In the meantime newspaper reporters had gone in a body to Dr. Regnier's and photographed the sleeping Botafogo from all angles. Then they interviewed the aristocratic and decrepit owner of the Angora cat, sitting in her apartment surrounded by collections of ribbons she had won in cat shows. They took pictures of my garden, the laburnum tree, and the balcony. The evening papers were plastered with my photograph and carried columns with the story, while the telephone rang incessantly. Only in Paris could such a thing happen. It made head-lines, and I received more publicity than any theater could have possibly afforded to give me.

Violette came up to Paris at once and introduced me to the

directors of the zoo, officials of the Board of Health, and even the great Chiappe, chief of police in Paris—resulting in the arrival of a car from the zoo for Botafogo the next day, where he was allotted a magnificent, air-conditioned, germ-proof cage, with scientific menus prepared especially for him, and a large brass tablet over the cage with my name on it. The newspapermen then raced to the zoo and photographed this, too, with Botafogo in his new quarters. The revues of the Casino de Paris and the Folies wrote skits about it for some of their scenes—so, like a butterfly emerging from its chrysalis, I basked in the full light of popularity the night I opened at the Théâtre des Champs-Élysées.

Then the strangest thing happened: from all over Paris, pet shops began sending me snakes on approval—little snakes and medium snakes—till life for the concierge became a nightmare filled with snakes. A man in Hyères, reading accounts of my parting with Botafogo and feeling the greatest sympathy for my bereavement, sent me a small red-and-black snake as a present, and the last person I would have thought capable of such a thing, Babe Barnato, sent an Algerian desert snake all the way from Whitely's pet shop in London. I kept the smaller one but succeeded in trading Babe's larger snake for a mate for Kimmie—a gray, sad-faced Lèvre Bleue lady monkey from the Belgian Congo.

The opening night of the Champs-Élysées was for a grand gala, and the boxes were crowded with celebrities. Rolf de Maré had adopted the charming fashion, originally used by Diaghilev in the old Châtelet Theater, of placing all the beautiful women in the front-row boxes of the balcony. Backstage we heard the reports of who was there, among them Cécile Sorel, Lina Cavalieri, the Duchesse d'Uzès with Violette Murat and Diane de Polignac, and in a box near them was Anna Pavlova who had played the same theater some weeks previously.

De Maré gave me an exquisite set of lights and a cyclorama of silver lamé that was simply lovely. Morgan had worked for a week on the staircase to enlarge it, and the steps now reached from the top of the stage almost to the footlights. Rainbow colors glowed through the crystal steps on my white ostrich-feather costume.

Nina brought Kies van Dongen, the painter à la mode, to my dressing-room that night. He had, of course, heard and read all about the Botafogo incident and like everybody else wanted to meet me. He was with his beautiful gray-haired wife, Jasmé, and they invited me to one of their famous receptions a day or so later. The parties given by the van Dongens were brilliant highlights of the Paris season. His house on the Rue Juliette-Lambert had an enormous ballroom and a dining-room with walls made of black marble on which van Dongen had painted figures of green centaurs. The table and furniture were of the same black stone, and the effect was astonishing. The first time I went there, the fête was in honor of the Aga Khan, and many of the favorite artists in Paris entertained. Walls of the ballroom were hung with portraits of celebrated artists and society women, so when van Dongen asked me to sit for him, it was a great compliment which I was naturally very flattered to accept.

He nearly always painted by artificial light and used one of the oddest implements to apply his color—an ordinary feather duster with a long bamboo handle, used by maids to dust cornices and picture frames. While he painted, he often wore a long gray overcoat and a basket, like a straw hat, over his eyes. I enjoyed sitting for him, although it was very tiring because he used powerful reflectors to light the color of the costume he had chosen to paint me in. It was an apple-green satin coat and trunks that I had worn for the Jardin, and the color interested him. In fact, he concentrated a great deal upon obtaining the effect he wanted with the sheen of the satin in contrast to the flesh tones. I sat for him off and on for five weeks and have an interesting photograph in my press book taken in van Dongen's studio by the newspapers, with a group around the picture consisting of van Dongen, his wife, Violette, Princesse Hélène Murat, Harry Wyndham, the English humorist and author, and myself. The

298

portrait was an oddly angular one for a dancer but was shown at the Paris Salon the following year, and critics raved about it. This was all magnificent publicity for me, since van Dongen was then at the zenith of his fame, and I have always been deeply grateful to him. He gave me an *affiche* for theater lobbies that he painted from the original, also a small head which was very good. Both, unfortunately, are in my Paris storage vaults—maybe!

During the last days at the Champs-Élysées, Rolf de Maré discovered a strange and extraordinarily clever American boy who did a trapeze act dressed as a girl. He called himself "Barbette" and was billed as the "Enigma," with a large question mark. In addition to doing a beautiful act, he was graceful and feminine and looked so lovely on the stage that the senile gentlemen in the stalls, licking their lips while he worked, were startled into consciousness when he removed his wig at the end of the act and they discovered he wasn't a girl.

Paris loved such acts when they were well done, and after de Maré had spent a small fortune dressing him in black paradise plumes and diamonds for the début, Barbette became a star. He hailed from Texas and was, when I first met him at the Champs-Élysées, a shy retiring boy who spoke little French and went through many stormy moments with the musicians in Paul Whiteman's orchestra, who worked on the bill and took a fiendish delight in teasing and tormenting him.

Violette thought he was wonderful and invited him to her house with Toni Ganderillas and Cocteau. He went from one triumph to another: books were written about him, and as his fame increased, he lost his shyness and became noted by every long-suffering manager in the theaters where he appeared for his demands upon their stage staffs and musicians, but as they have often told me, he was worth it. I have known Barbette for years: we have met and worked together in all sorts of countries and conditions. After the terrible illness that crippled him in New York a few years ago, the stage lost one of its finest performers.

Another odd personality from the United States appeared in Paris at that time. I first met him through a friend of mine from Argentina, a wealthy Australian divorcée, Nellie MacLennan, who 'phoned one evening and asked if she could bring an American friend to my apartment for cocktails. I was, as in Buenos Aires, always having crowds of people at my house, and on this evening Pepita and a nephew of the Khedive of Cairo were there for a drink before going out to dinner. Nellie arrived and introduced a small, rather commonplace man, who was definitely out of his element and appeared ill at ease. His name meant nothing to me then.

We barely noticed him and after dinner all went on to Bricktop's cabaret, the Grand Duke. Suddenly one of the colored boys in the band asked to speak to me privately for a moment. He warned me that the man in the gray suit (Nellie's boy-friend) was none other than the notorious Legs Diamond, said to be traveling on a ticket of leave from the American police because they wanted him out of the country for a while. The musician asked me not to mention the fact to our party or say who had told me—but to be careful. I talked to Bricktop about it; she said we had better get Nellie home while she still had her jewelry, for she was wearing a valuable collar of big diamonds and quantities of bracelets. Pepita and I decided to insist that Nellie, who was drinking and in the sloppy stage, come home with us. But there was no losing Legs Diamond: he came along despite our frank rudeness to him. Once in my apartment, Nellie passed out.

While I kept Diamond in conversation about this and that, Pepita adroitly removed Nellie's jewels, locking them in my desk. Then I told Diamond that we knew who he was. I am certain he had no intention of stooping to such a paltry crime as robbing our unconscious friend, for he admitted his identity, and I felt really sorry for him when he told me how lonely he was in Paris. He had rather nice eyes that were not at all shifty or mean but reminded me of a beagle hound.

300

When I confided the adventure to Violette the next day, she was so excited nothing would satisfy her but that I bring him to her house at once. She had always loved gangsters and read avidly all she could about them. There was a point, she said, that she and an antique duchess pal of hers could never quite clear up about a lurid underworld crime that had occurred in Chicago, and here was the golden opportunity for her to get the matter explained by one of the chief participants in the affair. Like the Spanish royal children who were said to collect detective magazines about the activities of Al Capone and whose dearest ambition was to have his autograph, Violette and her blue-blooded friend were far more interested in American gunmen than in the *Social Register*.

The next afternoon Legs Diamond called me up. He wanted, he said, some help from me in sending money to his wife and a girl-friend in New York, and would I meet him at the Café de la Paix to send the money for him? I told him I would, provided he accompanied me afterwards to the house of a very distinguished person whose name I could not tell him, and that he behave himself when he got there. I picked him up in my car as agreed and was shocked to see how ill he looked. I was touched by the gentle way he spoke to me about his womenfolk in the States and how he worried about their receiving the money—which was a very large sum. As we drove to Violette's house, I made him tell me all about himself.

It seemed that he lived in constant fear of some of his gangster enemies against whom he had recently testified and who might have come to Paris after him. In his nervousness he started at every traffic incident and kept twisting his fingers.

When we arrived at Violette's, she was alone and eagerly awaiting the guest. Evidently my cautions as to his behavior had taken effect, for he stared in awe at the butler, footmen, and palatial surroundings and treated Violette with such distant respect that she became impatient. She plied him with whisky after dinner, then sat down in front of him and said, "Now, tell me all about your murders—how many did you bump off?" This speech, coming from Violette, not only startled me but positively stunned Legs Diamond. He was shocked and so embarrassed that he turned scarlet, stuttered and stammered until Violette, to put him at his ease, went to the telephone for a moment. He took that opportunity of whispering to me, "Jesus, is that dame really a princess?"

Later that evening, he improved considerably and thoroughly enjoyed himself, while Violette took notes of all the gangster slang to tell the Duchess at the first opportunity. "She will be so jealous," she gleefully told us. I also introduced Legs to Jean Guérin, and there he made a great hit, enjoying himself so much that he asked me what he could do to reciprocate all the hospitality he had received. I told him that he was not expected to do anything, for like a movie star he was the "lion" of the moment and therefore a coveted guest. Before he left Paris, he did a very sweet thing, and that was to send me a gold cigarette case, in which was set just one large, very beautiful diamond. I suppose it was all wrong to glamorize a gangster, but in those mad, merry days anything new that was unconventional was sought after as a thrill.

After Deauville, I spent a week with mother in Jersey, where she was at last taking a rest. I had hopes of my father's coming across for a few weeks, but he did not, and the thought that he and my mother had now completely drifted apart saddened my holiday. I went to St.-Tropez with Nina and Violette on the latter's yacht, for the last days of August, and resumed work again in September at the Casino in Biarritz, doubling at the Caveau Basque, where Maria Koutnetzova and Dora Stroeva were singing.

Georges Baud appeared one night, with the Egyptian manager Gino Abouin who had been so disappointed that morning in the station after my arrival from Italy. This time, I was able to give him a different impression, which resulted in an engagement for Cairo and Alexandria for six weeks, to follow immediately after Biarritz. It was not only a high salary but the source of much satisfaction to Morgan, whose greatest desire had always been to get a look at what he called "that ruddy Spinx."

PART IV

XVI

WE LEFT Marseilles for Egypt with quite an impressive list of acts. Sascha Goudin and his troupe of Russian dancers, Mitty and Tillio, acrobatic dancers from the Casino de Paris, Pierrette Butterfly from the Champs-Élysées, and a girl called Musette who said she was English but might have been any nationality or any age. She dressed beautifully and had very well hennaed hair: her act consisted of playing the violin while doing an acrobatic dance.

Musette interested me from the first day. She had an extraordinary personality and was obviously hard as nails, saying little about herself, but I discovered she had traveled all over the world, especially in the Orient, and was the most self-sufficient person I have ever met. Gino Abouin and his wife also traveled with us. She was a pretty French girl with a set of diamonds that upset all the English and French matrons accompanying hard-working husbands back to their jobs in Alexandria.

Abouin seemed to know what he was about and arranged everything for our arrival in the most efficient and high-handed manner—so much so that somehow I managed to get Mascotte on and off the boat and into the Gezîreh Palace before I found out that a quarantine for animals existed as in England. I had left all these matters to Baud and Abouin while in Paris, having understood that no such procedure was necessary. As Abouin seemed to have unlimited authority with officials, I let him handle everything, little dreaming that later on it would cause me a costly headache.

Cairo was crowded with tourists of all nationalities but principally Americans, who stayed at Shepheard's in town, while the Gezîreh and Mena Palaces, some distance out, were full of British officials with their families, and members of the diplomatic corps. The dinner dances were especially elegant at the Gezîreh, and I noticed, when there were any Egyptians present, they were important officials invited by English officers. It was a lesson in diplomacy to watch André, the suave headwaiter, heading off a party of would-be diners when they were what the British described as "Gippies," if they did not call them "natives."

In a way, it was an extremely dull month, and had it not been for Musette's company, it would have been deadly, for on nights in the early part of the week we danced for the tables most of the time, and this, after Paris, was depressing.

I had received few letters from Leslie during recent months but knew he was stationed near Khartoum, and thinking it might be possible for him to obtain a furlough and come by military plane to Cairo, I cabled him about it. I wanted to talk over many things and learn what he intended doing with his life, for his letters were not communicative. However, he did not come, and I received a letter from him before leaving Alexandria, telling me his father was ill and he planned on going to London, so would perhaps look me up in Paris. But to come to Cairo while I was dancing at a hotel where most of his friends stayed would be a *faux pas* of the worst type for him, and he begged me not to mention to any officials I might meet that I was his wife. I concluded his career meant a great deal more to him than I did, and forgot the matter.

If I was not having too exciting a time, Morgan was. It was a pleasure to see him gloating over the mummies and Tutankhamen's tomb in the museum. He practically lived there, had spent nearly a week's salary having photographs taken of himself on camels with the Pyramids in the distance, and had visited the "Spinx" to his heart's content. When I told him that Anna Pavlova had spent an entire night alone in the desert, communing with the spirit of old Egypt, nothing could stop him from doing the same thing, so we took a car one night, and drove out to give him the thrill of seeing the Pyramids by moonlight.

With time on my hands in Cairo, I started seriously to study perfumes, their history and formulas, learning a great deal about them, and was deeply interested in knowing more about oriental essentials and fixatives. I went, with some friends of Abouin's who were research chemists for one of the big Paris laboratories, to the house of Ferhendi Brothers on the Rue Nalika Farela—one of the greatest of all oriental perfume exporters. I had been fascinated, the first day in Cairo, while passing a doorway of a perfumer near the Mohammed Ali Theater, by the odor of a fragrance I could not place but whose elusive quality haunted me.

Upon entering the shop and trying flacons of all descriptions without finding the one that had first intrigued me, I bought some attar of roses for mother and an *ambre chypre*—but they were not what I wanted. I searched and sniffed, till the day at Ferhendi's when suddenly, while one of their chemists was explaining a long and complicated combination of oils to Abouin's friends, I caught a whiff of the scent I was looking for. It turned out to be nothing more nor less than the humble Tonka bean, but its fragrance expressed for me the soul of the East.

I learned another interesting detail about rare perfumes: one of the most sought-after and expensive fixatives sold in Cairo is a civet obtained from the ordinary alley cat. These animals are possessed of powerful sweat glands, and the natives keep quantities of them shut up in a low-roofed room that is practically without air, starving the poor animals until they become weak and perspire so that their fur drips with moisture. This is collected with a wooden spatula, carefully prepared, and refined into little wax-like cubes which are then sold as a fixative for some of the most expensive odors. I brought a collection of essences and formulas back to Paris, which I kept more or less as a curiosity, for the heavy animal aromas predominant in oriental perfumes have never appealed to me, although they are interesting studies.

If Cairo had been almost too *comme il faut* and dull, Alexandria went to the other extreme. Gino Abouin had nothing to do with the direction of the Pavillon Bleu, where I was to fulfil the second part of my contract, so when he said good-by, he was profuse in his thanks and praise of my conduct but omitted to tell me what sort of place to expect upon arriving in Alexandria.

Morgan had gone to the theater early on the day we opened, to hang my rigging, and when I arrived later for band call, the expression on his face as he watched mine reflected acute anxiety for fear I would be too disgusted to work. The establishment was a tawdry, stuffy place with a tiny apology for a stage and a half-moon floor space. The orchestra appeared to be suspended in mid-air in a sort of cage—God knows how the musicians ever clambered into it or managed to play after they got there. They were a mixture of Italian, Greek, and Syrian, with a mania for marches, relying on the music of "Valencia" and Sousa's "Stars and Stripes Forever" to fall back on, in every emergency. There were tiers of boxes around the floor where Arabs and Greeks played dominoes and drank small cups of Turkish coffee.

The only acts that had come on from Cairo were Pierrette Butterfly, Musette, and myself as the star act, but at the rehearsal we met a dance team booked from London who were to fill out the bill, with the assistance of a magician from Marseilles. We were the distinguished imported acts, for in the lobby there were the usual attractions—Arab dancers who wiggled and jerked their stomachs to the wailings and thumpings of a native band, and who were fat, greasy, and depressing.

The place was simply unbelievable, and the dressing-rooms defied description. Preceding acts had scrawled their names in grease paint on the walls, with obscene comments about the establishment and its directors in five different languages. But the performance was the pay-off, for the audience (which consisted mainly of natives, with a sprinkling of French bourgeois and German tourists) were so absorbed in their eternal game of dominoes, they barely gave us a glance. Even Pierrette's high soprano notes failed to get more than a casual

310

applause, and after they examined me from all angles on the rope, they decided I was too thin, according to Morgan, who understood Arabic.

As the ghastly engagement drew to its close, I had a foreboding that something else unpleasant was about to happen. Sure enough, the bad tidings came in a letter from my brother, who had gone to Paris, alarmed by the news that mother was in my apartment, very ill with influenza, and had absolutely refused medical care. This was most unusual, for she had always been inclined to fly to a doctor at the slightest sign of ill health.

My brother's letter decided me to break my contract and return to Paris. After much argument and bickering, I finally came to an arrangement whereby the management would release me from the last week of my contract and I would waive the return passage to Marseilles in compensation.

I went to Cook's Tourist Bureau to arrange passages on the next boat to France for Morgan and myself, but there I ran into complications brought about by the officious Abouin and the lack of requisite quarantine certificates for Mascotte. I had already paid for Morgan's passage and my own before requesting a ticket for the dog. This, Cook's employee absolutely refused to sell until I produced the necessary documents.

I wandered down to the water-front to see what I could wangle, and after a series of complicated incidents, I managed to get the dog smuggled on board the ship, a proceeding that cost me fifty pounds. It was one of those chain affairs which always turn out costly. It started with a Romanian interpreter from the American Express Company, who found a steward on the ship, who knew another steward, whose brother did something in the engine-room. All day the chain of conspirators increased, until most of the crew, stevedores, and the beggars on the dock, were involved in the matter. When I explained the plan to Morgan he was horrified and upon boarding the boat the following morning wore such a guilty expression, I felt sure every one would think he was wanted by Scotland Yard.

In the end things turned out all right. I waited in my cabin until weeping relatives had said farewell to excited passengers and flustered stewards had got everybody's luggage where it belonged; then there came a timid knock on the door. An undersized and very dirty deckhand led me through passages and companionways to an insanitary and mysterious part of the ship, where I recovered Mascotte.

Musette came aboard to see me off and said she would be in Paris within a few months to arrange a tour through Canada, Japan, and China. She had a capitalist who often sent her on tours to the Far East with a unit of vaudeville acts, and if the idea interested me she would be happy to talk business. I promised to write her, and dismissed the matter from my mind.

When I arrived in Paris, I was shocked beyond measure to see how ill mother looked and how much she had aged in the past few months. The first thing I did was call in Doctor Gros of the American Hospital in Neuilly, despite her protestations, and when he arrived I had the greatest difficulty persuading her to allow an examination. When it was over, he had a long talk with me and very frankly said that mother was seriously ill, that unless she had complete rest from work, worry, and agitation, her illness could take a very dangerous turn. He had found her very hard to handle and had warned her as kindly as possible about her condition.

She was nervous and ill all through Christmas, worrying continually about getting back to work and my brother's needs. I wrote father about her health, begging him to come as soon as possible. When he cabled that he would be with us in early summer, she immediately decided not to be in Paris at that time, as she had every intention of rejoining the Swedish project.

Bunnie promised to stay with her while I went down to Nice for the New Year's engagement I had accepted some months previously for the Rhul. That was one of the saddest New Years I ever spent, for I had to work the contract and needed the money, but the thought of mother's condition was always with me. The only bright moment was the arrival of an old childhood sweetheart, Eric Farrant and his bride, a dark Irish girl who was so like me that everybody thought we were sisters. Eric was charming on New Year's Eve—he had a photo taken of our table with Eric between his wife and myself. "I want a souvenir of the two women I love best in the world," he said.

Upon returning to Paris, I signed a contract with Henri Varna for the new revue at the Palace, starring the great French clown, Grock, one of the greatest artists I have ever worked with. He was already a very old man but a master of violin, piano, and cello, working with a musical partner as a stooge. Their subtle, sly humor was one of the classics of the Paris stage and, for that matter, of the entire world, for Grock spoke many languages. He had his act translated into different tongues, conserving the same delicate *esprit* that is so typically French.

During the rehearsals, I decided it was about time for me to try my luck with some stage sets and see how they would be received in Paris. I designed a setting for the staircase, arranged as a glorified bar, with girls representing cocktails and myself, of course, the champagne, making an entrance from an enormous goblet perched at the top of the crystal stairs. Varna liked the idea and put it into construction immediately. This was my first tableau in Paris and called "Le Wonder Bar," a play on the German word. I also did my rope and the little piano number that was copied by everybody after the first week—dancing on my toes on the keys of a grand piano and tapping out a simple melody.

We had a mild March, that year of grace 1926, and mother began to improve. She went out a little but was still not herself and often felt very sad. It was hard for me, too. I could not be with her enough and do all the work I had contracted for, and I longed for my father to come over.

313

One day, while driving past the Banque de Varsovie, near the Bourse, I noticed the familiar figure of a tall elegant man dressed in livery, opening the doors of the bank to the callers. There was something about him that caused me to slacken speed, and as I drew alongside the curb, I recognized him as Prince Alexis, the husband of Helena Soltikoff, daughter of the Princess I had known as a child. He was so happy to see me again he nearly cried, and told me his wife and sister-in-law Choura were both sewing lingerie in the Galerie Lafayette (the large department store). I invited them all to dinner, and upon this occasion, mother, for the first time in weeks, perked up. We saw a great deal of her old Russian friends from then on, many of whom we did not even know were in Paris.

They were an extraordinary colony, most of them living from hand to mouth, but many working hard were getting along pretty well. Helena was nearly blind from embroidering the exquisite things she sold for a song, saving every centime in the vain hope of buying her son back from the Soviet. He was in a crippled children's home in Moscow, as far as she had been able to find out, and the U.S.S.R. had asked twenty-five thousand rubles to ship him to Paris. I had never heard such a preposterous story, but apparently it was true, for other friends of hers, the Mamoulasche family, had scraped enough money together to send for their father who had been condemned as a political prisoner to the salt-mines. But when he arrived, after they had paid an outrageous sum for his release, he turned out to be an old broken-down moujik they had never before seen. The Soviet did not exchange the merchandise.

Mother, always happy when she was exhausting herself running about for people she liked, had badgered all her friends into buying lingerie from Helena and Choura. She also obtained a position for Alexis with the Isola Brothers' offices at the Opéra Comique. As in Constantinople, Russians flooded the house, and those we could not help overflowed into Violette's château in Marseilles. One evening Alexis arrived at the Palace, where I was working, with another Russian friend, Prince Poutatine, to fetch me for a surprise party they were giving for both mother and myself.

The Poutatines had started a little hat shop near the Place Vendôme, where they barely eked out a living till Violette started bringing all the rich Americans she knew, who had a yen for princes, to buy the hats and accessories Princess Poutatine turned out. The prince, a very handsome man, delivered the hats to the purchasers. Naturally, the fair customers were so overcome with the novelty of having a real live prince delivering their millinery free of charge that business began to pick up.

The party was a typical Russian evening, held in the Poutatines' tiny house on the Cité des Fleurs, an ancient street in Montmartre where the houses seemed to be holding each other up as they sagged and drooped from old age. Our hosts' place was one of these and had three steps leading down to the front door, which had just given way under the weight of entering guests and were in consequence a trifle hard to navigate. Once inside, though, the scene was perfectly charming, for Princess Poutatine had somehow or other obtained a few portraits and souvenirs from Russia, and the rest of the furnishings were antiques bought for a few francs in the Foire des Puces. Restored and arranged with perfect taste, they made a delightful interior.

The rooms were lighted with candles, and there were flowers everywhere. Our hostess, a beautiful tall woman, was gowned, as were Helena, Choura, and the others, in perfect creations which must have cost all kinds of money. The élite of the Russian colony had gathered together that night, all the men in faultless evening clothes, and in the corner of the room were the inevitable Tziganski singers with guitars. There was even a beautiful Borzoi dog, and somebody's old family Cossack retainer who had got out of Russia on foot and walked through Germany and Belgium, taking two years to get to Paris and rejoin his former masters.

There was the old Grand Duke Nikolas Nikolaivitch, the young Grand Duke Dimitri Pavlovitch, and Felix Youssopoff, who, people said, had begun to think he was haunted by the spirit of Rasputin that never left him day or night, and was always whispering to him to poison some one. There were the Rodziankos, sons of the President of the Duomo under the Czar, old Prince Wolkonski, gentleman of the bedchamber to his late Majesty the Emperor, and scores of other guests, some of the greatest names in old Russia.

Tables were piled high with caviar, chicken, and buckets of champagne. There was an even more expensive Russian custom besides the classic one of breaking glasses, which consisted of a pyramid built with champagne goblets, over which a servant poured wine till it formed a cascade and spilled on to the floor. As each guest took a glass, drained it and hurled it behind him, the Tzigane songs rose to a wild crescendo. I was astounded at such a reckless display of luxury and wondered how on earth they had managed it. When I questioned them they said, "This is a party we will never forget. We want to be happy just this one night, even if we starve for the rest of the year. To-night everything must be perfect, like the old days in Russia. Please understand and enjoy yourself with us." I spent the rest of the evening reciting Pushkin, while mother sang the songs they loved. I think they were really happier than they had been for a long time.

I had accepted another contract to double at the Hollywood Club, which, as on previous occasions, kept me busier than ever, so that I had very little time to devote to mother—but it had to be done for financial reasons. The only real enjoyment she had was studying her singing with Zipilli, who had turned up at the Comique playing in the orchestra. I often took mother with me while rehearsing my tableau for the revue at the Palace—I knew she loved this. The Wonder Bar presentation did rather well, and I received an offer from Henri Hallais and the famous cartoonist, Rip, to produce and dance two more tableaux for a revue they were presenting at the Théâtre de l'Avenue early in May.

I accepted this offer, and there ensued a stormy scene with Henri Varna when I gave him my notice: he resented my leaving the Palace for another house, but it was an opportunity I couldn't pass up. Hallais, having heard about the work I did in Argentina and the famous *Ballet du Pissoire*, wanted me to repeat it in his show, which I did with nice success.

Mother spent a week or so in Spain, then went to England and wrote she was sharing a house at Marlow on the Thames— about an hour and a half by train from London—with the Australian singer, Nellie Melba. I gathered from the tone of her letters that she was feeling perfectly well and intended singing again in opera, for she spoke of studying two or three times a week in London. One night, just as I was going on at the Théâtre de l'Avenue, Marie handed me a telegram. It said: "Mother has suffered a stroke. Please come at once"— signed by a Dr. Maclean, and there was the address of a nursing home in Marlow.

I read it twice before the full horror of that short message became clear to me. Then I automatically went on and did the best I could with my dance. It was impossible to let the performers down because of a personal sorrow. When I came off, Halais was standing in the wings waiting for me, Marie having already told him the terrible news. He thanked me for dancing under the circumstances and very kindly told me to go pack a bag, and he would telephone the Imperial Airlines for a seat on the first plane to England.

I was worried to death about my brother, for fear they had sent him the same crude announcement, so while I packed Pepita put through a long-distance call to Jersey for me. It was as I had suspected. He already had the news and had caught the night boat for Southampton. I will never forget the kindness of my friends in the theater, for Mr. Hallais sent Jean Duvivier, the famous old character actor, before the curtain to announce that owing to the illness of my mother—

317

the celebrated opera singer Maria de Lisle—I would be unable to appear again that night. Zipilli, who dropped in to see me by chance at the theater, heard the news and came at once to the Avenue du Bois. He was very fond of mother and sat all night talking about her and the fun we all had working together. He drove out to Le Bourget and saw me off on the seven A.M. plane for Croydon.

I did not arrive at the Marlow nursing home until afternoon, and I learned that Dr. Maclean had been called the previous evening by mother's hysterical maid and found her condition desperate. He had judged it best to send for an ambulance to remove mother to a sanitarium, but on the way she suffered a further brain hemorrhage, and his hopes for her recovery were very slight. My brother had arrived several hours before me and was bitterly resentful that mother should have been moved from her own room without our consent, for he was certain the effort of the trip had produced the second hemorrhage.

For ten ghastly days we fought to save her life. The day following my arrival, I went to London and arranged for the best specialist I could find, Sir Frederick Treves, to drive down to Marlow immediately for a consultation. His opinion was that mother might live but would remain an invalid, partially paralyzed, for an indefinite length of time and that there was nothing science could do to effect a complete recovery.

When I met father at the boat train a week later, he looked so old and frail, my heart ached for him. It was not difficult to see that my mother's illness was the crowning blow to a long series of sorrows he had suffered all his married life and that the thought of losing her had completely unnerved him. He would not accept the opinion of either the doctor or the specialist, nor could he believe that such a brilliant, beautiful woman would be tied to a bed in helpless inertia, to drag out her remaining days in a way that would have revolted and horrified her.

During the third week of her illness, she improved enough

318

to speak a few words, recognized my father, and even smiled at the flowers he brought her every day. Father searched the village for lilies of the valley, big pink roses, and ice cream—the only things she seemed to enjoy. Sir Frederick Treves saw her again and said that mother's resistance was so good she could possibly live for two or three years, but as he had previously diagnosed, she'd never be anything but an invalid and both legs would remain paralyzed. She seemed happiest when I was with her and would spend hours holding my hand. I seemed to soothe her.

Father's finances were in no condition to stand the terrific expenses involved in a long illness, so I did what I could to help by making a quick trip to Paris to break my lease, if possible, and send Marie and the animals to Violette, whose sympathy and kindness, like that of such friends as Babe Barnato, Zipilli and many others, were beyond expression. I was trying to do some packing when I received a long-distance call from father. I could hear the anguish in his voice vibrate over the wire as he told me that Dr. Maclean had noticed a change in mother that morning and thought I should come back at once. Violette drove me to Le Bourget where I caught the afternoon plane.

When I arrived in Marlow at six o'clock that evening my mother was dead. The doctor cautioned me to get father back to the hotel as soon as possible, for there was a possibility of his having a complete nervous collapse. All sorts of sad details had to be attended to, so I begged him to stay with Bunnie at the hotel and let me do everything. I could not stand the look of utter misery in his tired gray eyes, and the thought of saving him a moment's sorrow that could be avoided strengthened me to spend the night in vigil beside my mother's body. As the nursing home was a Protestant one, father had encountered all sorts of obstacles in obtaining their permission for a priest or nun to remain with mother as he wished. Perhaps the only consolation to the whole tragedy was that she died in a coma, without fear or pain or ever realizing what happened. Her beautiful face was peaceful

319

as it rested in the pillows of flowers father had arranged. We buried her in the old Marlow cemetery, whose dead sleep beside the River Thames.

After it was all over, and the well-meaning crowds of people from the world of opera and theater had left us alone, I was able to get father to talk of the future. My brother, whose grief was beyond any attempt at consolation, planned on leaving at once for Jersey. I felt sure it would be the best thing for him and father as well to go there at once.

It was necessary for me to spend several days in London tracing all mother's effects in storage vaults and banks, and when this was completed, I took her dresses and hats to the nuns of the Sacred Heart Convent, for I did not want father to see them. After all this was accomplished, I traveled with father and Bunnie to Jersey, stayed there a week, then left for Paris to see about my own affairs.

Violette had interviewed the owner of the apartment house, obtaining a written consent for me to sublet with or without furniture, which was a comforting thought, but I had not time to do anything about it for the moment. I saw Mr. Hallais, and he told me the Avenue revue was closing in another two weeks, the end of the Paris season, so I accepted a contract at the Cirque d'Hiver for one month.

The old life of gaiety and bohemia had no appeal for me, and the only people I saw for a while were Olga and Nina. Violette went away for the summer and urged me to join her in Vichy whenever I could get a holiday. Before she left, one of the most touching tributes possible was paid to mother by friends.

I had arranged for a requiem mass on the anniversary of her birthday, to be held at seven o'clock in the morning at the church of St. Honoré d'Eylau, Avenue Victor Hugo. When Violette and I arrived we found nearly half the church filled with people I knew. Zipilli and Morgan had told everybody in Montmartre about it, and there were acts I had worked with in vaudeville and circus, all the Negro musicians from the Apollo and the Jardin, Bricktop and Florence, the

320

colored singers, and many other night-club performers who worked till five and six in the morning and had sacrificed their much-needed sleep to attend that mass.

I received all sorts of offers to go to Deauville and other pleasure spots of the summer *plages* in France but preferred to stay at the Cirque d'Hiver for as long as they wanted me. I spoke to father nearly every night by long distance—it was my only extravagance and well worth it just to hear his voice. He was remaining with my brother for as long as he could possibly afford, then returning to Canada, and said he understood my having to work, so not to worry about his feelings on the subject. I made up my mind that if he could not be in Paris with me, I was going to Canada if I could possibly manage it, so there would not be any lonely Christmas for him that year.

One of the attractions that had kept the Cirque d'Hiver open so late that summer (they generally closed before August) was an extraordinary act of sixty lions, handled by Marthe La Corse. She was a tall, powerfully built girl, with a mass of honey-colored, bushy hair framing the high cheek-bones of her face, and this, together with slanting green eyes, gave her an amusing resemblance to one of her own lions.

She worked almost nude, with a flimsy Greek tunic barely covering her body, in a gigantic cage supposed to represent a Roman arena where a Christian slave, in the person of the young lady, had been thrown to the lions. Instead of eating her, they did the most engaging tricks at her command. For the finale, they were all banked up on pedestals, while a group lay down in a heap of tawny fur with their trainer cuddled in the midst of them, her head in the mouth of a great black-maned Nubian lion from her own collection. No woman not possessed of the courage of ten men could possibly have whipped such an act together, and although the result was distinctly corny from an artistic point of view, there' was a savage magnificence about it that awed the public.

I became very friendly with Marthe La Corse and another girl called Nancy de la Mare, a beautiful blonde with the

sloping shoulders and frail beauty of an early Victorian miniature. She had a small private income which she spent almost
entirely on wild beasts, a strange contrast to her fragile,
delicate personality. Both girls lived in trailers, surrounded
by lines of washing strung up between cages of wild beasts
of every description, in the lot they rented, together with
other nomad acts, on the outskirts of Paris.

Nancy had a boy-friend who was not so interesting but was
also a trainer, handling some moth-eaten tigers in a *cirque
ambulante* around the small fair grounds. He was a coarsely
handsome Italian called Florio, with an evil and cowardly
disposition—the sort who wore a set of phoney medals on his
stage uniform. I spent a great deal of my spare time with
Marthe, and our friendship increased through an unfortunate incident that occurred in the menagerie of the Cirque,
when I was able to be of slight service to her.

One Saturday afternoon, a man had allowed his small son
to torment a lioness belonging to Marthe (on exhibition in
one of the cages), despite repeated warnings from the attendants. The boy slipped under the roped-off space between
the cages and the public and shoved his hand too near the
lioness. She grabbed his arm through the bars of her cage
and practically scooped half of him inside it. When they
finally got the boy out, he was dead. The father sued Marthe
and the Fratellinis as owners of the circus. It was then that
I introduced her to an influential lawyer friend of Violette's
through whom she was able to get a settlement adjusted.

Although it cost her money, she was lucky the affair had not
gone further, for at first the police threatened to suspend
her act. The fact that she had been decorated with a medal
for bravery the previous year was played up by the lawyer,
for she, alone and unaided, had saved the life of a soldier who
one night had crossed the lot where an escaped lion from one
of the trailers sprang upon him. Marthe had beaten and cuffed
the animal off the prostrate man and back into its cage before
it had time to injure him—so great was her courage and
power over animals.

Nancy told me a great deal about some of the rotten tricks that Florio was in the habit of playing, not only on her, but on his unfortunate animals, and I had witnessed several stormy scenes between the two. One hot August night, Nancy came crying to my dressing-room, to tell me a long story about how Florio had beaten one of his tigers brutally across the eyes with a whip, half-blinding the unfortunate beast, who was old and so crippled with rheumatism he was unable to spring or defend himself. I asked Marthe if she thought we could buy the tiger between us and by rest and treatment cure him sufficiently to be able to work him. Marthe knew the tiger Bengali well, and as he was a magnificent specimen, though old, she thought we could do something with him.

I was certainly in no position at the moment to burden myself with even half of a Bengal tiger but made up my mind that if Florio would sell him, I would go halves with Nancy, in the hope that Marthe could eventually use him in some way for her act. (I will not deny always having cherished a desire to have an act myself with tigers and leopards, but had never been able to amass sufficient capital to buy my own beasts.) So, on pay night we drove out to the fair grounds where Florio was working, near Vincennes and the trailer lot where the girls lived.

If I had any doubts about doing a reckless and extravagant thing, one look at the sick animal with bloody scars across his face, cowering and quivering in a corner of his cramped cage, decided me. Florio told us that the tiger had not eaten for several days, so he was disposed to knock off a hundred francs from his price of sixteen hundred, but that Bengali had been one of the most famous tigers in French circus history and had worked in great acts before coming down to his present misery. After a violent scene between Nancy and her lover, in which she tried to cut him across the face with his own whip, we pooled our money and bought Bengali, arranging for one of the acts to truck his cage to the trailer camp the next morning.

I was so excited I could not sleep that night and was out

323

at the lot bright and early, to find Marthe with some of her trainer relatives and neighbors looking over the sick animal. His eyes were still bright, and he snarled and zarped his great paws with unlimited energy, but there was no way to get him to eat. He was skin and bones, his fur filthy and matted, without luster, and it was difficult to prod him into the new temporary cage Nancy had fixed for him in her extra trailer, where it was warm and dry. She had sacrificed the only space she had for her kitchen to make the animal comfortable. He had more room to stretch and move but did not smell exactly of heliotrope, which meant another sacrifice on Nancy's part.

I telephoned the director Violette had introduced me to in the Jardin d'Acclimatation, and told him the story. He was very interested and at once sent up a veterinarian who found three huge back teeth with abscessed roots—one of the reasons why the animal could not eat and probably the main cause of the rheumatism or lumbago that had almost paralyzed his hind quarters. Nancy told us Florio had a habit of striking the helpless animal with his clenched fist, full on the jaws, to make him roar and excite the crowds. It was horrible cruelty, and although I had a vague idea that I was letting myself in for the main share of the expenses, I gladly paid the vet for injections and extractions of the teeth. This sort of thing went on through the last weeks of the Cirque d'Hiver, till I left for Jersey to see my brother and father.

While there, Morgan telegraphed that Georges Baud had a contract for two weeks at the Palladium in London, and although hating to risk leaving Mascotte alone so often, I felt I should accept and wired in the affirmative. I knew Baud thought it important for me to play London and the opening of the Palladium, for the autumn season was more or less of an event in vaudeville. Father intended joining me as soon as I finished my engagement, to arrange for the sale of some of mother's furniture and jewelry.

Almost the first person to come and see me in London was Musette. She had read of my opening in the papers and offered

324

me the contract we had spoken about in Egypt. She had formed a unit with six acts besides herself, all of them good performers who could do two or more acts in the show. From Southampton, the unit would sail to Halifax, Nova Scotia, and after playing there a week, would continue on to Montreal, Winnipeg, and Calgary, embarking in Vancouver for Tokyo. After a four-day contract in the Japanese capital, we would sail for Shanghai, where the new Summer Gardens, under the English management, were paying excellent salaries. I carefully calculated how long the trip would take and worked out a schedule so that I could catch a connection in Shanghai, after my engagement there, for a United States port, thereby avoiding any Canadian quarantine difficulties, and arriving in Toronto somewhere around the Christmas season to join father.

Musette was particularly anxious that Morgan earn extra salary by taking charge of the baggage and equipment for the troupe, so I called him into my dressing-room to discuss terms. While he was talking to her, I saw him glance at the list of artists, which was lying on the dressing-table. He turned white and mumbled something about "thinking it over," then rushed out of the room.

As soon as Musette left, I got hold of him and made him tell me what on earth was the matter. He pointed to a name on the list—it was "Honour Bright," tap and acrobatic dancer with four girls. "That," he said, "is my wife," and he explained he was not legally free from her when he had married his French wife, and therefore was in danger of being arrested for bigamy in British territory or the Dominions. According to his description of Honour Bright, she was capable of doing almost anything unpleasant—and though he was unhappy about the whole thing, nothing would induce him to accept the contract, nor would he allow me to tell Musette the real reason for his refusal.

I spent my last night in Paris with Violette and had a curious depressed feeling I could not throw off. For one thing, losing Morgan with whom I had worked so long, worried me.

I would miss his comforting presence. Pepita had disappeared, and here I was leaving all my friends to go roaming off again, half across the world from Paris which was my home. I realized more than ever what mother's death meant. She had been the object of all my hard work and planning, and now that she was gone, life seemed very empty. I will always remember Violette's words that night when I said good-by, for she read my thoughts so clearly—I could seldom hide any mood from her keen eyes. She said: "The time will not seem so long, and when you come back we will all be here just the same. Paris for you will never change."

That morning she had done another kind and thoughtful deed to please me, which was to obtain permission through her friend, the director of the zoölogical garden, to send Bengali down to the new Vincennes Zoo where he could have a proper cage for his recovery, and in the spring the first of the Mappin terraces would be completed, which would mean fresh air and sunlight for him.

Musette's unit had been arranged with a pleasing collection of people—typical international vaudeville variety—all of them young, with the exception of Honour Bright and the Pfeiffers, who had a performing dog act. Honour Bright was exactly as Morgan had described her to me, a hard-faced woman of about fifty, who worked her four girls relentlessly and seemed possessed of an inexhaustible supply of energy. She made all the costumes for the act and took care of the wardrobe, publicity, and bookings, in addition to working herself and rehearsing new numbers. Her own specialty was a number in Highland costume, on the music of "Loch Lomond" in three different tempos, to which she danced an acrobatic tap that was astonishing in a woman of her years. It amused me to see all Morgan's pet tricks that she had evidently learned from him and taught to the girls.

There were the Musical Madcaps, four singers—married couples of Italian extraction who played harmonicas, xylophones, mandolins, and accordions, harmonized choruses, and were so versatile they could be used to fill in for any emergency. Then there were the three Leroys, French acrobats and dancers, two men and a girl, whose acrobatic technique was outstanding. They, too, had a large repertoire, tossing the girl about between them and virtually turning her inside out in all their numbers.

Of the group, the Pfeiffers were the most picturesque. They were, of course, German but spoke every language, having toured the world for years. Madame Pfeiffer was still rather good-looking and had a beautiful figure, always working her act in a spangled evening gown with paradise feathers in her blonde hair. She was, so her billing claimed, the only woman living to present her animals in a "drawing-room" atmosphere with the same success as on the stage, so perfectly were they trained.

All the time I worked with these people, I was never quite certain just how many animals they were carrying, for they had twenty birds and sixteen dogs listed on their permit, but I kept seeing others of all sizes and breeds that Frau Pfeiffer kept in hat-boxes, dressing-bags, and muffs—fluffy poms and tiny yapping chihuahuas—till I lost count. Herr Pfeiffer was a character and readily admitted Mascotte was the only dog he could never get to obey him, although he was an excellent trainer of small animals. I asked him how he managed to get the varying numbers of dogs to coincide with the number on his permit. He shrugged his shoulders and said that if one of the lady dogs had a family en route, it wasn't possible for him to know the exact number of extra dogs there would be on arrival at their destination.

I used to help him exercise the dogs on the third-class deck, where they had been relegated with a special spot for their cages in a passageway that was warm. They all had German names, and it was an inspiring sight to watch Herr Pfeiffer struggling around the deck with an enormous spitz in a high wind, saying, "*Machs du schnell, Otto*"—and when the dog complied, he would say with exaggerated satisfaction, "*Ach, so ist brav.*"

Although I was attaining my object of spending Christmas

with father, I could not but regret wasting time with Musette's unit, for after all, I had the ability and opportunity to work in the best music-halls and revue houses in Europe and also had got a good start with my productions through the tableaux I had presented for Varna and Hallais. Baud had been more than a little annoyed with me for accepting a contract with what he described as *des saltimbanques* (barnstormers).

The only date worth playing on the entire tour proved to be Shanghai. The long trip across Canada on the Canadian Pacific was wearing on both the dogs and the performers. We played vaudeville houses all through Canada and doubled in Montreal at the Edward the Seventh Hotel. In Tokyo we opened at a "dancing" called the Palais de l'Orient near the Kagetsu-Tsurumi Gardens.

It was astonishing to discover that the tango was the craze in Japan, and Musette was heartbroken at not having engaged a tango band while in Paris. Practically the first person I met at the establishment in Tokyo was one of the Pizarro brothers from Buenos Aires, who, with his band, had been booked from the Bonbonnière in Berlin for a permanent engagement. Mingling with English and Americans were solemn-faced Japanese in tuxedos and black-rimmed glasses, shuffling around the floor to the strains of Pizarro's *bandoneons* and sentimental Argentine songs about *amor*. It was decidedly a change from the traditional geisha girls and samisens associated with Japanese entertainment.

When we docked in Shanghai, Musette introduced me to her mysterious capitalist who came to meet us complete with car and chauffeur and wearing the most magnificent pearls I have ever seen, except for my mother's. She was a tall, dark, and rather plain woman of about thirty-five, dressed in a perfect Patou ensemble, and seemed to have unlimited authority and respect from the officials, hotel managers, and everybody we came in contact with.

Musette told me little about her except that she had once been an English vaudeville performer—they had worked together for years when, with her husband, she played in a small-time comedy act. The husband, who drank and beat her, managed to get himself killed in a fight one night down at a waterfront dive, and his wife, penniless and destitute, had gone from one phase of misery and degradation to another. Finally, she ended up on one of the Chinese "flower boats" in the harbor, and there she met an Englishman who helped her to emerge little by little from the depths again, until she now owned houses in Shanghai and Hongkong that were known throughout the Orient for their magnificence. From the few guarded details Musette told me, I imagined she held gambling parties in these houses for huge stakes, inviting the richest and most important Chinese merchants, bankers, diplomats, and heads of large American and British concerns. I saw her only at the boat, for she was never seen anywhere in public, and remained about an instant in the foyer of the Cathay Hotel where she bought drinks for all the company. I noticed several people looking at her and nudging each other as she passed them on her way out.

The Summer Gardens, run by an English syndicate in combination with the Foster Agency of London, booked English entertainers almost exclusively, for ever since the World War, China had been satiated by Russian refugees with balalaika orchestras, singers, and dancers. The Gardens had a stage and floor show principally dedicated to the English colony and was situated near the Victoria Gardens in the International Settlement.

It was an innovation for the crowds of Chinese youth, whose leaders, educated at Oxford and Cambridge, gave large banquets for their societies and the new Chinese Youth Movement, which was then frantically combating the old traditions of opium-smoking and decorative oriental pastimes said to be undermining the morale of the country. There were always banquets going on, either for the Chinese students or for British and American businessmen. The two-week stay was thoroughly enjoyable, but I missed Morgan's reliable company for expeditions to all the places I wanted to see before leaving—

the fascinating water-fronts and the crowded Chinese quarter with the smell of rotten straw, fish, and wet bamboo.

About the second day I was there, Musette's friend sent a young Englishman to see me at the Gardens. He said his name was "just Smith." He was dapper, round-shouldered, and reminded me in some way of an insect. I tried to recall where I had seen such a face; then I remembered an enlarged photograph of a boll-weevil in a scientific magazine in the hotel reading-room that looked exactly like him.

Musette must have told her friend that I wanted to buy some embroideries and jade for Violette, so she sent this man who knew private places where it was possible to get ivories, jades, and ancient kakemonos superior to the usual run of merchandise shown to tourists. The things he brought to my hotel so mysteriously were all exquisite and very reasonably priced. He never would agree to take me to any of the places where he obtained them, but appeared almost every morning at the hotel with something so beautiful, I could not find its equal in any of the gift and curio shops.

I had never put up such heroic resistance to temptation and finally bought a group of ten pictures on eaglewood backgrounds, set with clusters of human figures in ivory and landscapes with trees in jade and lapis lazuli. I chose these pictures as a present for Violette and knew she would appreciate them. I felt reckless after the purchase of a jade collar for myself, along with a set of ancient silver perfume-burners and lamps that were far more than I could possibly afford, so hesitated over some embroideries that Smith showed me. I wanted them, but they were definitely beyond my reach, so, half-jokingly, I asked him please not to come back any more. I saw a similar piece of work in a shop on the Nanking Road, and upon inquiring as to price found that those Smith offered were a ridiculously low figure by comparison. I could not quite make it out.

The day I left Shanghai Musette brought me a large parcel, saying it was from our "capitalist." There were the embroideries I had wanted—a present. She was indeed a strange personality whom I would have liked to see more of in Shanghai. I was extremely grateful to her for those embroideries and fortunately had an opportunity to entertain her in Paris a year or so later, but in Europe she was a completely different woman from the dramatic, unreal personality of Shanghai. Not that there had ever been an attempt on her part to imitate a "Mother Goddam," even in China, but in Paris she played to perfection the rôle of a rich woman business executive on a well-earned holiday, concerned only with the hotel rates in Switzerland and her mother's "cure" at Marienbad.

Fortunately, I was able to obtain return passage direct to Seattle on a passenger and cargo steamer of a west coast line with the odd name of the S.S. *Shikshinny*. I cabled father advising him that this was the best combination I had been able to make, although unless I traveled overland from San Francisco I could not arrive in time to spend Christmas Day with him. He cabled me to stay on the boat and rest till Seattle, where he would meet me. I had a most enjoyable trip as the ship rolled and bucketed through the heavy Pacific storms after Nagasaki, on to the Golden Gate, and then up the coast.

XVII

I T WAS BITTERLY cold in Seattle. Father's object in having taken the long railroad trip to meet me had been in the main to carry out a cherished plan of his which I'd long forgotten about. Often he'd spoken to me of an eccentric elder sister of his residing in a small village near Grand Forks in the Turtle Mountains of North Dakota. She had lived there since the death of another brother, whose farm in British Columbia she had administered with a great deal more tenacity and success than had her menfolk.

Her own farm, with its rolling land hidden in pine and cedar forests at the foot of the low mountain range, was a large one, where she lived completely alone except for her Scotch overseer and the farmhands who had cottages on the estate. It was a most beautiful place, with air like dry wine in the mornings. I loved it so much I would have been happy to dream on there till spring came to the valley. In spite of the zero weather, father taught me to walk on snow-shoes, and we used to go for long sleigh-rides through the forests.

What I liked most about my Aunt Caroline was her love of animals, and her downright, almost masculine character. She had never married, was a very tall, strongly built woman, and must have been over sixty, although I never knew her exact age and father was not quite certain about it either. But she could ride like a man, was a noted big-game shot, and by shrewd thrift had succeeded in buying, little by little, additional acres of good land for her farm, until it had become one of the most prosperous in the district, and her imported Jersey cows had made history.

One of the nicest memories I have of her was that one morning when an old Indian with a little boy brought a tiny furry bear-cub for sale, she immediately bought him, making a warm corner in the barn for him with the horses and cattle. He was of no possible use to a busy woman with a large farm to take care of, but, she told me, she often bought orphan bears, because her conscience bothered her about the many occasions she had been obliged to kill marauding grizzlies for food during her pioneer days. She therefore felt she was in some way repaying the debt of slaughter by taking in the little ones and raising them till they were big and strong enough to be set free and return to their wild hills again.

It was a happy holiday, and the trip ended with father and me spending a few days in New York.

Upon my return to Paris, Georges Baud offered to book me at the Scala, Berlin, for two weeks beginning about the middle of February, then the Hansa Theater, and the Alcazar Balhaus in Hamburg for one month. It was an excellent contract, and I accepted at once.

My hunt for Morgan began and I found that he had left in October to work for a circus in Cuba. Lucille, his wife, told me the British consul, on orders from Honour Bright, had been making inquiries about Morgan with the help of the police from the Sûreté. Evidently Morgan's first wife had nosed out of Musette the history of his working for me in Paris and without saying a word had ruthlessly started on his trail. The police had made several visits to their rooming-house, until poor Morgan, in deadly fear of an impending scandal, obtained a contract for the Anselmo Circus in Havana and fled. He was sending all the money he could to his family, but I gathered from Lucille that they were having a tough time, so I did all in my power to help her.

An ensemble was engaged for our tour featuring the champion trap-drummer of the United States, Buddy Gilmore, who with his wife Mattie gave one of the most astounding performances in Europe at that time. I started rehearsals with them at once, for having such a master of rhythm to provide drum effects for my tricks was most important to me, in view of the publicity I had been promised.

333

But what to do with Marie and the monkeys? Kimmie's wife, Jenny, was going to have a baby. Violette was so thrilled by the fact, she told all her friends in the zoölogical gardens, and they could hardly believe their eyes when I invited them over to see the evidence for themselves. According to them, the little one should arrive about the first week in April, at which time I would be back from my trip, and I arranged for the services of the vet who had taken such good care of Bengali.

I went out to Vincennes on the day of my arrival to see the tiger, who was looking so magnificent, I hardly recognized him. He was sleek and fat, with beautiful soft fur and a proud arch to his neck. It was still too cold for the Mappin terrace, but I promised myself the pleasure of seeing him walk on to it for the first time, when I got back. I still had my old dream of an animal act, and of starting a collection of cats with him, but when I saw how happy he was and thought of all the hard work and traveling he'd gone through, I gave up the idea for his sake. The directors were so pleased with Bengali's progress, they talked of trying to breed him in the near future, for a cub from such a magnificent animal would be worth having for their zoo.

The situation as far as the four-legged animals were concerned was fairly simple, but regarding Marie, I found it was not so easy. Violette said the offer for her to live at Les Mées, doing a little light work for salary and keep, still held good. To my surprise, Marie told me that she had made other plans in my absence, having met some man (many years her junior) whom she was going to marry almost immediately.

This piece of information helped considerably in clearing up the mystery of the dyed hair that had always intrigued me. I knew she had saved quite a bit of money while working for mother and myself, and also that she had consulted a friend of mine about her investments. She was very mysterious and coy about her fiancé, telling me he was so impatient for the wedding she could not wait for my return from Germany but wanted to leave my service and get married when I left for

Berlin. Feeling sorry for her, and suspecting her life savings were the principal reason for the impatience on the part of her future husband, I could do nothing but make arrangements for the monkeys to board at the zoo till I got back.

Berlin proved to be a triumph beyond my expectations. The public was indeed crazy about the Charleston, and I took more applause with that number than with the staircase. In Hamburg the same thing occurred in the way of success at the Hansa, but I discovered that the Alcazar, where I was to double, was not at all the sort of place I would have accepted, had I known more about it.

The Alcazar Balhaus—*"Das Herz des Hamburg Nachtlebens"*—was run by two brothers whose names I can't remember, but the real force behind the place was their director, Herr Franck, a suave Russian, with a line of baloney as false as the artificial arm he wore to replace his own which he claimed had been shot away during some heroic engagement of the World War. Buddy Gilmore, who never liked him, told everybody he was certain Franck had lost his arm by putting it in somebody's pocket. However, he was a hard-working person, almost never getting out of evening dress or leaving the building of the Alcazar, where he harried the personnel and ruled the crowd of taxigirls with the despotism of a czar. He had a considerable staff of *konferenzien* and uniformed attendants to cope with the immense crowds that filled the house seats and restaurant every night, even Mondays. The attendants' presence was essential for that public was one of the roughest and most objectionable I have ever encountered.

The whole of the Reeperbahn, the street on which the Alcazar stood, had enormous colored photographs of me, bearing my name in large letters and the phrase *"Die Lola Montez der Charleston."* Just why they felt it necessary to compare me to the famous mistress of the King of Bavaria, I could not quite understand—but Herr Franck told me it was intended as a great compliment and the finest publicity they could think up for me.

As in Berlin, the staircase faded into insignificance beside the Charleston, which, although a good arrangement with clever, fast tumbling, could not compare with the tricky technical work on the bottles. However, the Charleston was what they wanted, and the public yelled and applauded until it was necessary to do an encore every show.

The second week in Hamburg I closed a contract, by cable, with the Colón Commission for an engagement in Buenos Aires. It happened that the director of *La Nación*, Señor Mitre, was about to pass through Hamburg to embark for Argentina, and the Colón wanted me to interview his secretary, giving him all the details and publicity from Paris and Berlin. The Argentine friends arrived on the heels of the cable and invited me to a reception given by their consul, arranging to call for me after the performance at the Alcazar.

On that particular night, I found myself obliged to bring my evening gown to the theater in order to dress there. I wore two diamond rings on this occasion—a thing I made it a rule never to do, for I could not wear any jewelry while working, or take the risk of losing real stones in such rough tricks as back somersaults or "butterflies." I arrived alone at the theater and on entering the stage door found Morgenstern, an old character actor whom I had employed as a "stooge" in the audience, sitting talking to the doorman. He offered to carry the grip containing my evening gown, and when we reached my dressing-room he noticed the rings gleaming on my hand. I was wearing mother's engagement ring, and this particular stone seemed to fascinate him. Morgenstern simply could not believe such a big diamond was real and kept asking the weight and value of it.

I decided to lock the jewelry in my wardrobe trunk and also to lock the door of my room. The star dressing-room was a flimsily constructed booth that had been built in without solid walls, and afterward we realized that any conversation within was perfectly audible to a person listening closely outside.

I gave no further thought to old Morgenstern, but when I

didn't see him coming through the public to take his customary
seat at the table near the stage for our scene at the end of
my Charleston, I thought it odd. I was particularly anxious
to get through quickly that night to join my friends, and when
I finished my dance, I noticed Herr Franck standing in the
wings, waiting for me to come off. This was not his usual procedure, but strangely enough, he kept that position all the
time I was working. At last, just as I was about to give up
the idea of Morgenstern's appearing, I saw him run quickly
to his seat—and so we finished the act. When I got back to my
dressing-room, I found what the detective magazines describe
as a "scene of indescribable confusion." The wardrobe trunk
had been clumsily broken open with an ax, the contents strewn
about the floor—and, naturally, the package containing the
rings was gone.

The news spread, and a few seconds later, all the acts remaining in the theater came crowding to my door. About the
first to arrive and start consoling me was Morgenstern. *"Ach,
mein kleine,"* he kept saying, "you are so good and kind,
who could have had the heart to steal your mother's ring?"
When Franck appeared, I asked him to call the police and see
that nobody left the stage door meanwhile. This he refused to
do, and when my Argentine friends arrived to call for me,
they, too, noticed his lack of interest.

The police were three moon-faced individuals, who, with
the usual thick-headed Teutonic love for doing things according to regulations, wasted half an hour questioning me as to
where I had obtained the jewelry and what proof I had, if
any, of being the owner, and wrote my replies in their note-
books with exasperating slowness. Señor Mitre's secretary,
José María Anadon (a very old friend of mine from Buenos
Aires), gave up his invitation at the Consulate to accompany
me to the police station. He did not speak German but wanted
to explain to the chief officer, Captain Rammig, that he'd
known me for years and was familiar with the stolen rings,
having seen them on several occasions in Paris.

I did not realize till later that the police captain knew far more about the theft than was natural. He listened to José María for a few minutes while I interpreted, then sent another policeman for a book. He thumbed through this for a minute or so, then showed us the picture of a villainous-looking dark-haired man, who in no way resembled the respectable José María. "This," he said, thrusting the book under Anadon's nose, "is the picture of a dangerous Chilean pimp we think is in Hamburg. I believe you are that man!"

I was so flabbergasted that for a moment I could not speak. Then I let him have my extremely frank opinion of his discourtesy and that of all his countrymen. He was furious, of course, and said, "Fräulein, you are in Germany, and now there is no longer a British occupation. Be careful what you say about the Germans." Finally, we had to telephone the Argentine consulate, requesting Señor Oyhanarte to be kind enough to come down to the precinct, since Captain Rammig refused to let José María return to his hotel.

It was then we realized that most of the officers loafing about the office understood Spanish and were well aware that both Anadon and I had called them everything we could think of in the purest Castilian. It was a ghastly night, for the eleven musicians were obliged to stay in the precinct till nearly four in the morning, while the police looked at their passports and questioned them.

During the time this was going on, patrolmen kept arriving, dragging in sailors with black eyes, cuts on their heads, and all the signs of having been brutally mistreated on the way. It seemed that no shore leave was permitted in Hamburg to sailors from certain lines docking in that port, owing to the dangerous reputation of the St. Pauli quarter; therefore, when the police picked them up, they were immediately taken to the Reeperbahn station. One of the men brought in was an enormous Swede, who spoke very little German. He was not very drunk, and not at all disrespectful, but during the captain's questioning he answered something which evidently annoyed the officer, for he struck him full in the face, taking the man off his guard. As he fell, both policemen that had brought him in kicked his head savagely with their heavy boots.

At last the consul arrived and managed to get Anadon released; also, a little more interest was shown and the regulation telegraphic alarm sent out to all jewelers, diamond cutters, and pawnshops throughout Germany, Holland, and Belgium, giving the details of the stolen stones, in order to stop any sales.

The following morning at seven o'clock, I was awakened by a loud thumping on the door of my room in the Hotel Esplanade. When I opened it, there were four more fat pig-faced individuals from the police headquarters, with orders to search my luggage They explained that the police, and Captain Rammig in particular, did not think I had ever been robbed at all but had hidden the jewels in my effects with the object of getting publicity. They were very proud of this astute reasoning and their knowledge of the crafty tricks foreign women think up to get their names in newspapers. When I pointed out that all Hamburg was plastered with my pictures, and therefore it would seem hardly necessary for me to go to such lengths to obtain more notoriety, they simply proceeded to search everything I had, which was not only an outrage but also a costly operation, for one of them took a razor blade and cut out the lining of my dressing-case to see if there was anything hidden behind it.

I went to the station demanding to see the chief of police. I could not get an interview with that functionary, so as there was no matinée that day, I caught the next train for Berlin and went to see everybody of influence I knew there. I found Henrietta von Friedlander-Fuld and told her my story, asking if she could get her brother, one of the richest lumber kings in Europe, to get in touch with the chief of police about my affair. I then called on Baron Hermann Saxe-Weimar, an old friend of mother's who had known me all my life. He was horrified at the story, especially since he had been educated at Oxford and affected the decent ways of the English. The Baron got hold of the Berlin chief of police on the telephone at once and really went to town on the subject of my treatment by the Hamburg officials. The result of this was a call twenty minutes later from the station in Hamburg, with Doktor Slambusch, chief of police, personally apologizing and requesting I call upon him immediately upon my return.

I went to see the interesting Doktor Slambusch the next day, and after the first three minutes of conversation became convinced he must take benzedrine in large quantities. He was a short, bristly individual, with high blood-pressure, duelling scars criss-crossing his face, and thick eyeglasses. Never before had I seen any man holding a responsible position jump about all over his office like a flea on a hot plate, as he did. He warned me at the top of his voice that it was extremely dangerous for me to remain in Hamburg, also that my presence was hampering the recovery of my rings. I pointed out to him that I had a jazz band of eleven men to think of, who needed to earn their living, also that I was not disposed to be frightened into giving up the substantial salary I was collecting at the theater, especially after such a costly loss as my rings. It was an instructive conversation, for I managed to get on the wrong side of the man almost at once—which, though unfortunate, could not be helped. And although I did try to smooth him down with the flattery that seldom fails to work on the paranoiac mentality of most Germans, I had a feeling he thought I was pulling his leg.

In answer to his insistent warning that something worse would undoubtedly befall me if I did not get out of Hamburg at once, I told him nothing could frighten me in the least but that if he felt I was in some kind of danger, I should appreciate his permitting me to carry my revolver, so that if the occasion arose, I could demonstrate to him my complete ability to take care of myself. He jumped to his feet and bellowed "Fräulein Davis, if you want to fight with Germans, why don't you wait till the next war!"

My answer was that I did not need to wait for any war to fight Germans, but then I pressed him for an explanation of his words "the next war." He bounced over to the window of the office, dramatically pointing to the gardens below. "Look, Fräulein!" he bellowed. "There is the future German Army we have bred for the next war!" Looking below, I saw a line of bespectacled school children, wending their way two by two through the gardens. I turned away in disgust, and I don't think the Herr Doktor liked this, for our parting was quite chilly.

I never expected any more help from him after our interview, but, to my surprise, the next morning, a heavy-set man announced himself at my hotel, wearing a massive watch chain and a bowler hat three sizes too small, crowning rolls of pink fat on the back of his neck. This was Kriminal Inspektor Furster, one of the best sleuths they had in the city. He had been expressly put on my case by Slambusch and was not only intelligent but rather humane for a German. We had something in common for he told me that his son, like my brother, was blind and paralyzed from wounds received in the World War when he was seventeen. Furster, the father, had been one of the most able spies of the German Secret Service in 1916, living and circulating in Belgium and Calais, obtaining information for his government despite a price on his head posted by the British and French Intelligence.

He liked me, and I wormed out of him the interesting fact that Police Captain Rammig and Herr Franck, whom he disliked, were in cahoots with some nice little side-lines, such as white slave traffic, dope running, and other winter sports. Bluntly I asked if he thought they had anything to do with the robbery. He said it was possible and perhaps one of the reasons Herr Slambusch wanted me to leave Hamburg. In the first place I was not convenient to any of them, for through my case, many things might become known. Besides, while I was in Germany, the thief could not attempt to sell the stones. There was a certain amount of logic to what Furster said, but I could not let the band down and needed my own money as well, so I determined to stick it out, prevailing on Furster to obtain a permit for my gun, which he did only after still another unpleasant experience that nearly drove the police frantic. I imagine Doktor Slambusch must have required a sedative when he heard about it.

Captain Rammig, as head of the St. Pauli precinct, arrested a stagehand named Witter—a nasty bit of work with a record a mile long. It so happened the man was innocent and I knew it, but Rammig, to stir up trouble, told Witter I accused him and requested his arrest. After four days the police released him, since there was absolutely no evidence against him, but when he returned to the Alcazar, Franck fired him. That night he waited for me at the stage door, accompanied by his wife, a frowsy wench who, as soon as I appeared, started insulting me. I happened to be carrying a roll of sheet music and clouted her over the head with it. She screamed and yelled, and the police had to rush around from the front of the house and arrest her, too. They merely protested feebly with me for creating more disturbance.

The next night, a Saturday, just as I was taking a bow after the Charleston, a glittering object whirled through the spotlight, brushed my hair, and, crashing, penetrated into the stage boards. My band, seated behind me, saw it and stopped playing, for they thought I was hit. A panic such as I had never seen before took place in the front seats. Women screamed and ran about shouting, *"Eine bombe,"* stampeding for the exits. I stooped and picked up the thing—it was a steel pipe about ten inches long and an inch and a half in diameter, sharpened at one end like a knife. I was so angry, I tossed it into the middle of the struggling mob, shouting, ''Here's your bomb, you lot of yellow cowards.'' Then turning to Sam Woods, the leader, I told him to play the ''march off'' the band always used for our exit.

For some reason, the boys, instead of playing the usual music, burst into ''Tipperary.'' This caused a considerably greater uproar. Men started yelling that it was an insult to the German public, but the band kept right on, and we all marched off to the historic melody. I must say, Sam Woods was at least three shades lighter when we all gathered together in the wings, and I could only sit down and rock with laugh-

342

ter. It was really funny. But not for Herr Furster. He came battling his way backstage, followed by two or three of his heftiest satellites, loudly protesting over what I had done. We had to wait for nearly half an hour before leaving the theater, and Furster insisted on driving me back to the hotel in a police car.

There we held another conference, with the additional presence of the two brothers who owned the Alcazar and Herr Franck. I expected they had come to the hotel expressly to fire me—but not at all. I was, they claimed, such an attraction, they simply could not think of dispensing with my services, for between the success of my act, and the to-do in the papers about the jewelry, there was standing room only every night. While we talked, a call for Furster came through from the station, informing him that the man who had thrown the steel pipe was none other than Witter, and he had been arrested trying to escape out of the top balcony.

What Witter said or did that night, I don't know, but he must have accused Herr Franck of being mixed up in the affair in some way, for the next day the police arrested Franck on orders from Slambusch. Once more I had to undergo a lot of tiresome questioning regarding what my Negro musicians said about Franck. At that time, I did not realize that Buddy's joke about the fake arm had spread abroad, along with his hints that if the police looked inside it, they might find not only the missing rings but also an ample supply of cocaine that Frank sold to the taxi-girls at so much per gram. Buddy had, of course, circulated this story as a joke, but the Germans, especially the police, took it very seriously, not being endowed by nature with anything resembling a sense of humor; so they corralled Franck, despite his indignant protests, removed his arm, and took it to pieces. It proved to be such an intricate and ingenious piece of mechanism that they were incapable of putting it together again— which of course necessitated their sending the arm to Elberfeld or somewhere, to have it put in working order. The sight of Franck's face when they finally let him return to the

343

theater, minus his arm, made me feel glad we were nearly at the end of our last week in Hamburg.

Before leaving, Herr Furster, who had convinced me of his sincerity, told me very frankly that he did not expect to retrieve my rings till some time after I left Germany, promising on his word that in one year from the present time, he would get them back. It was obvious to me that he had a very clear idea who the thief or thieves were, but he would not give me the slightest hint. I often had asked if he suspected Morgenstern, but he always attributed little or no importance to the possibility of his being connected with the theft.

The affair had depressed and sickened me, especially when I thought of the grief the loss of mother's rings would cause my father, should I eventually be obliged to tell him about it. Tactfully, before leaving, I wrote notes to Doktor Slambusch and to my friends in Berlin, thanking them for all the trouble they had taken to help me, and the only person I told about the affair upon returning to Paris was Violette. After I described Furster to her, she felt sure he would keep his word, and she advised me to try and forget everything for the time being.

I had not been home very long and was already starting to advertise the apartment for rent, devoting the weeks before me to straightening out my affairs prior to leaving for Buenos Aires—when, one afternoon, Marie turned up again. As I had anticipated, her young Lochinvar who had come out of the West had returned there, after taking every cent of her life savings. The foolish woman had placed her Titres des Rentes Viagères (French Government bonds) in the man's name, so there was nothing to be done, even if she had not married him. I felt sorry for her but could not take her back, having engaged a young Breton girl called Claire who was excellent and kept the monkeys far cleaner. Now that Jenny's baby was almost due, she was invaluable to me.

The night that event took place was filled with incident, for first of all I received a telephone call from Morgan, who had arrived from Cuba that morning and planned on taking his

344

wife and the children down to the country on the following day. I told him to come and dine with me, as I was not going out but awaiting the arrival of an addition to my menagerie.

We had a long talk after dinner, he telling me the saga of his troubles with Honour Bright and the circus engagement in Cuba, when Claire, who was watching Jenny, came flying in to tell me I had better send for the vet with whom I'd made arrangements.

The unusual feat of anybody's African monkey having progeny in captivity was another *cause celèbre* in Paris. Every one came to the house to admire the phenomenon, and the vet who had brought the baby monkey into the world was the proudest man in the zoo.

One evening, some people I had known in South America telephoned me—Jacques de la Melassie and his wife. They had brought a pet snake with them from Brazil and asked me to look at him and see if I thought he was poisonous. He was a pretty little black-and-white snake but had the classic arrow head of the poisonous varieties. I decided we had better use grandmama's old trick with the wine-glass, to milk out his fangs, but I must have been careless, for somehow he wriggled a little too far out of my grasp and bit me through the first finger of my right hand. Fortunately we were standing near the bathroom door, for the instant the poison entered my finger, I could taste the most horrible sickly almond flavor with a pungent sensation like raw alcohol. It made me so deathly sick and faint for a moment that I stupidly dropped the snake and rushed to the cold water tap. Luckily I had already got most of the poison out of his fangs before he bit me, but within a few minutes I felt so woozy I could not even help De la Melassie find the reptile.

We took the precaution of shutting Mascotte and the monkeys up where he could not get near them, then left for the Pasteur Institute on the other side of Paris. The young intern who opened and dressed the bite said nothing much could be done till the following morning, for it was indispensable for us to bring in the snake so that the laboratory could examine him and find out the exact type of poison, before prescribing an antidote.

The next morning I was still in a daze: my ankles and wrists were swollen, but that horrible taste in my mouth had gone. The condition of my eyes was possibly the worst part of the illness, for they pained so I could not bear to keep them open for more than a few minutes. I was in bed and under medical treatment for five days, and during all this time it was impossible to find the snake. This worried me greatly, on account of the monkeys and Mascotte, to say nothing of my own snake, little Pépé. It took quite some time for me to recover completely, and when I subleased and left the apartment some weeks later, I still didn't know what had become of that snake.

Violette planned to visit the United States in the fall, but allowed me to take the monkeys to Les Mées for the summer. We arranged a splendid home for them in a cottage where Violette had installed an old Russian gentleman who had lost everything in the revolutionary days, barely escaping with his life. The shock left him completely senile. He still wore an old and faded Cossack uniform, refusing not only to take it off but also to take a bath—the reason being that he considered himself a "forgotten man," and all frivolities, such as washing, were things that belonged to his past. It was an unfortunate complex, and Violette had to relegate him to the cottage as far away from the château as possible. She was getting a little tired of his inertia and complete refusal to interest himself in the gardens or offer to do any kind of work in payment for her hospitality. But there he was and, as far as anybody could foresee, there he would remain, till death or the Board of Health took a hand in the situation.

The monkeys, surprisingly enough, proved to be the only thing ever known to interest him. He brightened up at once and kept mumbling about the *oibisiani* (monkeys) till I told Violette that at last here was an ideal job for him. He became another man, smiling and playing with them and even cleaning their cage. It was a perfect arrangement, but when

346

I arrived in Buenos Aires, I received the pathetic news from Violette that in spite of the old man's care, the baby monkey had died. The old gentleman was heartbroken, crying and carrying on for days. He had suffered even more than the mother monkey, who savagely held on to her dead baby for hours, defying the vet to take his body away from her.

While Jenny lost her offspring, poor little thing, Bengali had become the father of a cub. All the papers reprinted his history and sent photographers down to take pictures of the magnificent cub, for the directors of Vincennes were justly proud of their triumph in getting such an old animal to reproduce. Nobody ever knew just how old Bengali was, except for his teeth, but we had, of course, donated him to the zoo to end his days there in a peaceful old age, with all the comforts he could possibly get in a state of captivity, including romance.

I received my passage orders from the Colón, to sail on the third of May, but it was not until the last week in April, when I had everything ready for storage, that a suitable tenant materialized for the apartment. He was an American doctor whose clientele of rich society women—tired of the novelty of the Piccinnini's Clinic for their nerves and hangovers—had switched their imaginary ailments over to this new man. He wanted an apartment with two entrances, and since his references were financially excellent, I was glad to accept his offer.

I found Buenos Aires much the same as when I left, except that many more modern buildings had appeared on the skyline. All my friends were there, Natascha, Mollie, the English girls, Nemanoff—now a ballet master for the Teatro Maipú—Matto, and all the old gang. I had traveled with many of the Argentine ministers and their families, and when the ship docked, newspaper reporters swarmed aboard and took pictures of me which appeared on the front pages the next day, flanked by the most solemn-faced and important personages with their wives. There must have been a considerable stir in Argentine society when they saw the photographs, for it was unheard of for an artist to be placed in such distinguished company.

During the excitement of the arrival, I had asked my old friend Dr. Fitzsimon, who had come to meet me, if he would mind holding Mascotte while I got my trunks through the customs, momentarily forgetting she was once more in a very amorous frame of mind. She immediately slipped her collar and dashed madly through the crowd and up a side street, leading from the quay to the town. Dr. Fitzsimon gave chase, together with his secretary and Alexandro Leloir, vice-president of the Argentine Bank of Commerce. These three dignified businessmen, whose sprinting abilities belonged to their younger days, were no match for my dog. They soon lost sight of her and were obliged to return, red and puffing, to break the news.

Leaving my trunks to take care of themselves, we jumped into Dr. Fitzsimon's car and began a frenzied hunt along the traffic-filled streets till we came to a tree-shaded plaza, near the Retiro Railway Station: there we found Mascotte, the center of a group of admiring dogs. Nobody present among the collection of bums taking their noonday siestas on the benches was sufficiently wide awake to inform us if the worst had happened, and I had hopes—but not for long!

I congratulated myself on finding a charming furnished apartment that overlooked the river and had a roof terrace and a large studio. There I installed my old Indian dresser, Flora, as maid, and really began to get after my work seriously, starting rehearsals for the official opening, the twenty-fifth of May (Argentina's Independence Day). Basil Romanoff was in charge of the ultimate production and choreographic end of the work, together with two members of the Colón Commission, painters and designers, so that all the different branches pertaining to the ballet were well organized, each person having sufficient time to produce a perfect job without overwork or last-minute scrambles.

After the opening, I found myself with a considerable amount of leisure, especially in the evening, and was approached almost immediately by several of the national companies of revue, to set tableaux in their productions. They were also interested in my personal appearance in their shows but I could not sign until my Colón contract terminated, and as yet I had not entirely made up my mind whether I wanted to stay on in Buenos Aires or return to Paris. Fate, however, decided the matter.

XVIII

A COMPANY of Don Cossacks opened at the Teatro Odeón in June, under the direction of a man called Kerensky, one-time choir leader in Moscow. Natascha attended their first night and came to my apartment early the next morning with glowing accounts of their tremendous success with the Argentine public and the beauty of their voices and repertoire. We went to see them that same night: everything she told me was correct, except that their presentation, uniforms, and general appearance were shabby, giving the impression that the show had been thrown together without careful placing of the men so as to grade their height or smarten up the general effect.

It did not take me long to discover that Natascha had another interest in the choir besides her love of the songs of her native land. After the show she introduced me to one of the tenors, a handsome man named Gregori Efimovitch Ianoushine. As a mere boy in Russia, he had been wounded in one of the last stands against the Bolsheviks, losing his left leg from the hip: Natascha told me that he wore a wooden one which permitted him to walk a little, that he was not strong, and that the miserable salary paid the troupe by their leader was not sufficient for him to have proper medical care. To please Natascha, I invited him up to my apartment for a drink after the show and found the story of the choir's formation an interesting one. They were, Gregori Efimovitch said, nearly all from a settlement of Russians that had come to Montevideo some years ago, on a grant of farm lands the Uruguayan government had made to all immigrants wishing to colonize the country. Only ten of them had come from a larger company playing in the United States, most of them having congregated literally from the ends of the earth.

The Cossacks were mostly ex-cavalry men—some of them had been officers—and as Gregori Efimovitch described his comrades, a plan began to form in my mind. I knew the tremendous success little rodeo shows always received every time they came from the States and toured the Argentine provinces, where the gauchos were wild about any form of riding other than their own. So I questioned Gregori as to how many of the men were riders with cavalry school training. He told me that several of the men living in Montevideo had worked in Paris some years previously in spectacles of Diguit and had been written about in the famous book by Kessel, *Nuit des Princes*.

Kerensky had about thirty men singing at the Odeón, and Gregori said there were many more who could be brought from other parts of the country for a good engagement. I found out that the troupe had only one month booked at the Odeón on a percentage basis, possibly with an additional two weeks in Rosario, provided their spectacle in Buenos Aires made good. Telling Natascha nothing about the idea I had had while talking to her friend, I began making careful calculations about the cost of forming a company of fifty or sixty men and a corresponding number of horses, to give spectacles in theaters with the choir and dancers, doubling with the Diguit horse show in the open air.

I approached several friends whose interest in the venture was of primary importance for obtaining contracts subsidized by the governments of Argentina and adjoining countries, in addition to theaters and show grounds functioning under professional impresarios. Government contracts were nearly always possible to negotiate when the spectacle was of an educational and artistic character.

Through the friendship and help of Teniente Coronel Roderiguez of the mounted police, I worked out a perfect plan for the horses. Roderiguez and his brother, both expert riders who showed their own horses at the annual Show in the Sociedad Rural, the Argentine Fairgrounds, were enthusiastic about my plan, helping me to get authorization to

351

pick fifty-two horses from the police remount department provided I put up the necessary bond of sixty pesos per horse, which would also cover saddles, bridles, etc.

The horses were to be stabled in Palermo and trained in the school there, until I took them on the road, after which I was to pay a monthly rental for them to be donated to one of the police charities. In case of injury or death of any of the animals, payment would be covered by the bond, but if they were brought back in perfect condition my money would be refunded.

For a time I went daily to the Receiving Depots to choose horses of the sturdy Anglo-Norman breed best suited for my purpose. I discovered a high percentage of them had to be scrapped because of a peculiar phenomenon frequently found in camp-broken horses. This is a form of "fit" or staggers caused by the native habit of breaking a horse by beating it over the head with the bolas, two lead balls on a rope intended for use in hunting ostriches. I have seen gauchos on friends' ranches breaking horses when they were not valuable imported stock and know just how an injury can be caused to an animal's skull through the force of blows given by the *domador* (trainer), who believes the quickest way to break a horse is to nearly knock its brains out. It is hard to understand how the Argentine gaucho, who is of a sentimental nature, a great lover of the animals by which he lives, can reconcile the useless cruelty of such a method with his love for horseflesh. The answer seems to be that gauchos for generations have been in the habit of breaking their horses in this manner to save time, for if they ruined a horse, all they had to do was go out with a lasso and get another from the herd running wild on the pampas.

Having solved the problem of mounts for the Cossacks, my next step was to get in touch with Kerensky. His proposition as to price was not a bad one. He paid his men in proportion to their vocal qualities: if a man had a good tenor he received a better salary than another whose vocal cords were not so

352

hot. It seemed an odd arrangement and turned out to be the cause of much discontent and jealousy among the men.

Don Faustino da Rosa, who was furnishing the capital for the uniforms, boots, and other necessary equipment, went into the project thoroughly, and upon Kerensky's return to Buenos Aires, held auditions with several other Russian singers we had in mind to strengthen the choir.

The entire tour was to run from the last week of August to about the second week in May, 1928, at which time I was to resume my second season at the Colón. After they had played a month at the Sociedad Rural in Palermo, doubling at the Teatro Cervantes under the direction of Da Rosa, I was to join the company the 20th of September after my closing date at the Colón. Under my direction the long tour would start in Rosario, pass through the principal towns of Argentina and across the Bolivian border to La Paz. Here we had government subsidy and the facilities of the mounted police.

After ten days in the Bolivian capital with a handsome array of private fiestas, we would continue by easy stages in order to give the horses every possible chance to become accustomed to the high altitude, then cross to Lima, Peru, via Jauja and spend fifteen days there for the Christmas and New Year fiestas. Thus the men could have a couple of days' holiday before taking the boat from Callao to Havana and a month with the Santos Artigas Circus.

Our return route was to play Panama, Bogotá, and Quito; then from Guayaquil we would go by boat to Valparaiso, Chile, for a two-week stay, followed by the long Trans-Andine route to Mendoza, Argentina, and Rosario again, ending our tour in Buenos Aires.

Knowing the Argentine percentage racket, I had been particularly careful to include trusted gate and ticket men among the personnel, using them also for the advance publicity and having them arrange for fodder and housing. I also took the precaution of obtaining insurance against more than five millimeters of rain, that being enough to prevent work. Al-

353

though we started in the month of August, when the rainy days of early spring were a menace, I felt that with the returns from the Cervantes, we would make out all right.

It was the most important undertaking I had ever contemplated and more of an adventure than a business proposition for me, but at the same time I had heavy responsibilities to face and so was careful of the people I engaged. As always, the men we needed most for their vocal ability and horsemanship were not always the most desirable in character, but to find perfection in an ensemble of sixty men was impossible. Fifteen of them were riders only, but among the forty singers there were twenty that also rode and were excellent dancers. In charge of the riders, I had placed the ex-Captains Schubert and Golovin—they organized the men on military lines—while the singers were under the exclusive direction of Kerensky.

Only one mistake was made by both Don Faustino and myself, which was to permit Kerensky to continue paying the men by the system he orginally used. He received a fixed sum per week which he was to distribute among the men at his own discretion, while both captains, Evar Mendez, and the other personnel were paid directly by me. The Cossacks were all so miserable and downtrodden when rehearsals first started that there was no discussion at all regarding salaries. It was impossible to give Kerensky a percentage of the takings above his own salary, and I later discovered he underpaid some of the singers in a most unreasonable way, thereby gaining more for himself. Natascha and Mrs. Schubert were engaged for extra secretarial work and supervision of the wardrobe, and, dressed in Russian Boyar costumes, sold photographs and programs during the charity functions.

The important long-distance jumps were to be made by train and boat, not such a formidable matter as it might sound on account of the excellent box-cars and general transportation facilities, for the principal industry of those countries is cattle and horses. Transportation of sixty-three persons was a much more costly and complicated matter and came under the jurisdiction of Evar Mendez, who combined the

354

passages allotted by each impresario from one point to another of the route, together with the advance in salaries indispensable to moving men.

The interest and enthusiasm shown by the Argentines, officials and men, were of greatest value. Many of them were excellent horsemen and took pride in helping in every way to make the show a success, especially for the Chilean public —for there had always been a rivalry between the two countries in matters of horseflesh and horsemanship, and the Argentines were anxious for their horses to make a good showing before the Chilean mounted regiments, in whose parade grounds in Santiago we were to give one of the shows.

The Cossacks of the Don and the Kuban sing in chorus as they ride, and sometimes their custom of whistling as they trot their horses is startlingly beautiful. Many file a tiny hole between their teeth to produce high sweet notes which, whistled by dozens of men in harmony, produce a thrilling effect. The more I worked with them, the more wealth of material did I find for a production that was worth all the preparation and hard work I put into it.

I chose gray uniforms with white sheepskin caps, black boots and accoutrements—first because of the dust problem, and second because this color made the men appear larger. Their "Tcherkess" coats had the cartridges picked out in silver and white, and many of the men wore colored decoration ribbons.

In theaters the formation on the stage was merely long lines of men standing on semi-circular platforms, facing their director, and behind them a heavy velvet drop. Perhaps the open-air night performance is the one most worthy of description.

The spectacle opened with a parade of horsemen riding four abreast. They circled the arena and then lined up around it while a group of singers seated at a long banqueting table, lighted by torches and silver candelabra, sang the "Black Hussars." Amplifiers picked up their voices and those of the men seated on the motionless horses.

In the light of the gigantic spot we carried, the group of men was thrown into prominence as they drank and clinked cups together, their song increasing in tempo until they reached the finale. The other riders, already in movement, trotted and galloped around them, whistling their war songs. They formed groups of figures, constantly gathering speed, until with wild shouts, first one horseman, then two, three, and finally four abreast, leaped over the tables and the seated men.

Then the different Cossack feats of horsemanship were displayed: wild riding, with tricks of vaulting and passing under the horse's belly, and upright balancing while in full gallop, and finally—the dangerous Diguit. This was a living pyramid of men mounted on galloping horses. The man at the summit, called a "top-mounter," had to control his balance by locking his knees around the shoulders of the men under him, holding aloft an enormous parade standard with the double eagles, together with the flag of Argentina or whatever country we were in. The entire pyramid moved around the arena, gathering speed, then wheeled down the center at full gallop, coming to a dead stop in the middle. It was a most thrilling and dangerous spectacle, requiring an extraordinary amount of balance and precision for both men and horses. I believe that only the Russian Cossacks can ever attempt it successfully, for they work with savage cries, intoxicated with the excitement and danger, in a manner that sweeps the public off their feet.

I have always felt certain that had it not been for the grounding in horsemanship and trick riding pounded into me by Ograinsky in my early youth, it would not have been possible for me to build the act without many more accidents than did occur. We were lucky, for beyond some tumbles, sprained wrists, and two broken ankles, there were no accidents, and not one horse was injured to any serious extent during the entire ten months of the tour.

While the rehearsals were going on, I was rushing madly from one thing to another, but managed to acquire a horse

356

called Montezuma, given me by an old friend and admirer, Don Benito Villanueva, and also a leopard cub two months old, which I bought from the drunken skipper of a "hooker" that came crawling into port from Senegal. In addition to these two absorbing pets, Mascotte presented me with a litter of woolly and plebeian puppies the night before the show closed in the Sociedad Rural.

It was a very cold but sunny afternoon when we gave our first performance—a Benefit for the Police Orphanage. The tremendous grandstand was packed. It was a popular audience, composed, naturally, of the police and military with their families and a sprinkling of the horsy crowd living around the Palermo racetrack, where the large stud farms are situated. At the last minute it had been decided that after the first group of horsemen entered the arena, I should lead the second squadron, and for this entrance, I rode Montezuma.

He was the first horse I had ever owned, and of all my animals except Mascotte, perhaps I loved him the best. He had been bred for a race horse, but had developed too much bone for the track and was too heavy. He stood about sixteen and a half hands high (a big horse for me to mount) and was a light golden bay. His delicate head and powerfully arched neck gave him the appearance of having Arab in him, although, according to the pedigree, this was not the case.

Montezuma was the son of an Argentine-bred horse named Barsac, of a fine imported strain from England, and his breeding showed in every graceful and powerful line. He had a perfect mouth but was a little nervous to ride, and from the beginning, I babied and spoiled him, till after a while nobody could exercise him but me. Peons and grooms got thrown off, rubbed off, and rolled on, till they gave it up. Another habit I never could break was his mania for destroying blankets— he tore up literally dozens to amuse himself. He was a stallion two and half years old, and the first day at the Sociedad Rural, when the public recognized me, the cheering crowds scared the life out of him. As we stopped to salute the President's box he was so wild it was all I could do to handle him.

With the exception of a few unavoidable rough spots, especially in the Diguit, everything went off perfectly, and the applause at the finale was terrific. The night show at the Cervantes was another triumph for both Kerensky and Da Rosa, for the improvement in uniforms, lighting, and general presentation was unbelievable. The men worked splendidly and everything was perfect. It was not until the company crossed the Argentine border into Bolivia that the inevitable troubles began to manifest themselves, for in Juyjuy we had bad weather and some shortness of gate receipts. We also had a long wait there, and the first signs of disorder began to show.

There is a drink called pisca sold in nearly all South American countries, particularly in the outlying provinces. In Santa Fé, the Cossacks, while guests at several ranches where we gave performances, had learned about it from the gauchos. It is a type of heady *aguardiente* and stronger than a mule's kick. This quality, together with the added advantage of costing only about two American cents per glass, was the source of endless delight to the men, who discovered they could get roaring drunk for practically nothing.

The twenty-four hours they spent in Juyjuy are probably still remembered in that sleepy provincial town, with its sober colonial churches and tree-shaded streets, for two-thirds of the troupe staged a spectacular drinking bout that ended in the police having to round them up in saloons and bars and intervene in a series of street fights. I spent hours straightening out their fines in the police station and battling with outraged bar-owners and rooming-house proprietors about the quantity of furniture they had smashed up. After this, I found it was more successful to speak to the men myself, more or less appealing to their sense of chivalry and making them understand that the contracts were my responsibility and that if they continued getting drunk and smashing up towns, there would be cancellations, with financial disaster for me. All went well until we arrived in Sucre where, except for the Cossacks, we all stayed at the same hotel. A scientific expedition, consisting of an assortment of learned professors, filled half the building.

I had known from the start that Natascha was madly in love with Gregori Efimovitch, but she had begged me to engage an old friend of hers, named Desiderio, as head ticket man. He was an Italian who for years had been house manager for the Teatro Politeama in Buenos Aires. I knew him as a seriously married man, an excellent and very honest person on whom I had grown to depend considerably for all the general accounting of the gate receipts. He had been of great service to me during the disturbances in Juyjuy, and for this reason I had asked him to stay in Sucre instead of preceding the company to La Paz.

For some days, I had noticed, he was depressed and gloomy, but I put it down to all the trouble we were having with the men and their pisca. It was very hot the night we opened, and after the hectic day and two shows, I was so tired I hardly noticed the strained atmosphere hanging over the hotel lobby. Gregori Efimovitch had taken a room at the same hotel rather than stop with the other men: according to Natascha he had not been feeling well and wanted to rest by himself. I observed that she and Desiderio were having a rather stormy conversation in the lobby when I said good night to them, and I was just dropping off to sleep about an hour later when I was awakened by a series of revolver shots, apparently in the corridor outside. Restraining the frantic Mascotte, I opened the door. The first person I saw beyond the rows of heads popping out of doorways was Natascha, clad only in a kimono, with the familiar storm signal—her hair floating behind her. She came flying down the hall pursued by Desiderio, a smoking gun in his hand. Evar Mendez and Captain Schubert grabbed him as Natascha, half-fainting, took refuge in my room, locked the door behind her, and gasped out that Desiderio had shot Gregori.

The entire hotel was thoroughly aroused, but nobody knew

where Gregori was till at last I found him in Natascha's room, lying on the bed, wearing only a heavy silver ikon on a chain around his neck. His artificial leg still draped in half of his trousers was propped up in the corner of the room. He had been unable to get up or defend himself without it when Desiderio broke in and fired at the lovers. Bullets had shattered the dressing-table mirror, but fortunately none of them had landed in Gregori. Explaining that he could not get up without his leg, he asked me for it. Somewhat embarrassed, I handed it to him and left the room with great dignity.

The hotel manager, to whom the matter of a jealous lover shooting up the hotel was apparently an everyday occurrence, shrugged his shoulders when I asked him to try and keep the whole thing quiet. It was, he said, none of his business, since nobody had been killed.

The next day we went on to La Paz, but Desiderio returned to Buenos Aires, for he had, he told me, suffered a great deal over Natascha's passion for Gregori and might kill her were he to remain anywhere near the two of them.

We played two or three unexpected stands en route, which enabled us to make the journey to La Paz on foot. As our caravan wound its way through the rugged country, sometimes the only living things we met were troops of llama and their shepherds, who solemnly stared at us and munched the leaves of wild coco. The peasants for centuries have had the habit of eating this plant in handfuls to give them stamina on long journeys. It is a mild form of drug but has the curious effect of making the native *paisano's* somber black eyes even more expressionless. Fortunately, this habit had no appeal for the Cossacks.

La Paz, although a good engagement in a way, did not prove too successful, perhaps because without Desiderio there were confusion and deficiencies at the box office, and at times the financial situation was tense. The men were grumbling about their salaries by this time, and Kerensky, instead of having the matter out with them, avoided holding a meeting. I had explained to them that the question of salaries was not my affair; they knew I paid Kerensky a round sum for all the men.

Everybody was nervous and on edge, partly on account of the high altitude, which causes insomnia for several days until one becomes used to the thin air: during the Diguit, three men became dizzy and fell in the pyramid. Some of the horses suffered severe bleeding from the nose and were obliged to be rested, with treatment from a local veterinarian for a day or so.

The short dates we played in Cuzco and Jauja returned a poor percentage, although we worked to such full houses there was standing room only, and the open air show was filled with gauchos in brilliantly colored ponchos who had ridden from miles around to see us. Evar Mendez was worried to death trying to get to the bottom of the box-office juggling by the local impresarios. The nights were so hot I had the animals picketed in a cow pasture reserved for them near the exhibition grounds, and I became so nervous on account of the drinking going on among the Cossacks that I spent several nights sleeping with the tethered horses rather than worrying in my stuffy hotel bedroom over the possibility of some drunken Cossack setting fire to the men's sleeping-tent and causing a stampede. Although I enjoyed this experience, I was worn out by the time we arrived in Peru, for in addition to all the other things I had to occupy my energy, it became necessary for me to ride at the top of the pyramid with the standard, replacing men that were injured doing this feat. Since I was lighter than any of them, the saving on both horses and riders was immense.

Lima was another story altogether, for there we had a sensational success not only in the big Teatro Lírico but also in the Diguit spectacles at the National Stadium. The matinées given for charity at the bullring in the center of town were jammed to suffocation. Juan Belmonte, the great Spanish bullfighter, although getting on in years, was fighting in Lima that season; also El Gallo, grandmama's old pal from Seville, the husband of the great dancer, Pastora Imperia. It was good to see old friends again.

At last the financial tide began to turn, and of course the Cossacks were elated by the success we were having, but not many days passed before they started asking again for a raise. The fiestas of Christmas were approaching, and they anticipated a holiday with unlimited quantities of pisca. This did not worry me much, on account of the horses being stabled in the police barracks only about a hundred yards from a large fire station, but what did worry me was the sulking and arguing that went on. Things came to a climax one afternoon when Kerensky paid their weekly salaries in my office at the theater. They demanded more money, and he could do nothing with them, while both Schubert and Golovin gave me a long complicated explanation about what the men thought and felt—which got nobody anywhere.

The ringleader was an enormous Cossack named Ouboukoff, who was never sober, always in difficulties over his room rent when we stayed at a hotel and in fights with the other men when quartered in barracks. He had instituted himself the spokesman for the whole crowd. The main part of his grievance was that now I was obviously making money and the houses were full. Why could it not be possible for them to get a raise? I argued with them for an hour, trying to get them to understand that I had taken a personal loss so far on the tour, as had Don Faustino, and therefore it was an impossibility at the present moment to pay extra money, until all the earlier losses were adjusted.

Any outside work such as private fiestas at the ranches, were always paid extra, and they had already played several more of these than had been anticipated, so they had done better financially than any of them expected. Talk did absolutely no good, so finally I left them still arguing with Kerensky.

I went back to the hotel and was sitting talking to one of the police commissarios on the veranda. Curiously enough, we were discussing a fire that had occurred that morning in

362

a downtown movie, when I heard a boy running down the street shouting something about a fire in the Teatro Lírico. When we got there, the engines were already pumping.

The Cossacks, Ouboukoff at their head, had piled all the uniforms, boots, caps, and what not, in the center of the stage where the velvet drop with its double eagles was already hung for the evening show—and had set fire to them. Only the bottom of the drop burned badly, for the streams of water from the hoses put out the flames before they did much damage, but a great quantity of boots and caps had been destroyed. I shall never forget the kindness of the gentlemen representing the Comisión de Fiestas, and the two Gardner brothers, owners of the theater. Although the show had to be suspended that evening, for nearly five feet of stage had been burned through, they insisted on paying me their share of the guarantee so I would not lose money.

We worked the Diguit with only twenty-five men, because of the loss of uniforms: I was so embarrassed and ashamed of the poor turnout we gave, I could have crawled into a hole and hidden myself. The police arrested the ringleaders but could do nothing with them, having no proof of exactly how the fire started. My own problem was far more serious. The question of uniforms and caps was more or less possible to overcome with the local tailors, who were very reasonable in price, but the purchasing of new boots was another situation. They were an indispensable part of the equipment and a very expensive item. With Evar Méndez I hunted for boots from one hot sunbaked street to another, while Kipling's famous poem drummed in my head—"Boots! Boots! Boots!"

Some of the men had only one boot still wearable; others had none at all, and the tongue-lashing I gave them on the subject was, I hope, something to be remembered all their lives. Like children, they were ashamed of what they had done, especially as I informed them that for each day they did not work there would be no pay whatsoever. Several of the other men, who took no part in the outrage, were justly indignant, so fights of every description came off, till the company looked

363

as if they had been through an authentic battle when they mustered for the performances—bandaged foreheads, shiners, and everything else. The papers came out with eulogies of the heroic fight the Cossacks put up to extinguish the blaze, which accounted for their honorable wounds. The police, managers, and myself writhed with helpless fury at the publicity which put the whole underhand business in a limelight of heroism. I had nightmares about boots until finally, at the cost of a great part of the profits made, I got the company fitted out again.

The celebrations held by the Cossacks on their New Year holiday resulted in my having to leave three men behind to fulfil prison sentences for knife fights and disturbances created in town. I had to post a bond and leave the deposit for their fares before they could be shipped on to Havana to rejoin the troupe at the Santos Artigas Circus. It was necessary to appear there with a stated number of men according to contract, and unfortunately these were all key men and not easy to replace in the Diguit.

The relative peace and quiet of the circus was heaven after all the trapesing about we had been doing and the constant nervous tension over the horses. At last I was able to get a little time to myself, and during the afternoons in the hotel garden had wonderful times with my leopard cub, San.

We returned via Panama, where on account of the heat and climate of the Canal Zone, I did not want to use the horses. We played Bogotá and Quito and embarked in Guayaquil, Ecuador, for Valparaiso, Chile. Financially, things worked out well, and most of our contracts through Chile were on a paid salary, happily eliminating the worry of gambling on a percentage basis. The excitement over our openings in Valparaiso and Santiago was immense, and although the weather was getting cold, the crowds that attended were even greater than those congregating at the racetracks.

Although we participated in one of the greatest successes any company ever enjoyed in Chile, and I personally was the object of the most cordial treatment, having invitations showered on me, I counted the days when I could return the horses to the Argentine police and end the strain and worry of the tour. Everybody said I had achieved the impossible, and the financial benefits from the trip were considerable despite losses at the beginning. I had been through plenty and had not yet come out of the fog sufficiently to feel proud of myself.

One of the principal difficulties that presented itself was that of the difference in class and education among the men. Political discussions were more or less taboo, but the wrangling and disturbances that arose and had to be settled began mainly through the complaints of some of the more refined souls who resented the primitive habits of their companions. The dancers and riders, in particular, were nearly all peasants and moujiks, addicted to such old-fashioned remedies as urinating on each other's feet after a long march or when they were tired. No amount of argument could induce them to stop this insanitary practice, for they claimed it was a sovereign remedy for athlete's foot and, in addition, rested and toughened their feet.

After ten months of wrestling with problems of this nature, I began to feel that a change of environment was needed, and even if the Cossacks nurtured a hope that I would continue with the company (as I knew they did) I intended unloading the lot of them as soon as we reached Buenos Aires. Poor Evar Mendez lost weight to such an extent he looked like "death in the afternoon," and our four gatemen, whom we had miraculously managed to conserve, had shattered nerves and calloused hands from counting the thousands of tickets at the Diguit ticket booths before we left Chile.

The matter of organizing our return trip across the Andes to Mendoza was greatly complicated by a series of strikes and litigations in progress with the Trans-Andine Railroad. They could not contract box-cars for the entire group of horses on the same trip and suggested we travel in two contingents— something that was utterly impossible to do and arrive in Mendoza on time to fulfil our engagement. Already the weather was getting too cold, and the impresario was impatient for the function to begin on time.

After much running about, I finally managed to get a plan, through the help of Sir Harry Farquharson, a Chilean millionaire of Scottish descent owning leagues of sheep ranches in the rolling country at the foot of the Andes. We obtained train accommodations for the horses to the Chilean frontier, where the mighty Christ of the Andes looks down through eternal mist on the Argentine border. From a junction there, we could take the horses and equipment on down to Mendoza by the old mule tracks, still in use by gauchos for their herds and small caravans. There was not much choice in the matter, although I was worried about fatiguing the horses, but with the regiment of guides Sir Harry had telegraphed for, I felt it was the only possible way of making the trip and arriving on time.

It was a great adventure, certainly, but it cost about three times the amount the train would have—and that was costly enough. When we left Santiago, the send-off at the station was of such proportions that Schubert, Golovin, and the ticket men were at their wits' end trying to find out if all the Cossacks were on the train—or how many were missing. It was not until we were fairly well under way and down the first pass heading for Argentina that I was told three men had missed the train.

The trip by road was a nightmare, for rain and wind such as I had never dreamed of, combined with ungodly thunderstorms, overtook us while we were descending a part of the road called "Boca de Lobo" ("Wolf's Mouth"). The horses slipped and struggled on the wet rocky ground, while the cursing Cossacks were forced to lead each horse that carried a saddle and heavy pack, and I had visions of the animals slipping, with broken legs as a result, if they did not break loose and run over the precipice that flanked the road. The Indian guides leading us grumbled and complained about the delay at the end of the convoy, where the covered carts—containing San's cage, the dogs, Natascha and Mrs. Schubert

—were, I imagined, the cause of our lack of progress. They insisted we had to hurry, storm or no storm, if we wanted to reach the next guard post for the night.

Giving Montezuma to one of the men, I hurried back to the end of the convoy as best I could to see what was detaining them and, through the stinging rain, ran straight into the astounding spectacle of a fat Indian girl with a face like an Eskimo, sitting on a miserable little pack mule loaded with bales of fodder. Of all ridiculous things, she was smearing

lipstick on her mouth with the aid of a small mirror. Dumfounded, I stared at the creature—she sat huddled in a colored poncho, with a preposterous hat topping her flat face, two plaits of greasy black hair dangling on either side of it.

"*Yo linda?*" ("Am I pretty?") she inquired. When I asked how in the name of God she had got mixed up with the convoy, she explained in pidgin Spanish that one of the Cossacks (whom she took to be a soldier) had taken her from her *casita* (brothel) on the outskirts of Santiago. There were, she informed me, two other *muchachitas lindas* (pretty girls) farther back in the caravan, who had also been invited by some of the men to accompany them into Argentina. This was the last straw!

I went in search of Golovin and Schubert, after telling the

Indian to get her fat carcass off that mule and walk before I threw her over the rocky chasm into eternity. Neither of the captains had observed any women getting on the train in Santiago with the men and were as horrified as I was. Eventually we found out that Ouboukoff and two others of the more moronic and troublesome riders were the authors of the invitation. They had, it appeared, become tired of the pisca and wanted feminine companionship for a change.

All three men were of the blond Tartar type of Cossack from the Don, and the swarthy corpulence of the half-breed *chulas* they had picked up held an irresistible appeal for them. Upon arrival at the next outpost, we managed to leave the three girls in charge of the guards and frontier patrols, who guaranteed to put them on the next train returning to Santiago, but the scene over the money the *muchachitas lindas* demanded for their services was a honey. Mendez and the captains between them finally got the matter adjusted, after Golovin knocked Ouboukoff unconscious so that peace could be restored.

For weeks after we returned to Buenos Aires and the company finally disbanded, the Cossacks hung about the city, not seeming to realize that there was no more Diguit. I felt terribly sorry for some of the nicer men, who tried forming a miserable little troupe with a balalaika orchestra. Others went back to their old occupations, while Kerensky got a few weeks in Brazil with the rest of the choir.

The letter of congratulation received from the police veterinarians on the excellent condition of all the horses made me feel both proud and happy. I had gone through hours of anguish over those beasts, and they were not only in better shape than when I took them out but had the advantage of now being perfectly trained, and that to me was a vast satisfaction.

I had been in Buenos Aires about a week when a cable arrived from Herr Furster of Hamburg, in care of *La Nación*, informing me that one of my stolen diamonds had been recovered. Furster had kept his word a little over a year from the time of the robbery. The thief was Morgenstern after all, caught while trying to sell the larger of the two stones, but despite all the police had done to make him confess what had become of the other ring, they had been unable to get anything out of him. He had been implicated in other thefts of importance, and later when I was in Germany again, I heard he had been sentenced to three-and-a-half years in prison.

It was quite a thrilling experience opening the envelop that contained the diamond. The stone had been dismounted from the setting, but it was wonderful to feel that something so intimately connected with my mother had at last returned to me. Herr Furster promised in his letter that should they at any time be able to trace the other ring, he would notify me immediately, and I should keep in touch with them, notifying them of any change in address. I did so for two or three years but never heard anything more about the missing ring. Presumably, Morgenstern sold it outside Germany in some way.

Having no time for any vacation, I commenced at once working at the Colón. The pleasure of being in my own apartment again was so great that the ballet seemed child's play after the last ten months. All was peace and quiet until I had some trouble with two old ladies living next door to my apartment in an enormous gray stone house. It had, like most Argentine residences, a flat roof where they kept chickens and hung out quantities of washing done by their own laundry maids. These anti-esthetic ways were common even to very wealthy people, who never allowed their laundry to go into strange places. As for the chickens, it is probably a good old Spanish custom that they would feel lost without.

San had grown so big by this time that I had been obliged to have a run built for her on the roof, where she could get exercise and fresh air. At night and when I was home most of the day, I kept her indoors, but she was inclined to be destructive, although very gentle and sweet. One afternoon she had spent her spare time clawing through a leg of my grand piano to give herself a manicure, while she lay lazily on her back underneath it. I just had time to drive her out before the instrument toppled over with a resounding crash that certainly would have killed her. After this experience, I was afraid to leave her alone in the house, for she had acquired some other extravagant whims as well, so I kept her a great deal in the open air. This was the reason for the beldames' next door going to the police. Legally I had no right to keep wild animals who could destroy human lives, in the city, and the police very nicely requested I send my leopard away. I refused, as her run was perfectly safe, and they themselves admitted there was absolutely no danger of her ever getting out of it. However, after two or three weeks of continuous conflict, these depraved old ladies had their favorite nephew (an unpleasant-looking youth with the aspect of a werewolf) shoot poisoned meat over on to my roof with a catapult.

Fortunately, Flora found it while San was trying to scoop a piece into the run with her paw. I took it to the pharmacy and had it analyzed. It was full of strychnine, one of the cruelest poisons that can be given to animals. There was no way in which San could be shifted out of their reach, and in the end I had to send her to the zoo. She was so affectionate and spoiled, this broke her heart, and for days she wouldn't eat. I used to get up at six in the morning, go out to the zoo, and exercise her on a leash before the gates opened for the public. Mr. Onelli was no longer director of the zoo, but in his place was a gentle old Austrian who always walked about the grounds with two spotted deer at his heels.

San settled down fairly well, but then to my dismay she suddenly developed abscesses in her ears. We lanced one after another, and the vets tried all sorts of injections unsuccessfully, until at last we had to give her an injection, putting her to sleep—for there was nothing further to be done, and she was constantly in pain. I went over to the cage and saw how she had torn the wood into splinters in her agony, and that her fur looked damp and unhealthy. I could not look into her big green eyes that were so understanding and had to rush away from her cage to keep up my courage while telling the vet to go ahead.

I never saw San again, and that sorrow was one of the reasons I wanted frantically to catch the first boat for Europe. Several contracts that meant a good deal of money had been offered me, if I would stay and produce some tableaux for the impresario of the Sarmiento and Maipú theaters, but I wanted to get home to Paris at any cost and see my brother, and I hoped that father would take a short holiday with me. I found Bunnie very much better than when I left Europe; he seemed to be more reconciled to his blindness. He was absorbed in music, composing songs, and writing articles and short stories for several of the current English magazines. We were both disappointed at receiving a letter from father saying that for numerous reasons he would not be able to join us for this holiday or at Christmas as I had hoped. Sensing there was something else wrong, I wrote immediately asking if he would like me to come over and see him. He replied that he would prefer me to wait till the following year when he felt that in all probability he could join me somewhere for a holiday. This answer mystified me considerably.

XIX

NO SOONER had I settled down to the joy of being in Paris again than a complicated proposal was made to me to appear in Russia in the acts that had done so well with Sam Woods' band in Germany. Stanislas Idzikowski, the impresario, arrived in Paris, and we concluded arrangements for five weeks in Russia and three in Bucharest, Budapest, and Vienna. It began to look like a very good thing.

Sam Woods, for years a martyr to lumbago, had retired to the United States, and the only Negro band obtainable for the engagement was a combination of musicians under the direction of two brothers, Julius and Washington Thompson, both from New Orleans. Their arrangements of spirituals and higher-class Negro music were outstanding, but in a completely different style from the jazz and blues that had been our success in Germany.

I began hurried rehearsals with the Thompson brothers. They were an unusually solemn couple of men for musicians, both college graduates and highly intellectual. In fact, the atmosphere at rehearsals was so refined, it became positively oppressive, and to build a vaudeville act with a colored band in an atmosphere punctuated with quotations from Freud and Einstein was something that, up till then, I had never encountered. The band had, as in Berlin, eleven men, all fine musicians with excellent voices: musically speaking it was perfection, but it ran to the concert type of work.

I was fortunate in getting hold of one of the boys who had sung for a short time at the Jardin de ma Sœur and whose tenor voice was something to marvel at—like deep purple velvet. He had been decoyed away from the "International Five" in those days by a wealthy, eccentric Englishwoman.

He lived with her in London for a year or so, till she grew tired of him and returned him to Montmartre. There were two or three other boys whose abilities for the real jazz and blues were exceptional, and when Zipilli and Violette came to rehearsals, they advised me to get some of that sort of repertoire ready in case of emergency.

Fortunately I had brought the staircase from Argentina, although I had never expected to do that number again for I was heartily sick of it. I tried to find Morgan, but there was absolutely no trace of him or his family in Paris. It was not an easy matter finding another man or any one willing to go to Russia, but after a good deal of hunting about I hired an Italian named Cesare Chichi at the last minute. It was with this odd collection of personalities that we finally started on our tour.

Since 1928, the year I journeyed through Russia, people have told me that the system of traveling has been greatly improved. I certainly hope so, for I would not wish my experiences on my worst enemy. After we had changed to the Russian railroad at the Estonian frontier, our real troubles started. Russian railways, like the famous Trans-Siberian on, which I frequently traveled with my mother in the old days, had always furnished the most luxurious means of transportation, but the train we finally got on after two hours of waiting in the bitter North Russian cold—while officials and frontier guards muttered over our papers, checking and rechecking our belongings—was a triumph of discomfort: not enough heat, seats of bare wood, no sleeping accommodations, and of course no class distinctions whatsoever. The windows were so dirty it was impossible to see out of them, for a sickly yellowish-gray light filtered through the panes during the short October day. At every little station the train stopped to admit more and more odd people into compartments.

A woman invaded mine with two children suffering from some particularly unpleasant type of skin disease. Next came an old bearded man with catarrh, also a wild-eyed younger one who kept staring at me till I thought Flora, my maid, was going to slap his face. An officer got in with an enormous bundle and four duffle bags which he insisted on keeping on the floor in front of him, then two "babas" (country women) came along and proceeded to eat dried fish out of a newspaper. Finally the stuffy compartment smelled so strongly of feet I thought I was going to be sick, so I went out into the passageway in the hope of getting a breath of fresh air. The wild-eyed man followed and cornered me, digging down into his top boot and producing a dirty little white paper full of cocaine which he offered me. He seemed so offended when I refused that I had to ask Chichi to sit with me in the corridor until we got to the end of the ghastly trip late that night.

Leningrad was a sinister, fog-enshrouded town, like a ghost of its former self. At the station we found Idzikowski's manager, a pleasant young Latvian, accompanied by a representative of the recently organized Intourist, the official travel bureau. They explained the endless slips of paper and tourist cards connected with our stay, telling where we could and could not go. The trips to be made to the Strangers' Bureau at police headquarters and regulations about this and that made life so complicated it did not seem worth living at all.

Our début was a strange contradiction of all we had expected, for the public seemed bewildered at first, although they applauded my staircase number with great enthusiasm, and seemed to enjoy the singing of such melodies as "Deep River," "Swing Low, Sweet Chariot," etc. Gershwin's lovely "Rhapsody in Blue," however, which was the *pièce de résistance* of the Thompson brothers, left them cold. The famous Charleston struck them as amusing but not anything to get worked up about, although they gave me fair hands. After leaving the stage, I whispered to Julius to play an encore on the "Tiger Rag" and to give it the gun. Fortunately he did as I told him and that saved the show, for then the public went wild. Reports in the papers confirmed their attitude, for contrary to everything Idzikowski said, they wanted to hear hot jazz and plenty of it—not a symphonic effort, which their own musicians played constantly and far better. We had a rehearsal early the following morning and changed the entire repertoire with the exception of the dances and spirituals which had gone over. Through this change, the evening performance was definitely a success, and we all felt much better about it.

There were quantities of German acts on the bill, and some of the girls were having affairs with different Commissars, who gave exotic parties in the traditional Russian manner after the show. These men obtained priceless furs and jewels from mysterious sources, which they occasionally gave to their lady friends, although it was supposed to be prohibited to take all *objets de luxe* out of the country, for they were considered the property of the Soviet.

The general aspect of everything was one of abject poverty, and the question of even having clothes washed became such an undertaking and so expensive that the musicians found it cheaper to buy clean shirts when they could find them, rather than tackle the laundries.

Idzikowski hinted to me that although there did not seem to be any visible evidence of our being too much controlled in our movements, I would do well to advise the musicians that when they wished to drink and have a good time, they should confine this sort of activity to the bar in the Tabarin where we performed or a cabaret, Le Coq d'Or, that existed under the theater. I had looked in once and found it to be a very expensive place, beautifully decorated—a lighted cellar in the Russian style, with groups of haggard, sickly-looking girls waiting hungrily for some man to buy cigarettes or *champanski* for them.

The manager of the hotel whispered to me one morning in the hall that he would take it as a personal favor if the crucifix I always hung over my bed were kept out of sight. I then began to notice other things, including the daily searching of my grips, papers, etc., when Flora and I were out. Thereafter I never left Mascotte alone, for fear if she were in the room when somebody came in, she would fly at him and fireworks would follow. There was an unpleasant feeling that everybody distrusted everybody else, and a sordid, morbid atmosphere about the few people I met, except for a Swiss friend, Frederick Ruckli, whom I knew from Paris. He had an enormous apartment all to himself on the wide Yaroslavl Boulevard, with all sorts of good food and wines, being a privileged member of the diplomatic corps. Ruckli told me a great deal about the evolution of the Russian people and their great strength waiting to be organized, saying I had visited Russia ten years too soon.

The newspapers wanted interviews, and I met two of the more advanced-thinking young men and women writing about art and the theater, among them a friend of Olga Gougoutchieff, Vera Missin. She was a strange intense girl who shared a studio with three others near the old Probrejensky Barracks. In fact, none of the girls I met seemed quite normal: they were obsessed with patriotic fervor, and like the majority of Slavs had absolutely no sense of humor, so when they questioned me on the outside world's opinion of Russia and the effort the Soviet was making with the five-year plan, I tactfully said I considered myself too stupid to have any ideas at all about politics—that as a rule such topics bored me. This seemed to stupefy them. Nevertheless, they were useful in obtaining passes for me to attend the schools of ballet and dramatic art, which proved to be extremely interesting.

Although I was impressed with many things in Leningrad, such as the projected "recreation grounds" with enormous gymnasiums for aërial exhibitions in the open air, I heard that Moscow, as always, was the center of Russian art and theater. I attended one good representation of Russian modern opera, the *City of Kitzeh,* which proved to be a revelation in color and stagecraft, but the ballet at the Marinsky disappointed me. Perhaps because I still cherished the memory of all I had seen as a child, the whole thing now seemed coarsened and fleshy. The first dancer in the *Swan Lake* ballet at the Marinsky, though an excellent technician, was far too heavy and wore a pair of cotton tights in that virulent shade known as Italian pink, which completely spoiled the show for me.

What was rather sweet and touching was the children's delighted awe of the Negroes wherever we went. Generally I accompanied the boys on sightseeing trips, for they spoke no Russian and could not afford the exorbitant rates of a guide for everything we wanted to do. In the streets, white-faced, thin little children, bundled in ridiculous and inadequate clothing, followed us. Sometimes the Thompson brothers, who like all colored people loved children, stopped and tried talking to them. One would timidly and very solemnly stand on tiptoe to touch their faces with an expression of wonder in his big blue eyes. They rarely smiled, those children, and I noticed that most of the people we passed on the street, beyond a furtive glance or a half-resentful stare at the *chilooviki* (strangers) rarely laughed or smiled either.

Artists were by far the best-off people I met, for they had government subsidies for schools, art expositions, musical academies, and theaters, and there appeared to be a sudden wave of every branch of decorative art coming into being after the long famine of anything pertaining to beauty.

Moscow was far more intensely Russian, in atmosphere as well as art, than Leningrad, and at the same time life there not only was more complicated but had a more lugubrious feeling about it. Idzikowski had obtained accommodations for everybody in the Moscowskia Hotel across the bridge of that name. Rooms in the hotel had been divided into half their normal dimensions by means of wooden partitions, with spaces like transoms left at the top and curtains hung at the entrance of each cubicle. Fortunately I had Flora in the one next to mine: otherwise, such intimacy would have been intolerable.

Officials from the secret police arrived at all hours of the night to drag some unfortunate transient from his bed, screaming and protesting, down the corridors and out of the hotel to God knows what fate. When I complained to the manager, a mild Ukrainian man, he turned white and whispered that any criticisms or comments were sufficiently dangerous to cause serious complications, should they be overheard, and his advice was to ignore all such things while in Russia.

I visited many studios with a friend of Nina's and Olga's, Ferdinand Terin, who worked at the Maly (Little) Theater, and also went to the school of ballet at the Bolshoi Opera and the Soviet schools of painting and design. At the Moscow Theater of Art, I witnessed one of the most startling performances of Oscar Wilde's *Salomé*. All the décors were made of strips of ordinary oil cloth, painted and used in a dozen different forms and effects. The acting was something to marvel at, but the woman playing the rôle of Salomé, though a great Russian actress was quite old and possessed a definite rubber tire around her waist. This glaring defect was startlingly out of place amid all the talent, beauty of lighting, and stagecraft.

In nearly everything I saw, I could not throw off an impression that a primitive savagery had surged to the surface with the new era of Russian art, which—had it not been for the coarseness that permeated most of it—would have been intoxicating in its strength. I felt it would take a hundred years to regain the culture that the Revolution had destroyed and to recover that mystical beauty of the pre-revolutionary Russian compositions.

In many ways I was elated at all I was learning, and the copious notes I made, with sketches, amounted to a wealth of material of every description, especially color, which had not been affected by the new trend and remained as glorious as ever. But at the same time I was depressed, nervous, and anxious to leave a country where a sinister gloom had touched with blood-stained fingers everything I remembered.

The streets of Moscow were even more haunted than those of Leningrad, and the old familiar scenes were filled with phantoms of the dear dead friends I had known. I think the most poignant memory I have of that trip to Moscow is associated with the exquisite "Invitation to the Dance," for it was intimately associated with my childhood days in the old Russia. One afternoon in the Bolshoi Theater I heard it played again, but now in that inescapable atmosphere of fetid humanity. Closing my eyes I could see once more my first gala night in that same theater, its stalls and boxes filled with courtly men and gracious, delicate women, the faint fragrance of sandalwood perfume and imperial violets blended as a perfect complement to the orchestra. The illusion became so strong, I rose from my seat and left the theater. Hearing that music played in such a changed environment was as pitiful as the thought of a rose trampled underfoot in the mud.

Near the end of our last fortnight, I decided to undertake a mission I had promised to fulfil for Helena Soltikoff, which resulted in considerable unpleasantness. Before I left Paris, Helena had given me a sum of money she had scraped together through her lingerie work, and requested me to see her old housekeeper, now a matron at one of the Moscow city hospitals. This woman, Helena said, could give me first-hand news of the little son she had been separated from when the Bolsheviks shot her mother and she was put in jail.

I took an antiquated droshky that was sometimes stationed outside the hotel for passengers going to the train: the shortage of taxis was another of the discomforts of life in Moscow, for drivers hesitated to take fares in case the Commissars of the OGPU wanted them. The man who drove me was a ferret-faced individual who attempted to start a long conversation about how and why I spoke Russian. I did not trust him and suspected he was a spy for the police, so I did my best to make him think I was too stupid to bother with. As we plodded through the snowy streets, he kept turning around to repeat the price of the fare, in case I didn't realize it was an expensive trip.

We finally arrived at the house I was looking for, situated on a new street of workers' dwellings. I was lucky to find the woman, Anastasia Taitatcheva, at home, but at first she didn't want to know anything about why I had come or furnish me with information—evidently suspecting I was going to do something indiscreet and get into trouble. Despite what Helena said about her being a trusted family servant, I did

379

not like the woman. She was nosy, familiar, and altogether unpleasant, but I finally got a certain amount of truth out of the maze of evasive lies she kept stalling me off with, when I gave her (as Helena instructed me to) half the money. I was to hand over the rest if my informant furnished proof of the child's identity and if possible arranged for me to see him and judge his condition for myself. She told me he was in an asylum for feeble-minded children some distance from the town, in the vicinity of Vlovsk, and that although he was a normal boy mentally, he was kept there because of a crippled foot that had never been properly attended to. He had never been told who his parents were and had no idea of his name.

As she revealed these pathetic details, I became angrier and angrier and had a job controlling my temper, when I finally got up to leave. A dull red flush mounted in her face, and I realized I had struck a wrong note with some outspoken remarks. Greed getting the better of her fears, she promised to bring me a report about the boy, telling me to return two days later, at which time she would give me all the information required for the balance of the money. There was something about the woman's whole attitude I did not like, so before leaving the house I asked permission to go to the toilet, and there I carefully inserted the paper bills remaining from Helena's rubles into the sole of one of my shoes. As I left the house she kept insisting I take a certain road back to town, and the more she urged, the more determined I was to do just the contrary.

Driving to the center of town by a completely different route, I dismissed the droshky and walked several blocks to the hotel, stopping off at a big store on the way. When I reached the hotel it was nearly six-thirty, and as soon as I entered the lobby the Ukrainian manager came rushing out of his office to tell me I was wanted at the Strangers' Bureau of the OGPU at once, adding that he would require to show my room to prospective clients for he understood I would be leaving Moscow immediately.

380

I went promptly to the offices of the Bureau on the Loubianka. After waiting there about half an hour, I was ushered into an office where a man in uniform, with a green shade over his eyes, was busily looking at finger-printed documents. His first question was, "Do you speak Russian?" When I replied in the affirmative he commenced a long interrogation, ignoring my questions as to why I'd been brought there in the first place. The sum total of the whole thing, according to him, was that Anastasia Taitatcheva had telephoned the secret police the minute I left her house, telling them I was endeavoring to "kidnap a boy from one of the government institutions in order to assist the enemy of the Soviet, Helena Soltikoff."

This cross-examination continued for upward of an hour, when I was finally confronted with the money I had given the woman. This was the most serious part of the entire mess. The Commissar expounded all sorts of complicated rules and regulations about any one's having such a large sum, and suspected I had entered the country with it for the express purpose of bribing a loyal Soviet supporter. Naturally I told him the money came from my contract at the Hermitage and nowhere else, but when he obviously didn't believe me, I insisted he call one of the Idzikowski brothers for the double purpose of assuring himself of the sum they paid me and also letting them know where I was. At the rate we were going, it seemed probable that Idzikowski's star act would not be on hand to perform that night.

The Commissar, a disagreeable person with a long yellow face like an anemic goat and fingernails in the deepest mourning, would not let me talk to anybody on the telephone, but finally I persuaded him at least to 'phone Stanislas Idzikowski and tell him where I was. He left the room to do this, leaving another uniformed moujik to stand in the doorway and gape at me while he was gone. Upon returning, he went into an office next door to talk to somebody, and I distinctly heard the deep booming voice of Helena's trusted retainer—she sounded as though she were crying. When he finally came back to speak to me, his manner seemed just a trifle more amiable as he said that somebody from the theater was coming to talk to me at once.

Then Idzikowski arrived, and I saw by the expression on his face that the matter was not a very easy one to arrange. "Do you know where you are?" he asked me in English.

I replied that of course I knew not only that I was in the Strangers' Bureau, but that it was one of the most unpleasant places I had found myself in for a long time. He explained that the third-floor offices of the OGPU were a place that, once strangers got in, they rarely left except to go straight to jail.

Apparently Stanislas Idzikowski was on very friendly terms with the goat-faced one, for they got into a huddle in a corner and whispered together, Idzikowski gesticulating like a Shakespearean actor in a hammy production. At last he came over to me and said that Goat Face claimed I broke the laws of Soviet hospitality by attempting to bribe a loyal citizen, thereby extorting information that was none of my business, but that, in consideration of the fact that it was my first offense and he personally was anxious to render service to Tovarich Idzikowski, he would allow me to finish the present week of my contract, but I must be out of Moscow by the following Monday morning. The musicians could, if they desired, remain there the week that was still left to be played. Idzikowski motioned to me to agree with anything the representative of the Comintern proposed, and said that as he had made himself responsible for me, he hoped I would do exactly as requested.

We finally got outside and went to my hotel. The manager, when he saw me, nearly fainted. I suppose he thought I had left for good. Idzikowski told me, on the way to the theater, that the risk I had run by trying to help my friend about her son could have landed me in really serious trouble, and it was hard to tell what the outcome would have been. Luckily, the Commissar happened to be one of the most persistent grafters the Idzikowski brothers had to deal with in their establishment, and he hinted that the matter of getting me out of the

382

Loubianka "third floor" would cost him a considerable amount in "champagnski" before he paid the debt in full.

After the show that night we had another conference over a drink. Unfortunately he became so pressing that I decided, rather than accept his offer to try and "square" the affair and obtain an extension of a week to finish my contract, I preferred leaving on Monday as ordered, managing financially as best I could. The whole thing was awkward, and I had to tell the Thompson brothers the entire affair.

They were immediately sympathetic and charming about everything, saying they would not consider for a minute remaining in the Hermitage without me. The whole band was more than relieved to get away from Russia, especially since there was no American consulate in those days, all affairs being handled by the British, whose authority was limited. As for Flora, suffering from the cold, her joy knew no bounds.

Stanislas Idzikowski was really "heaping coals of fire," for he paid me two extra days' salary so that I could settle our hotel bill, which I promised to return to him after Bucharest. I was extremely grateful to him for getting me out of a bad mess.

Bucharest was, as always, a sleepy date with half-empty houses and inadequate lighting, but we were too relieved at getting out of Russia even to think of complaining. Budapest was heaven after all we'd been through, and the Parisian Grill, with its delightful, fastidious public and excellent food was indeed a contrast. We could have stayed another week or more, so great was our success there. All the numbers that had not penetrated Russian audiences were encored and cheered by one of the most critical, music-conscious audiences in the world. Vienna was also a successful date and as gay as a Strauss waltz. Many of mother's old friends came to see me at the theater and hotel. Still, I don't think I have ever been so happy to get back to Paris as on that snowy December day we arrived.

I felt very ashamed that I had not succeeded in my attempts

383

on behalf of Helena, and that some of the money she had earned through so much sacrifice had found its way into the palm of her persecutors. Any news I could give was enough to break her heart, and she had suffered enough already, so I told her husband first, letting him wrap up the truth for her as he saw fit.

It was a happy Christmas, even though father was not with me as I had hoped he'd be. I always missed him more at this time of year, for like many people who have never had a family life or a home, Christmas represented an unattainable joy for me. Violette had arranged a most delightful surprise— a few days' hunting with the stag hounds of the Duchesse d'Uzès in the forest of Rambouillet. It is a historic hunt, originally established by the Louis's, and the hunt clubhouse is a place to dream in, with its ancient cobblestone courtyard and great vaulted reception hall decorated with antlers and heads of sangliers. The late Duchesse d'Uzès was a great friend of Violette's and a magnificent rider to hounds.

French hunts do not have the same rules as the English packs but go through a great deal of ceremony before they start, with picturesque *cours de chasses* played by the green-liveried hunt servants on large coiled horns. This was all in such contrast to my recent adventure that I felt as if I'd been transplanted to another world living at least a hundred years earlier.

New Year's Eve I spent with Violette and a party of friends at the delightful old roadhouse, Moulin de la Biche-relle, in the valley of Rambouillet. The faces of those gay, carefree French people standing in a circle around our table, their arms linked and singing "Auld Lang Syne," often float before my eyes and I wonder what has become of them.

It was time to be off to Buenos Aires once more, and again I felt a wrench at leaving Paris. My short stay had been fruitful, however, for I had decided how to use the researches made in Russia, seen the acts chosen for Lombard's revue, visited my monkeys at the zoo (where they were quite happy

384

and had completely forgotten me), and also helped the Thompsons get bookings in South America for the near future. Pepita, of whom I saw very little, had a contract with Jacques Charles and expected to go there herself in June.

On my way out from Europe I disembarked in Montevideo, where, through the services of Dr. Fitzsimon, I obtained my liberty from Captain Strudwick. This was something I had long hesitated to do, for religious reasons, but father wanted me to be free, and after mother's death, we decided upon this course. Having heard nothing from my husband for several months, I felt there was no sorrow attached to the matter for him and that there was absolutely no future for us together. Occasionally I heard from friends that he was doing marvelously well in his career—a deep satisfaction to me, for I had always sympathized with his ambitions—and when I heard that his commanding officers referred to him as the "second Lawrence of Arabia," it made me very happy for his sake.

I arrived in Buenos Aires for the Carnival season, that mad holiday so dear to the hearts of Latin America, and spent the last few days of it with Matto on his yacht, fishing tranquilly in the waters of the Alta Paraná, one of the most beautiful spots in the world. The memory of the moonlit waters, with the distant throbbing music of guitars floating across from the river bank, is one of the cherished souvenirs of my life. Matto's marriage had gone on the rocks, and he was feeling so blue I was glad to spend a few days endeavoring to cheer him up. This I managed to do so successfully that all the crazy adventures we had in those few days would fill another book.

In Rio, the success of the Thompsons' band was a splendid one, especially in the cabaret of the Copacabana where I arranged for three men with exceptional voices to harmonize old Southern melodies very softly in the intimate atmosphere of the small *caveau*. The boys caught the carefree spirit of Brazil and changed such melodies as "My Old Kentucky Home" to more ribald ones like "Those Old Red Flannel

Drawers.'' It was all the same to the Brazilians, who were convinced they were listening to a sentimental song about home and mother.

We had a repeat date at the Grand Ciné Florida in Buenos Aires, after our appearance in Rio. I did not want to play this date with an acrobatic jazz ensemble for fear the Colón would frown on such a combination, and as I had requested a release from my fourth season contract (which had been granted) I wanted to make my last year with them a highly successful one—particularly on account of the maquettes I had prepared. The Thompsons had been so sporting about the Russian fiasco that I did not know how to get out of the engagement, and I was hunting for a reasonable excuse that would not make them think I was snobbish, when one night the staircase slipped on the polished floor of the *caveau*. Three fingers of my right hand were broken, and I suffered a touch of fever as well, so I was able to get out of the Florida contract gracefully.

It worked out very nicely in the end, despite the discomfort my hand caused me, for that season at the request of the Arts Commission, I made an educational film for the Colón archives, on ballet technique and especially on the method of placing and using the feet in toe dancing. The 1929 season at the Colón was a memorable one, for in addition to the film I won the gold medal given by the Press Societies for the maquettes I designed for an Argentine opera based on a poem by Manolo Guiraldes. It was on a fantastic Incaican legend and the use of color I absorbed in Moscow was what won me this distinction.

It was late in July when I got the opportunity to go for two days to Montevideo to take care of some legal details requiring my presence. War was imminent between Paraguay and Bolivia, and all better-class river boats that make the overnight trip to Buenos Aires from Montevideo were commandeered for transports. So on my return trip I was confronted with the unpleasant necessity of embarking on a third-rate paddle-wheel steamer, overcrowded with tourists coming back from one of the many Paraguayan fiestas. I was

386

traveling alone, having left Mascotte and Flora in Buenos Aires. I had not given much thought to the probable discomforts of the trip and at the last minute was glad to get an inside cabin on a lower deck.

As the old boat made her way up the mouth of the Plate, I was sitting in the recreation salon talking to some people about the Colón season. Suddenly the piano, with three musicians playing around it, started careering down the center of the salon. Chairs with their occupants and tables laden with drinks and coffee began to overturn. At first people laughed a little nervously, but when a burst of wind drove through the windows and a sheet of water drenched everybody, they began to get panicky. A terrific electric storm had struck with the violence of a tornado.

Women screamed as men tried to help them toward the doorway and down to their cabins. I would have preferred remaining where I was, but my friends, anxious to make their own cabins before things got any worse, insisted I go with them. I hate crowds and nervous folk so went to my cabin and began to read. The boat pitched and shook so that all the things fell out of the rack beneath the medicine chest. I heard people rushing madly about outside. Evidently they were abandoning the lower-deck cabins, so I got up, looked out into the passageway, and saw that water was slopping about the carpets and that doors of cabins stood wide open. A German radio officer ran past, carrying an apparatus that had obviously broken down. In answer to my query he hastily shouted, "Get up on the top deck if you can!"

I ran back to my cabin, tied my money and jewelry into a handkerchief and pinned them securely into my girdle, then started for the stairs leading to the upper decks. There things looked pretty sticky, for some of the men were waving revolvers and threatening to shoot members of the crew, who, they said, had been pillaging their cabins. Some of the passengers kept shouting that the crew were not regular licensed seamen of the legitimate merchant marine but longshoremen the company had picked up on the docks to man the ship at the last minute. Then shots rang out—several men were left lying in twisted heaps while the old red-faced German captain fought his way down the jammed staircase, also carrying a gun and spluttering about what he was going to do if order was not restored at once. There was, he admitted, danger, but if the passengers would only keep their heads and proceed quietly to the boat stations, all would be well, and they would be allotted places in lifeboats in due course.

Just then the boat gave a wild lurch. Several people trying to get up the staircase lost their balance, and their falling bodies hurtling against those of the people below caused a struggling knot of humanity to roll down the stairway. Then they started fighting madly to get up it again.

I certainly did not feel like attempting to battle my way through that mob of lunatics, but at the same time the prospect of being drowned like a rat in a trap did not appeal to me. I remembered seeing a second companionway a little farther down the passage and was making for it when I noticed an old Spanish lady in a black mantilla, with two little round-eyed boys, sitting placidly on a trunk in front of one of the cabins: she was praying very softly. A little farther on I found a girl about eight or ten years old lying on her face. When I turned her over I saw that she had a big purple bruise on her temple and was unconscious. I did not know what to do with the child but certainly could not leave her lying there to be trampled on. Lifting the limp body, I carried her back to the old Spanish lady, asking if she would look after her till I found some way for them to get help from the upper decks.

When I got to the companionway there was more trouble, but at last I decided to make a rush for it to see if I could fight my way up and find somebody to help me with the old lady and the children. The pitching of the ship seemed to drive the men and women pushing their way up the stairs into a frenzy of fear. Suddenly I lost my temper over the whole business—how I got to the top of that staircase I shall never know, but I found myself surging up and through the door on to the deck, nearly cracking a rib in the scuffle.

388

Finally I found a man I knew slightly from Buenos Aires. He somehow got down the stairs again, but returned saying that the old lady was no longer there with the children. I never knew what became of them.

After a struggle I managed to get up to the very topmost deck of all, just behind the bridge, and tried to find a place of shelter away from the rain and the terrific wind that did not seem to have any intention of abating. Squeezed into a fairly secure corner beside a ventilating shaft, I sank to my knees, for it was impossible to stand upright against the fury of the storm.

In a few moments I became aware of another woman, wrapped in a fur coat, crouching on the slippery deck. She tried to speak to me, and above the shouting, screaming, and roaring of the gale, I could hear her give rein to her feelings on the subject of the unseaworthy ship and "the thieves who sent such ships to sea along with an incapable German captain." The little I could hear of her speech was couched in unusually strong language for an elderly lady: I could not distinguish her face, but she seemed to be elegant and had rather a cultured accent. When I replied as best I could, she yelled back to speak nearer her ear as she was deaf and used an ear trumpet.

All through the hours that followed, while the helpless paddle boat was buffeted about by the storm like a flustered hen in a millrace, I shouted replies to one of the most unusual conversations I ever heard. The first thing she asked was if I had a man on board with me. Upon my replying I was alone, she congratulated me and proceeded to inform me she was a member of Argentine society, returning from a little amorous adventure in Montevideo with a gigolo whom she described as a "yellow bastard" and who, she cordially hoped, was already at the bottom of the River Plate. He had, she said, cost her a lot of money and when she needed at least some attention had abandoned her to save his own skin.

She continued to regale me, above the music of the storm, with spicy anecdotes of well-known members of Argentine

389

society and their private lives, while I grew hoarse yelling my own comments through her ear trumpet, till with the dawn the storm subsided. We were still wallowing in high running waves, and a steady downpour soaked us to the skin, when in the first pallid light I managed to see my companion's face. She was a woman over fifty, heavily made up, with dyed platinum hair and two magnificent diamond earrings. In fact, she was literally covered with diamonds, which I insisted she take off and hide on her person before some of the looters caught sight of them and hit her on the head. I did not know her name, and it was of no interest to me, but I admired her courage and her absolute disregard for the possibility of losing her life before we were through with the mess. "I'm old," she said, "and have had a good time. If I have to drown to-night, it's all right with me—but I hope that gigolo goes, too!"

With the coming of daybreak, the panic had worn itself out, and we were able to make our way from the top deck, where we had spent the night, to the more sheltered one below: all the others were under water. To get into the salon was an impossibility, for it was crowded to the doors with passengers, many of them wounded. Finally pilot tugs and coast-guard patrols from Buenos Aires hove in view and towed us to the Rada, the official quarantine limit outside the port, where maritime police and doctors came aboard.

While the more badly injured cases were removed by launch to hospitals ashore, the police instituted a court of inquiry in the main salon, checking passengers and taking preliminary evidence from those having complaints to formulate or testimony to give about the accident and shootings. When my turn came, I had little to tell, passing the police table almost immediately, and was on my way across the cluttered deck to take the pilot boat ashore when I spotted my elderly friend of the ear trumpet, sweeping by on the arm of a gray-haired man who resembled her so much I felt sure he was her son. Her make-up was now decidedly the worse for wear, but she made the triumphant progress of a faded coquette who had once

390

owned regal beauty. I knew she must have been some one of considerable importance, for she had not been obliged to pass the table for the inquiry, and I surmised her son had come aboard to get the old girl ashore before she mixed with the vulgar herd. I think she meant to pass me by without recognition, although I knew she'd seen me, but as our eyes met, she suddenly stopped and, extending her hand as if in a drawing-room, said, "Ah, there you are—so nice to have met you. I did so enjoy our conversation—I can't think of anybody I'd have preferred to spend a shipwreck with. Too bad we're not in the same set—well, well, perhaps we shall meet again in Paris. One never knows, does one?" With that, she teetered over the gangplank to the pilot boat and disappeared into a cabin.

Barely an hour after the last passenger had been transferred from the ill-fated Montevidean boat, she sank peacefully into the mud of the River Plate. From a passenger list and crew totaling approximately four hundred and eighty people, one hundred and forty were drowned, shot, or missing.

All sorts of acts and artists were coming to Argentina from Paris because of depression in the United States: this hit the theaters and cabarets in Europe as soon as the tourist trade began falling off. Among the more important débuts by Europeans was that of a writer and columnist of the newspaper, *Paris Soir*—Mademoiselle Madeleine de la Tour. She was giving a series of lectures entitled "La Mode à travers les âges" and "L'Amour à travers la mode." The topics sounded decidedly threadbare to me.

Some of the writers for *La Nación* brought her to my apartment. She was a charming Parisienne, told me this was her first attempt at lecturing, and begged me to give her some insight into the tastes and customs of the Argentine women. With her she had brought a most marvelous collection of gowns from leading Paris couturiers and her display of these was bound to make one part of her program a walk-over; but the lectures as she read them to me sounded incredibly dull. She

391

also planned to write a book on South America during her trip through Argentina and Chile.

She opened at the chic auditorium of the Wagnerian Society which caters to a blasé crowd of ultra-smart young Argentines. I had no time to attend the first lecture, but afterward, Mlle. de la Tour arrived at my apartment nearly in hysterics with a critic from the *Nación* staff. He had accompanied her directly to my place with the advice that she ask me to try to help her rewrite the script for the following day, thereby, perhaps, averting complete disaster. It appeared that the audience had tittered and been bored through all her talk, only showing a faint interest when she modeled the gowns—but they were not disposed to wait while she got into them by listening to a young lady with a harp playing the "Seranata" of Toselli.

To write an entire script for a total stranger out of the clear blue sky was not an easy task. However, I came home early after the theater and pounded out an idea that I thought might help matters. I also assisted in engaging a band and singers (playing at the Plaza Hotel), to fill in while she changed costumes. Happily, all the nonsense I wrote in the middle of the night was so racy it appealed to the audience and got them laughing heartily, especially since the script was liberally sprinkled with refined Argentine slang—which, when mispronounced by a pretty girl, was amusing and tickled the listeners. Madeleine de la Tour was so grateful for the improvement in her lectures that from then on she hung around my neck. I wound up rewriting the rest of her stuff.

For my engagement in Chile I intended going over the Andes by plane to avoid the long tedious train journey, leaving Flora and Mascotte in the apartment till my return. Mlle. de la Tour approached me with an offer to pay my expenses if I would travel with her and help write her book, the royalties to be shared between us. Of course I did not accept, but suggested if she would like to publish some of my sketches, crediting me with them in her book and paying for them, we could go together to Chile.

We had bad weather for the flight, and the Pan American pilot had some difficult moments to pass, fighting his way through it. Frankly, I was petrified most of the time and too thankful when we arrived safely to bother about my appearance, but Mlle. de la Tour was made of sterner stuff, for although she had been even more scared than I (and violently airsick) she reacted as soon as we circled over the airport. Hastily she applied plenty of rouge and lipstick, arrayed herself in a stunning bright red raincoat with a hat to match on her blonde hair, then gracefully descended from the plane to greet the press and cameras with an enthusiastic description of her trip and how much she enjoyed the impressive sight of the Aconcagua.

I decided I would return to Buenos Aires by train instead of facing that plane flight once again. Luck was with me, for the plane I would have taken crashed a few miles from the Argentine border, killing the pilot, radio operator, and four passengers. Mlle. de la Tour, however, made the flight safely a few days before I sailed for Rio for my last South American engagement of the season.

Upon arriving in Paris I found a letter from father, telling me my brother had been ill again and was under treatment at the Pagenstacker Clinic in Wiesbaden. I spent Christmas with him and found his health very precarious. He had been so much better when I left Europe that this was a very unpleasant shock to me. There was no use spending time and money hanging about in Wiesbaden when the only practical help needed was financial, so I returned to Paris with the usual hurried object in mind of getting work for my new act.

The idea I'd had the previous year for an aërial act that could play circus dates as well as vaudeville seemed to suggest the best paid type of work I could choose. As soon as it was more or less ready, I broke it in at that popular melting-pot, the Olympia, passing from there to the Cirque Medrano.

393

It was my first engagement at the charming little bandbox of a one-ring circus created by the well-known clown of the same name and conducted by his wife, for old Medrano was an invalid and rarely came to the cirque. Madame Medrano, a talented and clever business woman, had built up a reputation for her taste in entertainment by shrewd judgment in the choice of her artists. I found it extremely hard to drive a bargain with her, but after working my first engagement at her circus, I realized she could give me more valuable suggestions in five minutes than the average director could think of in six months.

After the Medrano I played the Maravillas Circus in Barcelona, where the success of my new act became assured. There also I earned the name which from then on was always used for my announcements. The reason for it was this....

Everywhere I played, the master of ceremonies or ringmaster announcing me never failed to hash up the names of various theaters I had played, but they refused to leave them out, on account of wanting at all costs to bring in the famed pleasure spots of Parisian night-life, the Folies-Bergère, Le Moulin Rouge, Le Théâtre des Champs-Élysées, and so on, with disastrous results for the audience trying to understand the announcements. Outside France the same thing occurred with the spelling on the programs and billboards.

On opening night in Barcelona, the well-intentioned ringmaster had to repeat three times an announcement the management had typed for him. This exasperated me, for I wanted to make my entrance before the public grew tired listening to him, so I whispered, "Cut all this out; just say, Señorita Esmé of Paris." The audience got that immediately and gave me a resounding applause while I was pulled up to my ropes. From that night on my entrance in rings and on stages all over the world was heralded by the simple words that never failed to get a warm reception. "Ladies and Gentlemen—Miss Esmé of Paris!"

After Spain I had engagements at the Houck Circus in Amiens and went from there to the Winter Garden in Berlin.

Before leaving Spain, I sent to Granada for a box of earth taken from the sun-soaked Sierras, and a handful of sand from the bull-ring. This I took with me to England and up to Aberdeen, an idea I had long desired to carry out. From London I brought a box of those small red carnations that look like Spanish claveles, and bunches of jasmine. They were hot-house flowers, difficult to obtain in winter and only faintly perfumed, but they were the next best thing to flowers from Spain. I took the box of earth and the flowers with me, and one gray cheerless day visited the tiny Catholic burial grounds hidden away far outside the town with its tight-lipped Presbyterian population, and placed them on grandmama's grave. After working the sand and earth through the snow covering her resting-place, I scattered the red carnations like drops of blood around the headstone.

Working at the Winter Garden was always a joy, for it held many memories of my childhood. Though Berlin never appealed very much to me, nevertheless it was the most cosmopolitan of German cities, and all artists found the public wonderful to work to. German theater-goers always displayed a weakness for anything Spanish and dark, so when I took my act there I set the entrance on the music of a *pasodoble*, with cape whirls, and I wore, as I nearly always do, a costume with diamond epaulets and bolero.

Berlin was very gay that year and becoming more and more like a "second Paris," as the Berliners loved to call it. There was an exodus from cabarets and bars of Paris that turned up everywhere, while the crowds of male and female streetwalkers of all nationalities that thronged the streets increased nightly. The famed "Unter den Linden" had two of the more notorious bars for men (*Puppenfeen*) run by Italians, called the Sapphire and Chez ma Belle-Sœur (At My Sister-in-Law's), where young boys expensively dressed as women openly danced together and flirted with their male admirers, often monocled captains and colonels of the German Army.

La Petite Chaumière, which had been closed by the police in Paris, reopened on the Friedrichstrasse for the same purpose, while stolid Berliners paraded by its open doors viewing the goings on inside without the slightest scruples or embarrassment. Paris unquestionably originated most of these places but had managed to prevent their vices from being offensive. If they became so, the police immediately closed the establishment.

I was a little uncertain about what would be the best course for me to pursue as there was a financial slump affecting vaudeville in Europe, and I had been offered contracts on several occasions for circus and vaudeville in the United States. I always hesitated to accept them, mainly on account of father, who had repeatedly asked me not to work in New York, where his relatives and friends lived.

Into the midst of this perplexity came Mr. Howell of Howell and Baud, representing a new circuit called "Continental Varieties" that sent large units and revues to Australia, South Africa, and the British Dominions. He was accompanied by a Mr. Potter, a true type of the English vaudeville manager, wearing at all times and seasons a black bowler hat and diamond horseshoe tiepin, and smoking a cigar stub. They had come to Germany to book the famous "Talking Horses of Elberfeld."

John Potter had a remarkable sense of humor and I liked him at once, which went a long way toward deciding me to accept the contracts he offered to play Australia with a circus unit. I was getting pretty sick of traveling, and craved the peace of an apartment in Paris and a chance for a little relaxation, but the proposition he offered was far ahead financially of anything available for the moment in Europe—so I accepted, embarking in Marseilles the second week in May.

XX

THE AUSTRALIA tour was the only long one on which I didn't get into serious trouble or even mixed up with the police. I can not remember a single violent episode taking place except for a nasty accident that occurred through the interference of a drunken wag.

During the act in which two Swedish performers (the Larsen Brothers) did a difficult balancing ladder feat in the air, the drunk sitting in a stage box had unfortunately been sober enough to notice the signals the acrobats gave each other in order to move simultaneously and preserve their precarious balance. These signs were generally the international expression "Hup!" This tickled the fancy of the inebriated one, who from the shadows of the box proceeded to shout loudly, "Hup!" just as one of the brothers was changing his position. Evidently he thought the signal came from his partner, with the result that the other end of the ladder tipped, swayed, and his brother fell, dropping into the orchestra pit like a stone. He died a few hours after being taken to the hospital. It was a stupid, unnecessary accident that upset all of us. We gave a benefit for the surviving brother to send him back to Gothenburg.

The Australian public was most charming to us. They are great theater-goers, and I enjoyed working for them and their warm appreciation. We had little time to do any traveling or sightseeing, since we worked three shows a day, but the climate and general aspect of the country I also enjoyed for it reminded me a great deal of the English section of Buenos Aires. One day seemed just like another. The company was not given to frivolity outside their work, and for recreation they wanted nothing better than to sit all day long playing cards, headed by the indefatigable bridge fiend, Mr. Potter, now named by all and sundry "Potsdam."

I arrived back in Paris in the middle of November and was idle but a few days, since Neumann engaged me almost immediately for the revue at the Casino de Paris, starring my friend Jenny Golder, Spadoni from Berlin, and the American dancer Harry Pilcer.

Before opening I went to Jersey to visit my brother. Father came over for a few days that Christmas to stay with him. I learned that his mysterious reticence about joining me the previous year had been because he was so seriously ill that the doctors forbade him to travel, and he did not want either Bunnie or myself to know about it. I could not get time off from my work to see much of him, but he spent three days with me in Paris, and I think he enjoyed the few little expeditions around our old haunts that we were able to make. He went over to England alone to visit mother's grave and from there left for New York.

I was longing for some sunshine, so at the end of February I accepted a contract to tour in North Africa, leaving from Marseilles and going to Algiers, Fez, Rabât, Tangier, and Lisbon, then back to Paris via Bordeaux. While playing in Rabât, I received a letter from Olga telling me Pepita had died in a sanitarium, having become ill only a few months after her return from South America. She had been acting in a film in the south of France when her health broke down completely. The doctors said tuberculosis had developed in both lungs. Her last picture, *L'Espion aux Yeux Noirs*, was shown in Paris shortly after her death, and it was heart-breaking for me to sit through it, for although she was still very beautiful, her face had begun to show the ravages of her malady. It was terrible to think of so much beauty gone forever and more bitter still to think of the brilliant future she might have had. Since her marriage to a French actor a couple of years previously I had seen little of her; my work and her love of hectic gaiety had gradually caused us to drift apart. Perhaps it is true that those whom the Gods love die young.

398

Some months later, I found myself again in the Argentine, after a tour through Cuba, Colombia, and Chile, during which I had run into a series of revolutions that made travel and engagement schedules almost impossible. I decided to put into execution a plan I had thought up. Not only would it give me something interesting to do until the politics and shooting died down, but it would provide work for the members of my company—for I did not want to leave them stranded in South America.

Buenos Aires had never had in its entire history a decent cabaret or night-club—only the dreary pseudo-French places where nice people could not go and whose acts were a lamentable collection of cheap cabaret singers and dancers from Marseilles. Knowing I was popular enough from Juncal days to create a small club where people could get a decent dinner and my company could entertain, I looked up Judge Jaime Lavalloe, one of the kindest and most understanding of my many good Argentine friends.

Jaime Lavalloe had an extraordinary personality. He was one of the severest judges in the annals of the Argentine courts and the terror of every criminal in South America. With the exception of his sister, I was the only woman friend he had. I often dined with him in his magnificent house filled with objets d'art and the best looking young men I have ever seen. Jaime was an accomplished violinist, and I think his friendship for me was based on the fact that I could play his accompaniments better than his professional pianist.

He owned an office building that had an enormous cellar with a beautiful marble entrance and stairs leading on to the Calle San Martín in the center of town. The rent was almost nominal, for Jaime wanted to help, although he was convinced I was mad to open a club without any experience. However, I took the place and started hunting around for equipment.

Natascha, Mollie, and other friends, still in Buenos Aires, helped me paint and decorate the walls with murals which I designed to represent twenty-four hours of gaiety—the daily round of pleasure enjoyed by the smart set.

399

I put up all the money I had saved for a rainy day, which was five thousand pesos. Mollie helped me out by introducing a picturesque pal of hers from whom all the English girls borrowed money in the old Colón days. He was never called anything but "Bon Soir," because of his habit of using the only French words he knew on every occasion. This gentleman in turn introduced me to a man named Enrique Seebers, who had just inherited some money and was looking for an investment. He was a very social young man with adenoids and a receding forehead but came from a good family, which was important for what I wanted to do. So I signed a contract with him on a fifty-fifty basis.

Most of the furniture we obtained on credit, also the wines, while the question of kitchen equipment, smoke exhausts, and other annoying details had to be paid for out of our modest ten thousand pesos. Fortunately, the company was held over at the Florida, with three exceptions. The generosity of all those performers was something I always like to recall, for they stuck by and gave me all the help they could.

I obtained a license easily enough but could not get a permit for dancing, which made the first days of my venture very precarious. The work of the entertainers, I was afraid, was insufficient alone, but I had the luck to find an American band that had arrived from Chile because of the same circumstances we experienced. They were young good-looking boys calling themselves the "Hollywood Students," not being, of course, students and never having seen Hollywood. Their leader was the exceptionally good-looking Don Dean.

While I was struggling to open the place and worried to death over the outcome, I received a telegram that shattered me so completely that for several days I was unable to talk to any one or even think. My father had died suddenly in Canada. It was a very considerate wire sent by friends who had known him for years and administered most of his affairs. The letter following gave me more details.

Father had been ailing for some time and had gone to spend a month near the friends' farm in Brampton, Ontario,

400

staying at the hotel in the village. Often he'd written me about these friends, their farm, and their herd of prize Jersey cattle he was so interested in. As he felt his health fail, he wanted to live in the country, with his great love for the soil and all things connected with it. He had, their letter told me, been reading the Bible in his room one night and died in his chair, the open Testament on his knees. There they found him the next morning, seated upright, his face calm. They didn't think he even knew of his passing.

The realization that I would never see him again was almost too much to bear and still go on about my business as usual. There was nobody I could talk with except Mollie: her sympathy and kindness helped me a great deal to get hold of myself and resume the task I had undertaken for the artists who trusted and depended on me. The thought that my father had died alone in a hotel room without any one beside him tormented me, but in his letters he'd given no inkling that he was again unwell to any serious degree. His death was the greatest sorrow I have ever known.

Everybody was very kind, but I could see the anxiety of my associates by the unspoken questions in their eyes. Their uneasiness was sufficient to put me on my mettle, and I tried resolutely not to think of my father all the daylight hours. But I could not sleep and went through those long nights well known to people who have suffered greatly.

I had been careful to invite the press to the opening of "Whoopee" (the name we chose for the club), and their support throughout the entire speculation was of inestimable value. I advertised it in the papers as "somewhere a man can take his wife." This, in addition to the idea of Whoopee being a rendezvous for English and Americans, did bring in a certain following, but the *élégantes* of Buenos Aires, although personal friends of mine, would not put in an appearance until the establishment was accepted by their leaders. This was more easily said than done, and the first few weeks were terrible, financially.

There were many nice foreigners who came and enjoyed

the band and entertainment, but they wanted to dance, and the fact that I didn't yet have a permit for this was killing the whole idea. While the final expensive permit was pending, my partner and I were on the verge of bankruptcy, and another revolution broke out. In a way this helped us, for we had an excellent excuse to give our creditors, and they couldn't press us for payments.

At this difficult period in my venture, I became aware of the invaluable help and advice I could receive from the manager of the Hollywood Students, a shrewd and eccentric New Yorker called Bill Quittner. He came to the Whoopee every night and spent far more money than he was making on the managing of the band, trying to help us out. There was an atmosphere about the little cellar that I had faith in, and I felt sure that when we eventually got hold of the permit and people could dance, we would make money. I did not know anything about this type of business, so all the practical help Bill Quittner offered was priceless.

The second and more violent of the Argentine revolutions— in the year 1933—was the Uriburu revolt to overthrow Vice-President Oyhanarte, brother of the consul in Hamburg. Nobody seemed to have a very clear idea what it was all about— least of all myself—but whatever it was they wanted, a great deal of killing went on before they got it. Uriburu managed to get part of the army over to his side and marched on Buenos Aires to take the government house, which was situated near Whoopee.

Of course we closed the club, but on the worst day of the whole affair, I had gone down with Seebers and the cashier to check over some accounts. We were sitting in the office when a fusillade came from the Plaza on the corner, galloping horses from the Squadron de Seguridad (mounted police) thundered down the street, and I trembled for the safety of my small roadster parked in front of the building. I decided to make a dash for it and took the car to a near-by garage, there being no possibility of driving home while the fighting was on.

402

When I returned to the club, I found Seebers white and shaky. He pointed to some men sitting at the bar. When I asked what they were doing, he told me that the revolutionaries had first opened the cages of wild beasts in the zoo, letting them loose on the town, then released about six hundred lepers from the lazareto. Some of these men had descended on the city, broken into bars and hotels, and demanded to be served drink. They were all armed, and even if they had not been, people dared not refuse them, on account of their pretty habit of scratching any one they didn't like with a long nail which they grew especially for the purpose on the little finger of the right hand. This nail, loaded with pus from some infected part of their body, is supposed to contaminate the person receiving a scratch from it.

The lepers were drinking our liquor, shouting, and getting rougher and more truculent every minute. Seebers and I kept ourselves as much out of their sight as we could, but the row attracted a police patrol passing our shuttered door. The officers knocked, demanding to know what was going on. Fortunately, when we opened to them, the lepers pushed past and ran down the street.

For a week the tumult and fighting went on, until Uriburu was victorious and took over the city. Just as suddenly as the whole thing started, it ended. With the change of government, I had many friends in power, with the exception of my old trusty, the chief of police, who fled to Spain with the proceeds of many years of successful nest feathering. I regretted his loss, but the man who succeeded him was almost as nice.

I got my licenses all in order with this new set-up and did a lot of advertising, presenting the club as the most exclusive place in Buenos Aires, with entry by election of the committee. The name Whoopee was registered as "The British and American Assembly League." To the Argentines, "Whoopee" stood for everything that was sedate and high-minded after my friends on the various newspaper staffs got through describing it.

Our first break came with a dinner given by the Argentine

polo team who had been victorious over the Americans led by Hitchcock. The banquet was written up in the society columns of *La Nación* and *La Razón,* and from then on things began to brighten up. It was necessary to engage more and more personnel, and we even had a secretary seated at the entrance, with a book in which all members had to sign and introduce their friends (paying at the same time a respectable entrance fee).

We had plenty of headaches with society youths of big families, who insisted on getting drunk and making fools of themselves—to quote Jacinto Benavente: "Good boys from bad families, and bad boys from good families." Where Argentine women congregate, these incidents can not be tolerated, so one bright morning, I found myself confronted with the job of getting hold of a couple of tactful bouncers. They were to be dressed in Tuxedos and mingle with the guests, if possible, with debonair nonchalance, until the moment when action was necessary; then they were to eliminate the obstreperous members of Whoopee with as little scandal as possible. Simmons, the colored barman, who was a great attraction because of his tap dancing while shaking cocktails, always kept a blackjack in a drawer behind the bar, but only once did we use it, and that was in our early days.

Gradually the fame of Whoopee grew to such proportions that we had to turn people away night after night and never served less than three hundred dinners, the most our kitchen could handle. The popularity of the band had a great deal to do with our success; also the two large hotels recently opened to accommodate the influx of foreigners arriving to work in the ever-growing industries of the country. I had rented an apartment, but most of my friends and staff lived at the City Hotel, whose management sent me tremendous quantities of new members and their friends.

This hotel had tourist accommodations arranged with all the larger ships coming in from Europe and the States, but its name was unfortunate, because the taxi drivers simply could not understand the English or American pronunciation of the first word. Visitors touring South America arrived at the docks and demanded to be driven to the City Hotel. Nothing happened until they showed their tourist reservation card to the chauffeur, who, if an Argentine, would immediately say, "Ah! El Tittie Hotel"—and if he happened to be Spanish, would pronounce the word "City" with Spanish *sh* before it. This never failed to produce a disastrous effect on maiden ladies journeying alone, who would bashfully go to another hotel rather than be obliged to articulate such a dreadful word every time they took a cab.

As money began to pour into the coffers of Whoopee, energy began to pour out of my body. I had practically all the work to do, for it was a personal contact job. The question of necessary diplomacy toward people wanting credit or checks cashed I always handled personally, for Seebers was not only unable to speak a word of English but had a gift for being tactless that was positively dangerous. With the dinner hour there was the job of receiving people who insisted on sending for me to meet their friends; occasionally there were conflicts because of one thing or another—pacifying women who hated each other and wanted their tables changed, and so on.

All this would go on till daybreak, at which time a discussion on the readings of the cash registers (which I could never understand) took place, plus the usual closing arguments with Seebers, who invariably started superfluous discussions at five in the morning. It was a terrible strain, but I was making money, had paid off all my debts, and had my artists' contracts taken care of in full.

Our public became a varied type—mostly wealthy society people, American businessmen, aviators from the Panagra Airport, and ship captains who practically lived in Whoopee while in port. Then there was the Russian crowd, introduced by Nemanoff and Natascha, and although refugees, they always seemed to have money for drinks and a good time. Where Natascha collected them was a puzzle, but she appeared at regular intervals with most peculiar people.

One afternoon a pal of hers, a Russian Swede named An-

405

derson, who had worked on a newspaper in Brooklyn, came in to see me before the club opened. His manner was very mysterious, and he insisted I exclude the bookkeeper and my secretary from the office; then he went out and a few moments later returned with a fat woman carrying under her arm a bulky package wrapped in dirty newspapers. As soon as my office door was closed, Mr. Anderson unfolded a most unusual tale about the package, which, he claimed, contained nothing less than the mummified head of his late Imperial Majesty, Nicholas II of Russia.

Before opening the relic, he showed me two photographs of the head—a full face and a profile. They were, if fakes, most perfect likenesses, to judge by various publication photos I was familiar with and my faint childhood memory of seeing the late emperor driving to a military review in Moscow. They opened the package and deposited on my desk the head. Undoubtedly it was a most amazing thing, for it had the texture of wood, and the dried, wide-open eyes still held a faint opaque blue, and although the features had been swollen in death, they retained a perfect likeness even more impressive than the photographs.

The hair, I noticed, had been dyed blond, but the roots had grown slightly after death, and these were white. The beard and mustache had remained their natural blond color, well sprinkled with gray. I sat and stared at the head, noticing that the neck had been hacked through with some heavy instrument like an ax, so that the vertebrae of the neck were protruding below the shriveled skin.

The woman, who spoke nothing but Russian, sulkily and very unwillingly told her story. She had been, she claimed, the mistress of a German doctor, an ex-prisoner of war who had been taken from a concentration camp several months before the assassination of the Imperial family and kept at the disposition of the Soviet, in Moscow. After the crime in Ekaterinburg, he had been instructed to embalm the head, which had been sent from Siberia and imperfectly preserved. The doctor, the woman said, was a specialist in embalming and had done a marvelous job for which he was to receive a fairly large sum of money. Half of this had been paid before starting work, but he never received the rest, for the Soviet evidently changed their minds about the advisability of putting the head on exhibition—their original intention—to impress the masses with the "tyrant's" uncrowned head, in the style of the French revolutionaries.

The doctor, having heard nothing further for several weeks, stole the head, telling his mistress that should anything happen to him she was to keep it hidden and her mouth shut until word was received from a certain Commissar friend about what she was to do. The following day the doctor was arrested and shot.

Months went by, and at last she received word from an Argentine consular employee, whose name she refused to divulge, saying that her late lover's friend, the Commissar, had approached him to furnish her with means of leaving Russia with the head. Once in Argentina, they would be able to sell it to the United States news agencies—or possibly to one of the White Russian organizations functioning in America.

The Argentine had been able to get the woman out of Russia, traveling as nurse to his family, and she was still employed by this gentleman. The Russian Commissar who obtained this position for her had been found dead on a bench in one of the public squares in Buenos Aires shortly after she arrived which so terrified her that she had kept the head wrapped in old newspapers and hidden under her bed until the day she met Anderson at a Russian festival, became friendly with him, and disclosed her secret.

It was a weird tale that might have been invented, but somehow the woman appeared to be speaking the truth. The reason Anderson brought her to me was primarily because I spoke Russian, knew everybody in the Russian colony who might be in a position to purchase the relic, and also because all the representatives from the various American newspapers frequented my club.

The woman said she had been told by her German doctor

that the head should sell for at least two hundred and fifty thousand dollars, and that fantastic sum had remained fixed in her obstinate peasant's head: nothing could move her. She was completely illiterate, could not read or write, and to reason with her was an impossibility.

I did not know quite what to do in the matter, although it interested me greatly. Finally I got hold of some of the older Russians I knew, who might have proofs that would definitely establish the authenticity of the head. As the woman refused to give me her name or address, I was completely dependent on Anderson.

I 'phoned a Russian doctor who had attended the Imperial family at one time in Tsarskoi Selo and had often seen the emperor. Then I called up a relative of Olga's, old Prince Gougoutchieff, who had emigrated to Argentina for the purpose of getting rich quick. His plan was to adopt somebody with money, who would give him an income for life in exchange for the title of Prince or Princess. This impractical idea so far had not produced tangible results, and the old man had to eke out a precarious living painting extremely bad water colors.

I got together four people in all, including a Swedish masseur who had attended the Czar up to the time of his imprisonment in Tobolsk. They all arrived in my office a few days later, and the Russian woman, surly and afraid, appeared clutching the head in the same dirty newspaper. My guests opened the proceedings by locking the door, and when they had taken a good look, an old Russian lady invited by Gougoutchieff fell on her knees weeping. Between sobs she complained bitterly that her emperor's head should have been reduced to the indignity of dirty newspapers as a covering, and she proceeded to place four lighted candles around it on my desk.

The doctor was far more helpful and told us that the late Czar had been operated on in his early twenties for a skull fracture and that English physicians had inserted a tiny platinum plaque at the base of the skull. Manifestly, it would

408

still be there if the head was genuine. The story of the plaque had never been published, for State reasons, and only the medical men attached to the court were aware that the emperor had ever sustained a head injury. Then there was the proof to be established by the teeth, two of which were visible through the half-closed lips.

It was agreed that if an X-ray would not show the plaque, a cut could be made by an expert, to reveal the metal, for the doctor saw plainly through the hair on the back of the head a white scar about two inches long. Prince Gougoutchieff disclosed the important detail that a nephew of his, now residing in Paris, had seen the Imperial family a day or so before they were taken from Tsarskoi Selo to Siberia under the orders of Kerensky and had observed the emperor bareheaded on various occasions, noticing that his hair had turned completely gray but the beard was still blond.

The conference about the Czar's head continued for several days at a great rate. So much running back and forth went on that at last the Russian woman, whom I now knew as Anna, became frightfully nervous and refused to carry the head around any more. I offered to keep it in my office, but evidently she mistrusted me, too, so after permitting the doctor to make an incision on the head, where he found the small oxidized plaque, she positively refused to come any more unless given twenty-five thousand dollars on account.

None of the Russian group had the money, and a friend I approached at King Features claimed he had received information from his home office that there were two fake heads floating around the Americas, so he had to be positive about this one and wanted more pictures. Anna refused, and the matter hung fire. The next thing that happened was a robbery in the house of a wealthy Argentine diplomat: Anderson told me this was the man who was shielding Anna. There had been no motive for the robbery, the police found, as no valuables had been taken out of the house, so Anna's employers suspected that some Soviet agents had got wind of the head, and they politely requested her to move elsewhere.

409

She went to the house of some other Russians in Rosario, informing only Anderson of her whereabouts. To write her was impossible, as she could not read, so selling the head became an extremely difficult proposition. My Russian friends had written the entourage of the Grand Duke Kyril, then head of the Czarist group in Paris. Letters and cables flew back and forth between Argentina and France, and the matter became complicated in the extreme. I was so overworked with Whoopee I had little time to devote to the affair, much as it fascinated me.

We managed to keep the club open all through the hot Christmas and New Year season and actually broke even during the summertime when most of the wealthier people were in Mar del Plata. But as the months wore on, I had the nearest thing to a complete breakdown I ever felt. Realizing I had to get away from the place or collapse, I announced to my partner that I was going to sell out my half and retire to Europe for good. I had made a lot of money, and it seemed foolish to get so ill I could not enjoy it.

Enrique Seebers decided to buy me out, continuing to run the place by himself. He made the irreparable mistake of firing the band, whom he never liked, and as soon as they left things began to slow down. I did all I could to warn him, but it was no use, so we divided the profits and sold my share of the wines, furniture, and so on, for a considerably larger sum of money than I had ever dreamed of having all at once. I sailed for Europe in December, 1933, very much alone, for in the midst of scenes and legal entanglements over the club, I received another bad blow. Little Mascotte died!

The reason was due partly to her insatiable desire for motherhood. She had given birth to three fluffy puppies, Wynken, Blynken, and Nod, earlier that spring, but was getting well along in years now, so that the strain of her family's arrival had weakened her considerably. She had a bad time and was seriously ill for some weeks after the puppies were weaned. The vet said her heart was affected, and she lingered a few days, unable to eat or sleep, till at last the end came. I have already told of her burial in a quiet spot out in the country, and with her passing I felt as though I had lost the only thing left me to care for.

The first thing I did on arriving in Paris was to find Violette; we then sent a telegram to Nina asking her to come over for Christmas so we could all be together again. Olga was in Berlin, but she too came, also our friend Adeline Malet from her villa in Nice. It was a lovely meeting, for never among any of us had there been an angry word or feeling—something very exceptional among women friends. I sent my brother a telegram announcing my visit to him immediately after Christmas, and his evasive replies worried me until at last I received a letter saying he had married his nurse—a little Jersey girl named Dolly.

The thought made me extremely happy, for he had been a lonely, morbid person, and the life he led in eternal darkness and alone often made me miserable thinking of it. I went at once to Jersey and met my sister-in-law, spending a long month in the wonderful old monastery my brother had adapted for a dwelling-house. Built in the time of Queen Elizabeth, the walls were three feet thick at some parts of the building, and the delightful wood paneling and rafters made the living-room with its glazed chintzes and gay bowls of flowers a restful, ideal home. Dolly was a housekeeper par excellence, managing her house with that efficiency I have always admired to the verge of awe.

The gardens stretched away in dewy green lawns down to the cliffs that overhung the black rocks and restless seas Bunnie loved so well. The study had his Braille books, piano, and guitar just where he could find them, and the few steps leading into the garden were so familiar to him, he could be alone and still not feel helpless. I returned to Paris very happy over his marriage, my mind at rest about his welfare for the first time since mother's death.

I found an apartment again—a real haven of rest situated near the Étoile on the corner of the Avenue Hoche and the

411

Rue St.-Honoré—a large rez-de-chaussée, looking out on an ivy-trimmed courtyard that gave one a feeling of being miles out in the country, for the noise of the street traffic never penetrated this cloister-like precinct. I hauled out all my household gods and put in weeks of delightful rummaging in antique shops, hunting for odd things I wanted, often spending week-ends with Violette either at Les Mées or on her yacht in the harbor of Toulon.

Before leaving Argentina, I had promised Olga's relative and friends that I would do everything in my power to interest the Russian colony in Paris about the Czar's head, and as soon as I had arranged my apartment to look more or less habitable, I 'phoned some of them. In the space of three days, my place looked like the audience chambers in the Winter Palace, with titled scions of Russian nobility arriving every few minutes to discuss the purchase of the head and the method of obtaining proof of its authenticity—without any one's offering to put up the money necessary to pay for it.

In the end, the excitement died down, for none of them could raise such a large sum, even by collection, and I became sick and tired of the endless discussions in my house. Finally I asked them all please to deal directly through Olga and her uncle in the Argentine. The last I heard of it Anna had disappeared—also Anderson, and I have often speculated on the whereabouts of one of the most tragic relics I have ever seen.

Among my old Russian acquaintances were the Ourasoff princesses and a very intelligent, charming woman, Madame Loury. They were making quite a good thing out of the Manioulieff perfume formulas, selling some of the original ones to their former users, now in Paris. Madame Loury distilled many of the oils from her own flower and herb gardens near St.-Germaine, buying the fixatives and other rare ingredients from importing houses and the famed distilleries of Grasse and Nice.

Neither of the partners in the business had any idea of

412

putting the perfumes on the market in a commercial way, but when I met them I began studying their methods and formulas, spending hours watching Madame Loury blend her fragrances. She had a rare gift for suiting the values of perfume to color and mood, and her library of antique recipes for all sorts of perfume blends was fascinating. Often they sold their perfumes in ordinary pharmacist's bottles to the connoisseurs, who preferred taking cherished scents home to their dressing-tables very secretly, not caring what they came in but guarding from all their friends the perfume that enhanced their personality.

Madame Loury and Princess Ourasoff between them gained a fairly substantial living from their work and made themselves responsible for Manioulieff's widow, Ludmila. She was the actual owner of the formulas but utterly incapable of utilizing them commercially, with the result that in moments of financial stress she would sell a priceless formula to any laboratory which would pay for it. Had it not been for her sister, Madame Loury, and other friends, the entire collection would have been muddled away or lost.

Manioulieff had been one of the greatest perfumers the last century had known in Europe: from being an obscure Georgian chemist, he had risen to fame in the whole of the Old World. When forced to flee from the revolution, he had left thousands of rubles stuffed in the upholstery of his chairs and cushions in the ultra chic little shop in Moscow where I had first become conscious of the beauty in perfumes.

Few of his scents had ever been named, except the famous "Imperial Violets," said to have been first made for the Czarina and later introduced to England by Princess Soltikoff as a young woman; and his "Jersey Lily," blended to suit the white skin of the famous Mrs. Langtry. The majority of his rarest triumphs, however, were bottled in heavy crystal flacons, with tiny coronets, or just the initials of their distinguished users—thus the secret perfume of every beautiful woman in Russia was carefully guarded and never allowed to become an item accessible to the world in general.

The more I worked at the bewitching study of perfume, the more I mentally registered an intention to take it up seriously on a commercial basis at some future date, for after all, it was a thing of beauty that required the glamour of the stage with the imagination of the artist, to present it adequately.

I commenced training at my old Gymnase Pons that spring and had several prospective engagements lined up, when one afternoon while practising a new trick I fell and broke my jaw. A splinter of wood I had struck with my forehead cut my left eye badly, and I was, when reaching the ground, not unconscious but decidedly woozy, not fully realizing the extent of my injuries.

This accident was a link in a long chain of mishaps that seemed to form a cycle of bad luck I could not get away from. For the past few years I had worked steadily without any accidents, even with the dangers of the Cossack tournée. Suddenly, however, everything seemed to go wrong.

I was not able to work again until May, when between practicing and odd dates here and there, plus the season of open-air work in the Fêtes d'Aviation in St.-Germaine, I began to feel more confident again. I had worked out an idea of a rope ladder suspended under an airplane, with safety loops for the hands and feet on which it was possible to do a limited number of tricks visible from the ground, and had tried it out successfully in a small aërial gymkhana at Vincennes.

The principal function at St.-Germaine was suspended on account of the tragic fall of the young Californian "Bird Man" who descended from a plane with mechanical wings attached to his shoulders. The apparatus failed in his descent, and he crashed to the ground in front of the grandstand filled with horrified spectators. This accident made it difficult for the other performers to continue their stunt work, for even the most hardened are affected by such things, although they never will admit it.

There was a vogue for terrifyingly crazy stunts on planes that had been brought over from Hollywood some seasons previously, and Detroyat, the ace flier of France, was working in combination with Roland Toutain, whose trick of suspending himself from the wings of a plane by his feet and picking up a handkerchief as the plane dipped to the ground was one of the sensations of the Fêtes.

Roland Toutain went absolutely mad because of all those death-defying stunts he thought up, which caused him so many bad accidents he began to behave strangely and people were afraid of him. Violette had admired his nerve and invited him with Mrs. Toutain to dine one night, together with other friends, planning to attend the preview of Saint-Exupéry's film, *Vol de Nuit*, after dinner. We were all in evening dress, and at the theater I was placed on one side of Violette, Toutain on the other.

Violette must have been rather bored, for she fell asleep. Suddenly I smelled the acrid odor of burning silk. Then I saw her full taffeta skirt burning and noticed Roland Toutain with a cigarette lighter in his hand and the most insane expression of impish glee, calmly igniting the dress at its hem. For a moment I was too astounded to do anything—then I quickly dragged Violette out of her seat and slumber, while our agitated friends extinguished the flames before she received any serious burns. Needless to say the party broke up at once. It was an object lesson to stay away from any more stunt work, before I got like Toutain and acquired the urge to set my friends on fire publicly.

I played Italy again that fall at the new Barberini Palace in Rome, instead of old rowdy Salone Margherita, and gave four shows a day instead of the old-fashioned three as a maximum. Time was indeed marching on. At every one of those four shows the public gave the same nerve-racking demonstrations as they always had. On my return to Paris, I played the historical "Festival of the Dance" at the Salle Pleyel, that I have already described, and from there opened after Christmas at the perennial Empire in Paris, now under the direction of Rotembourg and Mitty Goldin.

There were not so many vaudeville acts playing Paris as before, and the circuit ran from the Empire, Bobino, A.B.C. theaters and the Moulin Rouge (recently converted to a movie house with vaudeville) on to an eight-week tour of London's Victoria Palace, Pavilion, and two French revue houses. I played the entire circuit successfully and was booked for a return engagement at the Moulin Rouge in May, when I had to engage a new rigging man.

I took on a Breton recommended by friends, but he was of a rather dictatorial disposition and I had arguments with him about the setting up of my apparatus correctly after every performance. I was using a parachute snap acquired during my plane work, and this released the crossbar on which I worked. This snap had to be carefully closed every time it was used, and my rigger was obliged to climb the ropes between shows to adjust it before the next performance. He did not feel particularly energetic over this detail, and I was to blame for not personally seeing that everything was in order. However, with four shows a day on one of the hardest types of work in the world, I did not have a superfluity of strength.

During the Wednesday matinée, while working with the usual confidence that everything was in perfect order, I threw my legs over the crossbar to execute a movement. The imperfectly closed snap opened: there was no time to grab anything or attempt to save myself, and down I came, striking the apron of the stage with my shoulders, the nape of my neck fitting nicely into the footlights. I felt a grinding crash as my hips struck the ground, remaining perfectly conscious of everything that was going on around me.

The manager ordered the curtain closed, but my body protruded outside it, and the doctor would not permit me to be moved for several minutes, while he knelt beside me watching my face intently. I asked for a cigarette: somebody lit one for me, then I passed out. Friends in the audience afterward told me that while this went on, the manager, to keep the attention of the public off the accident, sent one of the *commères* out on the stage. She was just a little French show girl dressed in an enormous crinoline *robe de style*, but she made a valiant effort to hide me from the audience as she sang some song about *"C'est Paris, toujours Paris,"* cleverly dropping her skirt over my head and shoulders, until the doctor finally allowed my removal.

Partially recovering consciousness in the ambulance on the way to the American Hospital, I could sense that this time I was badly hurt but somehow managed to ask Cécile Sartoris (who had rushed backstage from the audience and remained with me) to get hold of Violette at once. Between lagoons of coma, I could just recognize her kind face leaning over me all night, and hear her promise not to write my brother about the fall.

For the first few weeks I lay in the hospital going through one unpleasant phase of suffering after another. Violette never left me, and the nurse later said that night after night she came to the hospital, even when I could not realize she was there. She insisted I have one of the best rooms, took care of all my affairs, the apartment, and my dog, and when I was recovering, the kindly American Dr. Charles Bove, who saved my life, often told me that Violette 'phoned him at all sorts of hours asking about my chances for recovery. She accepted the unfair responsibility of keeping my accident secret, as I had requested when so ill I didn't know what I was asking. Never for a moment did she hesitate, as many would have done, for I was very near death several times.

Leaving the hospital in September, I was too weak and lame to walk or go out except for short drives, and even these were torture for a long time afterward. I had of course badgered Dr. Bove about returning to work, but he warned me never again to attempt any of the spinning tricks that had brought me so much success. Violette had gone over to London on a belated visit, and foolishly I began to practise again in a new gym belonging to some friends, where there were no other performers to speak of, standing around watching my

417

first painful efforts to get into shape again. Several times while disobeying the doctor's orders and attempting my spins, I became so ill and dizzy I had to stop work and remain in bed for a few days. Of course I did not tell the doctor what I was doing until one afternoon when I was obliged to send for him.

His arrival coincided with an amusing incident. When I arrived home that day, Cécile Sartoris dropped in and became alarmed to hear I had been taken ill in the gymnasium. Immediately she sent for Dr. Bove, and while we were waiting for him, Buddie, a French bulldog I had bought in Argentina, took an epileptic fit.

We shut the dog up during the doctor's visit, and no sooner had the door closed on his last words, "Absolute quiet and rest," than Cécile rushed for the dog's bottle of medicine. Getting it confused with a prescription of mine, she gave the dog my medicine and me a strong dose of the dog's. We never told the doctor!

I did not make a good convalescent, and the forced inactivity got on my nerves. I had to work at something, so did a vast amount of reading in French history, digging into Violette's library, which contained collections of original documents and letters on the Napoleonic epoch, the last tragic days of the French Revolution, the romance of Marie Antoinette and Fersen, and the countless incidents of the false dauphins who appear from time to time. These themes were as interesting to me as they were to Violette, who had made a study and research of the unedited data connected with them. I also commenced working seriously on perfume presentations, the technique of flaconage, and wrote some articles I thought might be interesting for Madeleine de la Tour's columns, both for *Paris Soir* and *L'Intransigeant*.

Both Nina and Olga were enthusiastic over an idea I had made notes on: to write and illustrate sketches about the women's night courts and the human derelicts floating in the Salle des Pas Perdus (Hall of Lost Steps). This name always enchanted me, and I had long wanted to do something

418

on it. The articles I wrote for Madeleine de la Tour were a series called *Moineaux de Nuit* (Night Sparrows), using the Parisian slang term which describes so perfectly the little street gamins of Montmartre.

Right after Christmas I began practising again in the gym of Maurice de la Grange and his wife Chrysis, whose aërial work was beginning to be well known in Paris, and the three of us built all sorts of tricks and stunts. To get back to activity and excitement after months of deprivation of any sort of muscle-building exercise was a tremendous moral help, and despite Nina's and Violette's protestations that I stick to writing and illustrating, or accept some production work, I could not resist the fascination of the profession I had worked so hard and suffered so much to master.

I started work again on the Pathé circuit of vaudeville and movie houses and was at the St.-Marcel Pathé when two friends, Tommie and Katherine Molony, introduced me to a charming and interesting person, Sonia Mannerheim, daughter of the Baron Gustave Mannerheim of Finland. Sonia was a distinguished, aristocratic woman, whom I saw for the first time entering the door of my dressing-room during a function when one of the singers on the bill, Gaby Montbreuse, was demanding from the call boy through the door of her loge if "that ——— long-winded singer" had finished his act. This somewhat embarrassing speech by my fellow artist heralded Sonia's dignified entrance. To my amazement, she simply loved it and all the picturesque backstage atmosphere which was so completely foreign to her. She lived in an apartment near the Avenue Victor Hugo, around the corner from the perfume studio.

When I returned from the Pathé tour through France, I found that Violette was ill. She reminded me of my father in her unselfish way of making light of her own troubles, and although I knew her great friend and physician Dr. Charles de Martel was constantly in attendance, I did not attach a greal deal of importance to what I believed to be a temporary indisposition. She was unhappy in Paris, wanting to live at Les

Mées, and told me her reason for remaining in town was to organize her affairs in case her illness became worse.

I was working at the Cirque d'Hiver again, now under management of the Bouglioni brothers (the Fratellinis having undergone a financial débâcle in which they lost the Cirque), and followed this engagement with one at the Medrano, whose hours enabled me to be constantly with Violette during those weeks. I realized, perhaps better than ever before, her marvelous courage and unselfish devotion to the charities she sustained and the private persons she befriended anonymously almost every week. In her consideration and affection for the people of her house and estates, she always found time to listen to their troubles, no matter how ill she was.

Whenever I broached the subject of her health, she would say, "De Martel saved my life during the war. He can do it again." One afternoon when I met him leaving Violette's house, I told him this. He looked at me for a moment, then said softly, "She is a grand person; there is nothing I would not do to help her—if help is possible now." That was all he would say.

It was the last time I ever spoke to that great-hearted doctor whose heroic death during the German occupation of Paris reached the American newspapers in 1940. He had been told by the German Kommandant to remove his patients and French wounded from his own hospital, in order that Germans might benefit from his skill as the greatest brain surgeon in Europe. "We want your brains, Dr. de Martel," they reiterated.

When the day came for them to take over his hospital, Dr. de Martel met them on the steps and stood bareheaded while the deputation of Nazi officers marched to meet him. "You want my brains, gentlemen," he said. "Here they are"—and putting a revolver to his temple, he literally blew his brains out at their feet. It was a strange but glorious end for one of the most brilliant surgeons and humanitarians of modern times.

It had been arranged that I drive Violette to Versailles for several days, and on the afternoon before we were to leave, she 'phoned me about one of her kindest actions, which was the purchasing of the grave of Yvonne George, the singer, whose family had no money to maintain it in perpetuity. I promised to arrange the details connected with the buying of the burial ground, as Violette didn't want any one to know of her part in this transaction. While I listened to her instructions, her voice over the telephone began to fail, becoming so weak I could hardly hear her. The next morning at dawn, she died.

Perhaps one of the most sincere tributes paid to her memory was that of the veterans of the Invalides, to whom she'd given so much all her life. They marched to the funeral services at the church of St.-Honoré d'Eylau, and placed over her bier before the altar an arch they had constructed themselves, with pathetic blue tinsel ornaments. Its tawdry appearance assumed the proportions of a glorious banner, with the words that followed her name: "And the greatest of these is Charity." I sat fascinated by this modest but glorious tribute to my friend, which stood alone in its simple truth above the magnificent wreaths and blankets of costly flowers that bore ribbons with coronets and the greatest names in Europe.

The memory of the requiem mass held for my mother, to which Violette had accompanied me in the same church, surged back with its poignant grief. I would have preferred sitting alone in the crowd of quiet, sorrowing people of all classes and descriptions (humble folk to whom her death meant a tragedy so great it overwhelmed them), but I had received a very kind invitation from her daughters and son, on which was written, "Please sit with us, Maman was so fond of you." I could not refuse.

Near the altar there were ranks of uniformed officers and foreign envoys, and I could see her great friends, the old Maréchals Lyautey and Pétain, staring straight before them, their features tense as the veterans filled the aisle. Lame and armless men with sticks and crutches formed the long procession that wound its way before her coffin for the last sad honor of sprinkling the flowers with holy water.

It was a splendid but terrible farewell for me, and I thought

421

I would have to rush out of the church when the service ended, before the black-uniformed ushers (their long staffs tipped with black plumes) stepped forward to strike the marble parquet of the church, speaking the words that were a part of the French ceremony for persons of her rank. "Violette, Princesse Murat, Duchesse d'Elchingen, Princess of the Moskova—go in peace."

Upon leaving the church and getting into my car, I noticed several typical Montmartre cabaret singers, their tears mingling with last night's grease-paint on their faces, stumbling blindly toward the bus station already jammed with people hoping to follow the funeral cortège to the Père-Lachaise cemetery. I knew none of these persons but felt they were friends to whom Violette would have liked me to give a helping hand. I asked three of them, two shabbily dressed boys and a girl, if they would like to come along in my car. Gratefully they accepted and all across Paris spoke not a word but sat staring dumbly before them, in utter despair.

Slowly we filed down the Avenue Victor Hugo, where the police were holding back an enormous Communist demonstration headed for the Arc de Triomphe. I knew that the hearse bearing Violette's body had to pass before the Arch, in accordance with the custom in France for all princesses of the Napoleonic dynasty, *pour prendre congé de l'Empéreur* (to take leave of the Emperor). However, owing to the demonstration, the officials heading the procession were obliged to turn down one of the boulevards leading from the Place de l'Étoile, crossing Paris by another route. The whole cortège was disrupted, and it was not until late afternoon that the various officials arrived at the monument to Maréchal Ney, the illustrious ancestor in whose tomb Violette was buried.

For the first time in my life, I wanted to get away from Paris for a while, so I accepted a contract to work on the S.S. *Normandie* for a summer tour between Le Havre and Antwerp. It proved delightful, despite the difficulties of bad weather and working high over the decks and heads of thousands of Belgian tourists celebrating the Fêtes de Prince Badouin. Nightly I had to descend from my rigging drenched with fog, my costumes clinging to me, and make my way through crowds of well-intentioned and excited Belgians offering me champagne and shouting wildly, *"Bravo! Bravo! Mademoiselle, vous est magnifique!"*

Later, every time I drove past the tragic hull of that great ship, half-submerged like a dead whale, I recalled the moments of emotion I had experienced on her when she was a floating palace. Then I would get a queer tight feeling in my throat, set my teeth, and say, "She is symbolical of France—she is not yet drowned and will right herself again."

The first night I worked on the *Normandie,* I bought a new pulley rope to reach the great height at which I performed and told my new rigger (a man I called Broken Nose) to have some sailors stretch the rope across the deck before putting it through the blocks. This they did with such a will that it broke and had to be spliced. The recent fall didn't help my nerves much, and I still suffered at times from the fracture sustained behind my right ear. As I mounted in the reflector beam, up and up above the heads of the innocent cheering passengers, my eyes were on the spliced rope and I reflected that as my luck was certainly going through a slump, perhaps—perhaps this was IT.

The kindness of the crew members detailed to assist Broken Nose pull me up to my rigging, and the anxiety of Monsieur Villar, the charming commissaire of the *Normandie,* were very sweet. They worked with a death grip on my ropes, and when I was almost down, I could hear one sailor mutter to another, *"Mon Dieu! qu'elle est culottée—celle-là"* ("My God! she's got pants on—that one"), meaning I had nerve. We had a wonderful voyage, with dancing and nightly supper parties with the ship's officers. The acts were exceptionally good companions, which naturally made the trip unforgettable.

I played the Scala in Berlin again, returning to Paris and Madame Medrano's cirque. She had created a big blue traveling top for a tour through France. I seriously contemplated accepting her offer to join the circus, but the old wanderlust got hold of me, and perhaps the sorrow of Violette's death had dimmed the beauty of Paris in springtime.

I decided to try my luck in the United States, closing my apartment once more and storing my things. As yet America was an unknown field for me in aërial work. Since a restless desire to leave France haunted me, I contracted to play that Mecca of summer circuses, Holland. This enabled me to embark at Rotterdam for the States.

XXI

O N THE DAY we left, there was a violent dock strike in progress. Agitated tourists argued with adamant stevedores and porters on the subject of their luggage. It was 1937 and Europe was changing rapidly—this strike recalled my last days in Paris. There had been riots in the streets, Communists holding meetings at the Arc de Triomphe, and the helpless Gardes Républicains endeavoring to break up the mobs were pulled from their horses without being able to use their sabers or revolvers against the aggressors.

Ever since the riots of February 6, 1934, when the police fired on the veterans in the Place de la Concorde, the smiling face of Paris had been changing to a mask of distress and sorrow. I thought of Violette's grief over the occurrence of that fatal day and how we had stood together on the Champs-Élysées watching those grim old warriors, their faces set and white, march bravely down their beloved avenue, only to meet wounds and death at the hands of their own countrymen. With American friends, we were obliged to retreat, swept along with the frantic mobs of stampeding Parisians fleeing before the fusillade and trampling on the flowers and gardens, to reach the comparative safety of the Avenue Montaigne.

I had really chosen the Dutch contract with a view to embarking from Holland and thus escaping the wrench of leaving Paris. As the S.S. *Rotterdam,* crowded with American tourists, held on her course to the United States, I remembered my strange dream during the last night in my apartment, which now seemed clearer to me.

I had never been very familiar with New York, having only worked there as a young child, and except for a few days spent with my father there it was an unknown city to me. I arrived in August, and the heat, after Europe, was the first thing to attract my attention, principally because little Buddie's fits were getting worse and worse. Daily I drove from the Hotel Commodore to Central Park, trying to give him some cool air, and finally decided to move to the nearest hotel I could find to the park, the Hotel Wellington on Seventh Avenue. Then began my acquaintance with New York.

I wanted to see the city for myself, in my own way, so did not look up any of father's relatives or get in touch with performer friends. I visited, together with other tourists, the famous Chinatown, Harlem, and the Bowery, then took a taxi

to Poe's cottage, with its bitter-sweet fragrance of bygone days, which I loved, and after that, I inspected Grant's Tomb from the outside. From these sacred precincts I transferred my curiosity to the theatrical agents of Broadway and met many strange and rare creatures among them. Being in no hurry to work, I wanted to get the feeling of the New York public before trying my act on them.

Coney Island had a few good shows, but I wanted to see a real American circus, and everywhere I went, the announcements of something called the WPA confronted me. I thought they were the initials of the directors or the corporation running the show. After all sorts of difficulties I found my way to Jamaica, where the circus was playing. In the middle of a dusty lot I spied a ramshackle tent and entered.

426

Returning to town after witnessing the spectacle, I was completely bewildered and not a little disillusioned and told an agent about my shocking experience. He laughed till he nearly cried and explained the true facts of the case to me.

After a lot of hunting around, I found a little gym tucked away on West Forty-seventh Street, between Ninth and Tenth Avenues, where I could just manage to hang my rigging and practise. The proprietor was an old German who ran a bar in the front of the establishment, with the universal circus atmosphere that reminded me of the Gymnase Pons on Montmartre. The first time I worked the roof nearly caved in; nevertheless, it was the only place to be found in New York where aërial acts could rehearse, and gradually I met the best talent in town practising there. It took several weeks to find a suitable rigging man as assistant, but I finally ended up with a well-meaning man of German extraction called Hermann. (German riggers are always named Hermann. I don't know why.)

As in Paris, the agents wanted to see how the act impressed the public and insisted I break in at a theater with atrocious lighting in Brooklyn. I went there for the purpose of inspecting the stage for my apparatus, and took an elevated train. I began to feel terribly nervous as the cars swerved around curves and tottered perilously above crowded thoroughfares, till when we were across the river and somewhere near my station, I was nearly in a state of collapse. Leaving the train at the first stop, I took a taxi to the theater, returning to New York the same way. Never, since that first experience, have I been able to stand this terrifying mode of transportation, and while playing Brooklyn, I took taxis to and from the theater, never ceasing to feel the most sincere admiration for the stoic travelers having the courage to commute daily on the elevated railroads.

My opening there was not what I would describe as a happy one, for the orchestra leader was allergic to rehearsing, and on opening night Hermann lost his head completely upon receiving the news of the wreck of the *Graf Zeppelin*. America had

427

a completely different atmosphere from Europe, and gradually I began to realize that circus performers are regarded by most Americans as a type of exotic freak, who lead a charmed life amid reckless and chaotic disorder. To a certain extent this is true, for there is a lack of care in rehearsals and an almost offhand method of presenting an act that is hard to get used to. America, like all the world, loves a circus, but Americans do not have, I think, the deep respect for the artists' talents that is shown to a good performer in Europe.

Another strange phenomenon is the way in which one would be booked at Loew's State and Radio City, and after achieving success there, be transferred to the boards of a movie-house in Pottsville, Pennsylvania. This is most disappointing to a foreign artist but apparently a perfectly natural transition to the American vaudevilleans and their managers. In Europe, if an act accomplished success in a good house, they generally continued on the same stratum—but not so in the United States.

Everywhere I worked, agents came to see me and commenced their conversation by saying, "All acts from Europe are too slow. They must be streamlined and given greater speed." At first I listened to them but soon got all mixed up and didn't know where I was. Finally I put my act back exactly as it was when I first arrived. At once I began having success, and the same theatrical gentlemen who had criticized me were the first to come rushing with congratulations, saying, "Do you see how my suggestions have improved it?" Of course, I thanked them profusely, and everybody was happy.

Shortly before Christmas, I came back from an engagement in Baltimore and was informed upon arriving at Loew's State that my old friend Barbette, the Enigma, was ill at the Polyclinic Hospital. His condition, the hospital told me, was very grave. After playing in Providence, Rhode Island, at Christmas and at the State Lake in Chicago, I returned to find the brilliant, graceful trapeze artist still lying on his bed, completely paralyzed. As often as possible I visited him, continuing to do so whenever I was in New York. During the two years he was hospitalized, making a courageous fight to regain his health, he never lost his caustic satirical gift for criticizing everything and everybody around him or his great sense of humor.

As in Europe, I found the difficulty of securing a responsible property man for my act very discouraging. Hermann was an honest and willing person but simply could not get the hang of things, and after two or three mishaps in which I nearly broke my neck, I decided to get another man. Since I had engagements with the Frank Wirth and Shrine circuses in which I used high rigging, I finally employed a Russian named Stepan, who appeared to be excellent during rehearsals, was a hard worker and very enthusiastic about making good. When we finally started working, however, I discovered that after six in the evenings he developed a thirst that simply could not be controlled, and he would go through the entire act with a drunken dignity and glassy stare that terrified me. I knew very few people and hardly any of the performers working with me on the big Shrine indoor circus dates, of whom I could ask the favor of helping my act, as was often done in Europe, so I put up with him.

I found a strange difference in all the ways of running a circus. The dressing-rooms, where everybody dressed together as a rule unless there were special accommodations in the armories or gardens where we worked, were so overcrowded and untidy, I did not know how I was going to keep my costumes in condition. My Russian assistant, to whom I had mentioned this distressing situation, bought a small screen, a rug, and a folding table, and these he proceeded to install in a corner wherever we went. It was much more comfortable but produced the unfortunate effect of making some of my fellow artists furious. They thought I was "high-hat" and referred to me as "that million-dollar dame."

The climax came when I worked a date near New York and had the stupidity to call on my cousins and a sister of my father's. They were, I could see, curious but dismayed when I extended an invitation to them to run down by car and see me work. Evidently a cousin in the circus was not a very acceptable addition to the family, and I never should have asked them to visit this skeleton in the cupboard in its natural surroundings. I had almost forgotten about it until one Saturday matinée, when they arrived in an enormous limousine.

There were two dignified old maid cousins and my aunt, her nostrils quivering at the smells encountered on the way to my dressing-room. Mercifully, Stepan, the rigger, headed them off with a savoir-faire unusual in rigging men and did his best to deter them from penetrating the area around the dressing-rooms, where the parade was just lining up for the "spec." Stumbling over ropes and tackle on the ground, despite Stepan's guidance, they managed to get inextricably mixed up with the elephants and some performing seals.

My relatives were nearly hysterical by the time I had thrown on a robe and steered them out of the mêlée, sending Stepan with them to obtain seats. When I entered for my act I didn't see them anywhere, and later on I received a little prim note thanking me for the tickets but saying they would return to see me again when I "played Radio City."

If vaudeville was on the wane in Europe, it was definitely a fadeout in the United States. Everybody excused the muddled rehearsals and various drawbacks by saying that variety had been destroyed by the movies and that I should have been here when the Palace was open. This, of course, was probably true, but it did not do me any good. All important houses had four to five shows a day, which undermined my strength considerably, and although I had a personal success and was becoming known, I had made up my mind to play the parks and fairs through the summer—one or two good circus dates, then return to Paris.

After my Russian assistant got through the bulk of Shrine circuses by the grace of God, he wound up his service to me by losing all my luggage while returning from a date in Philadelphia. It took me several days to retrieve it; then I had to start all over again to find another man, rehearse, and break him into my routine.

I had introductions to several agents in New York from those in Paris, but for circus and fair dates my act was handled by George Hamid, the most reputable agent in New York for my type of work. His office, then in the Bond Building on Broadway, always made me think of a scene from *Alice Through the Looking-Glass*. Hamid was rarely to be pinned down in any business conference with his acts, but with an affable smile, if they were good, he would wave them to the care of his two managers, Messrs. Blumenfeld and Solti. If they were not good, he'd stalk past with the same unyielding expression Meissonier has painted on Napoleon's face in his famous picture, "The Retreat from Moscow."

Mr. Blumenfeld, a suave diplomat, always made me suspect that in his Teutonic forefathers there had been more than a dash of Irish blarney. He could talk an unwilling artist into accepting the most extraordinary traveling combinations, involving endless expense and exhaustion, making them believe he had done them a tremendous favor. Dave Solti, who at the start of the century had been a famous dancer, was far more blunt. His critical artistic sense was the terror of the little acts auditioning for him, to whom—after they had gone through superhuman efforts to impress him—he would invariably say with a steely glint in his eye, "It vas lousy!" He was so delightful to me that I got the greatest joy out of listening to him, and although I appreciated his keen judgment of an act, I would sometimes have an uncontrollable fit of laughter in the office. Every one would stare at me as if they thought I was mad.

Under these circumstances, it was only natural that the rigging men Hamid's office disinterred for me were also personages from *Alice*, varying from the Mad Hatter to the White Knight. Hence I set out on a series of fair dates (a brand-new experience for me) with a veteran of the Spanish-American War called Bill. He was willing, if a bit shaky, and had an incorrigible habit of addressing me as "Honey" on

431

all occasions. He meant well, though, and during the first days of my tour, I watched with an eagle eye to find out if he drank. I had bought a car, the most practical method of transporting my heavy outdoor steel rigging to the different points on my route, and some of his erratic maneuvers in traffic gave me food for reflection. However, he convinced me that in this respect he was trustworthy, and always at the close of a date he would tell me he was going out for a few drinks now that his responsibility was temporarily ended. Never once did he drink on the job.

Some of the park dates around New York were charming, such as the Palisades and Rye amusement parks, also the Steel Pier in Atlantic City, where I felt more at home than I had since coming to the United States, for there were Ostemann, the German equestrienne, the Flying Otaris—old friends from the Hugo Stinnes Circus—and other acts from Medrano. The first fair I played was in Pennsylvania, and I shall never forget it.

It was the Harrisburg Fair, with many performers playing on the stage facing the grandstand and track, where the dust raised by the trotting horses hung in the air like an orange mist between races, when the acts worked. It filled our lungs and nostrils with a fine powder, and as if this were not enough, the star attraction was a man called Lucky Teeter and his Hell Drivers. They were rightly named, for never in my life had I seen so much hell raised anywhere as during his act. They lit fires with gasoline on the track, over which cars were driven at breakneck speed, and when the autos turned over they caught fire, blazing merrily away in the gasoline flames, while heavy black smoke got into everybody's hair and make-up.

I worked fairs till late in the fall, when the evening spectacles became difficult with the heavy dew soaking my ropes, causing them to tighten up and become dangerous. My act had been very well received and written up. I seemed to have made a good impression in open-air work, and nearly all the fairs requested repeat bookings for the following year.

At the Metropolitan Theater in Boston, over Christmas and

432

New Year's, my rigging had to be hung directly over the heads of Little Jack Little's band playing on the stage. Although the musicians and management did everything possible to make things easy for us, Bill had a lot of nervous tension to support while controlling my high swings over the band and the crowded first six ranks of stalls. I think this must have got him, and it wasn't until I returned to New York that he told me that he'd once suffered from shell-shock and that at certain times this had a very bad effect on his sangfroid. The tension is great for any aërialist's assistant, who from the ground carries a heavy responsibility—not only for the artist, but for the safety of the audience as well. When I played the Victoria Palace in London, a pregnant woman in one of the top balcony boxes instituted a lawsuit against the management, claiming that one of my more sensational tricks had frightened her into having a miscarriage on the spot. On our Boston date we did not encounter anything as serious as this but found hysterical women in the public who shrieked and swooned when I did certain feats above their heads. Male escorts dragged them out, protesting loudly to Bill, who was obliged to work the act from the audience.

Some agents were anxious that I enlarge my apparatus for the Madison Square and Boston Gardens, always played by the Ringling Circus with whom they were negotiating for my act. Any alterations in the length of my ropes meant that the timing had to be changed, and this required careful rehearsals. At once I started making these changes, using the rather inadequately sized gym on Forty-seventh Street, where the iron girders disturbed my high swings and leaps.

One morning the agents dropped in to see the progress of my work, and their presence had an unnerving effect on Bill, who was still very uncertain of himself, with the result that in a particularly high swing that preceded my ankle leap, he lost his head when he saw mine nearing the girders and threw his entire weight on the rope attached to my trapeze. The impetus of my swing was broken with such violence that the ropes snapped like a bowstring under my weight, literally throwing me up and off the crossbar. I fell with a terrible force, and only the fact that my feet were caught in the rope loops saved my life, but my body swung sidewise crashing into the wall, and then to the ground.

I tried to rise to my feet but couldn't, and remembered nothing more till I found myself in the emergency ward of the Polyclinic Hospital, with a broken hip and dislocated vertebra. I knew nobody in New York and lay in the hospital for days before 'phoning my cousins and aunt. They were most kind on this occasion and came nearly every day, until I insisted on retiring (still in a cast) to the hotel. It was a foolish move, for I had internal injuries that flared up, and was sent to another hospital, this time the Presbyterian.

Four and a half miserable months were spent in getting over this fall, until I was able to walk again, and the despair of Bill over what had occurred was very sincere. In a sense it was not his fault, for he had simply acted on a reflex through pure nerves, so I promised to give him another chance if ever I got well enough to climb a rigging again.

While laid up in my hotel, I received visits from many people who I never dreamed would have the kindness to think of me. The news of my fall had spread until it even reached the ears of acquaintances from Europe and South America. One of them materialized in the form of the internationally known German Intelligence agent, Kurt Ludecke, recently escaped from the friendship of Adolf Hitler which had culminated in a concentration camp for Mr. Ludecke. He came to visit, armed with a copy of his book, *I Knew Hitler,* and told me of the lectures he was about to give on the subject of life under the Reich. I had known him in Russia, Paris, and the Argentine: it is curious how pennies, good and bad, keep turning up in the lives of most performers.

Many acts I worked with saw the announcement of my accident in *Billboard,* that colorful journal for the theatrical world, and came to sit with me. The effect produced by their conversation on my starched and socially minded nurses was very interesting. On returning from the hospital, I was still

434

unable to move out of the brace on my back, or stand as yet, so there was nothing to be done but manage with a night and day nurse—which like everything else about my accident was both trying and expensive.

Among the friends that were so kind to me was George Frame Brown, whom I had met at another sickbed, that of Barbette. George had a heart of gold in addition to a great sense of humor and remarkable talent as a radio artist, and I know of no better bedside manner than the one he acquired from continually visiting sick friends. George has definitely a mothering complex which, together with his keen wit and brilliant conversation, is a wonderful tonic. When I was able to walk again, I gratefully accepted his kind invitation to convalesce at his country home in Saugerties, New York.

While talking over the visit, he suggested I bring my rigging with me, also Bill, and try to practise a little again, with a view to building up my morale. The doctors had been dubious about whether or not I could ever work again, on account of the back injury, but that very doubt made me more determined to have a try at it anyway. Other aërial artists who visited me were dead set against my ever attempting to use Bill in my work again and offered to find a more responsible person—a younger one—who could be depended on to hang my apparatus safely.

They brought a young man to see me one evening, when I was still far from well enough even to talk intelligently or pay very much attention to his personality, but I did notice that in neither appearance nor manner of speaking was he the usual type of rough-and-ready rigger from the circus. He was working with the Ringling show, somewhere near New York, and when he left, I forgot all about my promise to let him know when I needed some one for my act, nor did I remember it when setting out in the car with old Bill and my dog for George Brown's place in the country.

That was a memorable visit at one of the most health-giving spots imaginable. George had arranged and modernized a very old Dutch settler's farm into a delightful country home, at the foot of Rip Van Winkle's mountain. Upon arriving, I found a party of friends all from the world so familiar to me, of talented Bohemia, with that *joie de vivre* that such souls never seem to lack. It was the perfect atmosphere necessary for forgetting that things hurt when I tried bending my back, and that I could not walk very far or play tennis.

Gradually I became strong enough to swing again and soon realized I would be able to prove to the doctors that they had been overcautious. My greatest ambition was to send them the programs of my next booking. So, setting my teeth, I worked to the limit of my endurance.

Before leaving for New York, George, who had watched me practise every day, said very seriously that I should get another rigger. His imitations of Bill swinging me, and the fact that he was so jittery that an audience was bound to notice it, convinced me he not only was a drawback to the act but also could mean another disaster before long. Upon my return to town, I reluctantly let the old man go, feeling sorry about it but realizing George was right.

I was still in no condition to take any dates as yet but was contemplating employing some one to practise with a few hours every day, when I received a letter signed Robert F. Matz, Jr. This was the young man from Ringling's whom my friends had recommended. He asked me to reply if I was ready to use him, and suggested leaving his present occupation immediately and coming to New York. I hesitated engaging a full-time assistant when I was not able to work, but before I had time to answer his letter, the young gentleman in question arrived at my hotel, announcing his readiness to begin work at once.

The more I talked to him, the more I realized that a rigger with his build and appearance was too rare an asset to my act for me to let go. He was tall and very fair, in his lean thirties, with Nordic blue eyes and a smile that had sunshine in it. When I discovered he had an unusual love for all animals, which gave us much in common, I started practising with him, hiding my aches and pains as best I could. As the days went by, I learned his story. . . . He was a graduate of Laurence College, Wisconsin, came of a good provincial family in Appleton, and had left home and a humdrum job for a quantity of reasons—principally boredom—and joined the circus out of devilment.

From New York I transferred my rigging to a lot in Long Island, where there was plenty of room and height, and all through the beautiful summer days, as we drove to and from New York, I found out he especially liked dogs, and that I liked him. To make a long story short, I accepted a date at Playland, Rye Beach, without the slightest idea as to how I would get the strength to work but feeling that I had to get started for pressing financial reasons. While struggling through my act and suffering the tortures of hell, our romance grew, and through that, I somehow got the necessary will to keep going—though several times I nearly fell from weakness.

It was an odd interlude of happiness, mixed up with pain and fear and the most peculiar people who were on the bill with us. The day I arrived to work, I discovered that a man had fallen the previous week while doing his own act on a high pole which had suddenly snapped. He had crashed, with part of it still strapped to his wrist, clean through the roof of a soda fountain. The broken pole, with his torn and blood-stained clothes, had been left forgotten in my dressing-room and was the first thing I saw upon entering.

Next door to me was the star act, and never, in a long experience of eccentric performers in circuses and theaters, have I seen his equal. He was a most charming and amusing person in private life, but when working his nerves gave way completely, and for the hour he was on the amusement lot he raved and cursed at his assistants and riggers, going through an unspeakable agony of nerves before working. His act was a highly dangerous chute, down which he descended from a height of eighty feet, riding a bicycle. On reaching the end of the chute, this machine leaped over the public into a tank of water, from which he would emerge dripping and perfectly at ease. Before he went on, his wife would pace up and down in front of their dressing-room praying, while his assistants bit their fingernails and fumed inwardly.

We used to walk down the Mall together, with the other act, five blonde maidens calling themselves the "Juggling Jewels," between lines of applauding public, to the riggings placed in the section of the park referred to by the undignified name of "Free Acts." There the star would shake everybody by the hand, bidding them good-by in a voice tense with emotion, while his assistants clambered to the top of the gigantic chute. He would scream at them from the ground to ascertain that no blankety-blank sea gulls had done their business on the apparatus, for should this be the case, nothing would induce him to go up.

That was a wonderful mad fortnight at Rye Playland, though the only playful thing about it, as far as I was concerned, was its name. After finishing there, Bobbie and I drove down to Baltimore and, with my dog as best man, were married. We spent the rest of the summer in a cottage on Long Island, where Bobbie prepared his own trapeze act and I endeavored to get my health back and practise with him. We played the usual tour of vaudeville houses all over the states, and my act, which now included some double tricks with him, began to get good press notices.

In January we were in Boston again, when the combination of an eccentric light man blinding Bobbie while working, and his breaking all rules of theatrical superstition by whistling in our dressing-room, caused him to have a serious fall one night. It was a nasty crash into the audience, in which he injured his head and smashed his left wrist so badly it had to be operated on the same night. This was his second bad accident, and it took some months before he was well enough to work again. The sight of his fall had a curious effect on both of us, for I could not bear watching him work after that, and he was always on edge when I worked. But we battled it through, playing vaudeville and fair dates that summer of 1939, with better salaries and reputation than ever.

After the incident of the careless spot operator in Boston, I decided to have Barbette travel with us to style the act in his inimitable way, also to wrangle with the lights, orchestra, and other problems which are exhausting for an artist to cope with in addition to working several times a day. Almost miraculously Barbette had recovered enough to walk and use his hands but not to work in his act again. Our wanderings throughout the United States and Canada, in circus and vaudeville, were varied and picturesque, for the *Looking-Glass* gentlemen in Hamid's office gave their imaginations full rein by sending us one month to a gigantic state fair and then on to an ox-roast for the benefit of visiting firemen, in some obscure village. We played only one ox-roast, to be strictly truthful, for I felt certain that if there were any more, Barbette and I would have a nervous breakdown. It was a very nice ox-roast, and the firemen were perfectly charming, enjoying the act tremendously and entering into the spirit of the thing by focusing on me the enormous search-light on the front of their firetruck. This blinded me every night but lit up the countryside for miles around.

We were playing the Erie Fair when the declaration of war came over the air one quiet Sunday afternoon while we were in our hotel. As we listened, a chill crept over me, and an icy hand seemed to be crushing my heart. The people around us listened with grave faces, but few of them knew as I did the real meaning of war. My thoughts flew to my brother in England and all he had gone through. Down the long vista of the years, I could see again the dressing-stations of Bois Clausair.

When we arrived at the fairground that afternoon, a strange thing happened. I was in my dressing-tent, waiting for my act to go on, when suddenly instead of the familiar music of the "Beer Barrel Polka," which the band played for one of the acts, I heard the stirring strains of the "Marseillaise." My hands grew cold while listening, and I questioned a passing performer about the reason for it. He answered that nobody could understand why the band played it, unless by mistake, having got the score mixed in their music in some unusual way. At that moment, my dream in Paris became very clear.

I had had no complaints about my bookings and success all during those months, but I had always hoped to return to Paris with Bobbie and work our act there. Now that dream was at an end. I received a cable from my brother, saying he intended remaining in his own house and would not, under any circumstances, come to America. I had cabled, begging him to do so, and had it been possible, I would have gone across to try and convince him to return with me. In May, 1940, the Germans invaded the undefended Channel Islands, by sea and air, while the helpless population was evacuated at the last minute amid a scene of indescribable havoc. My brother and his wife managed to get away, leaving their house as it stood and taking only a suit-case. They finally reached England and settled in Wales, where, after a long illness, my brother died.

The thought of his last years being saddened by the horrors of war, that had robbed him of his sight, was a very cruel one; also that his manuscripts and writings, many of them unpublished and of great promise, should be lost forever in the bombarded ruins of the home he loved so much.

After a summer of fair dates in 1939, I was quite ill for some weeks and had to undergo an operation for complications resulting from my last fall. While recuperating I began thinking again of perfumes and the possibility of putting into practice in the United States my plans about them. Curiously, the same week I was giving serious study to the idea, a letter arrived from my Russian friends in Paris, saying they were leaving for Switzerland and had an opportunity to send me the formulas through friends coming to New York. There was, Madame Loury wrote, a marvelous opportunity to make money in America now that the European perfumes were rapidly becoming a thing of the past.

I promptly took advice on the subject of such a venture from perfume experts and essential oil houses and found the

440

information of Monsieur de la Vigne, of Maison Roure-Dupont et Cie of France, of the greatest assistance in deciding the first steps necessary to the formation of my project. Through his practical guidance and kind interest, I was able to obtain a reserve of necessary oils and fixatives required for the formulas when they arrived. Chemists and expert blenders went through long tests and research, growing more enthusiastic daily after translating some of the old formulas with solidified ingredients into the more modern liquid preparations.

With these we chose some of the more exquisite fragrances and timidly launched them on the New York market. Their success was astonishing, especially since at that time, 1940, French scents were still procurable, many of them being manufactured in America. Of course we made the usual mistakes, having no idea how to start a business, plunging into too many perfumes and too many expensive packages at the same time—but we learned, and a year later were on our way toward making a go of a delightful and absorbing business. I never attempted handling anything but the artistic side of the affair (in its way just another branch of show business), such as the creating of titles, packaging for the perfumes, advertising, promotion, and all the *mise en scène* indispensable to presenting them.

Perhaps some of my happiest perfume titles of recent months have been thought up during long hours spent driving for the American Women's Voluntary Services' Motor Transport Corps—the group of volunteer women who give their time and cars to the services of the Armed Forces. When I first started driving for them I was assigned to the United States Coast Guard in Hoboken, where during the hot summer months I spent many hours on dock detail. The beauties of the Jersey water-front will linger long in my memory, particularly an unusually strong-smelling fish market near a ferry outside which I frequently parked; also the intriguing odors of the Gowanus Basin. Life is indeed full of contrasts.

The financial details of our project were left entirely in the hands of my husband, whose business sense developed with surprising rapidity and whose personality has done much to build our clientele. As our little venture grew, we gradually built an office in the penthouse we found on a hotel rooftop, then a showroom, and then we rented a plant and warehouse downtown, with salesmen and employees. We also bought five dogs—three Bostons and two toy poodles.

The enthusiastic publicity which the fashion and beauty editors gave our perfumes while they were yet in their infancy was so gratifying that I felt extremely happy my old hobby had become of tangible use. When our real good fortune began

to establish itself firmly (although it had cost much hard work and sacrifice), it sometimes frightened me. I had become so accustomed to earning my living by intense physical effort and the domination of all self-pity or fear that the comparative ease with which our business grew did not seem real at times. I would wonder if it were only a dream and would suddenly end one morning when once more I would rise to take my rigging to some high tent or theater and look my old friend Death in the face again for eight long minutes.

I still practise nearly every day, for the feeling of the free air rushing against my body and the thrill of a high swing, would be too hard to give up. So I keep my rigging on the roof-garden, and often on summer evenings I steal out and climb high above the lights of the city to dream a while.

Newspaper reporters and writers have been kind enough to give me a great deal of amusing publicity on this famous trapeze, which is the delight of my neighbors and a distraction for the patients in the dentist's offices overlooking our building. On Sunday afternoons it is especially gay, when other aërial friends come to visit us and enjoy themselves on a busman's holiday.

From the sunny roof around our penthouse, I have learned to know this city of New York in many moods. In lavender spring twilights and on stormy nights when the wind wails like a lost soul, I feel again the lonely thrill of being on a ship far out at sea. In hot summer, I have listened to the city gasp under the night, and sometimes when I watched the sunset I have felt like the monk Paphnus gazing over Alexandria, the city of Thaïs, who felt the spirits of the people rise up to the rooftops where he went to pray—their joys, their sorrows and tragedies, their loves and lusts, welling up to the clearer air like a chorus of voices.

To the north lie the green stretches of Central Park, and over the treetops rise the towers of apartment houses that sometimes, in red autumn sunsets, lose their modern outlines till it is easy to imagine they are medieval castles—castles in Spain, which they probably are in reality to many people. All around our roof there are tall buildings, and when they gleam like opals in sunlight, I know they are the buildings of my dream in Paris.

High above the city it is very quiet, and the roar of traffic is almost inaudible. Here it is easier to think and reminisce for the throbbing life of the streets seems very far away. Here, too, when the March winds bring spring again, and the last snows have gone, we plant a Victory Garden, with morning glories on a white picket fence, spinach, and beans, that battle bravely for existence against the smoke of incinerators.

There are also fat gray pigeons that come from Central Park, looking for the rice they know I will give them—to the great annoyance of my dogs. They strut and preen themselves, perching on the rigging of my trapeze, which hangs between two slender white poles with dangling ropes against the sky. That, too, reminds me of a ship and a voyage through summer seas. For there is a feeling of expectancy about this place, and perhaps a promise, just enough to set gipsy wits a-wandering, that when the waiting is at an end and the holocaust of war is past, there will once more be ships and travelers and the old familiar places that beckon like a shrine.

CURTAIN

(1)